TRANSCENDING THE MATRIX
OF THE
IMPOSTER GODS

RECLAIMING THE HEART'S INTELLIGENCE

LARK ALETA BATEY

BALBOA.PRESS
A DIVISION OF HAY HOUSE

Balboa Press books may be ordered through booksellers or by contacting:

Balboa Press
A Division of Hay House
1663 Liberty Drive
Bloomington, IN 47403
www.balboapress.com
844-682-1282

Print information available on the last page.

ISBN: 979-8-7652-3884-4 (sc)
ISBN: 979-8-7652-3883-7 (e)

Library of Congress Control Number: 2023902679

Balboa Press rev. date: 02/23/2023

To all who search, look to your heart
It will show you the way.

∞

This book is dedicated to the enduring Human Spirit
And to the Infinite Being
that resides within our hearts
Waiting patiently for us to acknowledge
It's divine Presence.

CONTENTS

PART FOUR
ARCHITECTS OF A NEW PARADIGM

PART FIVE
RECLAIMING OUR HEART'S INTELLIGENCE

ACKNOWLEDGEMENTS

WRITING A NON-FICTION BOOK IS never a one-person endeavor, and this book is no exception. I owe a debt of gratitude to every person who was inspired to explore the subject matter that resulted in the books and articles that have supported my climb up the mountain of information to this place of understanding. It takes the focused interests and dogged determination of many people to tease a variety of valuable concepts and ideas from the deep reservoirs of our collective memory to the surface so they can be explored and shared. Each work contributes to the expansion of our understanding.

This book and the realizations I have written about within these pages has been a lifelong journey filled with many teachers, internal and external. They have taken many forms including movies, classes and seminars, long conversations with friends and family, and many, many books, as well as inner promptings of inspiration brought to me by meditation, active imagination, and journaling. All these experiences have come together into a grand gestalt that has prepared me to recognize the importance of the information that would compel me to write this book.

I am deeply grateful to my husband Bob for his patience and unwavering support in this endeavor and for being my editor-in-chief. The quality of this book has been enhanced many times over due to his patient and meticulous editing and his astuteness in catching passages that needed more clarity by asking pertinent questions. I have immensely enjoyed our editing sessions and the wonderful conversations that often ensued during that process. He has a penchant for organization that is truly a gift, and I am blessed to be the recipient of that. He has spent long hours checking the accuracy of the many footnotes and organizing the bibliographies to make them reader friendly.

A special thanks to Darlene Berges, publisher of the WingMakers Materials, for giving me permission to quote and write about this paradigm- changing information. I am grateful for her guidance and suggestions in this endeavor, as well as for the heart-to-heart conversations we have shared that have helped me to better understand this groundbreaking body of work. I am humbled by her trust in my understanding of the materials and how I have incorporated it into this book.

My deeply heartfelt gratitude to James Mahu, creator and translator of the WingMakers Materials, for his unwavering dedication in bringing forth this prolific body of consciousness awakening materials that include e-books, philosophy papers, intensely compelling novels, and activating music and paintings. I am in awe of his vast understanding and his ability to articulate his insights with an eloquence that is not only inspiring but transforming. To say that this planet is gifted with his Presence is an understatement of immense proportions!!

As I write, a photo of my maternal grandfather sits on my computer screen. He was a railroad engineer, and this is the retirement picture of his last run. It is a close-up of him sitting at the instruments in the cab of the engine. I vividly remember the shirt he was wearing and the bib overalls that were part of the uniform all engineers wore at that time. It's as though I could reach out and touch him.

Each day as I open my computer and am greeted by the picture of that dear man, I think of him, and I am reminded of my ancestors and the lineage I am a part of. I know his life was very hard, and yet he was a kind, generous and deeply compassionate man. He and my grandmother were larger than life figures in my childhood and played a huge part in my internal development, acting as catalysts to my yearning for truth. It was through their response to everyday situations and the stories they told me that I witnessed post World War II resourcefulness, deep wisdom, resilience, and strength in action. I was so in awe of these two people and their ability to push through the darkest days as beacons of light.

One last acknowledgement and that is the deep well of gratitude I feel toward my Wholeness Navigator who has steered me through this life and compelled me to take a second look at what it knew would be important to the discoveries I was destined to make. What is it that triggers a recognition that leads to a discovery? I can only say it is something deep inside that is a part of the mystery of life, and we are gifted enormously when we respond to that trigger.

PREFACE

FROM MY MIND'S EYE

I see it all now so clearly as it unfolds in my Mind's Eye.

AS AN INDIVIDUATED CONSCIOUSNESS, I am mandated to explore the outposts of the material worlds and in my creative endeavors find ways to expand the principles of Source by transmitting them into those faraway worlds.

I've been on this journey for as long as I can remember; I often lose sight of my original mandate, but even then, I continue to respond to an internal impulse that I was born to heed, and wherever it directs, I feel compelled to explore.

My current assignment found me awakening in a human female body on planet Earth. I spent years of what I refer to as my caterpillar stage of life just learning to navigate the story I found myself born into. I grew up, married, birthed, and raised children—all the while accumulating unspoken questions that began to fester within my psyche, causing a deep internal unrest that resulted in a type of psychic pain that could not be ignored. It was those questions that wove the cocoon of isolation that would ultimately be the catalyst for my awakening.

As part of my liberation from the confines of the cocoon, I came to understand that my heart began beating in this body through the loving impulse of an Energetic Heart [1] sent by and connected to my Individuated Sovereign Integral. [2] My first breath was given to me by that same Sovereign Integral, and from those first Magnificent Impulses, this life as a human began.

In keeping with ITS promise not to interfere, once my heart began beating on its own and became the catalyst for all the other processes that would result in a fetus growing into an infant destined to be delivered by my mother, this Magnificent Being sat back to watch. It watched me grow and waited for that time when I would consciously ask IT to come into my life and be a Presence of Love and Guidance.

You see, the whole idea of coming into a physical body and into the Play of Separation was to enhance the understanding of the material worlds as a Sovereign Being and ultimately of our Source from which all Sovereign's are offspring. Source's Magnificent Plan was to

---

[1] See **Energetic Heart,** Appendix A - Glossary
[2] See **Sovereign Integral**, Appendix A - Glossary

learn about ITS creation by sending out individuated fragments of ITSELF to experience it. We are those fragments, and our purpose is two-fold—for Source to experience the material worlds and for us to be the emissaries that would bring Source's attributes into the world of separation and duality.

So, I have come to understand that my mission assignment as a flawed human, fraught with problems and pain that sometimes even leads to despair, as well as fun and love and the accouterments of family and friends" career, everything—all the experiences of physical life are sacred ones, a fact-finding mission of sorts. All are allowed by Source and therefore not judged in the way we were led to believe we are judged.

You ask, "How have you come to see it all now in your Mind's Eye?" And "What do you mean not judged in the way we were led to believe we are to be judged?" And "What do you mean your Sovereign Integral agreed not to interfere?"

I know, I know. In just sharing a few ideas, I have raised so many questions. As I tell you my story, I may raise even more questions than I will ever provide answers to. Let's just see where the journey takes us.

This morning my Mind's Eye revealed the set up for this Play of Duality. The material plane is a structure built to hold belief systems, societal organizations, and information known and yet to become known. We could call that structure The Field of Separation. Within that Field is a level of consciousness we have come to call the unconscious. The unconscious holds the record of experiences on the physical plane of everyone. (You dear reader may be tempted to call this level the Akashi Records, but in the language that will be used in this book, this part of our consciousness will be known as the Genetic Mind.[3])

The next level is the subconscious. That level is directly available to each of us, as it holds the beliefs and customs and predispositions of the ancestors of the families we are born into. During the time we are growing in our mother's womb, we are being programmed from the subconscious to help us assimilate into those families. We hear our mother's voice and even become familiar with the rhythm and syntax of the language we will later speak. School and college and life experience will acquaint us with more of the material in the unconscious. Much will depend on what we choose to do with our life as to what we will discover or bring into our awareness from the subconscious level of the Field of Separation.

All of this reminds me of what we have learned about the unconscious from pioneers of the mind like Carl Jung. He understood how humanity shares dream symbols and art forms across ethnic and global boundaries through the deep undercurrents of the unconscious. Psychology has also learned of how impulses from our subconscious can influence us. We

---

[3] See **Genetic Mind**, Appendix A - Glossary

talk about subconscious drives and compulsions and how a person can be so like a relative they have never met.

What I began to understand this morning, however, was that all those dynamics set up for us in the material world are somewhat of a loop to keep us stuck in the Play of Separation. As long as we are continually responding out of our programming from our subconscious and pulling information from the unconscious, we remain stuck in a game that has become old and tired.

Earlier you asked the question about our Sovereign Integral agreeing not to interfere and what I meant by that. Well, I think it works like this. This Play of Separation is set up for us to have choice. Remember? Choice and free will are the mantras of the material world. We believe we are free to choose the life we want to live and how we live it. We are free to make our own decisions and that includes whether or not we accept guidance. We are free to choose whether to stay asleep or to awaken, to search or to just live, to dive into the darkness or seek the Light.

I honestly think that choice and free will are a part of the Play of Separation and not true in the largest meaning of the word freedom. But I am getting ahead of myself and will explore that idea further on in this book.

If we choose the transformation road by inviting the Sovereign Integral State of Consciousness [4] to be a part of our human expression, this activates our ability to grow to access a level of awareness that will ultimately loosen the grip and influence of the Play of Separation. This process will trigger a transformation within us that will inspire us to want to create a more inclusive, harmonious, and heart-centered life and the Field of Separation will lose the stronghold over the individual it once had.

The Sovereign Integral exists both inside and outside material reality. Initially the Field of Separation was formed as a tool to be utilized to explore the physical world, but through events we will be exploring as this book unfolds, we will learn that we have allowed it to become a contrivance that controls us through deception and keeps us locked into suppression and limitation. In order to attain or transform into the Sovereign Integral level of consciousness, one must come to understand what the Field of Separation is all about and how it keeps us in a loop.

There is a way for us to move beyond the Field of Separation and transform into Sovereign Integral Consciousness, and that is through the Intelligence of the Heart.

Remember when I said that my Mind's Eye saw how the impulse from my Sovereign Integral began the beating of my heart? I actually saw a tether that connected straight from

---

[4] See **Sovereign Integral,** Appendix A, Glossary

my heart to my Sovereign Integral. The significance of that revelation is that each one of us has a direct connection to our Sovereign Integral. We don't need an intermediary; we need only gently pull on that tether to get our Sovereign Integral's attention. Our Sovereign Integral is also tethered to Source, and in that way, so are we connected directly to our Source.

I have come to realize the importance of understanding the distinction between the Field of Separation and the Field of the Heart. The difference in those two dynamics is profound. The Field of Separation helps us to maintain our limitations and nurtures our ideas of finiteness. It nurtures our differences and keeps us locked in polarized belief systems. Living in this field forces us to navigate through the material world as limited, deceived humans.

The Field of the Heart, once activated, helps us to connect with our Sovereign Integral Selves and that is where life will get interesting on a level unprecedented in this world. Activating our Field of the Heart begins the process of waking us up to our potential as Sovereign Beings living on this earth. As we work with the Prizm of Love we know as the Virtues of the Heart [5] —Appreciation, Compassion, Forgiveness, Humility, Understanding, and Valor—we begin the process of bringing our Sovereign Nature into the physical world. And by the way, it is through working with those qualities of the heart that we pull on the tether to our Sovereign Integral and expand its influence in our lives.

When we live locked in Separation, we do not know that we have direct access to Source, and therefore we think we need an intermediary or savior. This model of existence has been one to give hope to us while in separation and keep us searching for guidance. Without that drive to search for guidance and ultimately a way out of the game, we would not ever find the Field of the Heart and learn about our original Sovereignty. Once we learn that we have direct access to our Source through the Field of the Heart, we can begin to understand the Field of Separation and its limitations. This initiates the transformation that will bring Sovereignty Consciousness to us while living in the physical plane.

The other question you asked was regarding judgment. Think of it this way—we have been sent to explore, experience, and experiment with the material world. All of our experiences become part of Source memory as fragments of the play of life.

As we more deeply internalize and utilize the qualities of understanding, forgiveness, and compassion, we come to realize that all people act out of their perception of whatever circumstances they find themselves in. We are all at different levels of the awakening process, and that old teaching that we will be judged…I think it is more of a projection of how we

---

[5] Appreciation, Compassion, Forgiveness, Humility, Understanding, and Valor are known as the Six Heart Virtues in the *WingMakers Materials* and will be used in that context throughout this book. Chapter 25 offers an in-depth exploration of the Six Heart Virtues

feel about ourselves in the un-awakened state…we are unforgiving and judgmental towards ourselves and others as we do not understand our magnificence.

That old teaching of a Judgement Day was created as a scare tactic to keep humanity obedient servants to imposter gods who imprisoned us in a hologram of suppression to serve as slaves. If you don't believe me, take a few minutes to list the many ways your everyday life is enslavement. I'll wait.

In my Mind's Eye, I see a world where lights are popping up everywhere, like fireflies on a warm summer's eve, as we as a species start to wake-up to our true origins and begin to understand how to bring our true Divinity, our Source, into the material worlds.

INTRODUCTION

THIS BOOK IS ABOUT US. It begins with an alternate story about our origins as a species and continues through our early history, but most of all it is a book about where we are going. It began as a revision of my book *Breaking Free from the Tyranny of Beliefs: A Revolution in Consciousness* [6] (*BFTOB*). As I continued this unique writing journey, it became clear to me that I was birthing a fresh message that needed to pick up where *BFTOB* left off.

To be sure, some of the history presented in *BFTOB* will be discussed here and built on; however, I have come to the conclusion after a year of writing what I thought was a revision that the old book needs to stay as it is, warts and all. It is a chronicle of where I was at the time that I wrote it. For some who may feel daunted by the tasks and changes ahead, the humble beginnings that became *BFTOB* stand as an example of how a profound journey of exploration can begin.

Writing *BFTOB* became a catalyst that nudged me onto a trajectory that would ultimately guide me to a new threshold. The experiences of living the discoveries that inspired that book and writing about them brought me to the brink of a new paradigm. But that is where it stopped—with the wistful anticipation that a future I saw as a vague outline on the horizon would come to fruition. Since the publication of *BFTOB*, I have discovered some astounding information that is so transformative and exciting in its implications that we would be remiss not to at least take a look and ponder its message. The Universe is a vast and mysterious place. We do injustice to ourselves when we close off ideas that might not fit into our current paradigm and owe it to ourselves to at least examine them with an open mind before we make our decisions about what we might accept or reject.

Our story is complex and holds multiple nuances. In order to tell it, we must give ourselves permission to consider profound ideas outside the boxes of our current accepted realities. This book attempts to do that by building on one message that progresses through five parts: Part One: Paradise Lost—The Matrix Naiveté Built; Part Two: The Ruse That Built a World of Oppression and Separation; Part Three: Searching for Truth Through the Mirror of Perception; Part Four: Architects of a New Paradigm; and Part Five: Reclaiming Our Heart's Intelligence.

Why do I use the phrase *Transcending the Matrix* in the title of this book? In *BFTOB* I introduced a Core Belief Matrix that I felt was a confining mold that has formed the basis for

---

[6] Batey, Lark Aleta, *Breaking Free from the Tyranny of Beliefs: A Revolution in Consciousness*, Balboa Press, A Division of Hay House, 1663 Liberty Drive, Bloomington IN 47403, 2012.

the beliefs we hold today in most parts of the world. It was the reason we as a species seem to be trapped in a constant replay of a type of continuous self-repeating loop reminiscent of the movie *Groundhog Day*. Now I have discovered that there is way out of the Matrix and far more to our collective story than we have been previously told, thus the new book. When I wrote BFTOB, I recognized the limitations and suppression caused by the beliefs of the Matrix, but I did not know that it was created by imposter gods as a hologram of deception. The myth that begins this book identifies the imposter gods; the trajectory of the book helps us to understand how to transcend the Matrix, their creation.

Part One sets the stage of our continuing journey of exploration with a mythological story. A myth can have several meanings. In this book the myth is being used as a tool to introduce an archetypal story or model of probabilities designed to help us consider some important concepts from our ancient history that contributed to the formulation of the matrix. The middle sections of the book begin the process of building a bridge that will help us transcend the matrix as we find missing pieces that help us to reclaim our Heart's Intelligence. The last part offers a way of experiencing the world that is not only liberating but can create new paradigms as our heart-centered approach becomes a way of life.

If you find the myth or any ideas in this book outlandish, set aside your skepticism and disbelief for a time—you can always go back—and see how you feel at the end. All myths are outlandish but usually have some truth buried within them, and in order to discover those buried treasures, we have to give ourselves speculative license to broaden our understanding of what might have happened. This book is designed to expand ideas into new possibilities.

I have fashioned the chronology of the book to show a fascinating trajectory of how we were plunged into the Matrix as a species of consciousness. We have spent centuries seeking understanding of who we are and why we are here, but we only seem to get so far, and the ultimate answers that would liberate our species seem to be just out of reach.

If there is anything we can be sure of it is this: our species may be trapped or feel stuck, but we are an intelligent species with origins that are far beyond anything we could have ever dreamed. Because of our embedded innate intelligence that is a part of WHO WE ARE, we will find the way out. It is inevitable. As each of us as individuals becomes ready, we will recognize the inner guidance that will show us the path to our ultimate liberation.

In the long voyage of my lifetime, I have been inspired by others who have led me to information that was helpful at the time and became an important chapter of my life's journey. I am grateful for each phase. I am also aware that as we climb our mountain of transformation, each new plateau shows us an entirely new vista that transcends the one we just left. The expansive outlook at the top reveals a different world entirely compared to the hills and valleys and paths of the incremental journey that we traveled to get there.

To transcend is the "act of rising above something to a superior state." It comes from the Latin prefix *trans,* meaning beyond, and the word *scandare,* meaning to climb, to go beyond ordinary limitations.[7] As we embark on the transcendent flight of this bird's eye view of our story, a sense of who we are will begin to reveal itself in breathtaking wonder, opening us to a vista of a liberating future before us. The Matrix will continue in the three-dimensional world for a while. As each individual learns to transcend the Matrix, it loses its grip, ultimately allowing us access to higher dimensions of the Multiverse.

We develop the ability to transcend the matrix by *reclaiming our Heart's Intelligence.* The amazing ability of our Heart's Intelligence cannot be explained in a short introduction. It is the story this book will attempt to identify and explore. I have come to understand that reclaiming our Heart's Intelligence puts us on the trajectory to surpass all that has suppressed us and held us in suspension as a species. It is the key that will open the door to our birthright. It is the passage home.

The realizations I share in this book could not have been written had I not discovered the *WingMakers Materials* that were translated by James Mahu and began arriving on the planet in 1998. I discovered the materials sometime in 2011-2012, around the time that *BFTOB* went to press. The experiences that led me to write *BFTOB* prepared me for the possibilities presented in the *WingMakers Materials.* When I discovered these materials, it was like arriving at a bountiful oasis of rich soul food after a long, often desperate, and desolate journey of my hungry heart and soul. My life has always been about searching for truth and the bottom line. Each piece of the puzzle brought me closer, even though it was only a piece or two. I couldn't quite get the whole picture to come into view.

When I stumbled onto this treasure of the *WingMakers Materials,* I was quickly catapulted into the long dive that would take me to the depths of deeply transformative realizations and to a message of Love and Liberation. The materials tell a story that has contributed significantly to my understanding of the undercurrents and ramifications of some of our most ancient history, including our origins as a species. They have shed a clarifying light on the questions that have plagued and driven me my entire lifetime and introduced me to an unprecedented philosophy of inclusion and wholeness that is activating my own awakening. These materials offer a "missing link" to our liberation by showing us how we have become imprisoned by our intellect, cutting off some important parts of ourselves. We are shown the way out of that prison and into the reclamation of our long-lost selves through the development of our Heart's Intelligence.

---

[7] "Transcendence," *Vocabulary.com Dictionary,* https://www.vocabulary.com/dictionary/transcendence

I have found that the *WingMakers Materials* are like a never-ending story—one grows to meet them. When I first discovered them and began pouring over the materials, they spoke to my heart and soul, and I opened to them with eager gratitude because I felt they were what I had been searching for my entire life. What I soon learned was that after weeks and months of pondering what I had read, I could go back and re-read the materials, and new understandings would pop out that I just didn't see before, and because of that, they hold my interest and continue to deepen my understanding of myself, of others, and of world events. Aside from the *WingMakers Materials'* powerful and life affirming message, if there is anything magical or mysterious or potent about them, it is this.

As you embark on the journey of this book with me, dear reader, please know that I offer my understanding and experiences as <u>one</u> explorer navigating a bridge that began in the old belief system of personal growth that centered on the "I" development of the ego and intellect and then crossed over into an inclusive new world of "We" that focuses on heart-centered practice and exploration that loves and respects all of humanity, not just a chosen few. That is the trajectory our species is being drawn to discover and explore. Through the course of my process, I discovered a new standard of relevancy for any material's authenticity as truth—it must teach inclusion, unity, equality, love, and understanding and not encourage exclusivism, isolationism, separation, and hate. Those parameters have become my benchmark for any material's ultimate significance.

I offer this book as an example of one person's journey to discover a Wisdom Path. I do not in any way set myself up as an authority; I see myself more as one of a growing group of explorers of this new quantum territory and possibly a contributing mapmaker of that territory we are collectively discovering. If one chooses to refer to this map, keep in mind that it is an interactive map, still being created and never concrete, as each explorer will fill in their own experiences which are both valid and unique. This map is a group undertaking and will constantly change as we grow in understanding.

Richard Bach in his book *Illusions* said, "You teach best what you most want to learn." In my case I write best what I most want to learn. I write about this because in the practice of writing, my immersion takes me deeper and my understanding expands. I humbly share this work with you my reader from that point of view.

I am convinced that our species is headed toward an unprecedented liberation. We are at the foundational stage of this new paradigm that is being constructed by those who have prepared and are choosing to participate. We are finding our way. This foundation is important as the entire structure of a new paradigm will be built on it, and our deepening understanding will be what strengthens it.

The *WingMakers Materials* are profound and offer a compelling message of love and unity in a world programmed to keep us in separation. The materials present truths that although they initially seem new to us are very ancient and part of our original heritage. These truths have the power to guide us to important portals that can take us into a heart-centered world changing paradigm. The materials offer some important information, terms, and concepts for the ultimate understanding of our species; how we got here and where we are going. Where appropriate I will be incorporating the terminology of the *WingMakers Materials,* as it is part of the new language being introduced to the planet. For the reader's convenience, I have included a Glossary defining new terms in Appendix A.

I want to be clear on one point. The *WingMakers Materials* don't need anyone to build on or interpret them, and my intent is to do neither. I write because it is in my DNA to do so. It is how I integrate information. My life has been about searching for the bottom line, and I write to help myself understand. My intention with this book is to share a deeply personal voyage of discovery and the perspective its impact has had on me. As I have explored this material, I have come to appreciate the transformative significance of what it means to reclaim one's Heart's Intelligence and to recognize heart-centered innovations of others. My understanding has set me on a trajectory that has become an integral part of my everyday life.

I am sharing my discoveries and insights as an example of one person's journey and experience with this information. The *WingMakers Materials* offer us a powerful benchmark of standards to aide us in our transformation as a species. In this book I will hold some existing beliefs and materials in which I have been personally interested to the fire of that benchmark. It is my expectation that this process could lead to the understanding of lost truths that have been hidden in plain sight that are compatible with the new paradigm, as well as reveal the petrified densities that have kept the old order program running far too long. Our new standard can help us know what to keep and what to discard as old material that has served its purpose and is no longer relevant. This exploration will also delve into some long-held questions about our history.

We have been given a great gift. Built within the practice of developing our heart-centered Behavioral Intelligence [8] is a process that will show us how to manifest the most profound transformation our species has ever experienced. The deepest truth exists, and it is certain that it exists within the parameters of this new benchmark of love, equality, and unity.

---

[8] See **Behavioral Intelligence**, Appendix A - Glossary

It is important for us as a species to work together as we awaken from the Matrix to communicate and contribute to the foundation that is being constructed. I offer my experiences and understandings in this book as the possibility that these might be an event string[9] for some.

"The term WingMakers is encoded:

'Wing' is derived from the term wind or blow. It is the active force of setting new states into motion. 'Makers' is the plurality of the co-creators—that being the collective essence of humanity. Thus, WingMakers means that from the collective essence of humanity new states of consciousness come into being. This is the meaning of the term WingMakers, and it confers to humanity a new identity.

... humanity is transitioning to become WingMakers."

James Mahu, excerpt from Collected Works of the WingMakers, Volume 1

---

[9] See **Event String**, Appendix A - Glossary

THE WANDERER

I have felt a yearning for as long as I can remember; a yearning to know. I am not even sure what I yearn for. I lost something—I don't know when or how, but that sense of loss has driven me to search for whatever will fill the void for a long, long time. Is it a thread, a key, a knowing? Is it something or someone? I won't rest until that void is filled; no matter how many lifetimes it takes me.

I experience myself as a wave of self-knowing— hard to describe—this wave that fragments itself and dips into time and space, animating a physical body. But even as a wave experiencing many lives simultaneously, I still don't feel complete.

How I think those dips into many lifetimes will help is beyond me, but they are my only options right now. And that is where the sense of loss comes in. In my deepest yearnings I think I should have more options, should know more—but I don't. I remain stuck, in lives or between lives—wandering, always wondering. What is missing? Since lifetimes on earth are my only options, the clues have to be there, hidden in the threads of experiences that color the tapestries of physical life. So that is where I search.

From the point of existence where I express these thoughts, I am known as The Wanderer. It is only a title, though, that expresses the task at hand. I do think I have another name. I search for that name; I know it is out there somewhere, and I will find it. And when I find it, I will know who I am and what this yearning is all about that drives me so.

PART ONE

PARADISE LOST-THE MATRIX NAIVETÉ BUILT

*Our history is full of stories of how humanity
individually and collectively
has given away personal power
to the spiritual and/or political leaders of the day,
allowing them to dictate what is "evil" and what is "good."
In doing so, we have collectively sanctioned atrocities
against others who believe differently,
always in the name of the spiritual or political leader
who happens to be in power.*

1

ON BEING BLINDSIDED AND OTHER RUSES WE DIDN'T SEE COMING

"The Might that came upon the earth to bless, Has stayed on earth to suffer and aspire. The infant laugh that rang through time is hushed: Man's natural joy of life is overcast And sorrow is his nurse of destiny." Savitri—Sri Aurobindo

HOW IT BEGAN—MAKING A CASE FOR A MODERNIZED MYTHOLOGY

ONCE UPON A TIME, A very ancient time, before there was a marking of time, a Vast Field of limitless, immensely alive Consciousness bursting with possibility and a magnificent and unfathomable potential for creativity known as First Source lived in and was an integral part of The Grand Super Universe.

In one of those events the human mind is unable to comprehend or explain, this Vast Consciousness found a way to divide itself and The Grand Universe as well. From the Archives of Existence, we are told that over eons of time The Grand Universe became seven Super Universes. First Source's initial offspring became the Seven Genetic Archetypes, and from these Archetypes, a Central Race of Individuated Sovereign Entities for each Super Universe came into being.

We live in Super Universe Seven and are associated with the Seventh Archetype. It is this expression of First Source that interacts with and governs our universe.

The Seven Archetypes reside within the Seven Tribes of Light known as the Central Race, sometimes referred to as the Elohim or the Shining Ones.[10]

Within the Central Race is a sub-race known symbolically as the WingMakers, and within the WingMakers is an order of beings known as Lyricus, or Lyricus Teaching Order. It is from this teaching order that humankind is ultimately destined to understand their purpose on Earth.

Our Earth is part of the Seventh Super Universe. A biogenetic template of the Central Race, known as the 7th Archetype Soul Carrier of the Individuated Consciousness of First Source, was used to develop a soul carrying species of Individuated Sovereign Entities based on this genetic template. These soul carriers were designed to exist in various levels of density throughout the Seventh Super Universe. A planet's level of density would determine the vibratory condition and characteristics of a species of humanoids living on that planet.

Species of intergalactic Sovereign Entity explorers traveled interdimensionally, settling on planets that corresponded to their vibrational density. At first these explorers remembered themselves to be part of the Whole, and yet separate, and reveled in their ability to travel through multi- dimensions and galaxies and colonize planets that suited them. Each colony adapted to the planet they occupied and developed characteristics and abilities that were compatible with the one they inhabited, or they found planets that were well-suited to their needs.

These Sovereign Entities were mandated to explore the outer reaches of the Multiverse and record their experiences in the Vast Memory of Super Universe Seven for the purpose of understanding and inhabiting the Cosmos.

As eons of what we call time went by, the Sovereign Entities drifted further and further away from the memory of their origins and forgot that they were a part of the Great Source. They questioned where they came from and began looking for a God outside themselves.

In those ancient cosmic eras, before Earth humans were created, the Individuated Sovereign Entities manifested in a myriad of personality expressions as they colonized the Multiverse. They developed many sibling rivalries as they sometimes defended their

---

[10] Mahu, James, "Lyricus Discourse 2: Calling Forth the Wholeness Navigator," *WingMakers*, Lyricus, https://wingmakers.com/writings/lyricus/discourse2/

The terminology introduced in this myth—Central Race, WingMakers, Lyricus, Lyricus Teaching Order, Seventh Super Universe, Individuated Consciousness, Soul Carrier— are all concepts that are also found in "Excerpts from *Liminal Cosmogony*" at https://wingmakers.com/writings/lyricus/liminalcosmogony/ This describes the goal for humanity in the broadest terms.

Where indicated, some of these terms will also be found in Appendix A - Glossary and/or scattered throughout this book.

understanding of reality in order to preserve their individual and developing species. It is important to remember that all of these species were offspring of First Source.

One group of these Infinite Beings was a colony of Sovereign Integrals. [11] They were etheric beings, humanoid in appearance, yet not as physically dense as humans are today. They understood themselves to be Sovereign and individual and also integrated with all others of their species. They could function individually and at the same time communicate and function as One Being. The Sovereign Integrals were a species of consciousness that specialized in expressing the Prism of Love as a Behavioral Intelligence. They were gentle, kind, and compassionate, and lived in loving harmony with each other.

At some juncture in these long-ago times, a planet came into being that resonated with a frequency that matched their consciousness. It was filled with breathtaking landscapes and pristine waters and was a paradise to all who knew of its existence. A colony of Sovereign Integrals was mandated to be the guardians and protectors of this exquisite and untouched planet. That planet is the one we now call home.

Those Sovereign Integrals came to be known as the Atlanteans. They began experimenting to learn what they could about adapting to the planet. A variety of different creatures took form on the earth, and the Atlanteans learned that they could project a fragment of themselves into these living beings, as well as plants, and experience what it is like to be a tree or a lion or a lizard. Over eons of time different creatures were created or allowed to evolve and adapt to this world. Some were able to survive; others became extinct. It is not known how long the Sovereigns/Atlanteans lived thus before things began to change; but in a dynamic universe, variation is inevitable. Long before the introduction of the human species, developments were experienced by them in the most unexpected way and rooted in those developments is the legend of how we began.

Deeply hidden in the archives of our existence there lives a story of intrigue and mystery—powerful and far-reaching—waiting to be told. How is it that a species of Sovereign Beings changed from being whole, loving, compassionate, and collaborative into a territorial, self-centered species living in fear, separation, and polarity, strongly controlled by belief systems?

FROM COLLABORATION TO MANIPULATION

Earth was a beautiful and unique planet, and it was of interest to many species of the Multiverse, not just the Sovereigns/Atlanteans.

---

[11] See **Sovereign Integral,** Appendix A - Glossary

Sometime in this ancient of ancient times, eons before we began marking time, the story goes that a species known as the Anunnaki [12] arrived on this planet in desperate need of a gold-like substance in order to help their own planet's atmospheric shields. They had discovered that a fine gold dust was the only substance that would mend the atmosphere of their planet which was having problems with temperature control. Workers and explorers were sent out to search for this gold. It was discovered that Earth had a plentiful supply. Permission was sought by the Anunnaki and granted by the Atlanteans to mine the gold. Being a cooperative species—curious, friendly, and collaborative—they allowed the Anunnaki to mine the needed substance as they saw no reason not to be helpful.

Over time, the Anunnaki became tired of constantly having to mine this gold and went about creating a workforce of earthlings who could do the slave labor for them. Since the Atlanteans were able to animate creatures, the Anunnaki negotiated with them to use their life force in creating these slaves. These initial primitive workers were human-like, but more like clones than today's humans. They could not procreate, so when one expired, another had to be created to replace it. This process also soon became tedious to the Anunnaki in charge of the mining project. Eventually these clone-like beings were destroyed, and a new species of humanoids was created that could procreate. The Anunnaki partnered with the Sirians and other inhabitants of the Multiverse, and each brought their special abilities to help in this endeavor. The Anunnaki had already convinced the Atlanteans to lend their life force to the first work force, and the second creation of this slave force of humans also received this same life force; and so, a great collaboration was underway. Beings from Sirius helped with the design so that these earth creatures could procreate; and a species known as Reptilians seeded the earth with foods that would nourish the new creations.

The Atlanteans' life essence entered the newly created human instruments through the breath.

Now the Anunnaki and their leader Anu were a very cunning and manipulative species, and they considered it quite an achievement to convince the Atlanteans to use their life force to animate these creations. Once Anu observed how the Atlanteans had begun to forget their origins, he plotted to trap them indefinitely in the human bodies he and his cohorts had created. His ultimate plan was to rule over them as their god. A veil of deception and suppression was created to obscure the consciousness of the Atlanteans once they entered human instruments; the programmed veil concealed their true identity. This was seen as a clever and great victory.

---

[12] See **Anunnaki**, Appendix A - Glossary

The human instruments [13] created by the Anunnaki were programmed as obedient slaves with a powerful instinct to survive and a strong fear of death. They were given egos that were oriented to the physical world and the programming that animated their bodies steered them into becoming focused and conforming to the material world. In this way the Atlanteans became human, and their forgetting-over-time became complete.

Anu, the powerful and diabolically intelligent leader of the Anunnaki, designed an elaborate mythology centered on his return to rule the earth one day as the savior of the world. This powerful belief was incorporated into the religions and programming of the humans to give them something not only to believe in, but also to act as a behavioral regulator. Obeying and pleasing what they believed to be their God was a way to keep them in line and conform to the programming. This also helped to maintain the illusion that they were growing and developing spiritually.

An intricate Hologram of Deception [14] was created as a program on Earth designed to perpetuate the entrapment of the Atlanteans in human bodies. Through genetic engineering, a royal bloodline of humans was created by inseminating human females with the bloodline of Anu. This gave Anu and his cohorts a loyal ruling class that would keep alive the belief systems perpetuating the return of Anu as savior and ensure that the programming continued.

The Human Mind System [15] that the Anunnaki and their cohorts designed is a veil of distortion connected to all Human Instruments. Because it distorts reality and entraps the Human Mind in a suppression framework, causing separation and a fear and survival mentality, the vibrational density of Earth has become much darker and more concrete. Anu and his cohorts did not want to get imprisoned in this suppression system, so he made the decision not to return as their ruler because he didn't want to become ensnared as the Atlanteans had. The story of Jesus as savior was eventually created as a useful substitute to keep the Sovereigns/Atlanteans trapped.

The Anunnaki, having fulfilled their mission of attaining the needed gold for their planet left Earth and its inhabitants to continue indefinitely in the programmed hologram.

The Atlanteans, now trapped in human bodies, remained connected at the deepest level through a Genetic Mind. [16] This mind held all of the memories of their origins and also the programming of the beliefs that Anu had set in motion, namely separatist, survival, and fear-based ones.

---

[13] See **Human Instrument,** Appendix A - Glossary
[14] See **Hologram of Deception,** Appendix A - Glossary
[15] See **Human Mind System,** Appendix A - Glossary
[16] See **Genetic Mind,** Appendix A - Glossary

But not all the Sovereigns became trapped in human instruments.

Some, when they saw what was happening, fled and did not participate in these experiments. They became known to the ancients as the Guardians, the Elohim, the Shining Ones, and now to us as the WingMakers. They would occasionally offer glimpses of the truth in dreams or inspiration to individuals who were subconsciously more resistant to the programming.

For example, the Gnostics, an early group of esoteric Christians, taught about a Demigod named YVHV or Yaldabaoth who was the creator of this world. They believed that what they called the Unknown God (First Source) was greater than this Demigod.

The Sovereigns continue transmitting their life force through the breath and the Energetic Heart, [17] an energy field around the human body that animates the human heart and transmits loving characteristics of the Sovereigns such as compassion, understanding, and forgiveness. The Anunnaki could not interfere with that transmission as it was the only way the human bodies could be animated.

The elaborate programming of the human instrument by the Anunnaki and their cohorts was a program of separation and focused more on the development of the ego and the intellect in order to keep the Energetic Heart from having much impact on the humans, but its characteristics were there nonetheless and were and are accessible to humans in varying degrees.

As time progressed, understandings came to light to give the human species hints that this world *as it is known (the Hologram of Deception)* was created by the Anunnaki. Scholars who discovered and translated the Sumerian Tablets recognized the Anunnaki as the creators of the human body and gave them credit for being the creators or gods of this world.

The Old Testament of the Bible and similar writings found worldwide all have stories of how these civilizations have interacted with Anu and his sons Enki, Enlil, and Marduk, who all became known as the gods of this world.

They demanded exact obedience and were gods of cruelty and vengeance. It is these entities who cemented the "fear of god" into the human psyche.

What got lost in translation, however, is that the Sovereign Beings are the offspring of First Source, trapped in bodies programmed by a sibling god. You see, all these species are basically siblings as we all come from the same Source. Some may be more evolved, but none are greater than the other. We have discussed from the beginning how each species specialized in certain skills and characteristics. Anu was especially focused on power and

[17] See **Energetic Heart,** Appendix A - Glossary

control and aspired to be considered as God. Because he was very much aware that he was an infinite being, he developed a great deal of power. He wasn't impressed with the loving and compassionate way of approaching existence that the Sovereigns held, and it was a great coup to trap these loving and somewhat naive beings for his purposes.

In Anu's mind, power won over love and was more important. The human species was programmed with that same belief, and so love was vilified as a soft and weak emotion, and power took center stage.

Anu and his cohorts programmed humans in such a way that it would be difficult for them to believe this deception story because one could reason that if the Sovereigns were infinite beings, they would be impossible to trap. The program contributed to keeping human minds closed and confined by the keeper of all the beliefs of humankind, the Genetic Mind.

This is the conundrum the human species must wrestle with as we examine this new mythology of our origins and try to make sense of one of the greatest stories of sibling rivalry ever told.

Once the Sovereigns/Atlanteans were anchored into the human instruments, they plunged deeper into separation created by this program of deception and completely lost the memory of their identity. The human ego was masterfully created by the Anunnaki to function within the system of polarity and separation. The slave mentality is deeply embedded in the human psyche and has run rampant in all the cultures of the world since humans began. Throughout humanity's journey on this earth, there has been a tendency for one class of a civilization to dominate and enslave the other class or classes of humans living within that society. If a population is conquered, the inhabitants are enslaved by the conquerors. In every walk of life, we see examples of how we are enslaved.

The Anunnaki weren't sure how long it would take for the Sovereigns to figure out their ruse of deception, so to give the humans some feelings of self-empowerment, they embedded within this programmed system the illusion of free will through choice.

You see, in the realm of free will we actually only have two choices: either to stay in the program or to leave it. Within the program and living in duality, we exist within the illusion of choice. We have choice when we are presented with everyday situations where we have to make a decision, but ultimately any choice we make is just another experience in the program. When we use our free will to begin examining our lives and our belief systems in order to break free from the deception and leave the system, this choice activates a whole new paradigm within our consciousness, and that is ultimately what this book is about. But I digress; let's get back to our story....

Initially inspired by Anu, the ruling class put belief systems into place to maintain the agenda of servitude and keep their subjects obedient. Religion was a useful tool because it perpetuated into the belief systems the idea of a Higher Power to be obeyed without question, giving rulers a powerful way to subjugate whole populations. After all, who could argue with an omniscient off-planet being?

Once a belief system was activated, it began its insidious influence to maintain the established way of life because the offspring grew up in the customs and belief systems of the parent. Thus tradition, culture, and belief systems were passed down through generations. Nations developed their unique flavor of belief systems and traditions and customs. Each country established a border and fought to defend their little corner of the world. National boundaries maintained even more levels of division. The ruling classes understood that as long as humans were fighting amongst themselves, this would keep them distracted and occupied—too busy to ever discover their true origins.

The momentum has been so effective that as eons of Earth-time have continued to pass, humans have become more deeply entrenched in earth's reality. Even upon the release of death, they could no longer return to their original state where true rejuvenation between lives would help them to release the experiences of the incarnation just completed. Instead, they went to a place that gradually became an extension just beyond Earth where the environment replicates the after-death beliefs taught to individuals in various cultures. In this way these lost beings have never been allowed, even upon death, to understand that they are Infinite Beings. From this world of the dead, they usually reincarnated into a new body very quickly, often without clearing the old life out of their energy field. They began to reincarnate often with past life issues imbedded into their energy fields, perpetuating a continuance of these issues in their new lifetimes. These Grand Beings were trapped in a vicious cycle with little hope of escape without some form of help.

Earth—once a paradise—gradually became a place of suffering and strife. The once pristine waters and natural resources were taken over and polluted by those whose only interests were in keeping humanity enslaved and working to support the greedy and powerful. Religious and territorial wars causing great suffering and atrocious acts of domination became the norm for this great planet.

Down through the ages, a concept of God began to form. This God was believed to be a powerful and terrifying being who banished us to earth to seek redemption because of something we did. This created a belief in a "fall" of some kind. The most prevalent teachings centered on us being exiled to this planet to "work out our salvation" through suffering, and these belief systems generated guilt and shame from those original feelings of abandonment. This led to the reasoning that maybe through suffering on Earth, God would see our plight and take pity on us and forgive us. In this state of mind, it was quite easy for humans to latch onto the idea of a savior, a redeemer, to show us the way home; not realizing that we are living on the planet that is our home, locked in a program of deception that hides our Sovereignty and true origins.

Our belief in the need for a savior began to manifest teachers who were willing to show The Way. However, while we yearned for a savior, unless that "savior's" teachings reinforced what was already believed, the teacher would be judged an infidel or a product of evil, trying to lead us astray. Many have been tortured and slaughtered throughout history for trying to help us wake up from the nightmare in which we are trapped. Thus, we find ourselves in a cosmic Catch 22 as we perpetuate the cycle of limiting and suppressive core beliefs.

Male and female bodies were created with a strong attraction between them, and the act of procreation became the method for birthing into this world. With this split into masculine and feminine consciousness, a powerful precedence was set for polarities to manifest upon the earth. As a split consciousness, it has become more difficult to think, feel, or create from a unified state. Humans have become more specialized by focusing their understanding of reality from the fragmented point of a masculine or feminine view while in a physical body.

The characteristics of the masculine energy were perceived as active, aggressive, and focused; the feminine characteristics are receptive, passive, and intuitive. While both sexes have retained the ability to utilize the characteristics of both genders, one basic set of gender characteristics generally dominates, leaving the other characteristics in a recessive but accessible state.

As the feminine characteristics are basically receptive, peaceful, and nurturing, it was easy for the males to subjugate the females, setting precedence for male domination.

Another factor that contributed to male domination was the way humans set up their societies. They began grouping in small communities and often had to fight other communities to keep their homes and families safe. Since the women bore and cared for the children, it became the male's lot to defend them. Thus, a warrior mindset began to manifest on the earth as dominator characteristics took a firm hold on the masculine psyche.

All was not lost, however. As briefly mentioned earlier, not all the Sovereigns were tricked into giving their life force to the humans on the planet. Some refused to participate in this scheme of Anu and fled. They remained in their etheric form and became the Guardians (Elohim, WingMakers) who watched over their trapped siblings. Throughout history there have been those who are not as susceptible to the programming as their fellow humans and are open to inspiration from the Guardians. In this way new and innovative ideas have been gradually introduced to the world. Our history tells us that new ideas typically come at a great price to the innovator because they are generally resisted by the status quo. This helped me to better understand why humanity is so dogged resistant to new ideas— we are programmed to be that way. It all makes sense.

Some might ask: if there are Guardians who know about this entrapment, why didn't they just free their siblings from this prison of deception? Aside from the fact that the programming of the humans was extremely hard to penetrate because it was set-up in such a way as to be self-correcting, the Guardians were initially curious about the experience of limitation. To have some of their species trapped and living as embodied beings who had forgotten their origins was something they could learn a great deal from. The experiment was allowed to continue, at least for a time, so all the experiences of physical life would go into the Collective Memory to be tapped at any time throughout eternity.

As the Guardians watched over their siblings, they began making preparations to eventually bring this Grand Experiment to a close and to awaken the Sovereigns to their place in the Multiverse and as the rightful owners of the earth as it had been in the beginning. It was important that the preparations be covert, however. The program is powerful and has the ability to self-correct,[18] so the process of infiltration that would eventually free their siblings is painfully slow. Any knowledge that the trapped Sovereigns received concerning the deception was stopped, or the information was made to look foolish so as not to be believed, or the messengers were executed, or their message was utilized to the advantage of the Anunnaki.

The Guardians studied the situation for eons of time and watched as very dark times settled over planet Earth. Throughout the course of history, the progress of technology has made it possible for them to facilitate the awakening of the Sovereigns as they learned ways to "hack" the program. Progress, albeit slow, has been happening all along.

A team of Guardians has now incarnated on Earth. Each member has a specific task to do in building the foundation upon which the suppression can end and the new paradigm begin. They stay out of the limelight and work behind the scenes. One of the members of this team, James Mahu, has begun the long process of preparing cultural activating materials in the form of music, story, and artwork to begin the awakening of those prepared. As those who are ready receive this information, they strengthen the foundation as they

---

[18] Spivak, Nova, "Is the Universe a Computer? New Evidence Emerges," http://www.novaspivack.com/uncategorized/is-the-universe-a-computer-new-evidence-emerges
Maryland physicist James Gates, Jr. has discovered an error-correcting code embedded within the equations of supersymmetry that describes fundamental particles within the law of physics. Gates explains: "This unsuspected connection suggests that these codes may be ubiquitous in nature and could even be embedded in the essence of reality. If this is the case, we might have something in common with the Matrix science-fiction films, which depict a world where everything human beings experience is the product of a virtual-reality-generating computer network."

begin working on the grid surrounding Earth to change the resonance from a self-centered paradigm to a heart-centered one.

Others will incarnate at a later time and pick up the gauntlet to carry the new paradigm forward with assignments specifically for their time—moving humanity towards a momentous discovery that will help mankind remember and know without a doubt who they are. This is known as the Grand Portal, [19] or the irrefutable scientific discovery of the soul.

The day is coming when humanity will realize that we did nothing wrong. We trusted and we collaborated, and our siblings took advantage of us. In the process, however, we have come to learn some valuable and far- reaching lessons, and that is what we will take with us as we move forward into the liberation that is also a part of our story and our heritage.

Certainly, we have lost our naiveté in our journey through the Grand Experiment, but we are also becoming expanded, wiser Sovereign Beings. If we look at this experiment of forgetting on Earth as a training ground and prerequisite for creations and experiences in the future, possibly even preparing us for the creations of other worlds, we have learned a great deal about the experience of finiteness and who we share our life force with when we collaborate—on any level.

The Guardians planted certain information to be discovered at a time in the planet's history when the beginning of the end of this Grand Experiment is near. As the human self is activated and reaches toward our Source by grasping new concepts, and Source reaches toward the human as we open to Source, this expansion of dimensions makes it possible for new developments to occur on earth that will eventually bring about a mass awakening.

The present human body is designed to hold a certain amount of electrical energy and resonates within a limited range of frequencies. The Grand Beings we came from resonate at a much greater expanded range of light frequencies while staying connected to the human to give life to the body. It makes sense that as an individual begins to release the core beliefs that create limitation, the body's energy will start to clear and have the capacity to tolerate a more expanded range of light frequencies from our Sovereign Integral.

If that is so, then as evolving humans we can expect to have the ability to hold an increasing expansion of Light and frequency ranges from our Sovereign Integral, expanding our awareness exponentially while still living in the human body. The Light field of the Love of our Source is our original state of consciousness, and it hovers around us, waiting to be summoned and integrated. Embedded within each of us are triggers that can be activated

---

[19] See **Grand Portal,** Appendix A - Glossary

by encoded material, given to us by Lyricus and the WingMakers that will help us to wake up from the programming of limitation and separation.

The most important part of our awakening at the level of consciousness where we are now includes learning how to reconnect with that Love that is our Source through the virtues of the Energetic Heart. Meanwhile, what has our species learned during our sojourn in the Hologram of Deception? We have learned a great deal about what it is like to live in and experience the limitations of a physical body. We have come to understand intimately the trauma of separation and felt and learned to overcome the hardship and pain of fear, war, starvation, and oppression in many different time periods and with diverse tools to work with, from the very primitive to the most technologically advanced.

We have experienced first-hand what happens when we feel lost and hopeless and disconnected. We have lived through countless variations of aloneness that lead to suicide and the desperation that leads to crimes of passion. We have come to understand that when there is no hope and humans are in an emotionally or physically weakened state, individuals and societies are more vulnerable to corruption and oppression. We have also experienced the resiliency of individuals who give themselves strength and hope in a myriad of ways to survive through difficult times.

The Love of Source, so much a part of our birthright, is a part of us in spite of the efforts of the program to block it. We have known the incredible feelings of love that can grow as we become attached to a newborn infant or a new pet, as well as the feelings of devotion, loyalty and love that can arise out of human relationships. We have learned what it is like to come out of darkness into light, whether it is through a life-altering insight, a breathtaking view on a mountain top, or the magnificence of a sunrise that promises a new day, regardless of the darkness of the previous one. We have learned the power of hope and character and resiliency in the midst of limitation that can sometimes be crippling.

We have had experiences of being wealthy and poor, and all the degrees in between, and discovered what brings happiness and what doesn't.

We have lived through countless experiences, both positive and negative, that have created an expanding memory of consciousness for the Whole, as well as for each individual Sovereign Being. When we return once again to Sovereign Integral Consciousness, we will all have access to these countless memories and lessons experienced through a variety of perceptive lenses.

Humanity has arrived at a crisis in the collective history of the earth and those who inhabit it. The outcome of this crisis is like no other because if we work through it successfully, we will find ourselves in a new era with the potential of being fully aware while still in a physical body, knowing that we are no longer separate, but rather Sovereign Beings and connected to Source. As we grow in our understanding of that connection, we can finally realize that all the splits and polarities and traumas we have experienced in this world are part of a grand experimental illusion, and we can awaken to our wholeness and embrace our divinity. We can hasten our individual trajectory to our Sovereign Integral state of consciousness, or we can choose to slow it down; the choice is ours.

Do we allow ourselves to wake up to who we really are, or do we remain asleep, hypnotized by the suppressive schemes that are destroying the resources of this planet and keeping us trapped in deception and limitation?

The rest of this book will flesh out our story as we explore keys to this awakening process. We have the opportunity to awaken to the Sovereign Beings we once were while retaining the memories of what it was like to be asleep.

Our first step will be to go back in time and trace how our current belief systems became embedded in our psyches so that we can better understand how the program suppresses and limits us.

If we as a species can grow to understand how we have been deceived and suppressed and begin to awaken, that accomplishment has the potential of creating a powerful and far-reaching metamorphosis for all humankind, maybe even all consciousness. As we awaken from the illusion and claim our Sovereignty, we will bring a completely new way of being to Earth. It is in activating and utilizing this new way that we will find the solutions to the crises that plague us now.

EXPLORATIONS

(Throughout this book I will be suggesting explorations that will help to take your understanding of these concepts to a new level. A journal dedicated to these ponderings might be useful as you journey through this book.)

1. Points to Ponder:
    a. What makes gold such an important commodity in this world?
    b. Slavery has been around since the creation of humans—is it something in our DNA? Many references to slavery are found in the Bible and down through history. Think of all the forms of slavery we find ourselves in, even today. Can we see for ourselves that indeed the Human Instrument has been programmed with a slave mentality?
    c. Why the belief in the need for a Savior? Have we been programmed to believe we are "lesser than" and in need of someone "greater than" us to redeem us as a way to keep us enslaved to belief systems and hierarchies that serve the ruling classes?

    d. A survival-based belief system is also a fear-based system and demands conformity. Ponder and journal how issues of survival, fear, and conformity manifest in your life.

2. Keeping the above points in mind, think about your life events and make a list of the main ones. From this list answer the following questions:

    a. What do I see or feel or experience as the overall theme of this lifetime?

    b. What do I have to believe about myself to have these life events?

    c. Where have I been successful?

    d. How did that success feel? How did I respond?

    e. Which of my experiences have I labeled as failures? How did I respond to them?

    f. Describe what success and failure means to you in the larger scheme of your life.

    g. What do you feel your mission is for this lifetime?

HOW WE LOST OUR CONNECTION TO OUR HEART'S INTELLIGENCE

Lost

Sovereign Explorer
Lost in the dream of time
Origins forgotten
Distracted by the seduction of ego
Donning countless disguises
Unaware of inner guides

Fragmented Consciousness
Projected into Human Instruments
Sustained by the biosphere
Confined to the senses
Suppressed by deception
Trapped in limitation
Weathered into submission
By the ravages of countless lifetimes

Event Strings
Messages for you
Expose the ruse of the programmed mind
Stirrings—questionings—insights
Awaken from the dream
Inspired by the Wings of Light
Navigate into the realms of wholeness
Appreciation—compassion—forgiveness
Resonate—activate—reconnect

2

THE RIVER OF BELIEFS AND ITS TRIBUTARIES

*"It takes courage to knowingly read a book that is
challenging some of your cherished beliefs."*
— Mokokoma Mokhonoana

A RIVER OF BELIEFS FEEDS the Collective Consciousness and has since the beginning of the history of humanity, defining the restrictions of how the human species has lived in separation. Individual cultures have given the customs and practices of these beliefs distinctive flavors. The main river of beliefs has fed all cultures a similar story, and the tributaries of that original river still exist today.

It is not within the scope of this work to define in detail every ancient belief system; however, I do want to give some examples that have played a significant role in developing the cultures we have today to help us see how we have been immersed in that river and where that river has taken us.

THE TOWER OF BABEL MYTH

Mythical stories give us a way to explain what we don't understand. Take the myth of how we became divided into different cultures and languages, for instance.

The Old Testament story of the Tower of Babel is an archetypal story that has attempted to explain why our species developed a variety of languages and cultures. The story goes that at a time when all of Earth spoke the same language, the people chose to build this massive tower that would reach to heaven. God says in Genesis 11:6 that "If as one people speaking the same language they have begun to do this, then nothing they plan to do will be impossible for them." Genesis 11:7 "...let us go down and confound their language that they may not understand one another's speech." The Tower of Babel story gives us some clues that take on a whole new dimension of meaning and significance when we consider it in light of our myth in Chapter One. As a parent we want our children to succeed beyond our expectations. Why would our "creator" not want the same for us??? What was this creator afraid of??

This god who we now know is Anu and/or his sons—Marduk, Enki, and Enlil—were afraid that if the people remained unified, they could accomplish impossible feats and maybe even discover the deception of how "god" enslaved them. It is very plausible that after the human instrument was created and the Sovereign life force was used to animate the bodies, Anu and his cohorts did not know for sure what it would take for the Sovereigns to regain their memory, so they did everything they could to make sure that would not happen.

One sure tactic to keep a species deceived would be to make it difficult for them to communicate. Inserting different languages into the civilizations scattered over the earth would be an effective way of isolating them and keeping them from being able to communicate with one another and to create wariness of the "other." Suspicion of what we do not understand, i.e., other languages and customs and beliefs, has been highly effective in providing the rationale to defend our territories, even if it meant war. This was a cunning strategy for keeping populations distracted from their true heritage and purpose for being on this earth.

Now our technological devices have the ability to translate languages for us, so language barriers are becoming less problematical, and computer "language" is universal. The same language is used to program computers, regardless of the nationality. James Mahu, around the year 2000, predicted that the internet would become what it is today. He identifies it as the OLIN (One Language Intelligence Network) technology [20] and explains that this technology will play a large part in breaking down global language barriers.

Another factor that is helping to unify us globally—English is becoming a common language around the world, and when one language is known worldwide, that alone is unifying. The time of separation is coming to an end as we enter the era of transparency and expansion. The Tower of Babel story gives us a mythical or archetypal story to explain how we might have been sent further into separation. Now as we head into an unprecedented new era in humanity's long sojourn on this earth, the internet is changing all of that and making it easier for us to communicate and grow in our understanding of one another which has the potential of breeding compassion and cooperation.

---

[20] Mahu, James and John Berges, *Collected Works of the WingMakers, Volume I*, edited by John Berges, Egg Harbor, NJ: Planetwork Press, 2013. The complete explanation can be found in "The WingMakers Glossary," p. 669. I have added a short paragraph to the **Genetic Mind** definition in the Appendix A - Glossary.

As we grow in our understanding of one another and share our traditions and myths, we learn that the ancient history in all countries includes similar stories and shares similar archetypes. The great flood is an example of an historical event all civilizations have in their past. Carl Jung discovered that we all share similar dream symbols, regardless of our nationality or ethnic background. In spite of our perceived differences, it is amazing how many commonalities we share worldwide. We are coming to understand that on a very deep level we are all connected in more ways than we could ever imagine.

GOD INCARNATIONS, VIRGIN BIRTHS AND OTHER ANCIENT MYTHS

Our current religious belief systems maintain many of the same doctrines that were a part of the early polytheistic, pagan, and Mystery religions. There are basically few differences from what they were thousands of years ago, long before Christianity came on the scene. Each culture had its own pantheon of gods and goddesses that were worshipped or called upon for help and guidance with the various events of everyday life. If we were to explore the stories of the pagan gods in any culture, we would discover not only many parallels to the story of Jesus, but to our overall collective belief systems as well. Why is that significant? The story goes that Jesus was crucified for his message, and yet the religion that has become Christianity is—as you will see—the very same teachings, customs, and beliefs that were alive and well at the time he supposedly lived.

One of the most popular beliefs to illustrate my point is the Virgin Birth. The following short list is an example of ancient, pre-Christian religions that believed in a Virgin Birth. A factor to consider when we think of the Virgin Birth archetype that is found in Genesis 6:2 and 6:4 where we read that the "sons of God saw the daughters of men that they were fair; and they took them wives of all they chose…When the sons of God came into the daughters of men and they bear children to them, the same became the mighty men which were of old, men of renown." Some say the "daughters of men" were impregnated by a form of artificial insemination while others believe they were simply impregnated in the usual way and thus a "god" would impregnate a human virgin. Regardless of the impregnating method, it is possible that the Virgin Birth archetype/myth began way back then. These "Virgin Births" brought forth kings and the ruling classes.

As I studied this information, I was astounded at the similarities in terminology utilized by these ancient belief systems and Christianity.

Osiris—an ancient Egyptian god—was believed to be virgin-born. His sufferings, death, and resurrection were celebrated in the annual mystery play at Abydos around March 25 or at the Vernal Equinox. He was called Kryst or the Anointed One. He was born of the Virgin Isis Meri and laid in a manger; a star announced his birth, and three wise men came to him. Osiris was reported to be a teacher at the Temple at age twelve, disappeared for eighteen years and was baptized at age thirty by Anupt the Baptizer who was later beheaded. He was betrayed and crucified between two thieves and rose on the third day. He was called by many names including The Way, The Truth and The Light, Messiah, God's Anointed Son, the Son of Man, the Word Made Flesh.

Horus—the son of Osiris—was worshipped three thousand years before Jesus. Many ancient Egyptian statues of Mother and Child that have become equated with Jesus and Mary were originally statues of the baby Horus and his mother Meri Isis. The parallels between the Jesus story and the Horus story are numerous: the names of their mothers—Meri and Mary; the virgin birth; the baptisms of each: Horus by Anupt who was later beheaded and Jesus by John the Baptist who was also beheaded; both had twelve disciples, walked on water, cast out demons, healed the sick and raised the dead; Horus was taken to a high mountain from Armenta to be tempted by Set; Jesus was taken to a high mountain from Palestine to be tempted by Satan; both successfully resisted the temptation; Horus raised his father Osiris from the dead, and Jesus performed the same miracle with Lazarus; Horus was born in Anu (the place of bread), and Jesus was born in Bethlehem (the house of bread); both delivered a sermon on the mount, and both were crucified. [21]

Krishna—believed to be a Hindu incarnation of God—is born of the Virgin Devaki, and a star heralded his nativity. Krishna's story parallels many other events depicted in the birth of Jesus.

Buddha—an enlightened being followed throughout the East—was born of a Virgin mother named Maya. His birthday was celebrated on December 25, and he was visited by wise men who acknowledged his divinity.

Mithra—an important god in Persian polytheism—was born to a virgin mother in a cave. The believers in Mithraism celebrated his birth on December 25 and his resurrection in the spring (around Easter time). Mithraism existed in tandem with Christianity in the first three centuries AD. Mithra was reported to be the most widely venerated deity in the Roman Empire at the time that the historical Jesus was believed to have lived. He participated in a supper with his twelve apostles (signifying the twelve signs of the zodiac) before his crucifixion and ascended into heaven at the time of the spring equinox.

---

[21] "Not Just Jesus: Other Virgin Births," *Law of Attraction GPS,* 2010, http://www.lawofattractiongps.com/living-law- of-attraction/not-just-Jesus-other-virgin-births/#axzz3vXbC6S8Q

Mithra was also known as Sol Invictus or the Invincible Sun. In the ancient Zoroastrian religion of Persia, Mithra was the spirit or archangel of the sun and of fire. Mithraism evolved within Persia as a religion separate from Zoroastrianism, and Mithra was worshipped as the sun god. [22]

Dionysus—the Greek god of fertility—was born to the Virgin Semele.

Quetzalcoatl—an Aztec deity—was born to a virgin mother Chimalman. The Aztecs were expecting his second coming when the Spaniards invaded their country in the 16th century.

Savior/salvation—all of the above ancient god figures and more were sacrificed and expected to come back as saviors to save the world. This was an especially important belief that was central to most religions of the world.

The pre-Christian "sons of God" (i.e., Osiris, Mithra, Dionysus, Heracles, and others) were believed to be born of a virgin, either in a cave or cowshed, and placed in a manger. Several of them were announced by a star and attended by wise men bringing expensive gifts. Stories of healing the sick and walking on water are attributed to them as well. Most were crucified or sacrificed in some manner to save mankind; they were entombed in a cave and rose on the third day at the Spring Equinox. Names given them include Good Shepherd, Alpha and Omega, Master, Redeemer, King of Kings, Only Begotten Son, Savior, Sin Bearer, and Prince of Peace. [23] Practically every detail of the recognized story of Jesus Christ that forms the foundational teachings and doctrine that the Christian Churches are built upon was taken from the mythologies of the pre-Christian era. These are the teachings that were in vogue at the time Jesus supposedly lived.

All of the above mentioned "deities" were saviors long before Jesus Christ was deemed to be the savior by the Council of Nicea, and their mythologies were transferred to the story of Jesus.

THE MYSTERY SCHOOLS

The mystery schools were comprised of various secret cults of the Greco-Roman world that offered religious experiences not provided by official public religions. The Mystery

---

[22] "What does Sol Invictus mean and how did it affect Christianity?" *Answers*, https://www.answers.com/Q/What does Sol Invictus mean and how did it affect Christianity

[23] Hoeller, Stephan A., "The Gnostic World View: A Brief Summary of Gnosticism," *The Gnosis Archive*, http://gnosis.org/gnintro.htm
Information taken verbatim in part and excerpted directly in part from this article.

religions reached their peak of popularity in the first three centuries AD. Their origin goes back to the earlier centuries of Greek history.

The word mystery is derived from the Greek verb *myein*—to close— referring to the lips and eyes. Mysteries were always secret cults, and the person had to be initiated or taken in. [24]

Other than Judaism and Christianity, the Mystery religions were the most influential ones in the early centuries before and after Christ. They involved secret ceremonies known only to the initiates. The major benefit of these practices was thought to result in redemption.

Basic characteristics of a Mystery religion:

1. Each mystery school centered around an annual growing cycle in which life is renewed in the spring and dies in the fall. Practicing rituals in these specific times of the year gave the participants deep symbolic significance to the cycles of growth, death, decay, and rebirth.
2. Each cult had secret initiations to give the participant information about the cult's god or goddess and included teachings on how to achieve unity with that specific deity. This was always secret knowledge.
3. The mystery of each school centered on a specific deity, and that deity either returned to life after death or triumphed over enemies. A theme of redemption from the earth and material planes was usually a part of this. The mystery was enacted as a sacramental drama that appealed largely to the feelings and emotions of the initiates. The religious ecstasy experienced was symbolic of beginning a new life.
4. The mysteries had little or no use for doctrine or correct belief. Each cult had its own means to bring about union with the deity such as processions, fasting, plays, and acts of purification, blazing lights, and esoteric liturgies.

   This lack of any emphasis on correct belief marked an important difference between the mysteries and Christianity. The Christian faith was exclusive in the sense that it recognized only one legitimate path to God and salvation, Jesus Christ. The mysteries were inclusive in the sense that nothing prevented the believer in one cult from following other mysteries. [25]

---

[24] Merkelbach, Reinhold, "Mystery Religion - Greco-Roman Religion," *Encyclopedia Britannica*, http://www.britannica.com/topic/mystery-religion

[25] Nash, Ronald, "Mystery Religion: What Were the Mystery Religions?" *Christian Research Institute*, http://www.equip.org/article/mystery-religion-what-were-the-mystery-religions/
Information about the basic characteristics of a Mystery religion was paraphrased or excerpted from this article.

5. The goal of the initiates was a mystical experience that led them to believe they had achieved union with their god and some kind of redemption, salvation, and immortality.

Most mystery schools were based on sacred stories often involving the ritual reenactment of a death-rebirth myth of a particular deity. [26] In classical antiquity the most celebrated and earliest mysteries were the Eleusinian rites of ancient Greece which were based on the growth cycles of nature.

These myths told how the seasons came to be through the story of Hades, Persephone, and Demeter. Hades abducted Persephone and took her to the underworld; her mother Demeter became so angry that she caused a complete failure of crops. Zeus ordered his brother Hades to return Persephone to her mother; Hades tricked Persephone into eating some pomegranate seeds before leaving the underworld, thus sentencing her to live part of the year in the underworld as his wife and part of the year in the world with her mother. This myth tells a story of how the seasons of the year came to be. The Vernal Equinox celebrated the return of Persephone to the upper world each spring. The Autumn Equinox began the time of hibernation, where life is naturally drawn down into the planet when Hades would once again take Persephone to the underworld.

PAGANISM

Paganism can be described as a group of religions and spiritual traditions based on a reverence for nature. It is still practiced today.

Pagans venerate Nature and believe there are many deities, both goddesses and gods. Pagans believe that the model of spiritual growth and renewal is tied to the cycle of the natural year. Each season brings different emphases. Pagans see the earth as sacred and recognize the diversity of Nature. Some pagans such as the followers of the goddess Isis see all goddesses as a composite of the one Great Goddess and all the gods as a composite of the one Great God. Some pagans believe in a supreme Divine Principle, the origin and source of all things.

Pagan religions all recognize the feminine face of divinity; some include ancestral deities. Paganism sees Nature as a manifestation of the Divine and accepts divination and magic as

---

[26] Karoglue, Kiki, "Mystery Cults in the Greek and Roman World," *Heibrunn Timeline of Art History, The Metropolitan Museum of Art*, 2000, http://www.metmuseum.org/toah/hd/myst/hd_must.htm The information on the Eleusinian mystery is taken from this article

a part of everyday life. Pagans usually believe that the divine world will answer a genuine request for information, and the practice of magic is accepted.

To most modern pagans the whole of life is to be affirmed joyfully and without shame as long as others are not harmed by one's actions. "Modern pagans who are not tied down either by the customs of an established religion or by the dogmas of a revealed one are often creative, playful and individualistic." [27]

Pagans usually have respect for all life and a desire to participate with rather than to dominate other beings.

PLATO AND NEO-PLATONISM

Our journey exploring the tributaries of beliefs wouldn't be complete without a brief mention of the impact of the philosophical belief system made famous by Plato (born in Athens in approximately 428 BCE), a student of Socrates and Aristotle's teacher. This lineage of philosophy has shaped centuries of thinking and can be found as an influential undercurrent through many if not all religious ideologies. One of the famous Neo-Platonic philosophers was Hypatia of Alexandria. We will talk about her life in Chapter Four, but first, what made this particular philosophical belief system stand the test of time?

> One of the main reasons for Plato's primacy is that in Plato we have the first collected body of philosophical literature. Unlike Socrates, who did not write at all and unlike the pre-Socrates whose writings were retained in fragmented form, in Plato there is a body of work which scholars have poured over for centuries. .... Plato did not write in the form of philosophical treatises; rather he chose to write in the dramatic form of dialogue. .... they approach philosophical subjects through conversation of characters who pose questions to one another. In most of the dialogues Socrates figures as the protagonist and a number of interlocutors are defeated by his logical form of questioning. [28]

---

[27] Jones, Prudence, "What is Paganism?" *Pagan Federation International*, http://www.paganfederation.org/what-is- paganism/
Information about paganism is excerpted and paraphrased from this article.
[28] "Plato," *New World Encyclopedia*, 2015, http://www.newworldencyclopedia.org/entry/Plato
Special note: When writing the segment on Plato and Neo-Platonism, I went back and forth between three websites cited in this chapter and found in footnotes 6, 7 and 8. The information, if not directly quoted and noted as such, was paraphrased from these sources.

The article quoted above goes on to explain that the nature of the dialogues changed over the years. In the early years Plato was believed to have been writing actual conversations with Socrates, while the later dialogues were entirely Plato's thoughts. Through the works of Plato, we have a large body of ancient writings that still exist and have been studied extensively by scholars down through the centuries. The writings have cut a deep groove of influence throughout human culture. Plato's works are considered to be classics of Western civilization. He introduced dialogue as a philosophical form of discourse and through the dialogues, indirect teaching allowed readers to draw their own conclusions from the discussion.

Plato believed in the immortality of the soul and taught specific doctrines about justice, truth, and beauty. He offered ethical teachings that encouraged students to develop virtues and grow in their ability to reflect or consider philosophical ideas as a way to attain a good and happy life. Moderation of the physical appetites was important, courage was an important virtue of the spirit, and wisdom was the virtue of the intellect. Plato taught through the Philosophy of Recollection that the teacher was a midwife whose job was to help the student give birth to gestating concepts.

Neo-Platonism is a modern term for a Hellenistic school of philosophy founded by Plotinus in the third century AD. The term "Neo-Platonism" itself was not used in ancient times; in fact, it was not coined until the early 19th century, and Neo-Platonists would have considered themselves simply Platonists.

The ideas of Neo-Platonism demonstrate significant differences from those of Plato. Neo-Platonism is generally regarded as a religious philosophy that combines a form of idealistic Monism (everything is derived from the One Source) with elements of Polytheism (the belief or worship of more than one god). It teaches the existence of an indefinable and transcendent One from which emanates the rest of the universe as a sequence of lesser beings. Later Neo-Platonic philosophers added hundreds of intermediate beings such as gods, angels, and demons. [29]

It is not easy to generalize about Neo-platonic philosophy; however, the following ideas generally seem to be included:

1. There are many levels of existence or being arranged in a hierarchical descending order, the last and lowest comprising the physical universe which exists in time and space and is perceptible to the senses.

---

[29] Mastin, Luke, "Neo-Platonism," *The Basics of Philosophy*, 2008, http://www.philosophybasics.com/movements neoplatonism.html

2. Each level of being is derived from its superior, beginning from the original emanation and ending in the worlds of time and space.

3. Each being is established in its own reality by turning to its superior through contemplative desire which is contained in the original creative impulse that it receives from its superior; thus, the Neoplatonic universe is characterized by a double movement of outgoing and return.

4. Each level is an image or expression of the one above it. The relation of archetype and image runs through all Neoplatonic schemes. (Archetype = original pattern).

5. Degrees of being are also degrees of unity; as one goes down the scale of being, there is greater multiplicity, more separateness, and increasing limitation—until the atomic individualization of the spatio-temporal world is reached.

6. The highest level of being originates from the ultimate principle which is absolutely free from limitations and transcends any conceivable reality, so that it may be said to be "beyond being." Because it has no limitations and has no division, attributes, or qualifications, it cannot really be named—but may be called "the Good" as the source of all perfections and the ultimate goal of return.

7. Since this Supreme Principle is absolutely simple and undetermined, human knowledge of it must be radically different from any other kind of knowledge. It is not an object…hence it can only be known if it raises the mind to an immediate union with itself which cannot be imagined or described. [30]

In summary: Neoplatonism had strong religious and mythical elements such as the Doctrine of Emanation—we emanate from the One in increasing levels of separation until we reach the material plane of existence. All comes from One Source and ultimately returns to Source. It was taught that emanation occurred due to an overflow from the fullness of being in the One.

Neo-Platonists did not believe in evil; they compared it to darkness that only exists in the absence of light. Evil is considered to be the absence of good and lacking in perfection. Forgetfulness of our origins resulting in dark behaviors would be considered to be evil only because we forgot our Source.

GNOSTICISM

Gnosticism is a complex belief system and Mystery religion that thrived before and in tandem with early Christianity and Islam until it was practically annihilated through

---

[30] Armstrong, Hilary A., "Platonism," *Encyclopedia Britannica*, http://www.britannica.com/topic/Platonism

persecution as the two later religions began their insidious spread over a large part of the world. There were sects of Christian Gnostics, but they were persecuted and either murdered or went into hiding.

> Gnosticism flourished from about 100 to 700 AD and stressed salvation through secret knowledge or Gnosis. They understood that the Unknown God was not the creator. The creator was known as the Demiurge or YHVH. Their system was based on the division and antagonism between the Demiurge or creator god and the Ultimate God. Gnosis taught that the world was in error due to a fall of a deity and that humans could become conscious and could know the Ultimate God through a "knowing" or Gnosis attained through a series of initiations into the Mysteries. They would become illumined as the spark of the Divine entered them.
>
> Gnosticism is the teaching based on Gnosis, the knowledge of transcendence arrived at by way of interior, intuitive means. Although Gnosticism rests on personal religious experience, it is a mistake to assume all such experience results in Gnostic recognitions. It is nearer the truth to say that Gnosticism expresses a specific religious experience, an experience that does not lend itself to the language of theology or philosophy, but which is instead closely affinitized to, and expresses itself through the medium of myth. Indeed, one finds that most of Gnostic scriptures take the forms of myths. The term "myth" should not be taken here to mean "stories that are not true" but rather, that the truths embodied in these myths are of a different order from the dogmas of theology or the statements of philosophy. [31]

This article goes on to explain other interesting beliefs Gnostics hold which I will paraphrase here: The Genesis myth teaches that the world is imperfect due to the transgressions of Adam and Eve. Gnostics teach that the world's failings are a result of the creator YHVH, who they believe is a lesser god also called the Demiurge which is not the Unknown God. This ultimate and transcendent God is beyond all created universes and emanated forth from Itself, the substance that is in all the worlds, visible and invisible. The Gnostics believed that intermediate deific beings called Aeons exist between the Ultimate True God and humans.

---

[31] Hoeller, Stephan A., "The Gnostic World View: A Brief Summary of Gnosticism," *The Gnostic Archive,* http://gnosis.org/gnintro.htm
Information taken verbatim in part and excerpted in parts from this article.

According to the Gnostic view, one of the Aeonial beings named Sophia (Wisdom) came to emanate from her own being a flawed consciousness, the Demiurge who became the creator of the material and psychic cosmos—all of which he created in his own flawed image. Not knowing his origins, he imagined himself to be the ultimate and absolute God. Since he took the already existing divine essence and fashioned it into various forms, he is called the Demiurge or "half-maker." His cosmic minions are called Archons. He is mistaken by most as the true God.

Gnostics believe that humans are generally ignorant of the divine spark within them, and that the Demiurge and his Archons are intent on keeping humans ignorant of their true nature and destiny. By being attached to materialism, it is believed that we will remain enslaved to these lower cosmic rulers indefinitely. Death releases the divine spark from its lowly prison, but if there is no substantial work of Gnosis undertaken by the soul while on earth, it is hurled back into another body in the physical world.

DIGGING DEEPER INTO THESE TRIBUTARIES

If we read between the lines of all these ancient belief systems, we can see that the savior/evolution model of existence [32] is woven throughout the teachings. All of the above religions encourage a relationship with a teacher/master. Now we are learning that this was by design. James Mahu in his "Project Camelot Interview, Question/Answer 2" outlined the *Human Mind System* and its eight components. The Human Mind System is the program that makes up and controls our unconscious, subconscious, and conscious realities. It is the program that was put into place when the Human Instrument was created to keep us from understanding who and what we are and where we originated from. It is the Matrix we are all "plugged" into.

The part of the Human Mind System I want to focus on here is what James calls the *God-Spirit-Soul-Complex*. He explains that this is the central element of the Human Mind System and a crucial part of keeping us in separation. It is a program of fear of death, fear of separation, and fear of non-existence. It teaches us that we have a soul and programs us to yearn for a master to teach us how to be saved and live a moral life in order to earn eternal happiness. This model teaches "ascension" as the way to God. [33] According to the God-Spirit-Soul-Complex, once you are "saved" you are released from self-responsibility for

---

[32] See Appendix D, **Models of Existence Table**
[33] Mahu, James, "Project Camelot Interview," *WingMakers*,
https://wingmakers.com/about/interviews/project-camelot-interview/

the world and rewarded with eternal life. The "soul" is a substitute term for our real divine Source which is our Sovereign Integral. If you look back over all these belief systems, you will see this undercurrent.

At the same time, we learn that down through the ages some Entities have entered into the world to insert ideas to move us along to the time when we would ultimately know the truth about ourselves. I named them the Guardians in my myth. I believe that Plato may have been one of these Entities because of what he taught and his use of discourses as his teaching method, similar to the format of the *Lyricus Discourses* [34] in that they are conversations between student and teacher. Plato's teachings have enough parallels to what is taught in the *WingMakers Materials* that I have found myself wondering if Plato may have laid some important foundational groundwork for information that would come much later. Truth is hidden in the nooks and crannies of the history of this world if we are willing to remain open and explore.

SOME THOUGHTS ABOUT THE ORIGINS OF THE CONSERVATIVE/ LIBERAL DICHOTOMY

Freke and Gandy [35] identify two schools of thought that arose out of ancient belief systems: the Literalists and the Gnostics or Mystics.

The Literalists interpreted the Jesus story as a literal historical event. Once the Roman Catholic Church incorporated the Literalist interpretation of the Jesus story into their doctrines, they did everything in their power to eradicate the old pagan religions, even though they both told the same story, so that the Jesus story would be the only religion, and the Roman Catholic Church would thrive with total control.

The Gnostics or Mystery Religions believed the stories to be metaphors of our journey on the earth—symbolic and archetypal—not literal.

The Mystery Religions taught initiates in increments. The Outer Mysteries—or literal story—told the story of a dying godman who was resurrected as a savior of mankind, but as the initiates were taken deeper into the mysteries, they learned that the story was not an actual historical event, but rather an allegory for the individual's journey on earth, as each

---

[34] See **Lyricus Discourses,** Appendix A - Glossary
Lyricus Discourses 1-6 can be found at https://wingmakers.com/writings/lyricus/
[35] Freke, Timothy and Peter Gandy, *The Jesus Mysteries: Was the Original Jesus a Pagan God?* Three Rivers Press, Random House, 1999.

of us is a god man/woman. The Inner Mysteries taught the way toward Inner Knowing or Gnosticism.

Now fast-forward to the present, and we will see how the Outer Mysteries or the Literalist interpretation morphed into our fundamental and mainstream religions. The Literalists taught that the story of Jesus and salvation through believing in Him actually happened in the way it is described in the Bible. They were fanatical about having all others believe the same. The Gnostics took a mystical approach, teaching that one must seek direct experience of the Divine or Gnosis (knowing), and that Gnosis could happen through deeper exploration of the Mysteries. The initiate would learn to transcend matter through this deeper knowing. The literalists were intolerant of other's beliefs; the Gnostics were tolerant because they understood the progression of evolution of a person's spirituality.

Now let's take a long and hard look at the continuum that contributes to maintaining rigid, control-driven belief systems. They generally have the following characteristics:

- Belief in an authoritarian god who is believed to be male;
- Male supremacy, privilege, and domination;
- Often racially bigoted;
- Misogynistic and persecuting non-heterosexual gender orientation;
- Territorial thinking that rationalizes warfare;
- Rational, linear, logical, literal, and "better-than" thinking;
- Exploitation of people and the earth's resources for whatever cause is currently in vogue;
- Strong resistance to progressive change of any kind;
- Fundamental dogmatic, literal religious beliefs;
- Exclusivist ideologies both national and religious;
- Support of the growth of big business at the expense of the individual.
- Support of the exploitation of natural resources and disregard for the impact of that exploitation on future generations.

As we look at the characteristics just listed, we can recognize them as the current Conservative political philosophy, the ideological descendants of the Literalists. To get a glimpse of what is needed to balance that continuum of beliefs, we only need to look at these counter characteristics:

- Belief in a Universal Source with both masculine and feminine characteristics and/ or a Supreme Being or All That Is that is beyond gender;

- Acceptance of all humans regardless of gender, race, or sexual orientation; equality and partnership of the sexes;
- Inclusion of the intuitive process in decision making;
- Recognition and acceptance into our belief systems of dimensions beyond our five senses;
- Fair treatment for all;
- Strong investment in finding peaceful win-win solutions;
- An understanding of metaphorical expansive and inclusive spirituality and thinking;
- Concern for the survival of the global community and global resources, not just national and personal survival;
- Holistic, nonlinear creative thinking;
- Responsible ecological stewardship of earth's resources and fair- trade policies that do not exploit;
- Practice of the Golden Rule in all endeavors.

The threads of these philosophical traits descend from the Gnostic mindset into beliefs with a Liberal ideology.

If you take a good long look at especially the way the United States is structured, you will see a strong overlay or blanket of belief that has all the characteristics of the Literalists. These characteristics are blatantly apparent in the bureaucratic systems that govern this country, the "good ole boy" networks that are rampant in our legal and political systems, as well as the leadership in most of our corporations. Many of our global corporations have become behemoths of control that rival dictators of old.

So, we have a River of Beliefs that has fed humanity through the centuries in one form or another. The mythologies of all religions, including Christianity, have many of the same characteristics and players and basic beliefs. The names and places may be different, but the stories are surprisingly similar. The remaining chapters of Part One will continue the story, adding more details about how our current beliefs made their way to the present. Along the way, gems of truth were fed into this great River of Beliefs, but they were generally rushed over by its enormous power and buried deep in the riverbed. Our job as we explore our beliefs is to go panning for the crystalline gold gems of truth that are hidden, and when we find a gem that feels like truth, hold it up to the Emerging Light now descending onto the planet and let that Light illuminate it. If it doesn't hold up under the Light, then let it go.

How do we tell the real crystalline gold from the "fool's gold"? That is our journey.

3

"OH WHAT TANGLED WEBS WE WEAVE ..."

"Any belief worth embracing will stand up to the litmus test of scrutiny.
If we have to qualify, rationalize, make exceptions for,
or turn a blind eye to maintain a belief,
then it may well be time to release that belief."
— Laurie Buchanan, PhD

SOME THOUGHTS ON THE JESUS QUESTION

IN THE LAST CHAPTER I discussed the River of Beliefs that flows through our current belief systems. In this chapter I want to focus on a specific tributary of that river because of the significant and overpowering impact it has had on our world.

We pick up the thread of our story at the Council of Nicea, convened by the Roman Emperor Constantine I in 325 AD. The decisions made in this meeting created and helped to perpetuate the foundational belief systems of the Western world that remain entrenched to this day.

The official story reports that the Council was an important initial ecumenical meeting of about three hundred bishops from across the Roman Empire. Since it was such a significant meeting for the early Church, documents have survived from that time. [36]

For the first time in the history of the Church, representatives of all of the bishops convened with the purpose of resolving disagreements and creating a unifying doctrinal statement. The Council was historically significant because it was the first effort to attain consensus through an assembly that represented all of Christianity at that time and was considered to be the first "ecumenical council" of the Church.

---

[36] "Council of Nicea," *ReligionFacts*, 10 November 2015, http://www.religionfacts.com/council-of-nicea Information gathered and paraphrased from this source.

Part of the reason for this Council was to resolve the dispute over the teachings of Arius, a priest in Alexandria, Egypt who held that Jesus Christ was greater than man but inferior to God and had not always existed with the Father and had been begotten by Him before the world was created. The counter argument was that Jesus had always existed and was the same as God the Father. Constantine called this meeting to see if they could work out their differences.

Arianism was condemned by the majority of bishops at this Council and decreed to be heresy. One of the most well-known outcomes of this convention was the "Nicene Creed." This creed was formed using specific language designed to refute Arius' teachings.

Like many historical events, this bit of history has more than one version. I discovered an interesting "unofficial story" of the Council of Nicea in an article titled "The Forged Origins of the New Testament"[37] that sheds an entirely different light on the Council. The information from the article quoted below was written by Tony Bushby, an Australian magazine publisher for Australian and New Zealand markets. The article describes the Council gathering as a "bizarre event that provided many details of early clerical thinking and presents a clear picture of the intellectual climate prevailing at the time." Bushby goes on to explain that about four years before the Council, Constantine had been initiated into the religious order of *Sol Invictus*, one of the thriving cults that regarded the Sun as the one and only Supreme God; the other was Mithraism. By most accounts Constantine held pagan beliefs throughout his life. He wanted a state religion, however, and convened the council for that purpose.

The following paragraphs quoted or paraphrased from Bushby's article are very telling:

> One of the attendees, Sabinius, Bishop of Hereclea said 'Excepting Constantine himself and Eusebius Pamphilius, they were a set of illiterate, simple creatures who understood nothing.' (*Secrets of the Christian Fathers*, Bishop J.W. Sergerus, 1685, 1897 reprint)
>
> Dr. Richard Watson (1737-1816) a disillusioned Christian historian and one-time Bishop of Llandaff in Wales (1782) referred to them as a 'set of gibbering idiots' (*An Apology for Christianity*, 1776, 1796, reprint; also *Theological Tracts*, Dr. Richard Watson, 'On Councils' entry, vol. 2 London 1786, revised reprint 1791). From his extensive research into Church councils, Dr. Watson concluded that 'the clergy at the council of Nicea were all under the power of the devil, and the convention was composed of the lowest

rabble and patronized the vilest abominations.' (*An Apology for Christianity*, op. cit.) 'It was that infantile body of men who were responsible for the commencement of a new religion and *the theological creation of Jesus Christ*.'

In this same article (quoted and paraphrased in part below), Bushby explains that Constantine's intention was to create an entirely new god so his empire could unite all factions under one deity. He invited the presbyters to debate to determine who their new god would be. The names of fifty- three gods were tabled for discussion as they came up with five prospects: Caesar, Krishna, Mithra, Horus, and Zeus (*Historia Ecclesiastica*, Eusebius, c 325). Since Constantine was the ruler, he would ultimately decide on the name of the god for them.

To involve factions of Britain, he chose the name Hesus to be joined with the Eastern Savior-God Krishna (Krishna is Sanskrit for Christ), and thus Hesus Krishna would be the official name of the new Roman god. The Council voted, and both divinities became one God. A new god was proclaimed and ratified by Constantine (*Acta Concilii Nicaeni*, 1618) that legally placed Hesus Krishna among the Roman gods as one individual composite. "That abstraction lent Earthly existence to amalgamated doctrines for the Empire's new religion; and because there was no letter 'J' in alphabets until around the ninth century, the name subsequently evolved into *Jesus Christ*."

A variety of historical resources tell us that Constantine had found a way to join church and state into a universal code of dogma that included the cults of the day combined into a monotheistic state religion that he could have control over. Constantine was a member of a pagan religion that worshiped the Sun God,[38] and his reign was called a "sun emperorship." (He did not actually "convert" to Christianity until he was on his death bed. The story goes that he "converted" as he believed that was a way for him to be forgiven for his sins. At the time of the Nicene Council, Constantine was mainly looking for a way to unite his subjects under one religious ideology that he could control.)

Once the Council achieved its objective by agreeing on a universal doctrinal statement called the Nicene Creed, Constantine used the power of the state to enforce the Council's edicts. The doctrine and its enforcement by Constantine's government created a powerful and all-encompassing entanglement of church and state. This establishment of the Roman Church was the beginning of a dominant international organization whose influence and impact on the world's belief systems would last for centuries.

---

[38] Freke, Timothy and Peter Gandy, *The Jesus Mysteries: Was the "Original Jesus" a Pagan God?* Three Rivers Press, Random House, 1999. This book presents the story of how the Roman Church falsified history to its and Constantine's advantage and how Constantine used the Council of Nicea to enforce standardized decrees and dogmas for the Roman Church.

With the founding of the Nicene Creed, precedence was established for a statement of beliefs to be universally accepted and unify the Roman Church. The joining of church and state imposed a belief system on the masses whether they chose it or not. This set a precedence that would ultimately result in untold suffering over many centuries.

At that first Council there was debate about whether Jesus was "begotten by God" or was "created by God." It was finally decreed that Jesus was begotten, not made, thus asserting he was equally eternal with God. In essence Jesus Christ was *decreed to be divine* at that council, as part of the creed tells us:

> We believe in one Lord, Jesus Christ, the only Son of God, eternally begotten of the Father, God from God, Light from Light, true God from true God, begotten, not made, one in Being with the Father …

The Jewish people kept Saturday as the Sabbath Day, and the early Christian Churches also worshipped on Saturday. The council made the decision to worship on Sunday. Constantine worshipped on Sunday as did many religions of that day that celebrated and worshipped the Sun as God.

The early Christian Church celebrated the Jewish Passover. The Council made the decision to change the Christian celebration of the Passover to the first Sunday after the Jewish Passover which coincided with phases of the moon and was always celebrated on the 14th of Nisan which could fall on any day of the week. The Council decreed that the Christian Passover would always be celebrated on a Sunday. In subsequent years, the name of Passover was changed to Easter in the Christian churches, as the Church embraced more pagan traditions and moved further away from Jewish traditions. [39]

We discussed earlier that Easter was a pre-Christian festival celebrated at the vernal equinox, symbolizing the time when the Sun God is resurrected from his winter death. The celebration represented the *resurrection of the Sun God* long before Jesus Christ came on the scene. Easter was named after the pagan goddess Ishtar, and the celebration of the rites of spring and resurrection/rebirth are very old traditions.

As far back as ancient Greece, there was a custom of making a person a "scapegoat" who would symbolically take on the sins of the people. He would be fed pure foods at public expense, be dressed in holy garments, and wreathed in sacred plants. On the day of his sacrificial death, he would be insulted, beaten, and killed. This was meant to atone for the people's sins and was one of the many forms of the need for a savior that was incorporated

[39] Chamberlain, Rick Aharon, "Anti-Judaism and the Council of Nicea," *YashaNet*, http://www.yashanet.com/library/antisem.htm Information about Anti-Semitism

into belief systems. Many of the pre-Christian religions believed sacrifice of either a human or animal was needed to atone for sins. Some of the Mystery religions maintained a doctrine of original sin. This belief in original sin and the practice of killing a sacrificial scapegoat in order to be cleansed of sin was carried over into Christian mythology, and Jesus became the "scapegoat."

Many pre-Christian religions taught that humans were born of the original sin of being in separation from God and that the sacrifice of an animal (often a lamb) was metaphorically the death of the animal nature of the initiate. Initiates were bathed in the animal's blood (washed in the blood of the lamb), therefore facilitating a rebirth into their divine nature and union with God.

Originally the cross was a pagan symbol representing the intersection of heaven and earth. It was also a symbol of the Tree of Life. During the reign of Constantine, the Roman Catholic Church took this ancient symbol and converted it into the defining symbol of Christianity.

The Roman Catholic Church established other customs after the Nicaean Decree, such as the celebration of the birthday of Jesus on December 25. There is much controversy about the date when Jesus of Nazareth, a Jew, was actually born. If Jesus was a Jew, and if he had been born the way it is portrayed, his birth would more than likely have been in the autumn. This coincides with the Feast of Tabernacles, a Jewish Holy week, held in the fall after harvest time when taxes would be paid. This, of course, depends on whether there is any truth to the story of his birth, i.e., they came to be taxed, there was no room at the inn, etc.

Practically every detail of the recognized story of Jesus Christ that forms the foundational teachings and doctrine upon which the Christian Churches of today are built was taken from the mythologies of the pre- Christian era. These are teachings that were in vogue at the time Jesus supposedly lived.

It doesn't make sense that Jesus would be killed for teaching what was being taught already, if indeed he was. Something in his teachings had to be radical enough to incite a movement and dangerous enough to the powers that be to send his followers into hiding to practice these new beliefs after his death and to be willing to die for them.

Freke and Gandy in their book *The Jesus Mysteries* offer an alternate fascinating and plausible explanation of the Jesus story. They explain that the Jews were repeatedly conquered by other nations, and the integration of Jewish and pagan culture happened over centuries of time. According to these authors, it was quite common for the pagan religions to localize a deity to make it more palatable to the indigenous population. The book goes into great detail about the history of the Jews and their absorption into the various societies that had originally conquered them. At the same time, Jews worked extremely hard to maintain their identity as Jews. The authors explain that

By the time that Jesus was supposed to have lived, Galilee was surrounded by Hellenized cities, which were the home of eminent Pagan philosophers and centers for the Mysteries of Dionysus. [40]

The Jews believed that a Messiah would come and free them from the Roman occupation that they were enduring. In order to attempt to integrate the Jews, a Jewish "god-man" was created and given a Jewish name. So, Jesus became the godman of the pagan religions and the Messiah of the Jews, a composite figure with a story fabricated to bring the Jews into the pagan religions with their own savior. Ironically, the Jews would have no part of this scheme and ultimately dismissed the story that Jesus was their savior.

In Chapter Two I brought to your attention the Literalist and Gnostic- mystical dichotomy. This polarized paradigm takes on deepened significance when we look at the following.

When the Council of Nicene set the Universal or Roman Catholic Church in motion, they used and strongly enforced the Literalist way of thinking, and over time it became the dominate belief system, eradicating any others that contradicted their teachings. As the centuries progressed, the Gnostic or mystical version of Christianity went underground and became secret, as those who were Gnostics faced persecution and death for their beliefs.

Why would Constantine and the Church fathers use the literalist interpretation of Christianity as the state religion? One would think that many were aware of the teachings of the Inner Mysteries. Constantine himself held pagan beliefs. Some interesting insight into this question comes from *The Jesus Mysteries*. First it is explained that the Roman Emperors needed "one faith," a universal religion. Several had been tried, but without success.

In the first half of the fourth century Emperor Constantine tried Christianity. It was an ideal candidate for the role. The Romans needed a Mystery religion because they were always popular with the people. But Mystery religions were led by mystics and philosophers, who had the audacity to question and undermine the authority of the state.

Literalist Christianity, however, was a Mystery religion that had purged itself of all its troublesome intellectuals. It was already an authoritarian religion, which encouraged the faithful to have blind faith in those holding

---

[40] Freke, Timothy and Peter Gandy, *The Jesus Mysteries: Was the "Original Jesus" a Pagan God?* Three Rivers Press, Random House, 1999.

positions of power. It was exactly what the Roman authorities wanted—a religion without mystics, the Outer Mysteries without the Inner Mysteries, form without content. [41]

So, the Roman Catholic Church under the auspices of Constantine added Jesus of Nazareth to a long list of deities with the same mythology. This gave the church a way to unite a plethora of beliefs under one universal belief system and aided in uniting the Roman Empire, both church and state, under one government system, giving Constantine total control.

Whether Jesus actually lived or not, Constantine and his cronies created the belief system of Christianity that exists today, and the world is still reeling with the fundamentalist mindsets of self-righteousness and better-than/less-than that evolved from this.

The Roman Catholic Church created a massive monster and gave the state the power to dictate what people would believe. Using their belief in a singular supremacy and its hierarchy, the RC Church began an insidious and cruel campaign to convert the world to one belief system through the campaigns of the Inquisitions and other religious wars. Unspeakable atrocities were instigated throughout a long bloody history to defend beliefs enforced by people who became powerful by claiming they were given their authority by God. The violent aftermath of that first Council has rippled throughout history with a vengeance. As the RC Church began to enforce its beliefs, humanity's progress was not only halted but actually reversed as blind faith replaced scientific and historical investigation, and the population was forced into the Dark Ages—a period of time roughly between 500 and 1000 CE.

During the Crusades, many attempts to purify the Christian world of all non-Christian "infidels" were carried out. This began with the purge of any beliefs that were not sanctioned by the Church, and there were many. Crusaders sought out and slaughtered the much-respected Cathars and Gnostics, as well as Jews, Muslims, and those labeled pagans or gypsies— anyone who practiced pre-Christian or non-Christian traditions.

I find it paradoxically ludicrous that while the Roman Catholic Church incorporated many pre-Christian "pagan" traditions into its code of beliefs, it still fought to eradicate all those who continued to practice any tradition that smacked of paganism that was not included in the Catholic dogma. The reason for this probably lies in the need for these charlatans to cover their tracks so that what they put into place became the major not-to-be-questioned belief system enabling them to maintain control.

---

[41] Ibid.

Another paradox is the anti-Semitism that began to take hold when the Jews rejected the teachings that Jesus was the Messiah. Anti-Semitism became more widespread as Christians blamed the Jews for the death of Jesus. It seems a strange irony that the Roman Catholic Church established after the Nicene Council and founded around the *resurrection of Jesus* blames anyone for his death. According to the story and that particular belief system, if Jesus had not died in the way he did, there would be no savior or Christianity as it is practiced today. All the eggs of Christianity are in this one basket of a sacrificed and resurrected Jesus saving the repentant from their sins, and yet Jews are blamed for his death. If this reality is indeed true, then Jews should be praised for the part they played in this cosmic drama.

According to the story, on the cross Jesus said: "Forgive them for they know not what they do." If we follow the story line to its ultimate conclusion, Jesus by asking that "they" be forgiven would also be pointing to the bigger picture that included his destined martyrdom, which meant no one person or group was to blame.

During the crusades, the Church guaranteed that any soldier who enlisted would be forgiven for sins past, present, and future, and that anyone who died in the attempt would go straight to heaven. "What goes around comes around" springs to mind. It appears that our modern-day radical, fundamental Jihadist terrorists aren't the only ones who fight "infidels." It also gives us a deeper glimpse into the fierce enmity that is still going on today between fundamental Christians and radicalized Muslims and the Jews.

Many of the books that were originally written as part of the Bible were later termed heresies and deliberately excluded by the Church. They now exist in separate texts called the Apocrypha.

Freke and Gandy tell us that there were hundreds of Christian gospels. The Bible as we know it now has been through countless translations and revisions in order to make it tell the story to support the Literalists' deception. The story of how certain books came to be included in the Bible is also full of deception and cover-ups and omissions, and yet it is considered by many fundamentalist/literalist Christian groups today as the inspired word of God. Every word is believed to be the unalterable, literal, inspired truth—never to be disputed.

Another strand of this tangled web that also leads us to a man called Jesus tells a different story. Some fascinating information is found in the book *Holy Blood, Holy Grail* [42] in the chapter titled "The Secret the Church Forbade." The authors present the theory that Jesus was an aristocrat, a legitimate claimant to the throne, and that his messages were meant to gain the allegiance and support of the people. He was trained in esoteric traditions that could

---

[42] Bagent, Michael, Richard Leigh and Henry Lincoln, *Holy Blood, Holy Grail*, Delta Tradeback Edition, Bantam Dell, 2004.

very well have included the healing arts. His message was one of "hope to the downtrodden, the afflicted, the disenfranchised, and the oppressed. In short it was a message of promise." They believe his message was targeted to a segment of the population in order to unite them to a common cause of overthrowing a despotic regime, the Roman occupation. (The book is well-researched and builds a strong case for this.) According to the authors, Jesus was executed, or the population was led to believe he was executed, but his message of hope lived on and became a strong movement. This book focuses on the preservation of the royal bloodline of Jesus, which included his marriage to Mary Magdalene and the child or children that they might have had.

In *The Jesus Mysteries*, Freke and Gandy explain that there were many teachers, and that Joshua or Yeshua were very common names, and that crucifixions were widespread.

There could easily have been a man who lived who fit the description mentioned in *Holy Blood, Holy Grail*, a man named Yeshua who began a movement to take back his rightful throne. It is plausible that the mythology of Jesus was originally created from the life of that man.

Bottom line, however, is that whoever this person was; he is not the person who is worshiped today as Jesus Christ because as we have seen, that man is likely either a composite character or a fabricated mythological figure made to fit the needs of the rulers and the theology of the day. While that is neither a good or bad thing in and of itself, the havoc that the enforcement of those beliefs has wrought on mankind is unconscionable.

Throughout the long and cruel history of Christianity, one belief system, compiled and agreed upon by a group of men (of questionable character by one account) and enforced by might, slowly became the accepted "word of God" to be obeyed by everyone. Millions suffered and died for any beliefs they held or were suspected of holding that conflicted with the prevailing belief system, and that mindset continues to this day in many parts of the world.

Decades ago, an extremely dangerous movement was begun by the Christian Right to bring Christianity to the White House and make it part of our government. Hopefully enough level-headed people will continue to elect members to Congress to ensure that this never happens. Thankfully, the division of church and state is a part of our Constitution and for very good reason. The founding fathers of this country fully understood what religious oppression could do and wrote the United States Constitution to counteract that tendency and preserve the separation of church and state. That is an extremely important right we must hold sacred. It would take an amendment to the Constitution to change that right which would be difficult to do, but the potential is there, nonetheless. For anyone interested in pursuing the subject of the attempt to turn the United States into a theocracy, I refer you to *The Family: The Secret Fundamentalism at the Heart of American Power* by Jeff Sharlet. A five-part docuseries by the same name has been released by Netflix featuring this book.

It is disconcerting, to say the least, and important information is presented to improve our understanding of this issue.

The thinking of a radical interest group is dangerous to the religious freedoms we enjoy in this country. If we should learn anything from history concerning the enforcement of religion, we need to remember that the enforcers of a belief system can become brutal and vicious very quickly.

As we can see, there are many theories about Jesus and his origins and what he truly came to give the world and whether or not he actually existed. As I see it, we have a combination of the Old Testament history of violence and exclusivism catalyzed by the jealous God Jehovah and the traditions of the Mystery religions married to the story of Jesus created by the Roman Catholic Church to enforce their beliefs and stay in power.

We have to ask ourselves: if a Great Being did incarnate on this earth to bring change, what would he or she have taught? What would be the point of reinforcing the current flawed belief systems set up to support the continued rule of the ones already in power? The teachings would have to be so radically different from the current belief systems that it would rattle the foundation of the status quo to its very core; and that would be grounds for execution by those in power determined to maintain their positions.

REFLECTIONS ON THE ORIGIN OF THE SAVIOR BELIEF

Another aspect of the Jesus story that I came across while researching this segment has led me to some hunches that I think should at least be noted as food for thought. First a review of some history already noted earlier in this book to set the stage for my hunch.

We have learned about historical documents that have surfaced that tell a story of the Anunnaki being our creators. In the myth that began this book, I added that we, the Atlanteans, in our original state as Sovereign Beings and initially in cooperation with the Anunnaki, used our abilities to give the breath of life to the slave bodies created to mine gold. The story goes that Anu initially planned to come back and rule the world and thus began to perpetuate the story of a redeemer who would come to save the world. This was the beginning of the *evolution/saviorship model of existence*. [43] He and his cohorts put a ruling elite class into place programmed to preserve this plan. They are known in modern

---

[43] Mahu James and John Berges, "Chamber Two Philosophy: The Shifting Modes of Existence," *Collected Works of the WingMakers, Volume I*, edited by John Berges, Egg Harbor, NJ: Planetwork Press, 2013. Also https://wingmakers.com/writings/philosophy/chambertwo/
See Appendix A - Glossary for a short definition of the Models of Existence and a table of the models in Appendix D.

day vernacular as royalty, the Illuminati, the Incunabula, and other secret societies that rule behind the scenes. According to James Mahu, that plan has changed because Earth is too vibrationally dense now for the Anunnaki to return. If they were to, they would be trapped here like we are. However, the program that was put into place continues to run—the *Matrix* film stories as a metaphor are something to consider—and the world awaits and continues to teach about the return of a savior. (I will have more to say about the *Matrix Trilogy* in Part Five of this book.)

I have wrestled a lot with trying to understand the part that Jesus played because there are so many conflicting stories about him. It seems pretty certain that a being lived who had a major impact on the world. I have puzzled over what message he would have brought that would cause such a commotion that it made the ruling powers afraid of him and resulted in his crucifixion, if indeed he was crucified, or at least the creation of a crucifixion story.

I have a strong hunch that the Being who became the human Jesus is a member of the Guardians who did not participate when many of our species became entrapped on the material plane in programmed bodies. It is very plausible to me that He remains working behind the scenes to bring the real truth of who we are to all his brothers and sisters living in suppression. It is very possible that he is part of the group who watches over us and was one of the volunteer teachers who came to insert a liberating message into the collective consciousness. For the times in which he lived, his ideas were too radical and infringed on the status quo too much, so he was silenced. They silenced the human, but the message he brought is forever in our collective consciousness and can be accessed by any who open their hearts and minds to it.

His statement that "the Kingdom of God is within" is a message to us to take responsibility for our actions and to look within for guidance. Teachings that have survived that are attributed to him encouraged humility, mercy, and pureness of heart; peacemaking over power; love and acceptance. Love Wins. It is a powerful energy that will ultimately win out over all the hate in the world because it is part of who we all are at the deepest level of our Beingness. I believe that might have been the message that was being conveyed. Because he was such a popular figure, his life was used by the powers that be to build a religion around him, but the religion they created just perpetuated the belief systems of the day, keeping the savior/evolution model in place.

I think his actual message might have been one of taking responsibility for personal transformation, and I believe that he is actually our brother. We are ALL the offspring of First Source.

The *transformation/mastership model of existence* (see Appendix D) offers an alternative way of being in this world and a way to begin to deprogram oneself from the *saviorship/ evolution model of existence*—and was more than likely the message the powers that be wanted to silence. If that is true, then Jesus came to begin to insert the ideas into the program that would ultimately free us from it. He was setting the stage for events that would happen long after his human life on Earth. (Reminder: our world is a fractal, which means that when an idea or concept is inserted in one place, it becomes embedded and spreads throughout the fractal—more about that later.)

I personally think that the Old Testament is a collection of stories about humanity's creation by and relationship with the Anunnaki before they left. The New Testament gives us a story to replace Anu with Jesus as the savior who would return to perpetuate the *saviorship/ evolution model of existence*. Remember that this model was in place long before Jesus was believed to have lived.

Personally, I think the Bible should be titled The Book of Anu.

If we look at the basic story of Jesus perpetuated by Christianity, we see another narrative of an awaited savior. Thus, the powers that be at the time of Jesus took his story and constructed it in such a way as to keep the saviorship/evolution model of existence alive and well.

In my twenties, I became involved with a church that interpreted the Bible very narrowly and literally and was quite strict about mandating their membership to follow the laws set forth in the Bible. They believed in Jesus as Savior, but since He was a Jew, they believed we should keep the Old Testament Jewish holy days and obey the Jewish teachings such as dietary restrictions and honoring Saturday as the Sabbath. They didn't believe in keeping the Christian holidays because of their pagan origin. We studied the Bible constantly which means that I have read the Bible—all of it. I have an old, dog-eared Bible that has tabs for each of the books and many notes in the margins. We sat through two-hour sermons every Saturday where the Bible was expounded in great detail.

As I look back, I don't believe this church was a cult, but it was close to it. By the time I came to my senses and left with a group of like-minded members, I had experienced a deep despair brought on by the church's suppression of my entire being. I cannot read any of the Bible now without triggering those same feelings of despair again. So, I speak from extensive experience with the Bible and how it can be literally enforced as a highly effective suppression instrument which is especially brutal towards women.

I think the church I was involved with and the whole of Churchianity missed the important point that the true Jesus would have brought an entirely new way of being, suggesting that it was time to leave the Old Testament teachings behind along with their hateful and vengeful god. Instead, churches did nothing but "rebrand" an old system of control by latching onto the messenger but missing the message and instead retaining the old message and reinforcing the worship of a lesser god.

What good is faith if it causes <u>pain</u> for another? What good is religion if it does no good? What good is any belief that leads to hate? [44]

> Morality doesn't mean 'following divine commands.' It means 'reducing suffering.' Hence in order to act morally, you don't need to believe in any myth or story. You just need to develop a deep appreciation of suffering. If you really understand how an action causes unnecessary suffering to yourself or to others, you will naturally abstain from it. People nevertheless murder, rape and steal because they have only a superficial appreciation of the misery this causes. They are fixated on satisfying their immediate lust or greed, without concern for the impact on others – or even for the long-term impact on themselves. Even inquisitors, who deliberately inflict as much pain as possible on their victim, usually use various desensitizing and dehumanizing techniques in order to distance themselves from what they are doing.
>
> — Yuval Noah Harari, *21 Lessons for the 21ˢᵗ Century*

TAKING A DEEPER LOOK INTO OUR CURRENT CORE BELIEFS OF SAVIORSHIP/EVOLUTION

What belief system and its banquet of trappings could have forced mankind to be willing to perpetuate the atrocities and enforce the religious laws and dogmas we see touted in our major belief systems? What could be so powerful as to take away the personal sovereignty of each individual?

Helen Ellerbe in her book *The Dark Side of Christianity* [45] makes a couple of powerful points that I think are relevant to our discussion. The first point is this:

> As people believe that God can have but one face, so they tend to believe that worth or godliness among humans can also have but one face. Different genders, races, classes or beliefs are all ordered as better-than or less-than one another. Even the notion of two differing opinions existing harmoniously becomes foreign; one must prevail and be superior over the other. Within such a belief structure, God is understood to reign singularly from the

---

[44] Brock, Jared, *A Year of Living Prayerfully: How a Curious Traveler Met the Pope, Walked on Coals, Danced with Rabbis, and Revived His Prayer Life*, Grand Rapids MI: Ann Spangler and Company, 2015.

[45] Ellerbe, Helen, *The Dark Side of Christian History*, Morningstar & Lark, PO Box 153, Windermere FL 34786, 1995.

pinnacle of a hierarchy based not upon love and support, but upon fear. The Bible repeatedly exhorts people to fear God.

Her second point is: "One's beliefs about God have impact upon one's beliefs about society."

We see her astute and important observations played out so clearly in far-right belief systems that tout white supremacy and other beliefs that exclude everyone but a chosen few. My feeling is that a belief system that originates from the origins of our true consciousness would teach inclusion of all, as we are all ONE, and we all come from the same Source.

James Mahu takes us to a deeper level of understanding of these ideas in the *WingMaker's* "Chamber Four Philosophy: Beliefs and Their Energy Systems" [46] by explaining that "All beliefs have energy systems that act like birthing rooms for the manifestation of the belief." He goes on to identify the strongest undercurrent of belief that humanity has, and that is survival.

When I read and pondered that information, it felt like a huge missing piece of the puzzle in the creation of what I had identified as the Core Belief Matrix fell into place. James gives us an equation:

Survival Based Energy System + Galactic Time = Conformist Life Experience = Belief System

When one looks at a survival-based belief system, one sees not only conformity, but also fear-based thinking and enslavement. It is all there in that one equation. This belief system creates a hierarchical ruling structure. What kind of belief system would we need to develop to pull ourselves out of that equation? James gives us a hint when he explains that our way out is through an explorer-based energy system. Hmmm… (Note: I have gone into greater detail about the Models of Existence in Appendix D.)

Keeping a survival-based energy system in mind, let us put our newly discovered equation to the test as we look at the major principles that have perpetuated our current system of suppression and separation:

- We are born of original sin. We somehow "fell" from the good graces of God and thus we are inherently evil, and therefore we cannot trust information that comes

---

[46] Mahu, James and John Berges, "Chamber Four Philosophy: Beliefs and Their Energy Systems," *Collected Works of the WingMakers, Volume I*, edited by John Berges, Egg Harbor, NJ: Planetwork Press, 2013. Also https://wingmakers.com/writings/philosophy/chamberfour/

from within (fear of our ability to trust thinking for ourselves). This is a direct teaching against Gnostic or inner knowing. That belief if strongly driven into people, gives the church authorities a great deal of power. They teach that we are given a Source, i.e., holy books as the supposed final and only Word of God, but only those ordained by God are qualified to interpret those books. These so-called holy books give the laws for mankind's supposed redemption which is really a form of control (*Conformity*). The belief is that because we are inherently evil at worst, and flawed at best, we cannot make spiritual decisions for ourselves or look within for answers. We must turn to the leaders of the church for interpretation and enforcement of the Bible and the "holy" laws. Teachings that have survived that are attributed to Jesus suggest that the *Kingdom is within,* and yet heads of churches demand obedience and looking outwardly to them for answers—not within.

- o   I am approaching this belief from the premise that there is truth to the myth of how our bodies were created by the Anunnaki. To keep us little Earthlings in our slave mentality and believing that we are less-than those in authority, we are taught that we are sinners and must be guided and controlled by our "wise" church leaders. What we are not told is that the Essence that lives in and animates this "space suit for the soul" or "human instrument" is infinite. Our pathway out of the suppression is in developing a relationship with that Infinite Being that animates us with its Life Essence. (Survival is moot; we are infinite beings.) That relationship will be taken up in more detail in subsequent chapters.

- Men have been given dominion over the earth and everything in it, including women and children. Anything to do with sex is inherently sinful unless it is for the procreation of children, and even then, it is suspect. Women have been looked upon as the temptresses. Starting with the story of Eve, it has been taught that women have led men astray, and they must be ever on guard against the wiles of women. (This perpetuates inequality, distrust, and enslavement of those who are believed to be lesser-than.)

- o   Let's look a little deeper…we recognize intuition as part of the feminine principle or feminine characteristics. In order for humankind to lose that trust and connection in their inner Source of Direction, the intuitive processes must be undermined, and that includes anything coming from the feminine or females. The word dominion (sovereignty—self- rule, independence) has been misconstrued to mean domination or control by power. That destructive set of beliefs has its tentacles in every facet of our lives and has caused unconscionable suffering. Women and girls down through the centuries have endured unspeakable abuse because of this belief, and it is still happening publicly and privately in many parts of the world. Men and boys who have a more dominant feminine nature are also shamed and abused in a myriad of ways. This belief has caused separation and polarization at the subtlest levels of existence.

- We are caught between God and the Devil or the forces of good and evil, and both are vying for our souls. We struggle with the pressures of sin and guilt. Since we are inherently evil, we must obey strict rules and laws in order for God to consider accepting us, and in order for us to stay in line. A message that was empowering would be threatening to ones who wanted to be in control. Being caught between God and the Devil makes us fearful pawns to be manipulated, powerless against unseen forces such as the unknown. We enslave ourselves to dogma to save ourselves from the wrath of god.
    - o This teaching is a way to keep us in separation and keep us polarized. Evil is the absence or suppression of Light; Truth and Oneness have nothing to do with two Infinite Beings vying for our souls.
- There is nobility in suffering and sacrifice. If we sacrifice on earth, we will be rewarded in heaven. One way to get on the good side of God is to sacrifice ourselves, and the more we suffer, the more we show God that we are determined to get back into His good graces. This coercion to suffer results in wealthy, so-called religious leaders manipulating their naïve flock to give them money, often money the person can ill-afford, as part of that "sacrifice," and a way of buying their place in heaven or god's good graces. Some believe that God applauds this suffering as a mark of devotion. Think about it, if suffering is so important, why aren't the religious leaders "suffering" and sacrificing instead of sending their followers on guilt trips because they do not pay enough or do enough?
    - o Think of the self-debasing and self-flagellating practices of many religious orders. Doesn't that seem a bit sadistic? What need would a loving and all-powerful Source of All fill by being sadistic??? If our self-debasement fills a need in a so-called god, I would have to wonder about the validity of that god as the Source, the First, and the Unknown God.
    - o Sacrifice happens at times by those who work to bring truth to the world, but there isn't some God looking down demanding it as a form of torture or rite of passage.
    - o The Anunnaki created a doctrine of fear in order to keep their slave labor in order and obedient. They were to be feared as they were unpredictable and cruel beings, but they are not the true God—our Source.

- We need a savior to submit to the ultimate sacrifice for us since we are so inherently evil, we cannot redeem ourselves without one. God shows us how much he loves us by sacrificing his own son, thus demonstrating to us the level we are expected to sacrifice. Churches will teach that we are forgiven because of the sacrifice of Jesus, but then turn around and coerce members into sacrificing by making them feel guilty for not doing enough or sending enough money, etc.; you know the drill. (Power of the Hierarchy)

  o James Mahu tells us in "The Fifth Interview of Dr. Neruda" and in the "Project Camelot Interview" that Anu originally planned to come back to Earth as ruler and "Savior of the world." The need for a savior belief system was initiated by that plan. However, James said that scenario is now off the table. With Anu's return being the plan, humanity was programmed to live within the "savior/evolution model of existence" in expectation of that prophecy being fulfilled.

  o Humanity can move beyond the programming of the savior/evolution model of existence by understanding the transformation/mastership model of existence also explained in the "Chamber Two Philosophy" paper.

- God is an authoritarian deity—angry, jealous, demanding, dangerous, and capricious. This god is usually considered to be male and is much feared. At the same time that the Judeo-Christian God is all the above, he is also said to be merciful, loving, and compassionate to those who believe in him while punishing those who don't. This is a strong belief in an exclusive god, and its members are caught in a quagmire of dogma that must be followed in order to be loved by this god. This creates a doctrine of exclusivism and separation; if we follow this god, we are saved, if we don't, we spend an eternity in the punishing environment of hell. Unfortunately, this teaching also includes either persecuting non-believers or trying to force the rest of the world to become "saved," and we know the suffering those beliefs have caused.

  o We now know that this "authoritarian god" concept originates from Anu and his sons and is not our Ultimate God or First Source.

  o If we use some common sense and basic psychology, even without the story of Anu, we see in the beliefs above the dictates of a very needy god. Could he be afraid of being found out for the imposter he is?

Throughout my book *Breaking Free from the Tyranny of Beliefs: A Revolution in Consciousness,* I explored this core belief matrix from several angles. It is a matrix that has seeped into the collective consciousness of the world and influences most if not all belief systems in some way and in so doing has stripped us of our sovereignty. Many of the mystically or atheistically or agnostically inclined within the collective in different parts of the world have been able to break free from some or all of these beliefs. But for the vast majority of humanity, the undercurrent of beliefs continues to be held in place by this foundational matrix. In various degrees of entrenchment, this matrix affects everything we do from our everyday lives to the type of government we create and the way we do business.

The information, references, and inner work offered in this book can be used as a tool to help transcend this paradigm of deception.

EXPLORATIONS

1. As an exercise in understanding where you are on the continuum of beliefs described above, choose one or more of the beliefs listed and journal or write a short essay about how this belief has affected your thinking and your life.
2. Now take this belief and see if you can trace it to your childhood or the time-space event where it was implanted into your psyche.
3. Journal how this specific belief has affected your interaction with others and your perceptions of others.
4. Explore your own belief system with the intent of finding any beliefs that nurture the idea of separation and exclusivism and then journal how each of these beliefs makes you feel toward others. Do you feel loving and accepting, or do they feed the ego drive of "better than?"

4

HYPATIA AND THE FALL OF ALEXANDRIA, EGYPT

"It is from the Bible that man has learned cruelty, rapine, and
murder; for the belief of a cruel God makes a cruel man."
— *Thomas Paine, The Age of Reason*

THE LAST CHAPTER TOLD THE story of the Council of Nicea that convened in 325 AD and set the precedence for Christianity to become the official religion of the Roman Empire. Let's sail across the Mediterranean to the famous Port of Alexandria, Egypt and visit this city for another important chapter of events that changed the course of history around the same time.

Alexandria was founded as a port city about 331 BCE by Alexander the Great. It is famous in antiquity as the site of several landmarks including the great lighthouse, considered one of the seven wonders of the ancient world, and the Temple of Serapis that was part of the renowned Library of Alexandria. This library was legendary to the world as the repository of everything known up to that time. The Library of Alexandria was begun under Ptolemy 1 (305-285 BCE) and was completed by Ptolemy II (298-246 BCE) who sent invitations to rulers and scholars asking them to contribute books. It is not known how many books were held in the library but estimates of 500,000 have been made. [47]

Alexandria was once the largest and most prosperous city in the world. It grew from a small port to the grandest and most important metropolis in ancient Egypt and attracted scholars, scientists, philosophers, mathematicians, artists, and historians. According to Mangasarian, [48] in the year 400 AD Alexandria enjoyed a population of 6,000,000 inhabitants and covered about fifteen square miles. It was free from poverty. No one was idle and work

---

[47] Mark, Joshua J., "Alexandria." *Ancient History Encyclopedia*, April 28, 2011, http://www.ancient.eu/alexandria/ Information in the first two paragraphs paraphrased from this article.

[48] Mangasarian, M.M., "The Martyrdom of Hypatia," *Wikisource*, https://en.wikisource.org/wiki/The_Martyrdom_of_Hypatia

(A speech given to the Independent Religious Society at the Majestic Theater in Chicago, May 1915)

brought good wages; even the lame and blind found suitable work. The Alexandrians manufactured papyrus and knew how to blow glass and weave linen.

It was an eclectic seat of cultural exchange and home to many belief systems, including the Gnostics and other pagan religions, as well as the early Christians. Remember that Christianity was formally decreed as the church of the Roman Empire in 325 AD. It was being enforced in the Roman Empire and gaining ground and influence in other parts of the world, including Alexandria, at the time we pick up our story of Hypatia.

Hypatia was born and raised in Alexandria during its last days as a seat of cultural exchange. There is speculation about her birth date; some scholars put her birth at c.370 CE while others put it at c. 350 CE.

Considered by some scholars to be among the most brilliant women who ever lived, Hypatia was one of the most famous and revered women of her generation. She was the gifted daughter of Theon of Alexandria, a mathematician and philosopher of considerable renown. He tutored her in math, astronomy, and the philosophy of the day, including Platonism. He raised her as he would have raised a son by allowing her to apprentice with him and by teaching her what he knew.

Her fame as a lecturer of philosophy brought students from Rome, Athens, and other great cities of that time. She was considered an extraordinary woman and led the life of a respected academic at Alexandria's university. She never married and devoted herself to the study of many subjects including mathematics, physics, biology, astronomy, literature, and geography. All who write about her are in agreement that she was a woman of enormous intellectual power. Cyril, the Christian Archbishop of Alexandria, saw her intellectual abilities as a threat. He felt that Hypatia's power as a teacher made her a dangerous influence because she gave the existing Platonic Mystery Schools credibility and kept them alive, thus obstructing the progress of his new faith, Christianity. He hated her because as a mere frail woman she dared to think for herself. He became obsessed with the idea that she was inhibiting the growth of Christianity. Mangasarian states that "Cyril was a barbarian, and the doctrines of his religion only sharpened his claws and whipped his passion into a rage." [49]

Hypatia was a great power in Alexandria and the most popular person by some accounts. According to Mangasarian, when she appeared in her chariot on the streets, people threw flowers at her and applauded her. Poets called her the Virgin of Heaven. Some even said that her beauty made Cleopatra jealous. However, she was very modest and focused on learning

---

[49] Ibid.

and teaching. She was the last known teacher in the tradition of the Platonic Mystery Schools.[50] (See Chapter Two to review Platonism.)

In 415 CE while on her way home from teaching at the university (other accounts say she was going to work), Hypatia was attacked and murdered by a mob of Christian monks.

According to the account written by John Lamb Lash, [51] Peter the Reader, a zealous convert to Christianity, led the mob sanctioned by Cyril. Lash describes her death in graphic detail. Reader called her a vile heretic and a witch who beguiled people through her beauty and branded her teachings as the works of Satan. She was dragged from her chariot and down the street to a church, stripped naked, and beaten to death and burned. Her body was pounded to a pulp, her limbs torn off her torso. The mob was so frenzied and the attack so ferocious that it was impossible for anyone to intervene. Once she was dead, it was said that this wretched mob took razor-sharp oyster shells and scraped the flesh off her bones and took the scraped bones to a place called Cindron and burned them to ashes. No one was ever prosecuted for the death of this most beloved icon.

Alexandria, a great seat of learning during the early days of Christianity, began a rapid decline after the death of Hypatia. Joshua Mark states:

> It is by no means an exaggeration to state that Alexandria was destroyed as a centre of culture and learning by religious intolerance and Hypatia has come to symbolize this tragedy to the extent that her death has been cited as the end of the classical world ... Hypatia's death has long been recognized as a watershed mark in history delineating the classical age of paganism from the age of Christianity.[52]

Carl Sagan described the cultural dynamics of Alexandria in the following passage taken from *Cosmos*:

> The Alexandria of Hypatia's time—by then long under Roman rule—was a city under grave strain. Slavery had sapped classical civilization of its vitality. The growing Christian Church was consolidating its power and attempting to eradicate pagan influence and culture. Hypatia stood at the epicenter of

[50] Mark, Joshua J., "Hypatia of Alexandria," *Ancient History Encyclopedia*, September 2, 2009, http://www.ancient.eu/Hypatia_of_Alexandria/

[51] Lash, John Lamb, *Not in His Image: Gnostic Vision, Sacred Ecology and the Future of Belief*, Chelsea Green Publishing, 85 North Main Street, Suite 120, White River Junction, Vermont 05001.

[52] Mark, Joshua J., "Hypatia of Alexandria," *Ancient History Encyclopedia*, September 2, 2009, http://www.ancient.eu/Hypatia_of_Alexandria/

these mighty social forces. Cyril, the Archbishop of Alexandria, despised her because of her close friendship with the Roman governor, and because she was a symbol of learning and science, which were largely identified by the early Church as paganism. In great personal danger, she continued to teach and publish until the year 415, she was on her was to work she was set upon by a fanatical mob of Cyril's parishioners. (He goes on to describe her murder.)

The glory of the Alexandrian Library is a dim memory. Its last remnants were destroyed soon after Hypatia's death. It was as if an entire civilization had undergone some self-inflicted brain surgery and most of its memories, discoveries, ideas and passions were extinguished irrevocably. The loss was incalculable. In some cases we know only the tantalizing titles of the works that were destroyed. [53]

Hypatia's life and accomplishments and the eclectic citizenship of Alexandria are examples of the best of humanity. Hypatia's tragic fate and the fall of Alexandria are significant historical events for us to contemplate in our present political and religious climates. While Alexandria was tolerant of many belief systems, it flourished. Once Christianity began to take a stronghold narrowing the minds of its inhabitants by restricting what could be believed, this once magnificent city began a sharp decline. We also see the sprouting of the roots of prejudice towards Science that have carried through to this day by the Christian Right.

Hypatia of Alexandria became the head of the Platonic School in 400 C.E. and lectured on philosophy and mathematics to large audiences that included some prominent Christians … In addition to being a philosopher, mathematician, and scientist, Hypatia has been held up as an example of the Platonic ideal of equality of the sexes, and as a model of virtue by some early Christians. She also became a martyr and a symbol of the way in which early Christian zealots attempted to suppress the "pagan" Hellenistic thinkers.[54]

Paganism, Gnosticism, and the Mysteries were pre-Christian systems of belief. Most of these belief systems seemed to have an understanding of the ideas that we would eventually

[53] "Great Philosophers: Hypatia," *Oregon State University,* http://oregonstate.edu/instruct/phl201/modules/Philosophers/Hypatia/hypatia.html.
[54] "Hypatia of Alexandria," *New World Encyclopedia,* http://www.newworldencyclopedia.org/entry/Hypatia_of_Alexandria

go back to the One and that individuals evolve spiritually at their own pace. The teachings weren't forced or made mandatory. People were free to embrace the beliefs that resonated with them—until Christianity came along, that is. The great irony to this and succeeding horrible events down through history is that, as discussed in previous chapters, Christianity teaches the same savior story as many of the pagan and Mystery School religions, and yet countless humans have been brutally slaughtered and/or persecuted because their religions were considered pagan.

Some Gnostics embraced Christianity as they had the insight and spiritual understanding that helped them blend the two religions into a mystical version of Christianity. They were open to interpreting the metaphors and symbolism inherent in the story. But the Literalists would have none of it and became vehement in their campaign to eradicate all forms of Gnosticism, causing the Gnostics who survived the purge of all non- Christian religions to go underground. Apparently, Gnosticism was close enough to the truth of the origins of Christianity that it too had to be silenced.

A mystical belief system that taught direct contact with Source and cut out the "savior" middleman would empower the masses too much because they might stumble onto hidden truths through their own insights or mystical experiences. The belief that only a savior had the authority to show the way is an effective method to keep the masses controlled and unquestioning and doubting their own inner promptings. Subsequently, Christianity in the hands of the ruling classes became one of the cruelest and most powerful tools of all to suppress and control the whole of humanity in the Western World.

PART TWO

THE RUSE THAT BUILT A WORLD OF OPPRESSION AND SEPARATION

SHADOW ON THE BORDER OF ISOLATION

A shadowy territory on the border of isolation
Hovers at the edge of my psyche
Where darkness masks despair
An invisible veil molds to form
Concealing an alien world
Too dangerous to reveal
Stay neutral—neatly confined—defined

What happens if the veil is removed?
Will it reveal a stark land of desolation?
With its gnarled roots of distorted memories
Rising out of the depths of hopelessness
Haunting the stumbling traveler
Overcome by despair?

Shadow on the Border of Isolation
Forbids my rendezvous with light
Blocking the Silence I seek
And long to penetrate and absorb
My passage out of the prison
Away from the desperate world of shattered dreams

The Shadow whose name is Deception
Blocks me from crossing the bridge
With taunts about boarding my ship of foolish Dreams
Attempts to bar me from voyages awaiting me
Beyond the darkness of despair

Fear holds me—dreams call me
Teetering on the threshold
Two distinct paths reveal a future
Separation on one side—Oneness on the other

Determined to face my fears and
Defying Deception's taunts
I gingerly peel away the veil of oppression

For I have come to claim the Dagger of Light That
Illuminates the Path over the Border
I must slay the Shadow of Deception
That guards the Bridge of Silence and Truth
So that Unity can find me and align with the future
Away from isolation into my homeland of Oneness

© Lark Aleta Batey 2015

5

THREE REVOLUTIONS—THE WHEELS OF THE SCIENTIFIC REVOLUTION ARE SET INTO MOTION

INTUITIVE VS. INTELLECTUAL FUNCTIONING

> The last three millennia have witnessed the development of the logical, thinking human being. Beginning with the ancient Greeks, Western civilization has marched inexorably toward the elusive goal of the autonomous, rational human. Through the emergence of Christianity, the awakening of the Middle Ages, the Renaissance and Reformation, the Scientific Revolution of Copernicus, Kepler, Galileo and Newton, the Philosophical Revolution of Bacon and Descartes, and into the Industrial Revolution and the modern age, Western consciousness has moved seemingly single-mindedly toward what may best be expressed in the Cartesian cogito—I think therefore I am. [55]

THE PROGRESSION QUOTED ABOVE IS a double-edged sword. On the one hand, humanity gradually developed a strong intellect which strengthened the ego and gave us the ability to make great strides in important technological and scientific developments; on the other hand, this same progression plunged us deeper and deeper into separation by insisting on rigid dogmatism and devaluing the intuitive function.

Three Revolutions operated in tandem—the Industrial Revolution, the Philosophical Revolution, and the Scientific Revolution. Prior to these game- changing revolutions and part of their catalyst was the invention of the printing press around 1450 by Johannes

---

[55] Miller, Jeffrey C., *The Transcendent Function,* State University of New York Press, 2004.

Gutenberg.[56] His initial venture was to print the Bible, the first book to be printed using reusable movable type. Other methods of printing were around long before his invention, but Gutenberg's method made books available to everyone through mass production of printed material. This moveable type press remained unchanged until the 19th century when steam-powered presses were introduced.

Gutenberg lived during the 15th century as the Middle Ages and the Renaissance were coming to an end and a middle-class culture based on commodities and money began to emerge. Gutenberg's era marked the beginning of a new chapter in human history. Inventions such as gun powder, the compass, the water wheel, the clock and expanding developments in medicine and other sciences, as well as the emergence of universities all over Europe, were the forerunners of these revolutions.

Interestingly, the invention of the movable type press and the mass printing of the Bible actually rattled the foundations of the Roman Catholic Church as new interpretations of the Bible became important instruments for breaking down its control. Prior to that, illiteracy kept the masses in line as they were told what to believe by their priests, and the Bible was only studied and interpreted by the clergy. That tendency was still the norm in Catholic circles way into the 20th century.

I remember as a young girl one of my friends was from a devout Catholic family. We had a discussion one day about the Bible, and I told her that my grandmother studied it a lot. She was a close friend, and I might have broached the subject to her that there were certain things we didn't believe in anymore. I know I was trying to get some point across to her about the Bible. My friend told me that they were not allowed to read the Bible, that the priest was the only one who understood it, and that it was their priest who told them what the Bible said. I remember feeling shocked by that statement. In her mind it discredited anything my grandmother would have said on the subject because she wasn't a priest. Now as I look back on this conversation from my childhood, I realize how powerful that rule was for many devout churchgoers given similar instructions. It feeds into the belief that salvation is necessary because all are sinners, and they cannot possibly know what God wants without an interpreter. That experience was also the first of many throughout my lifetime of what it feels like to come up against a mind closed by religious programming. It is like hitting a brick wall.

The original Bible was written in Latin, and it was actually a crime to translate it into other languages. Gutenberg printed his first Bible in Latin. William Tyndale, an Oxford Scholar

---

[56] Woreck, Daniel and Zora Parwini, "Six hundred years since the birth of Johannes Gutenberg—inventor of the printing press, an assessment of his significance," *World Socialist Web Site*, 3 January 2001, https://www.wsws.org/en/articles/2001/01/gute-j03.html
The information about the Gutenberg press is paraphrased from this article.

who lived in 1521, was shocked to find that most people in England were scriptural illiterates. He translated the Bible into English, arranged for it to be printed and illegally smuggled copies into England. In 1535 he was betrayed by a fellow Englishman and burnt at the stake.

I can't help thinking how absurd the law forbidding the Bible to be translated into the vernacular was. Latin was not even the language of Jesus or the characters of the Old Testament; it was the language used by the Roman Empire. Latin wasn't any "holier" than any other language. It certainly wasn't a sacred language. Keeping the Bible in Latin was an attempt by the paranoid religious leadership to ensure that few could read it and to maintain power through the mystique of the priesthood as god's called and chosen ones. Only the Church leaders knew the extent to which knowledge was suppressed, and they wanted to make sure their followers didn't find out.

The rise of universities during this era created new interests among the educated masses, and a shift from religion to earthly things added to the demand for printed material. As the rise of science and other secular subjects emerged, they took away some of the supremacy of the Church for the educated. The poor, however, continued to be enslaved as the Industrial, Philosophical and Scientific Revolutions developed.

THE INDUSTRIAL REVOLUTION

If we put ourselves in the place of the people living under the conditions I will be describing below as the Industrial Revolution began and gained momentum, we will see more examples of the control that beliefs have over a society. Take the belief that men were given domination over the earth and everything in it, including women and children. Add to that the belief in original sin, setting people up to believe that everything that happened to them was their fault or punishment from God, and stir the nobility of suffering into the mix, and we have a recipe for misery and submission to domination. Controlled, busy, overworked, and tired people lose their sense of self-worth and can be easily manipulated. If they find themselves in dire circumstances, it can easily be interpreted as a punishment or a trial for their sins.

The collective consciousness continued to be perpetuated by that river of belief set in motion so many eons ago that included keeping the masses in a slave mentality to serve the wealthy. This indoctrination of suppression in the form of hierarchies, customs, and societal expectations was handed down from generation to generation, creating a predictable and uniform way for our species to perceive and function in the world. It also set the stage for the creation of corporations and big business monopolies.

The Industrial Revolution that started in Great Britain in the 18th century began with cottage industries of homemade items in predominantly rural agrarian societies. Before this time, people lived in small villages and were either farmers or skilled craftsmen. The family lived and worked together, handing down skills and crafts from one generation to the next. They still often lived in poverty under feudal law, but an agrarian society at least gave its inhabitants access to nature and fresh air and relatively clean water. They were able to grow their own food and raise their own livestock.

As industrialization began to take hold, everything changed. People began to move to cities to find work in factories and were crowded into substandard and inadequate vermin-infested shanty towns that lacked clean water and safe sewage disposal. As sewage was dumped into the streets, cities became squalid cesspools of filth and disease. The air wasn't fit to breath. In these foul and putrid environments, disease and malnutrition became formidable enemies.

In the book *Dissolving Illusions*, a chapter titled "Suffer the Little Children" [57] describes these conditions in graphic detail. From the late 1700s into the 1800s and 1900s, as machines replaced the manual labor of skilled adults in the production of goods, manufacturers began using children as a cheap source of labor. Factory work for children was abusive and demoralizing. Many children were forced to work twelve hour shifts of backbreaking work in factories and mines. They began their lives in the coal mines at age five and were often kept in "apprentice houses" away from their families under the observation and "care" of matrons. It was a common saying that the children's beds never got cold as one set would be climbing out of bed to go to work and another would be climbing into the same bed. These children grew up in loveless, abusive environments where they were treated like slaves. Most of them were sickly, and many died at an early age.

The chapter "Suffer the Little Children" continues to describe despicable conditions where children worked: in glass-making factories, in canneries, and in cotton mills and other burgeoning industries. This chapter is very difficult to read, but it is important to understand how profoundly these children and families suffered in dangerous and humiliating work.

Think of what it would have been like when entire families, including the children, were forced to work in squalid slave-like conditions in order for them to survive, and they were

---

[57] Humphreys, Suzanne, M.D. and Roman Bystrianyk, "Disease, Vaccines, and the Forgotten History," *Dissolving Illusions,* 2013, https://www.dissolvingillusions.com/
For a jolting, eye-opening understanding of what the Industrial Revolution brought to the poor working class, this is a well-researched book with many actual pictures of the inhumane and squalid conditions of the early 19th century. The entire book and pictures can also be found free on their website, or the book can be purchased.

without health, safety, or minimum wage or age laws. Hierarchies ruled the workplace and the overall societal structure. Companies controlled their workers, even creating company stores where they were forced to buy their necessities. As I write this, I recall a song that was often played over the radio when I was a child. (I grew up in the late 40s and 50s.) The song was titled "Sixteen Tons." I am sure many of my older readers will recall this song. I remember a part of one verse:

> You load Sixteen tons, what do you get?
> Another day older and deeper in debt
> St. Peter don't you call me 'cause I can't go
> I owe my soul to the company store.[58]

My maternal grandmother was born in the late 1890s and used to tell me stories about the conditions of her childhood and early adulthood. She grew up in the Sandhills of Nebraska and lived under very sparse conditions. She said that her mother married at sixteen and had a baby every year for about ten years and then basically "gave-up" and withdrew from the family by isolating herself in her room. Grandma, being one of the older girls, was given the responsibility of caring for her younger siblings. She described conditions of excruciating poverty and long hours of hard work.

She used to say, "Don't talk to me about the good ole days, there was no such thing." After she married my grandfather, she became a nurse in her young adult years and would go to people's homes to care for them when they were ill or to deliver babies. She cared for people before antibiotics were discovered and worked many people through pneumonia and other such illnesses. She told me that she would go to the home of a family and stay there for a week or longer as needed. Her first order of business would often be to clean up the environment. She ate and slept very little when she was working. She lived an extremely hard life, and her health in her later years suffered from it.

For the times that she grew up in and lived out her life, my grandmother had a surprisingly feminist attitude. She had nursed people through countless illnesses and dire circumstances. She was psychologically strong, sure of herself and wise, and I admired her immensely. No one talked back to my grandmother. She was clearly the matriarch of the family, and we did as we were told. She was a loving monarch. Her word was law. We didn't dispute her. I used to wonder as a child listening to her stories how I could capture some of that wisdom and not lose it all when she died. She was my most influential role model.

---

[58] Travis, Merle, "Sixteen Tons" *Wikipedia*, 1946, https://en.wikipedia.org/wiki/Sixteen_Tons
The song has been recorded by many singers through the years.

My maternal grandfather was a fireman on the Union Pacific Railroad when he was a young man, and he would work twelve-hour exhausting shifts six days a week shoveling coal to keep the train engine running and earned about fifty cents a day. By the time I was born, he had worked his way up to being an engineer and drove trains between Ogden, Utah and Evanston, Wyoming. Life was much easier for him then.

My grandfather was a staunch supporter of the unions and was a union treasurer for years. I remember so well his co-workers on the railroad coming to visit him and pay their union dues. He had a huge roll top desk where his paperwork and the money were kept and locked. That desk always fascinated me.

Grandpa credited the unions for the improved working conditions, remembering what he and others had endured when they were young.

From the stories these two people told, I was given a glimpse of how difficult life was in the early 20th century, and why the improvement of working conditions and human rights and the creation of child labor laws and unions were and are so important. These hard-fought improvements rose out of the suffering of our predecessors and deserve our continued respect and support.

Born out of intense personal suffering and hardship, a legacy of workplace laws and regulations such as the forty-hour work week, a minimum wage, and child labor laws have been bequeathed to us by our grandparents and great-grandparents. These privileges and benefits should not be taken lightly.

If we look back at the history of our nation and our world and think about all the changes that have happened in our lifetimes, we can grow to appreciate the many covert undercurrents of progress and expansion that when inserted into our collective consciousness, stimulated subtle modifications, which over time became huge societal changes. The instigators of these new ideas invariably originated from liberal and progressive points of view.

For those who were influenced by that undercurrent of new ideas and became the catalysts for societal change, their lives were anything but easy. They often suffered painful consequences for the injustices they tried to correct as the more conventional points of view fought those changes.

All we have to do is remember the uphill battles fought to attain women's right to vote and the opposition to other human rights movements that continue to this day to get a taste of the kind of ostracism, resistance to change, and control society has wielded on its more progressive citizens. If we take an objective look back on the journey humanity has traveled over the centuries, we see that push-me, pull-you dynamic in all walks of life: progressives push forward—conservatives push back.

In incremental surges, humanity fulfills its caterpillar developmental tasks before a new order can insert itself, and then we soar into a flight of transformation as new ideas find a place and function in our world. This dynamic plays out over and over as new discoveries are introduced into the collective.

There are always those who are destined to be out in front blazing unknown trails and those in the back fighting to keep the status quo of the known. The Yin and Yang of this dichotomy inevitably urges humanity forward even though it is incremental and seems frustratingly slow to those with the vision of what the future has the potential to provide.

If we can catch a glimpse of the trajectory of our collective history, we have a greater chance of seeing the big picture of humanity's evolving journey to a whole new consciousness. It is to our collective benefit to be able to recognize that subtle and precious undercurrent of change and embrace its ability to inspire us in unique and mysterious ways. In so doing, we are nudged along a transformational course where we develop ideas that nurture our world and stimulate an evolution of our consciousness that will ultimately give us the perception and insight to see a whole new world of understanding unfold before us.

Keeping these ideas in mind, let's explore the phases in humanity's journey along the path of human development and evolution that have brought us this far.

THE PHILOSOPHICAL AND SCIENTIFIC REVOLUTIONS (1550—1700)

The Scientific and Philosophical Revolution was an important era on the trajectory of humanity's journey on this earth, entering on the heels of the Inquisitions and the Renaissance Age (roughly between the 1300s and the 1500s).

The Inquisitions began their insidious agendas beginning in the 12th century and carried through to the 19th century in various European countries. Their focus was mainly on forcing people to adhere to Roman Catholic religious beliefs. The first Inquisition began in 12th century France to root out the "heresies" of the Cathars and the Waldensians. The worst manifestation was in Spain where Jews and Muslims were targeted. The Spanish Inquisition was a dominant force for more than 200 years and resulted in over 32,000 executions. [59]

Napoleon abolished the Inquisition in France in 1806; Portugal abolished it in 1821; the last execution in Spain was in 1826, but it was not completely outlawed until 1834. [60]

---

[59] https://www.history.com/topics/religion/inquisition
[60] https://en.wikipedia.org/wiki/Inquisition#Ending of the Inquisition in the 19th and 20th centuries

The Renaissance [61] (14th to 17th centuries) inspired new values as humanity began to emerge from the economic, intellectual, and cultural decline of the Middle Ages:

- Humanism, the most characteristic value of the Renaissance, had three elements—a belief in man as a proper focus of study; a revival of classical learning of the Greeks and Romans; and a revival of classical texts and language and the creation of new works in the style of the classics. Renaissance thinkers believed that Man was created in God's image and was endowed with a "spark of the divine," the ability to create intellectually and artistically.

- Individualism—in the Middle Ages, identity was defined by the group one belonged to. During the Renaissance, individual thought and expression began to become highly regarded.

- Secularism—in the medieval world, the goal of life was to attain salvation in the next life. The Renaissance man was firmly planted in this world and strived to make this world comfortable and satisfying. They remained devout Christian believers, however.

- Materialism—The Church of the Middle Ages preached against the accumulation of wealth (although it amassed major fortunes) as indicative of the sin of pride and the corruption of spirit. The Renaissance saw no reason why the comforts and beauty of earth would create obstacles to heaven. If man-made artistic creations were the result of God's gift to man, how could they be bad?

- Civic Humanism—involvement in the politics of one's city-state and the giving freely of one's talents for the greater good of the community was expected.

- Appreciation of Nature/Naturalism—the Renaissance period encouraged men to enjoy and observe natural surroundings, and from their study and observations, they created accurate and natural depictions of the human form, the environment, the cityscape, and the flora and fauna.

- Virtu—an Italian word for "manliness" that in this period meant one had developed all of his skills and talents to the fullest. A Renaissance Man was expected to be familiar with philosophy, history, and rhetoric; to dress well and have a respectable home; to know quality; to have manners and gallantry; to know how to ride a horse and use a sword. He was expected to be a successful businessman and to be able to write in Latin, Italian, and Greek.

- Keep in mind that the Renaissance that occurred after the Middle Ages was male centered. It would be many years before women began to enjoy the rights that men

---

[61] https://www.vanderbilt.edu/olli/class-materials/Values_of_the_Renaissance.pdf The information in this section regarding the Renaissance was taken from this PDF.

had in any century. The liberation of the feminine gender is a story of its own, and not one I can do justice to on these pages. The focus of this book is the liberation of consciousness, regardless of gender, and to that end I continue.

The progressive thrust of the Renaissance Period was necessary as a precursor to the revolutions that followed it. This set the stage for those destined to challenge traditional thought in order to shift values from the religious to the secular.

Enter the Scientific and Philosophical Revolution and the arrival of the great thinkers of that era. Three of the most influential scientists of all times according to some historians lived during this period. They were Descartes, believed to be one if the greatest minds of the Scientific Revolution; Newton, called the most influential scientist of all time; and Bacon, one of the great philosophers of the Scientific Revolution. These futurists laid the foundations for the Age of Reason and Enlightenment which was to enter the world stage around 1650.

Rene Descartes (1596-1650) was a famous French philosopher and mathematician and is often called the Father of Modern Philosophy. He was a strong believer in mathematics and developed analytical geometry which linked geometry and algebra. He was also known for the development of deductive reasoning. This method had four premises:

(1) accepting as "truth" only clear, distinct ideas that could not be doubted, (2) breaking a problem down into parts, (3) deducing one conclusion from another, and (4) conducting a systematic synthesis of all things. Descartes based his entire philosophical approach to science on this deductive method of reasoning.

His famous saying was "I think, therefore I am."

Descartes wrote:

All science is certain, evident knowledge. We reject all knowledge that is merely probable and judge that only those things should be believed which are perfectly known and about which there can be no doubts. [62]

The Cartesian method of thought was systematic, bringing science into greater alignment with mathematics. "He invented analytic geometry—a method of solving geometric problems algebraically and algebraic problems geometrically—which is the foundation of the infinitesimal calculus developed by Sir Isaac Newton and Gottfried Wilhelm Leibniz." [63]

---

[62] Watson, Richard A., "Cartesianism," *Britannica*, https://www.britannica.com/topic/Cartesianism
[63] Ibid.

The Cartesian way of thinking has become a major part of the scientific method. It is a form of rationalism as opposed to the tradition of empiricism which originated with Aristotle.

Sir Francis Bacon (1561-1626) [64] was born and died in London, England. He lived under the reigns of Queen Elizabeth I and James I, and he was a Member of Parliament for thirty-seven years and was influential to James I. He was dubbed a knight in 1603. According to *Wikipedia*, Bacon became Baron Verulam in 1618 and Viscount Saint Albans in 1621.

It is also widely believed that he was an illegitimate son of Queen Elizabeth I, and strong evidence points toward the idea that he wrote the works attributed to Shakespeare.

He was an excellent writer and an unusually original thinker for the times he lived in. Bacon was an English philosopher, statesman, scientist, and lawyer who proposed the Experimental Method (inductive reasoning) where an experiment is done and then the conclusions are drawn. He is considered one of the great scientists for challenging old beliefs and creating new ones.

Descartes introduced deductive thinking; Bacon introduced inductive reasoning, "… a logical process in which multiple premises, all believed to be true or found true most of the time, are combined to obtain a specific conclusion." [65]

Descartes began with intuitively derived principles that were taken as the premises in the standard deductive method of reasoning. Bacon began with experimental observations that were used to inductively extract higher truisms. Descartes' background was science and mathematics; Bacon's was law.

Sir Isaac Newton (1643-1727) was born in England. He was accomplished in many fields such as optics, mathematics, gravitation, and chemistry. He is most famous for his work on gravitation and formulated the Law of Universal Gravitation. He is also known to have invented a method of calculus to solve some of his problems. He built the first reflecting telescope. In 1687 he published *Mathematical Principles of Natural Philosophy*, and it is believed to be one of the most important scientific books ever written.

Newton spent most of his life as a professor at Cambridge and is considered by many to be the greatest and most influential scientist who ever lived. [66]

---

[64] Quinton, Anthony M., "Francis Bacon: British author, philosopher and statesman," *Britannica*, https://www.britannica.com/biography/Francis-Bacon-Viscount-Saint-Alban

[65] "Inductive reasoning," *WhatIs*, https://whatis.techtarget.com/definition/inductive-reasoning

[66] "Newton, Bacon and Descartes," *Google Sites*,
https://sites.google.com/site/newtonbaconanddescartes/home/newton-bacon-and-descartes
Some information about Descartes and Bacon above are also taken from this article.

THE AGE OF REASON

At this juncture in history when the above revolutions were set into motion, several dynamics came into play. This period is marked by a passionate interest in the physical world and knowledge acquired from thinking. Mysticism and religion and the superstition of the Middle Ages were all being challenged. Individuals began to feel free to have and explore new ideas as the pendulum of beliefs began to swing in the direction of reason and rationality. Interests in life after death and other abstract subjects that flourished in the Middle Ages were losing their stronghold. Christianity began losing some of its power among intellectuals, but it was still the prevailing religion. The core belief matrix formed by the Church was still very much intact in the ethics and beliefs of the people, even though the focus began to change from the fear of God and faith in Biblical truth to a reliance on reason and rationality.

While upper class white men were enjoying the rights of a new age of individualism and humanity, encouraged to be well-educated with an understanding of the arts and sciences, women, children, and other races were still considered second class citizens. Upper class women could marry and escape the drudgery that was the lot of lower-class women forced to work long hours in factories and mills, but they were not welcome in academic circles.

During these times, women were expected to marry well and be loyal to their husbands and give birth to boys. They had few rights within society that weren't granted to them by men. The church had long ago put males in control, seeing females as having fewer mental faculties and at best only capable of bearing and raising children.

Nature has long been referred to as feminine, i.e., Mother Nature.

Even though new ideas were being introduced and utilized during the years that Descartes, Bacon, Newton, and other great scientific pioneers were making strong headway into the intellectual collective, intuition and all things attributed to the feminine continued to remain suspect, illustrating the attitude towards intuition that dominated the scientific community.

Only that which could be observed and measured was accepted (literalism); anything intuitive or subjective (gnostic) was held suspect. Science and religion were now at opposing ends of a rigid continuum of beliefs. The three Revolutions we have discussed in this chapter stimulated changes in humanity's belief systems that belittled intuition. We can see how a concrete frame of mind was necessary to get us where we are today.

Belief systems that perpetuated black-and-white, literal thinking influenced the mainstream way of life throughout this historical period up to and including the present day. They perpetuated our internal isolation from our true origins to maintain our external separation, i.e., God from humanity, science from spirit, male from female, nature from humanity, brain over heart, intellect over intuition, indifference over compassion, etc.

The basic belief that began to drive scientific exploration during the Age of Reason was based on the concept that the human is a physical machine powered by chemicals and genetics, detaching us from the intuitive or divine sides of our nature. Thus, a continuum of belief that began with religion and influenced science and industry has succeeded in keeping our true origins and identities hidden from us to this day. One could argue that the thinking that evolved during those revolutions was necessary for science and technology to bring us to our current threshold where intuition and the acceptance of the feminine can be invited into the mix. As we move forward into the 21st century, it is important to remember the lessons learned along the way.

I will end this chapter with a quote of Thomas Paine from his book *The Age of Reason* that articulates a clear message to humanity to examine our religious beliefs, so we do not fall prey to repeat the most devastating parts of our religious history.

> The most detestable wickedness, the most horrid cruelties, and the greatest miseries that have afflicted the human race have had their origin in this thing called revelation or revealed religion. It has been the most dishonorable belief against the character of the divinity, the most destructive to morality, and the peace and happiness of man, that ever was propagated since man began to exist. It is better, far better, that we admitted, if it were possible, a thousand devils to roam at large, and to preach publicly the doctrine of devils, if there were any such, than that we permitted one such impostor and monster as Moses, Joshua, Samuel, and the Bible prophets, to come with the pretended word of God in his mouth and have credit among us.
>
> Whence arose all the horrid assassinations of whole nations of men, women, and infants, with which the Bible is filled; and the bloody persecutions, and tortures unto death and religious wars, that since that time have laid Europe in blood and ashes; whence arose they, but from this impious thing called revealed religion, and this monstrous belief that God has spoken to man? The lies of the Bible have been the cause of the one, and the lies of the Testament of the other.

6

MEDICAL MODEL AND/OR THE NATURAL APPROACH—A QUESTION FOR OUR TIMES

A PERSONAL DISCLOSURE

AS I BEGAN RESEARCHING, SCRUTINIZING, and discussing what material I would include in this chapter, I came to realize that if I am going to write a book that examines our collective beliefs, I have to be willing to do the same for beliefs that I hold. It is difficult to look at one's own stuff, but look at it I must. So, in the spirit of fairness and disclosure, I will give you some background of where my biases and beliefs originated.

I was aware even as a young adult that what seemed to be the most common-sense solution, or made the most sense to me, often found me butting my head against the status quo or commonly held beliefs. I just seemed to perceive things differently and was mystified by why what seemed obvious to me was often not even on the radar of those around me. This was my experience almost everywhere I turned, regardless of the issue I was dealing with or the subject I was interested in.

Natural ways of living and staying healthy have been huge interests of mine most of my entire adult life. I raised a large family on an extremely limited income and without health insurance in the late '60s, '70s and '80s.

I became interested in nutrition as a newlywed. My introduction to the concept of the importance of nutrition was actually through a cookbook I received as a wedding present. It explained that the human body needed certain nutrients to function well. I was a young wife, finding myself with the responsibility of providing meals every day, and now I learned that food had a purpose—to provide nutrients to the body so that it functioned properly. I was fascinated by that concept. (That may sound tongue-in-cheek, but it isn't. Nutrition wasn't really on the mainstream radar that I was aware of in the '60s, nor do I remember much being taught about it in home economics classes.) It was one of my first "aha" realizations. Good nutrition became my first focus and study.

One of my first "mentors" was Adele Davis and her book *Let's Have Healthy Children*. There have been many books about nutrition after hers, but she put me on the path. This has been an evolving life-time study as has the field of health in general.

My limited funds while raising our children forced me to be very particular about what I spent money on. I tried very hard to get as big a "nutritional bang for my buck" as I could. I baked my own bread. I bought whole grains and ground them into flour or cereal or had them ground. I bought raw milk from a local farmer who had exceptionally clean practices in the way the milking cows were handled. I was a Licensed Massage Therapist and had a private practice in my home for about sixteen years while raising my kids and one of my clients provided us with farm-fresh eggs. I kept fresh fruit and popcorn for the kids to snack on. Soda pop was a treat, not something that was allowed in the house as a staple. I baked but kept sugar consumption to a bare minimum.

We took the kids to a doctor when they needed medical attention, but that was infrequent.

I had my last three children naturally with the help of Lamaze Preparation for Childbirth classes and began teaching the method while I was having my fifth and sixth babies. At that time, I also became a La Leche League leader and facilitated monthly meetings as support for mothers who wanted to breastfeed. I was available to help new mothers as well when they had individual breastfeeding problems. I participated in the battle to have fathers in the delivery room if they wanted to be there, and we promoted the idea of birthing rooms and babies "rooming in."

The town I lived in while raising my kids now has one of the best birthing centers in the state, I believe. It is gratifying to know that our group was instrumental in starting that ball rolling. I was able to be at the birth of a grandson and seeing this birthing center in practice was a rewarding and heart-warming experience.

I AM INTRODUCED TO THE WORLD OF HOMEOPATHY

I found homeopathic medicine when my sixth baby had some minor but chronic health issues. I met some Naturopathic doctors in Kansas while doing some research, and they helped me considerably. As I began learning homeopathy, I shared what I was learning with a friend. She was as intrigued with it as I was. We spent many hours together studying and discussing the uses of the homeopathic remedies.

In the spring of 1983, we learned of a two-week homeopathic training in Pennsylvania. We made arrangements and traveled to Millersville where healthcare professionals who wanted to learn more about homeopathy came from all over the world. It was an information-packed, unforgettable life- changing two weeks for both of us.

My friend and I created a Homeopathic Learning Center and developed and taught a six-week homeopathic first-aid class. We kept a supply of remedies on hand for our students to buy as needed. We did this mostly as a public service; we didn't make any money off the remedies. We used the money to increase our supply of remedies and to keep books on hand for people interested in the subject. We were careful not to prescribe (homeopathy), but to teach others how to use the remedies. We also had a segment in the course about when to seek medical help and not rely exclusively on the remedies.

The study of homeopathy opened my eyes to the history of medicine in this country, and while it is beyond the scope of this book to go into great detail about this fascinating subject, understanding how the medical profession developed might be helpful as we move forward into a new world where information, ideas, and policies are changing as fast as our hearts are beating.

Harris Coulter's book *Divided Legacy* recounts the history of the medical profession and its conflict with homeopathic medicine. The book begins by explaining that in the 1820s and 1830s American physicians enjoyed a well-established professional monopoly on the legal practice of medicine. As the century progressed, the profession lost its position of privilege and power to a series of competing and hostile groups of practitioners. According to Coulter, until the end of the 19th century there were four competing medical views:

1. The traditional medical doctrine—which was derived from the Solidist tradition represented by the Scotsmen William Cullen (1710-1790) and John Brown (1735-1788) and the American Benjamin Rush (1745-1813)—was upheld by the medically educated and licensed practitioners, known as "orthodox," "regular," or "allopathic" physicians.
2. A second doctrine was that of the "Indian Doctors"—practitioners who had never been to medical school and strongly opposed the therapeutics of the "regulars." They obtained their knowledge from the American Indians and from whites who had been in contact with the Indian medicine men. They were also known as the "herb doctors." Some early physicians who believed in their cause were called "botanical practitioners" or "botanics."
3. A third system devised by Samuel Thomson (1769-1843) turned away from school medicine and created a simplified system that involved copious use of steam baths and a native American emetic plant—*Lobelia inflata* sometimes known as Indian Tobacco. The Thomsonians and the Botanics fused in the late 1840s to form the Eclectic medical school.

4. The fourth system was homeopathy. This was the work of a German physician Samuel Hahnemann (1755-1843) and was introduced to the United States in 1825.[67]

Of the three "sectarian" forms of practice, homeopathy was the greatest threat to traditional medical ideas because it possessed and advocated an integrated and coherent doctrinal basis for its therapeutic practices, and it recruited practitioners from among the ranks of the orthodox physicians. Homeopathy had a well-developed philosophical base.

Until the end of the 19th century, the American medical scene was marked by incessant clashes between the homeopathic and allopathic physicians.

Coulter describes the thought process allopathic doctors use to diagnose and treat illness:

> …the problem which any medical thinker must face: (1) how is he to know what factors in disease are significant for therapeutic purposes, and (2) how is he to know what medicines are significant in a given case of disease?… To a hypothesized disease 'cause' a remedy of 'opposed' power must be administered…the 'opposed' remedy sometimes was thought to neutralize the disease cause, sometimes it removed the cause, and sometimes it moved the cause to another part of the body.[68]

Hahnemann's view of the therapeutic problem was quite different. He believed in the "law of similar" or "like cures like." Hahnemann was very quick to point out that he did not invent the "law of similar." He taught that it was a system of thought that originated with Paracelsus.

Hahnemann's interest in homeopathic principles began when he was translating Cullen's *Lectures on Materia Medica,* and he disagreed with Cullen's reason why quinine helped someone recover from malaria.

Basically—and this is a simple explanation of a very complex system— Hahnemann believed that a substance that would make a well person sick would make a sick person well if given in minute doses. He tested his theory out on anyone who would allow him to, and in his lifetime, Hahnemann personally conducted and supervised the "provings" of 99

---

[67] Coulter, Harris L., *Divided Legacy Vol. III: The Conflict Between Homeopathy and the American Medical Association*, North Atlantic Books, 635 Amador Street, Richmond CA 95805, 1999. (First edition published with the subtitle *Science and Ethics in American Medicine: 1800-1914*, 1973. Second edition, 1982.) Information from this book quoted and paraphrased.

[68] Ibid.

remedies. Today through the work of his followers, over 1500 remedies have been "proven" and can be found in the homeopathic *Materia Medica*.

A "proving" is conducted by having a well person volunteer to take the substance to the point where they develop symptoms, and those symptoms are meticulously noted. Once symptoms begin to happen, the substance is withdrawn. One has to actually look through a homeopathic *Materia Medica* to appreciate the depth and meticulous detail of the "provings" of the remedies. Every section of the body is noted with detailed symptoms experienced by the 'provers" of those substances.

In homeopathic practice when someone is ill, the symptoms are considered, and a remedy is given that most closely matches the symptoms being manifested. Results can be dramatic if a match occurs between symptoms and remedies.

This is a subject dear to my heart, and I could write on it in a lot more detail, but this book is covering a variety of subjects, and space will not permit, so I need to restrain myself and refer the reader to the resource below. [69]

An important difference between allopathic medicine and homeopathic medicine is dosage. Allopathic medicine typically uses large doses of medicines by mouth or intravenously; homeopathy uses exceedingly small, almost infinitesimal doses, usually dissolved under the tongue. It is believed by homeopaths that the remedies work on the Vital Force of the body; in contrast, allopathic medicine works directly on the physical body. I feel that homeopathy has been and continues to be way ahead of its time. It is an "energy medicine," and humanity is in its infancy regarding our understanding of how "energy" works with the body.

Homeopathy became very popular in the 1800s. By the 1840s allopathic medicine began a strong campaign to destroy homeopathy by labelling any doctor who practiced homeopathy or any other kind of alternative healing as a quack. During this time, the American Medical Association was formed as a national organization to train doctors in allopathic medicine and regulate the practice and ultimately the licensure of physicians.

This strict regulating of the health profession gives us a little insight into the long and difficult battle alternative healing modalities such as Chiropractic have had to endure in order to be considered as legitimate branches of health care.

The next part of the campaign to ensure that the AMA controlled medicine in the U.S. was to educate the public with the notion that medicine was far too complicated for anyone other than a trained physician to study and administer. Where homeopathic practitioners educated the public in the use of the remedies and encouraged patients to have a small

---

[69] Homeopathic Educational Services in Berkley, California for further information at https://www. homeopathic.com Dana Ullman, MPH owner, is a wealth of information and help.

supply of the basic remedies on hand, allopathic physicians made it a point not to explain their procedures to the public.

> Coulter states on page 193 of *Divided Legacy*:

> ... the urge to inform the public about medicine conflicted with all of medical tradition. The provision in the 1847 Code of Ethics against 'publishing cases and operations in the daily prints, or suffering such publications to be made' was by many held to prohibit any sort of medical communication in lay journals. [70]

So, we see the pattern set for the trend down through the next generations not to question one's medical doctor. Human health was put into the hands of the physician. The AMA took control of the medical profession, making it an immensely powerful organization that has monopolized medicine in the U.S. and dictated what would be taught and accepted as treatment modalities.

For example, most of us have heard or read how until recently nutrition was not even included in medical training, or if it was, it was only offered in elective courses.

RECOGNITION OF AND BREAKING FREE FROM THE SUPPRESSION PARADIGM

As a young woman, I became very frustrated and grappled with health aspects of the paradigm of suppression as I began raising my children.

Information on nutrition was hard to find. The general consensus was not to question our medical providers. I think anyone living during that time after World War II can remember those days. So, teaching Lamaze, Education for Childbirth in the 1970s and homeopathy in the 1980s went against the grain of the status quo. My generation didn't take well to being told they weren't allowed to question, and disillusioned rebels began coming out of the woodwork. Slowly, movements like childbirth education and natural health began to find their voices and exert their influence.

As we look back on the brief history of medicine discussed above, we can see the same trend of being taught not to question rearing its authoritarian head again, just like we saw earlier with religion. Sound familiar?

---

[70] Coulter, Harris L., *Divided Legacy: Science and Ethics in American Medicine: 1800-1914*, 1973. (See footnote 1.)

That paradigm thankfully has been changing for several decades now, and the internet has become a massive encyclopedia of information about almost everything. Finally, we as lay-people have at our fingertips the information we need to take responsibility for ourselves in order to make the decisions of what kind of health care intervention we are willing to accept and seek. We can ask informed questions and expect to receive informed answers. By allowing patients to be a part of the medical team with their providers and being able to discuss their treatment openly, an enormous amount of pressure can be taken off the doctor-patient relationship. Some doctors seem to find it refreshing to work with informed patients.

I find it interesting and somewhat entertaining that no matter how hard the powers that be work to keep information suppressed, it does not last. Eventually, the pressure that keeps the lid on anything that is suppressed builds, and the cover is blown.

What these big organizations like the AMA don't take into consideration is the human factor. It is true that some go into medicine for the money or power or prestige. But medicine by its very nature is focused on helping, and the biggest percentage of our health care professionals go into this field because they genuinely want to help humanity and make a difference. They make a decision from their heart to go into medicine and find themselves in a profession fraught with politics, irrational regulations, insurance company interference, and other frustrations. It takes tenacity, intelligence, and focused hard work to complete medical training, and those who make it through that arduous process come from our brightest. That wonderful intelligence is also an aide into seeing what is wrong with the system. Many doctors who began as orthodox practitioners are now becoming sympathetic to the idea of more natural approaches. They are encouraging their patients to understand their illnesses and the importance of self-care because they know that generally the less invasive they are, the better the outcomes. And if their patients feel that in all instances their doctors are truthful with them, they are more likely to cooperate if they do need a more intrusive kind of treatment.

All walks of life are beginning to feel the impact of the two dynamics of transparency and expansion.

We cannot allow the suppression paradigm to ever take over again. We have the right to know what is in our best interests and make decisions from an informed place with the help of professionals trained to guide and advise us.

We must without question have the right to choose the kind of health care we feel will work best for us personally—whether it is full-on traditional medicine all the way or a natural way or a combination of both. That should be the right of each one of us along with our medical team to determine what we feel works the best for us as individuals.

INTERESTING RESEARCH AND BIG PHARMA

I subscribe to Life Extension, a cutting-edge health magazine produced by a company that researches the use of nutrients for health. Some of their articles combine research in medicine with research in supplements.

In the January 2016 issue, I came across an article that illustrates the issue of Big Pharma's focus on making money titled "What Strikes Terror in the Citadels of the Pharmaceutical Industry." This was written by Dr. Ward Dean as a rebuttal to some "research" done on Vitamin D.

I am quoting the preamble to that article below because it illustrates in real time what we are facing with Big Pharma and some so-called studies done by mainstream medicine. Be wary. Some mainstream research gives good information, some others not so much. It is important to be informed and to do one's homework.

> In response to medical reports that are misinterpreted by the media, *Life Extension* has historically issued point-by-point rebuttals when the study's methodologies/analyses are scientifically flawed and/or the findings blatantly false.
>
> In response to sensationalize headlines appearing earlier this year about a flawed Vitamin D study, *Life Extension* reached out to a medical doctor who has been fighting the establishment almost as long as we have.
>
> Before you read Dr. Dean's detailed rebuttal to this study published by the American Medical Association, it is important for you to know why these kinds of reports garner so much media attention.
>
> In pharmaceutical corporate boardrooms charts are routinely presented showing how many people are projected to contract a terrible disease. Data about the potential benefits of a patented drug follows the chart projection. Then a financial calculation is done to show how much money will be made if the pharmaceutical company pushes this drug through the FDA's arduous approval process.
>
> An uncertainty has arisen regarding the lucrative financial projections coveted by drug companies. What if the chart showing growing numbers of aging Americans contracting a degenerative disease goes the other way…in other words declines? This destroys the profit expectation and incentive to spend hundreds of millions if not billions on a new drug candidate.
>
> The greatest threat to the profitability of Big Pharma may be Vitamin D. This vitamin costs virtually nothing and has an incredible amount of data

showing its ability to decimate the financial projections of drug companies who look forward to lots of aging Americans being diagnosed with some form of cancer every year.

Drug company ads dominate media advertising the way tobacco ads did in the 1950s through the 1960s. It is in the economic interests of Big Pharma for the media to air headlines warning Americans to avoid Vitamin D (and other supplements.) The more people who believe these flawed reports, the more money the pharmaceutical industry makes. As you will read, not only is this analysis attacking Vitamin D without scientific merit, but newly published data reveals Vitamin D to be more effective in preventing death and disability than previously known. Drug companies would prefer you not read these reports on Vitamin D. [71]

We see yet another area where information is being suppressed or there is an attempt to suppress it, especially where that information will eliminate the need for products or services of powerful corporations and special interest groups.

The drivers in the seat of our global crises are too often power and money and the belief systems of chauvinism born from these are the mutant monster offspring which propagate the world with pain and suffering. Do not be fooled; most large corporations do not have the public's best interests at heart. They are solely about profit.

Our beloved Earth is now in a critical stage of global chaos. The lack of responsible stewardship is causing the extinction of many plant and animal species that cannot live in the altered environments created by this greedy kind of "progress." If we continue on this destructive trajectory, many are saying that it won't be long before humans are included in the species that cannot survive on the planet.

Take heart because there is hope. A growing consciousness of stewardship is awakening in our country and across the Western World, and hopefully it will continue to gain momentum. Awareness of issues is the first step, and we live at a time in history where the grassroots level of the population has almost unlimited access to information that can be paradigm changing.

Articles such as those quoted above are becoming the norm as we grow in our ability to share information. It is becoming more and more difficult to keep secrets. As we continue on the journey of this book, we will explore additional information and discoveries that will give us hope for a more life-affirming paradigm as we move into the future.

---

[71] Dean, Ward, MD, "Rebuttal to JAMA Internal Medicine Report *Vitamin D ineffective for Hypertension*," *Life Extension Magazine*, January 2016

Please understand, I am advocating a heart-centered revolution, not a violent one. I am advocating that each of us as an individual becomes willing to examine where we are with an open mind. I am advocating that we learn what it means to study our belief systems from a heart-centered approach and collectively agree to support humane practices in the world and actively refute inhumane ones that involve other humans, animals, and the earth. Money talks and we can make a powerful impact that way.

We are caught collectively in a tyranny of belief systems that have created a deadly trap for ourselves. Those in control believe they have to dominate, lie, invade, conquer, and manipulate to get the results they want, and those who are being controlled believe they have to submit.

We would do ourselves a big favor by rethinking the belief that new ideas and innovations need to fall within the current basic collective framework of beliefs, because by doing so, we suppress new information. If we keep our ideas and discoveries within the confines of a specific continuum of beliefs perpetuated through time, we make it difficult if not impossible for new ideas to be considered. We have legitimized the belief systems inherited from the past that have brought about the mindsets that are creating the crises that plague us today. Unless we are ready to take an objective look at where we are going, we will stay stuck.

I have often puzzled over the question of what makes those beliefs so compelling. Why have we bought into them so completely and allowed ourselves to be so manipulated and controlled? What happened in our murky past to make us feel so powerless that we simply genuflected and submitted?

Some have rebelled and lost their lives in their attempt to overcome a belief structure that robs humanity of its sovereignty, illustrating how deeply power and control are embedded in this matrix of beliefs. Fundamental Christianity isn't the only rigid belief system that has embraced those restrictions; most fundamental religions on this earth are very restrictive and carry some version of many, if not all, of the beliefs of the core belief matrix.

Carl Jung contributed significantly to our understanding of how the matrix of beliefs is spread through what he termed the Collective Unconscious, [72] the undercurrent of consciousness from which we all are fed. Humanity shares the same symbols and archetypes regardless of where we live or what our culture is. A suppressive and limiting undercurrent of beliefs feeds our species through this same Collective Unconscious. This common sharing field is important to keep in mind as we move into the future, and I will talk more at length about this later in the book.

I have to ask the question, what is so GREAT about the status quo that it couldn't benefit from some improvements? The answer that pops into my head is that the collective ruling

---

[72] In our new paradigm language, the Collective Unconscious is the **Genetic Mind**, Glossary - Appendix A.

class is afraid of losing their power and will do whatever they must to maintain what they have, never mind the suffering, devastation, and destruction they cause in doing so.

We are at a crossroads. The Scientific/Industrial Revolution began as humans moved away from the absolutism of controlling religion, but the "Literalist" way of perceiving life still remained dominant. All that was accomplished was to transfer the literal-minded core beliefs and dominating modus operandi of religion to the study and development of technology and science.

Our arsenals are now loaded with weapons of mass destruction, as well as with lifesaving and life-evolving information and technology. Which path will we take now? Will we continue down the road of corruption and destruction where we allow greed and the hunger for power to make our decisions; or will we take the path of discovering our vast potential and embracing it in a new kind of evolution that includes a discerning, more comprehensive understanding of our origins and what we call "spirit/divinity/god"? That is the decision each of us must make.

7

SOME THOUGHTS ABOUT OUR HEALTHCARE

OUR SCIENTIFIC AND MEDICAL RESEARCH communities are being challenged daily by the expectations and rules of their establishments. In our laboratories of science and medicine, our most brilliant research scientists and doctors have been forced to sublimate their subjective hunches and exciting discoveries because they don't match existing criteria, or the new discovery will cause issues with an already established money maker.

Don't be fooled—the breakthroughs that get the most attention and are utilized are generally the ones that generate the most money, especially for the pharmaceutical companies, or that don't go against the status quo of those products already making money. A very obvious example is cancer research into natural solutions (low return on money) vs. chemotherapy and radiation—big money makers for all involved in cancer treatment. To those interested in making money in these endeavors, it is all about attacking the disease, not necessarily helping the patient gain back their health or overcome the disease process. The big money makers in many disease arenas seem to be more palliative, rather than curative.

It is true that Big Pharma has discovered some major medications that are extremely helpful. Have you ever noticed though that the most promoted drugs are the ones you have to take for life once the treatment has started? Big Pharma is very resistant to and spends millions of dollars to lobby against natural treatments and supplements and information that the public can access on their own because it cuts down on their profits.

New ideas are generally met with resistance, and that is OK to a point as they need to be tested out, but even common-sense solutions are sometimes ridiculed. Take for instance when medicine in this country was in its infancy; simple hand washing was scorned as unnecessary. It took the medical community of those early days a long time to accept this simple precaution as one of the most important steps in preventing the spread of disease and infection.

All that being said, the science of medicine has learned a great deal of valuable information about our bodies and how diseases affect us. We have learned through vigilant public health practices how to keep many infectious and contagious diseases from spreading. The fields of surgery and emergency medicine have accomplished amazing feats that border on the miraculous. We are at a time in world history when we theoretically have some of the most advanced technology and knowledge about how to heal the human body ever known, and yet we struggle with devastating health and ecological crises that threaten our very existence on this planet.

Our soils are stripped of precious nutrients by our farming practices; our air and water are polluted by incompatible manufacturing practices as well as inhumane farming methods that warehouse animals in huge stinking feedlots that pollute the air, water, and soil for hundreds of miles around them. Everywhere we look, humans are creating crises by the way we live, and the pursuit of money by big business contributes significantly to the problems we face.

Statistics report that iatrogenic illness and death alone have reached epidemic proportions and indicate that medical care is the third leading cause of death in the United States, after deaths from heart disease and cancer. At a time in history when medicine has unprecedented comprehensive knowledge of the human body and how it functions and how disease processes function; one has to ask how medical care could have such a negative statistic. Our knee-jerk response is to blame the medical community, but other dynamics come into play that have as much if not more impact. Along with how much of a money maker a treatment is and the influence of Big Pharma, we don't have to dig too deep to come up with another reason right off the top, and that is insurance companies. They are getting more and more restrictive on the kinds of treatments they will cover, and there are many stories about people having devastating outcomes due to not being able to access the medical care they need *that their doctor wants to provide for them* because insurance companies won't authorize the medicine or procedure. It is galling to know that insurance companies are dictating the decisions about what medical interventions people can receive based on costs to the insurance company instead of the doctor who studies for many years to learn how to diagnose and treat patients. That alone should be a critical argument for universal healthcare. Then add to that argument the obscene amount of money the CEOs of health insurance companies in this country make. They are among the highest paid CEOs of any corporations. If CEOs are paid according to percentage of profit for the company, and the policy of the company is to save money—period—what does that tell you about where an unfair share of our insurance premium money goes? It certainly doesn't seem to be about helping us when we need it. It would appear our insurance premiums are going to support the wealthy lifestyles of CEOs.

In an article titled "Skyrocketing Salaries for Health Insurance CEOs" dated June 9, 2014, Wendell Potter writes:

According to *Health Plan Week*, a trade publication, the CEOs of the 11 largest for-profit companies were rewarded with compensation packages last year totaling more than $125 million.

Over the past several weeks, several of them have told shareholders and Wall Street financial analysts that their companies likely will have higher profits at the end of this year than they expected, despite having to pay more medical claims as a result of the new Obamacare customers they picked up.

Those announcements have been music to the ears of shareholders, who are considerably wealthier today than they were this time last year.

Of those 11 companies (Aetna, Centene, Cigna, Health Net, Humana, Molina, Triple-S Management Corp., UnitedHealth Group, Universal American, WellCare, and WellPoint) nine saw their stocks close near 52-week highs this past Friday.

The biggest gainer has been Humana, one of the largest operators of Medicare Advantage plans, whose share price has increased more than 53 percent over the past year.

The increases have been equally impressive at most of the other big companies. Aetna's share price is up 31 percent, Cigna's 32 percent. United's is up 28 percent. And WellPoint's is up 39 percent.

But it is the CEO compensation that has been the most eye-popping, especially at two of the publicly traded companies that specialize in managing Medicaid enrollees in several states: Centene and Molina.

Centene's CEO Michael Neidorff saw his compensation increase 71 percent last year, from $8.5 million to $14.5 million. Even more impressive was the 140 percent raise Molina's J. Mario Molina got. His compensation jumped from $4.95 million in 2012 to $11.9 million in 2013. [73]

Who needs a $14 million-or $11.9 million-dollars salary a year? Think of how many people could be helped with that money. The first figures of $8.5 million and $4.95 million are obscene enough and should be more than enough money for one person. Why isn't the rest of that money put back into circulation where it can help people who are sick and could benefit from the help of their insurance companies? What percentage of our premiums goes to support CEOs of insurance companies???

---

[73] Potter, Wendell, "Skyrocketing Salaries for Health Insurance CEOs. Commentary: if they're making millions, should the rest of us have to pay higher premiums?" The Center for Public Integrity, June 9, 2014. http://www.publicintegrity.org/2014/06/09/14912/skyrocketing-salaries-health-insurance-ceos

One of my providers left town, and I needed to find a local doctor who could provide primary care. I asked the office personnel for suggestions and was told to be sure and find my new provider before I went on Medicare because many doctors won't take new patients on Medicare. If you are already their patient, then of course they will treat you, but since Medicare payments are so low, they don't like to take on new Medicare patients.

We hear so much about how Medicare and Medicaid are draining the system and needing to be cut back and how Obamacare is too expensive. According to the quote above, it appears to be all propaganda. It is apparent that we need to rethink what is really draining the system!

More and more doctors are leaving the insurance company game and the medical associations in their communities and going out on their own to practice the kind of medicine they feel is best for their patients. That is fine for people who can afford to pay their doctors out of pocket or foot the bill for large out-of-network deductibles. For those on very tight budgets who pay high premiums for insurance, however, their only recourse is to submit to the dictates of insurance company decisions, sometimes with devastating outcomes, or go untreated with often equally devastating consequences.

When health care is controlled by insurance companies whose only goal is to save expenditures so that their shareholders and their CEOs can make huge profits, it renders the system ineffective and abusive. Some areas where insurance companies are effective include car, life, and property insurance. However, we need them to get out of the medical field where they cause more harm than good.

This writer would suggest that it might be in our best interest as a nation to stop fighting over national health coverage. Many countries successfully provide full health benefits to their citizens, and it is an idea that could be adapted to an American version. Obamacare is a start. Medicare and Medicaid are starts. They are not the be-all-end-all system— they are a start.

We could look to European countries that have succeeded in providing national health care as examples. So many Americans are caught up in semantics—they hear the phrase "socialized medicine" and dig their heels in the sand and refuse to even hear what it is all about. We might benefit from an open-minded study of existing systems for ideas of what works and what doesn't and try cooperation and collaboration to bring about the changes needed to improve our health care system for administrators, practitioners, and patients alike.

PART THREE

SEARCHING FOR TRUTH
THROUGH THE MIRROR
OF PERCEPTION

PRISM OF TIME AND SPACE

Essence radiates through the Prism of space-time
Reflecting the fragments of form and experience
A time traveler playing in the illusion mirrored
A wanderer in the world of archetype, symbol, metaphor
Reflecting the experiences of consciousness exploring
Enforced amnesia—or so it seems

The prism holds many mirrors
Images filtered through a brain
Fashioned to perceive polarity and separation and form
Making it easy to become lost
In the maze of reflections
As we dance through space time

Beating in the center of this sacred mandala
The Energetic Heart emanates love-centered virtues
through the prism
Heralding a call to Oneness
Radiating spiritual equality into all the reflections
Activating the Divine frequencies of love
Calling us back to wholeness and home

Lark Aleta Batey 2016

INTRODUCTION

SOME THOUGHTS ON MIRRORS
AND PERCEPTION

As you live deeper in the heart, the mirror gets clearer and clearer.
Rumi

PERCEPTION IS THE NAVIGATOR OF our everyday life. It determines how we see the world in general and influences our responses to our experiences and to people who are a part of our experiences.

Each chapter in Part Three will attempt to explore an avenue of perception mirrored to us in the hologram. Do we respond with shame? Do we search for truth? What kind of information-seeking is on our radar? Are we influenced by archetypes, and if so, can we identify that influence and is that even important? Do we only give credence to what our senses can tell us? What factors actually contribute to our ability to create our own reality? How do we deal with death?

The above questions can be better understood by our ability to recognize what we mirror to the world and what it mirrors back to us.

The mirror is a rich symbol to explore spiritually, psychologically, and metaphorically. Physically a mirror reflects light and the world within its boundaries, but the concept of "mirror" goes much deeper than that.

Our culture mirrors or reflects back to us where we stand in relationship to our collective beliefs and traditions. Scientists have even discovered *Mirror Neurons*. They are described as a small circuit of cells in the premotor cortex and inferior parietal cortex of the brain. They are activated both when we perform a certain action and when we observe someone else performing the same action. Neuroscientist Marco Iacoboni was asked in an interview [74] how a mirror neuron works. He explained that mirror neurons are brain cells that seem to specialize in coding the actions of others and also one's own actions. He said that they are essential cells for social interaction. They seem to provide some sort of inner imitation of the actions of other people which in turn leads us to simulate the intentions and emotions

---

[74] "The Mirror Neuron Revolution: Explaining what makes humans social," interview between Scientific American writer Jonah Lehrer and Marco Iacoboni https://www.scientificamerican.com/article/the-mirror-neuron-revolut/

associated with those actions. Iacoboni explained that gestures, facial expressions, and body postures are social signals. Mirror neurons help us to code the actions of others and ourselves.

Iacoboni used autism as an example of how a deficit in mirror neurons would affect a person's ability to communicate. With a deficit in mirror neurons, an autistic person cannot read the social ques of others. Iacoboni said that the motor deficits in autism can be explained because mirror neurons are a special type of premotor neurons, brain cells essential for planning and selecting actions. If a person is deficient in mirror neurons, he/she isn't able to understand the other person's actions or mimic them. It is also believed that mirror neurons play a part in language development. Thus, a deficit in mirror neurons can account for the three major symptoms of autism—social, motor, and language problems. Iacoboni shared the following caveat about mirror neurons: they are critical for social interaction but can't explain non-social cognition. He added that every brain cell and every neural system is interconnected and does not operate in a vacuum.

Iacoboni believes that there is convincing behavioral evidence linking media violence with imitative violence and encourages more open discussions on this subject.

Depending on the reflections we perceive, our personal mirror can be bright and illuminated or twisted and dark. Our internal mirror begins to develop with the relationship between us as infants and our mother or caretaker. When mother responds to our baby actions in either a positive or negative way, she is mirroring our behavior back to us. At first, we see mother as part of ourselves, so we internalize her responses or mirroring on the unconscious level, integrating it into our developing psyche. As we develop as children and realize we are another to our mother, then the mirror becomes a part of the expectations we take with us into the world, and we measure the rest of the world through the internal images reflected in our inner mirror. That is one of the reasons as young adults we often marry someone remarkably similar to our parents. Our internal mirror searches out the matching reflection of familiarity.

Literally a mirror reflects a reverse image back to us of what we look like when we look into it. But it can also become a distorted reflection if what we see isn't what we want to see. We have subconscious expectations programmed into our developing psyches by our environment about what we *should* look like, and when the mirror does not appear to reflect that image back to us, we might explore the possibility that we have a psychological or self-image problem.

Women especially struggle with image issues. Has a certain body shape or type been programmed into her psyche by her environment, the media, and magazines as the only acceptable look and does her body measure up? What part of her body does she see in the mirror? Most women reading this know that they will focus on what they think is the most flawed part of their body first, and it may be the only part they will see in the mirror. That flawed part can be blown out of proportion to the rest of what a woman sees when she looks into the mirror distorting her self-image and self-acceptance.

Relationships are complicated, so the following examples are based on some extremely basic considerations of how internal dynamics develop as we grow up and begin looking for life partners. I do not understand enough about how mirroring works in homosexual relationships and/or attractions to address it here. I would assume some of the same general dynamics apply.

Of course, there will always be exceptions to the following, but generally in heterosexual relationships females, especially when young and naïve, will be looking for that subconscious image formed through childhood interactions with the important males in her life mirrored to her by fathers, grandfathers, brothers, uncles, male clergy, teachers, etc. That composite male becomes the *Animus* or inner masculine ("Animus" in Jungian Psychology, see Appendix A - Glossary) in her psyche. How the males in her childhood treated her and how she feels towards them will contribute to the patterns of behavior and attitudes she will be subconsciously seeking in any male who will become important to her. The same goes for a male. A man in relationship with a woman will tend to gravitate towards a female who holds the image of his *anima* or inner feminine, usually formed by significant females in his life growing up.

Part of the task of becoming a conscious adult is to become aware of the inner drives and promptings that form our internal mirrors. This is especially important for those individuals who have had a difficult or painful childhood at the hands of adults of the opposite sex. A person who is abusive or controlling will feel familiar, maybe even comfortable. Our subconscious tendencies will be to gravitate towards someone with those same innate characteristics. Unfortunately, many of us are not that much in tune with our inner worlds in our early adulthood and because of our lack of awareness, this dynamic can have a powerful effect on who we are attracted to as a partner.

The inner composite image is held up as a pattern in behavioral expectations men and women hold about their partner's behaviors in everyday situations as well as expectations about oneself. Do we get defensive or hostile in interactions with our partners (and others as well) because we feel that we do not measure up to some image or expected response we hold within ourselves that we thought we had hidden well or do not want to face within ourselves? Do we start a battle because our partner does not fit an expectation of how a mate should act based on the image we hold in our internal mirrors? Or is this person perceived as acting like a negative person from our childhood? Are we overly sensitive to what we *perceive* as negative intentions in someone close to us that mirrors or reflects an action from that inner *Animus* or *Anima* composite that has in our formative years been hurtful? Mirrors in relationship dynamics are complicated and fascinating to ponder if one has the inclination to do so.

Our programming can also include some very deep archetypal dynamics as well. For instance—the *Animus* in the female psyche can play a destructive role that is important to be aware of. Let's explore the story of *Snow White* in this context.

The following ideas are based on Nancy van den Berg-Cook's lecture "The Magic Mirror of Snow White."[75] She offers some insightful and powerful perspectives into the stepmother Queen's obsession with the Magic Mirror. She describes the Queen in the story as someone with a narcissistic personality disorder. She explains that this disorder is developed when a child does not receive meaningful mirroring from their caretakers as their psyches are developing, and they develop a very weak sense of self. This causes the narcissist to foster a deep sense of unworthiness that produces an inner rage to any change within their environment that destabilizes that weak sense of self.

In the Queen's case the negative mirroring would have come from the males in her life who set her up to be perpetually seeking approval from the masculine gender through her beauty. Dr. van den Berg points out that in most of the illustrations of this story the Queen's Magic Mirror is depicted as having a cruel and fiery masculine spirit. Jungian psychology would say that this Magic Mirror represents her *Animus* or inner male. Culturally for as long as we have recorded history, the female's beauty is an important if not the most important component of her existence. The Queen relies on this critical masculine authority to tell her she is the fairest in the land. As long as the Mirror answers that she is the fairest, all is well. But when it tells her that Snow White is now the fairest, she goes into a debilitating, murderous rage because her beauty is all that has ever been mirrored to her as important from her inner male.

Women especially in patriarchal cultures are forced to rely on their physical beauty as their primary sense of self. Even though we are seeing some improvement in this area, young girls are still being bombarded with the pressure to conform to very narrow standards of beauty and being physically attractive remains a very deeply embedded program in the female gender; this includes acceptable body types and weight. For a girl who does not fit the current archetypal mold of feminine beauty, life is often a very painful existence if she is not reared with a sense of self that can override societal expectations of how she *should* look. It takes astute and vigilant parenting of a daughter to help her move beyond this powerful societal programming.

---

[75] van den Berg-Cook, Nancy, PhD, "The Magic Mirror in Snow White," www.cgjung-vereniging.nl/home/files/nancy_vd_berg.pdf

The story of the stepmother in *Snow White* mirrors a very real and debilitating problem for women. This projection of expectations onto the female gender can contribute to the hidden resentment aging mothers have towards their beautiful young daughters as they see their own physical beauty fade. Our culture feeds into it. How many older men do we see leaving their aging wives for younger women, further intensifying this deeply hurtful psychological issue? It says to the wife that nothing counts but her external beauty when her husband does not recognize the gem within and support and respond to it. This perpetuates misogyny within our culture.

The flip side of that coin obviously is that a woman who has never worked at anything but keeping her external beauty alive or has never been encouraged to cultivate her own interests will be quite boring and superficial as she ages. A richly diverse and progressive society depends on encouraging females to develop themselves fully.

The Magic Mirror in this fairy tale is depicted as a threshold between the conscious and the unconscious and is a metaphor for the inner mirror we all carry and consult daily. An important part of our inner work to better understand how we are affected in our relationships is to become aware of our subconscious mirror and how we are programmed and driven by it. That awareness can help us learn to see ourselves and our partners for the unique humans we are. If we can become aware of the debilitating inner images we constantly see projected onto the mirrors of our existence and realize they are programmed responses, we have more of a chance of being able to overcome them.

We would make huge strides in our cultural revolution by mirroring to our children and grandchildren the understanding that we are all connected by reflecting behaviors of acceptance towards those around us regardless of physical appearance, race, religion, ethnicity, gender orientation, or other differences. By changing this one thing in our role-modeling behaviors, we would make significant progress in transforming our external world into a more positive and accepting one.

Here is where our hearts can become significant sources of inner promptings, as they play an important role in not only our mirror of perception but in what we reflect back to the world. Have our hearts become numb and closed down or are they becoming open to projecting such qualities as compassion and understanding and appreciation? What is our world mirroring to us?

Kabir Helminski put it beautifully in the following:

> The heart is an intelligence beyond the intellect, a knowing that operates at a subconscious level, and the only human faculty expansive enough to embrace the infinite qualities of the universe... The human heart is a kind

of mirror where divine qualities and meanings may appear. Those qualities are as much within the heart as within the thing that awakens those qualities within the heart. The situation is like two mirrors facing each other, the heart and the world, while the original reflection comes from a third source, a divine source. But choice appears to reside in one of these mirrors, the human heart.

He further explains:

Every quality that the human being recognizes in the world of outer appearances is derived first of all from the inner knowing of its own heart, which contains a complete sampling of the universe of qualities. The divine qualities are primary; the heart is the interior mirror, and the world is the outer mirror that reflects the heart's projections of these divine qualities. The significant conclusion we can draw from this is that while the mirror of the world can reveal to us what the heart itself contains, the qualities themselves are contained entirely within the heart. All of outer existence is merely a pretext for revealing to us what the heart itself encompasses.[76]

I find these to be such wise thoughts to ponder as I contemplate what qualities I mirror in my daily life.

The chapters in this section will explore some of the many mirrors that have been embedded into our psychological and spiritual make-up.

---

[76] Helminski, Kabir, *The Knowing Heart, A Sufi Path of Transformation*, Shambhala Publications, Inc., 4720 Walnut Street, Boulder, Colorado 80301, 1999, www.shambala.com

8

LOVE, FEAR, SHAME AND OVERLAYS

OVERLAYS

THIS CHAPTER DELVES INTO SOME of the variables and dimensions that come into play in the formation of psychological and emotional overlays in the creation of our cultural belief systems. We will be exploring this concept on three levels: metaphysical, emotional, and psychological.

It is very probable that the first layer of consciousness we bring into the material world are characteristics that come with us from the very Essence of our Sovereign Integral, and those characteristics may be a part of our original DNA. We could say this is the superconscious level. The next layer is the unconscious programming encoded in the DNA given to us by the Anunnaki and their cohorts when they created the Human Instrument.[77] This layer is also very deeply imbedded into our psyches in the form of functional implants.[78]

Under the surface of our conscious awareness, a current of subconscious ancestral traits passed onto us by our parents adds to our overall consciousness structure. Once we are born, environmental factors come into play to individualize and localize our personalities and belief systems. I like to think of each layer as an overlay. (We could also say that all the above form the internal mirror each of us holds up to the world as discussed in the Introduction to Part Three.)

I had a vision as I was pondering the concept of overlays and how we are programmed once we are born. The idea of overlays helped me to understand how our programming might work. I saw each overlay as an almost gauze-like layer of energy. The initial layers are the programming from the functional implants. Subsequent layers consist of the energetic

---

[77] See **Human Instrument,** Appendix A – Glossary
[78] Mahu, James, "Fifth Interview of Dr. Neruda," *WingMakers*, https://www.wingmakers.com/content/neruda- interviews/ Functional implants are explained.

memories of each experience or emotion as they are incorporated into the emotional bodies of infants and children, merging with their existing consciousness patterns, and creating unique belief structures. Young children lack intellectual filters or boundaries, so any experience that affects them emotionally becomes deeply embedded into their psyches, making childhood experiences very powerful in the formation of the individual.

As the child grows, these accumulated overlays develop a thick barrier of energetic padding between the individual and the world. This causes each individual to have a distinctive world view and fits right into the idea of living in a "veiled" existence. Astrological influences at the moment of birth may also add an energetic overlay onto individuals. Science is just discovering how much the fetus absorbs while in-utero. It is now believed that the fetus begins to pick up the language patterns of its mother during gestation, thus preparing the baby for language.[79]

Overlays of mass consciousness belief systems become a part of children's programming as they attend church, school, and social gatherings. All this adds to the "veiled" existence idea. It seems reasonable to consider that the "veils" of the overlays could be all that keep us from unknown worlds that may be closer than we realize.

Overlays play a fundamental role in the development of automatic impulses that drive our everyday desires and reactions. Our belief systems are imprinted onto our consciousness, causing each of us to have a unique perception of life and the world we live in.

Most if not all religions teach some kind of immortality or eternal life after death, and living on after we die is generally accepted. A logical question we might ask is: "Where did we come from if we didn't exist somewhere in some form before our earthly incarnation?" I personally find it easy to believe that I existed prior to this incarnation and will continue to exist after I have worn this body out and leave it. I remember as a child pondering the idea of a pre-existence, trying to wrap that idea around the finiteness of my small human self. It was difficult for me to imagine not ever existing. The idea of pre-existence and continuous lifetimes is an interesting subject to ponder in one's quiet moments.

Have we lived on other planets and maybe in forms other than the human form as we know it or in a formless state? We can only speculate at this stage of the game, but if we think of all the ideas humans have had about existence and pre-existence, we have to assume that

---

[79] "Study Shows Language Development Starts in the Womb," *The University of Kansas*, 7.18.2017, https://news.ku.edu/2017/07/13/study-shows-language-development-starts-womb
This study was funded by A National Institutes of Health Clinical and Translational Science Award grant. Kathleen Gustafson, Research Associate Professor in Department of Neurology; Utako MInai, Associate Professor of Linguistics and team leader of study.
This is one of many articles that can be found on this subject.

they came from somewhere. For the sake of this discussion, let's accept the premise that we are infinite beings and have lived before and speculate about what impact those lives might have had on us.

Many of us may go from one life to another without processing previous lifetimes, therefore bringing along baggage to each new incarnation. It is taught in some ideologies supporting reincarnation that when we are born into a new body, we bring old patterns or tendencies with us that have not been resolved and released. We may also be presented with opportunities to work on certain issues of our own choosing. It is highly probable that we could be living parallel lives, our Sovereign Integral Consciousness having all the experiences at once. We think linearly in this world because we are programmed that way, but other lifetimes could happen in all sorts of ways, so let's stay flexible and play with some of these ideas.

Below I have imported a list of examples from my previous book[80] of variations of beliefs supporting some kind of pre-existence as a review before I expand on this subject:

- We may bring one behavior pattern or emotion we want to focus on to a particular lifetime and stay with that issue until it is thoroughly explored and resolved. For example, we may want to investigate the spectrum of love in relationship. This could mean living dramas that illustrate to us what love is not; being involved in a variety of love relationships; or we might find ourselves grappling with the aftermath of experiences that have driven us to feelings of hatred or indifference in contrast to love. We might also experience an intensely profound love.
- We may have the opportunity to live a life that is exactly the opposite of the previous life just completed to explore another completely different view, such as incarnating to live as a pauper after being extremely wealthy or vice-versa.
- Some entities may choose to explore a difficult issue by living a life where they seem to be a victim of harsh circumstances. By doing this, they may hold an anchor for those who interact with them, facilitating questions, actions, and reactions from others. This type of situation can help others come to terms with their personal biases and bigotries and teach compassion. The story of *The Elephant Man—John Merick* could be perceived as an illustration of that concept.
- We may become attached to certain entities and incarnate with them over and over, playing different roles each lifetime. This enables us to explore a variety of

---

[80] Batey, Lark Aleta, *Breaking Free from the Tyranny of Beliefs: A Revolution in Consciousness*, Balboa Press, 2012. I borrowed the concept of overlays from here and have expanded those ideas in this book.

relationship roles with this group or single entity. This includes choosing our parents, culture, ethnicity, and the home environment we are born into.

- We may believe we have done something terrible and need to be punished, so we come into a life that seems to punish us; or conversely, we come into an easy life and may believe we are being rewarded for accomplishments of a previous life.

- We are multi-dimensional entities living parallel lives all at once in different frequencies and times. A variety of themes can run through all the lives at once, and as changes happen in one life, they may have an effect on all concurrent and/or parallel lives in some way.

- We exist in probable lives within one life, where we have probable selves living out variations on a current lifetime in the same time frame. It is helpful to contemplate this possibility when we are considering transcending a certain path we are headed down during this lifetime. If many probabilities exist, then we can shift our conscious awareness toward different choices to put us onto more suitable trajectories. A decision in this lifetime could also shift us onto a different trajectory than the initial one.

- After death, we go to a place where we become aware of a variety of environments we can be born into, and we are able to choose our new location.

- If we become too attached to the material orientation of the earth plane and don't evolve much during a given lifetime, after death we don't go far away. That earthly attachment causes us to eagerly take the first body that becomes available, and we may find ourselves incarnating into less than desirable places and circumstances.

- We decide on the focus we want to live in a given life and plan out a blueprint of possibilities. From this blueprint, we create a contract for the next lifetime. Variables are "written" into the blueprint so that we have some choice about which parts of the contract we will actually fulfill. In this model, it is thought that exit points are written into the blueprint. If a person at the juncture of an "exit point" chooses to stay, they may be confronted with a life- threatening illness or accident that they recover from, rather than die. This can potentially drastically change the course of the life lived so far and activate a latent part of their blueprint.

- Some who reach the stage we currently understand to be enlightenment come back to earth to help others, even when it is believed they could have stayed in the non-physical realms. The Buddhist term for this type of entity is Bodhisattva.

- I add a new belief and that is this: There will be one lifetime when we come to this planet for the specific purpose of waking up to the Sovereign Integral State of Consciousness and through a course of event strings, we will be led to the information that will help us to accomplish this. Once that happens, we no longer reincarnate, as we are liberated from the Hologram of Deception. We will then live in the world in the Sovereign Integral State of Consciousness. We don't know what that looks like yet, but it is something to anticipate and work towards.

My hunch is that as long as we are asleep within the hologram, we will reincarnate, and our particular beliefs will determine which of the above scenarios we utilize to incarnate into each new life.

Through the course of our long sojourn on this planet in various centuries and bodies, probably both genders, and varieties of life situations, we gain soul experience. We are born amazingly unique in temperament, personality, likes and dislikes, and abilities. Obviously, some of those characteristics can be attributed to genes, the in-utero environment, and the milieu we grow up in. It is quite likely, however, that other characteristics that make us unique accompany us into a lifetime and become the backdrop that will play against or with many other factors.

James Mahu in the "The Fifth Interview of Dr. Neruda" (*WingMakers Materials*) adds some important clarifications to this discussion about how our conscious mind functions and interplays with the deeper parts of ourselves in his explanation of the triad of consciousness:

Human consciousness is the key to suppressing an infinite being. Human consciousness or the triad of consciousness is composed of three interactive layers.

The first layer is universal mind or unconscious, and this forms the link between the individual and the entire species. This layer is what enables us to see what everyone sees, feel what everyone else feels, know what everyone else knows. It is the perfect way to unify a species in separation. In fact it is the way we feel unification, through the unconscious mind.

The next layer is the genetic mind, as the WingMakers refer to it or subconscious in the case of Sigmund Freud. This forms the link between the individual and their family tree or genetics. This is where the bloodline is expressed.

And then there is the conscious mind. This is the unique individual perception and expression—what most of us call our personality and character built on this layer.

The conscious mind is heavily influenced by the genetic mind, especially between birth and the age of seven or eight. By that time the influence is all-encompassing. Remember that the Anunnaki created the biological form—the body, the Sirians created the functional implants, and Marduk executed the programming of these functional implants so they would evolve along a programmed path, leading to the return of Anu. This was expressed in the hierarchal structure of humanity that speaks of gods and masters in religious and esoteric texts.

This was all part of the design, to create various religions and esoteric cults that would support a vast Hierarchy and order the human species into master-student relationships, and then create a multi-leveled afterlife that would reward those who believed and were obedient to their gods or masters.

You see the whole principle that was behind this endeavor could be summed up in on word: separation. Everything exists in separation within the earth plane and its afterlife planes as well. But according to the WingMakers, what is real is that we are all imbued with equality and oneness—not through the unconscious mind, which only links us in separation, but rather through the life essence that is us. And this life essence is sovereign and integral. It is I AM WE ARE. No one is above, no one is below. No one is better, no one is lesser." …

As the interview progresses, Dr. Neruda answers Sarah's question— "Everything we have been taught to believe in is a lie, a deception and how could that be possible?"

It's possible because the beings that have enslaved humanity designed a world to which we adjusted over eons of time. We evolved into it in such a manner that we became lost in our world. The veils that have been placed over us are opaque. So much so that people operate in human uniforms unaware that everything around them is illusory. It is a programmed reality that is not real. The WingMakers say that everything is sound holographically organized to look real.

There is so much to ponder in the above quote beyond the subject of this chapter, but for the purposes of this discussion, I see Dr. Neruda's statement as compatible with the many ideas about incarnating over and over. This is the planet of choice. Our many belief systems keep us distracted and give us a way to order our societies. In this way the deception is perpetuated without question as we recycle into new human instruments after leaving the old ones at death.

OVERLAYS AND THE DEVELOPMENT OF OUR UNIQUE PERSPECTIVE

Each infant born into this world is a fragment of an Infinite Being with distinct characteristics and a unique energy signature. Over this initial fragment the overlays begin to build the unique veil/mirror this child will perceive the world through and the filter through which all ensuing events are perceived and interpreted.

Anyone who has been around infants recognizes that right from the outset they exhibit huge differences in temperament, response, and ability to learn. This is apparent even in children growing up in the same family. Obviously, genes, nutrition, uterine, and familial environments contribute to the initial conditions. Consider these conditions married to the many belief structures we are born into, and we begin to understand how each of us becomes a unique individual.

Infants are born into families with distinct cultures and begin to have unique emotional, cultural, language, and somatic experiences. Each of these factors contributes to the emotional body memory of the child on a minute-to-minute basis by forming overlay on top of overlay in response to life experiences. Infants and children are mostly emotional bodies as they do not have the filters that give them the ability to censor or intellectually process incoming stimulation. Every event in their lives, especially in the pre-verbal stages, is incorporated into their body-mind memory as an emotional experience and lays a strong foundation from which inner response to further stimulation occurs.

Now, this collection of overlays becomes the unconscious impulses from which we act and react in our daily lives. Every action we take, every decision we make, and the unique way we see the world—all are factors that include those initial overlays which create our singular experience of the world of density and illusion.

It may be difficult as an abstract idea to understand the concept of the world as an illusion, but it makes sense in a basic way that the world each of us lives in is an illusion because we experience it through our unique perceptions or overlays.

To be released from this illusion would mean to peel off the overlays, one layer at a time, allowing the Sovereign Being living deep inside as a latent potential to come forth. The analogy of the healing process being like an onion, peeling away the layers of limitations, beliefs, neuroses, and behavior patterns, etc., is an old but excellent one.

Basically, that is what the journey of spiritual awakening has always been about—the attempt to reach some stage of advanced knowledge. Most of us who have been on any kind of spiritual journey have participated in the clearing work of self-examination that has included learning to peel off layers of shame, self-doubt, constricting emotions, and limiting beliefs.

The "clearing work" spoken about in spiritual growth circles could be thought of as the conscious work to release the overlays from our energy fields, bringing us closer and closer to the hope that we are "lifting the veil" of illusion. When we begin to understand that we are not our jobs, or our gender, or the roles we play in relationships—then we can begin to realize that we are so much more than our overlays; this thick veil of perception is not who we are. It is the lens through which we experience life uniquely, but it hides our true selves. But who or what is our true nature? That is the question that has always plagued and eluded us.

Personally, I have come to believe that many of the answers are on the other side of gaining proficiency in working with the Six Heart Virtues and developing our Behavioral Intelligence.

James Mahu defines the Six Heart Virtues and Behavioral Intelligence by explaining that

> The six heart virtues are the "rooms" in the home of love. They are not word-concepts; they are behaviors. The acquisition of Behavioral Intelligence is the task each of us is performing day-to-day whether we realize it or not. It is what life brings. We are all learning to forgive, to be humble, to express compassion, to be empathic and understand the other's point of view, and so on. These are the qualities of love, and if we can pay attention to the branches of love, then love is expressed more completely in our lives.
>
> This is the equivalent of consciousness, because consciousness is love. Thus if you want to bring more of your Self—your consciousness—to this reality we call human life, then the Six Heart Virtues and their expression, is a good way to do it. [81]

As we embrace a heart-centered approach to transformation, we are moving into exciting territory from the human standpoint.

It takes courage to allow what we identify with as our ego selves to be released or even questioned. If we let go of all of that, what will be left? Will we be bare, raw, and unprotected? Will there be emptiness or nothing? Will this Sovereign Integral, once revealed, be able to live in this world? Those are all fears that have the potential to keep us locked into our familiar worlds, afraid to change. As clothes give us a feeling of protection by allowing the world to see only what we want it to see of us, so the veils hide and protect our True Selves. If we strip away the veils and allow our Selves to be seen by the world, can we survive?

---

[81] A New Journey in Consciousness: An interview with WingMakers creator and author James Mahu by Darlene Berges of Planetwork Press," http://planetworkpress.com/pwpcart/index.php?main_page=page&id=9

History tells us that the world can be quite brutal to those who have attempted to show their real Selves, and yet for the game to change, we must collectively honor and support this transformation for those who choose to make it and be open to what each one finds. Every individual who accomplishes a heart-centered transformation blazes the trail for more to engage in the same process.

Part of the important preparation for a heart-centered paradigm is exploring beliefs and attitudes that formed the old overlays and created the layers of densities that keep us stuck. This is the work that will prepare us psychologically and spiritually to be open to a heart-centered approach to events and relationships in our everyday lives.

Most of us on a spiritual path have encountered the term "emptiness," and trying to figure out what that entails can be a bit daunting. What is it, and how does it fit in with attaining advanced states of consciousness? James Mahu offers a definition of emptiness as *"empty of illusion—the deceptions of the Human Mind System."* [82] What is the Human Mind System? James defines it as the secret framework for the suppression of the Sovereign Integral. It has three components—the unconscious or genetic mind, the subconscious mind, and the conscious mind. James explains: *"The Human Mind System is the most opaque and distorted veil that has stood between humanity and its true self, perverting its self-expression within the domains we call reality."* [83]

Another important part of this paradigm is in achieving the awareness that we are in this together as a species. On this wisdom path, we will come to a level of understanding where we begin to realize that it isn't all about us as an individual; it is about all of us collectively. We are making progress when our focus begins to evolve from an individual self-serving life-view to an inclusive life-view of world-serving.

Our transformation work isn't a competition to see who advances the best or the fastest. It is about bringing the Six Heart Virtues into one's life and learning how to transmit them into the world and apply them to everyday situations. As we learn to do that, our own understanding of ourselves and our life on this earth begins to change and evolve. Working with the virtues and sending them out into the world is very powerful work. As we breathe each virtue into our hearts, we bring potent energies into our bodies that will gradually enhance our ability to be a conduit for those energies. We transmit those energies out into the world as we consciously focus on them as we exhale. If we practice this work diligently and consistently, we are in the process of developing Behavioral Intelligence.

---

[82] "James: The WingMakers Interview," written Q and A initially published in *Project Camelot* and later added to the *WingMakers* website. https://projectcamelot.org/james_wingmakers_sovereign_integral.pdf
[83] "A New Journey in Consciousness: An interview with WingMakers creator and author James Mahu by Darlene Berges of Planetwork Press," http://planetworkpress.com/pwpcart/index.php?main_page=page&id=9

We may be surprised to find that as we transform with the help of the Six Heart Virtues, we no longer aspire to the goals we thought we had when we began this journey. Since our hopes and dreams are initially ego driven and a product of the illusion we are in, there is no telling what is in store for us without the overlays to cloud our perceptions. As we begin to explore the heart-centered approach to transformation, we will be overcoming the great deception we all have been subjected to. This will make room for new solutions, ideas, and dreams to come into our conscious awareness allowing us to find win-win solutions for the earth and for ourselves, instead of win- lose ones.

For example: instead of continuing to pollute our environment, allowing only those in control to profit, we could be inspired to find solutions from a more advanced consciousness where the environment is preserved, businesses prosper, and pollution is controlled, allowing the earth and all its inhabitants to flourish. If that is a hope that we harbor and nourish, we may be able to attain that result. We have arrived at a time in our collective history when we are reminded that it is time for each of us to take responsibility for our lives and the world we live in. We are also learning that we have the power to manifest a fuller dimension of life on earth for everyone, not just an "elite" few.

Impulses from within are motivating many of us to begin the work of transforming into our Sovereign Integral while continuing to inhabit a physical body. We have to be courageous in our willingness to examine ourselves because what we uncover during this process could be quite difficult to deal with at times from an ego perspective. We begin to find our way out of our predicament when we realize we live in an illusion of deception, separation, and suppression.

Individually we accomplish our release by being willing to explore our overlays through the lens of our hearts without judgement. This includes forgiving ourselves for our "blindness" and our "mistakes," realizing that in the final analysis they were experiential gifts we gave to our Integral Self. As we clear and remain in the same body, if we continue to have memories of what it was like to be veiled, that can serve to keep us humble in our newly expanded state.

As we let go of each layer of our overlays, our world will shift, and that can be challenging. We have a knee-jerk resistance to change, but that is only because we have worked for so long to keep the game in place. It can be an exhilarating realization once we begin to understand that we can change the world we live in through a more heart-centered approach to life, and that we are so much more than we have been taught to believe we are.

We can help ourselves move into this new paradigm by learning to identify some of the overlays that have kept us locked in a suppressive reality. Below we will explore some examples of overlays and discuss their impact on keeping us in separation and suppression.

DYNAMICS OF SHAME IN THE FORMATION OF OVERLAYS

"When I feel guilt, I feel that I have made a mistake, and when I feel shame, I feel that I am the mistake." John Bradshaw

Shame is an insidious energy that can cause great stress and deep- seated damage within the human psyche. A shame-based belief system is responsible for political and religious fanatics, eating disorders, child abuse and neglect, and many sexual addictions and aberrant behavior. Shame drives to the core how one feels about oneself; it affects our ability for intimacy, our ability to feel compassion, and creates feelings of not being good enough no matter how hard we try. Shame causes these feelings to become beliefs.

The March 2002 issue of *Scientific American* features an article by Mary Katherine Armstrong titled *"Child Abuse, Shame, Rage and Violence."* She quotes Martin H. Teicher saying that:

> …recent brain imaging surveys and other neurobiological research show that child abuse and neglect can cause permanent damage to the neural structure and function of the still developing brain of the child. [84]

Teicher goes on to propose the idea that surviving harsh and/or violent conditions actually changes the way the brain develops. The individual becomes hyper-vigilant and reacts aggressively to challenge without undue hesitation. This is important to understand when we think about how we grew up, how we were parented, and also how are we parenting our own children.

History has given us information to help us understand that a shame- based belief system can do great damage over several generations.

One of the most graphic illustrations of the effects of a shame-based belief system comes to us from Germany. Armstrong in her article explains the mindset of the Germans prior to the rise of Hitler. The children of Germany were "…raised with a pedagogy which was thorough and exact in its instructions on how to raise an abused child right from babyhood."

It was called black pedagogy (*Schwarz pedagogic*). Armstrong explains that intense shaming was deliberately built into this system of child rearing. The parents were instructed from the day a baby was born to "master the crying baby by frightening it." The concept was that the parent would be master of the child and from then on "a glance, a word, a

---

[84] Armstrong, Mary Katherine, "Child Abuse, Shame, Rage and Violence," *The Primal Psychotherapy Page,* 2003. http://primal-page.com/childabu.htm

single threatening gesture will be sufficient to control the child." This form of parenting also discouraged any physical demonstrations of love such as stroking, kissing, or cuddling.

Armstrong goes on to explain that children were raised according to detailed rules designed to humiliate them and control them in order to produce adults who would always obey authority figures. This dependence on authority and the intense shaming of children produced the generation of Germans who obediently followed Hitler, and "found their emotional release in carrying out atrocities." This type of child rearing causes the adult products of such practices to develop within them a shame/rage/violence cycle, and they took that shame/rage/violence "out on the Jews and others who reminded them of themselves when they were helpless children." Armstrong explains that Hitler himself was beaten and shamed by his father "to the point that he was unable to feel the beatings." Hitler's cure for his own shame was a whole regime created to help him feel superior. "His many obsessions with superiority-inferiority, racial purity, pollution and contamination are typical ways of bypassing feelings of shame."

Psycho-historian Lloyd DeMause takes us into an even more detailed account of German childrearing practices in his speech on September 28, 2005, at Klagenfurt University in Austria titled "Childhood Origins of the Holocaust" to help us understand how a mind that believes in genocide can happen.

> Just as psychiatrists have found the motivations for murder involve extremely low self- esteem—the murderer saying, "I never got so much respect before in my life as I did when I pointed a gun at somebody—and just as suicidal individuals are found to have inner parental voices that tell them they are "bad" and demand their deaths, so too nations that commit genocide are in fact punishing themselves. They are not just *"being aggressive"* or *"being greedy"* as realist theories of war claim. Wars I have shown result from fear not "greed" or "aggressiveness" as most theories of war claim. They are outcomes of early childhood fears of helplessness—creating a "time bomb" set to go off when adults believe too much freedom is resented by the inner parental voices. These voices that command them to kill--whether they are labeled God or Providence or Motherland—are implanted during childhood in their dissociated early fear network. The voices tell them they are bad for wanting things for themselves and must be punished, and the child— rather than losing the parent's care—fuses with the persecuting parent and punishes someone else as a "Bad Self" scapegoat. This group-fantasy of a fusion with the Powerful Motherland always takes place before wars and

genocides, showing itself in the familiar grandiose feelings of being swept up and transformed by the nation and then accusing enemies of what you were accused of as a child.

The killing of "Bad Self" enemies is done so that the Punitive Motherland will once again love and care for you once you have purified your sinfulness. The Holocaust was very much a "Victory through Sacrificial Purification" group-fantasy. …Every sinful attribute ascribed to the Jews is a repetition of "sinful" qualities German and Austrian parents routinely ascribed to their own children. The psychodynamics of wars are exactly the same as in the self-destructive behaviors of individuals—like self-cutters, who satisfy the inner voices demanding they suffer for their sins by making token cuts to their arms. The Holocaust was a similar self-destructive sacrifice of a part of the body politic to satisfy the parent's punitive voice in their head.

Self-cutting like genocide makes people feel alive, reborn. …. The Jews had to be "cutout" of Germania to "purify" it to remove its "badness" which was really the "badness" ascribed to itself as a child, saying it "must have been" the reason for mommy not loving it, for her abandoning it, for her torturing and assaulting it. [85]

The above quote is just the tip of the iceberg to a long article that explains in graphic detail the kind of torture and humiliation the generation of German and Austrian children endured who grew up to become the adult perpetrators of the Third Reich insanity. The article is difficult to read but one I strongly recommend because it helps us as a species to better understand what we do to children when we shame and abuse them. It may help us to recognize deep-seated dynamics at play in our own psyches. This is especially critical to understand for those who have been subjected to extreme and abusive parenting practices, and it may help us recognize those traits in our leaders. The generations since the Third Reich are not far removed from the generation of parents who raised Hitler and his cohorts. Some of those ideas have filtered down into parenting practices and must be recognized for the heinous destructive ideologies they are.

In a shame-bound system, it is believed that it is better to shame another than to have one's own inadequacies exposed. Shame is created in each member and passed on or projected onto others in a shame-based society or family. The scapegoat or one who carries

---

[85] deMause, Lloyd, "Childhood Origins of the Holocaust," *The Association for Psychohistory*, 2005, http://psychohistory.com/articles/the-childhood-origins-of-the-holocaust/
(Speech given on September 28, 2005, at Klagenfurt University, Austria)

the projection of the family sins helps to alleviate the stress on each member of the family caused by the shame.

For those who ascribe to a shame-based religion, they find relief from that shame by projecting it onto the ones who are not members of that particular faith. The outsiders become the "bad guys," giving the members of that particular congregation feelings of "better than" which helps to alleviate some of the shame that is foundational to their psychological make- up.

Shame is a means of displacing an unwanted feeling onto another in order to protect oneself from it. Shame is an internal, subjective experience. It is a judgment of the self. Shamed persons see themselves as inadequate, inferior, worthless, and defective. In a family belief system where shame exists, the core feeling of all the members of the family is inadequacy.

In families where child abuse or neglect occur, or where religious fanaticism is the core around which the family is built, shame often is the foundational overlay upon which all other overlays grow, and it will probably be the last overlay to be understood and released. Shame is the ultimate suppression that literally paralyzes one's ability to develop self-esteem and self-worth until the dynamics of the overlay are understood.

THE CYCLE OF BONDING AND ATTACHMENT [86]

Bonding is the first and most basic link of trust that needs to develop between an infant and its caregiver, usually the mother or a mother figure. Attachment is the second stage of this fundamental developmental stage in the life of every infant. When this process is interrupted, it creates many obstacles to the developing child's ability to form adequate and viable relationships with others through the course of their childhood and adult life.

The crucial process of bonding develops during the first six months of life through the repeated completion of what we call the bonding cycle. The infant has a need and usually feels it through increased tension which leads to crying, the parent responds and attends to

---

[86] There is a great deal of information about bonding and attachment. As a childbirth educator during the years I was having my children, and later a social worker, I became interested in the subject. I had the opportunity to attend a teacher training facilitated by the Child Welfare League of America (CWLA) in San Francisco to train foster parents. They provided a wealth of information about the various aspects of child development as it pertains to foster care, and concerning abuse, neglect, and trauma. http://www.cwla.org Another extremely useful resource is the Child Trauma Academy http://childtrauma.org/ Dr. Bruce Perry is a pioneer in the work of brain functioning, brain development, and the effects of trauma on the developing brain. His books are available on his website. His work is groundbreaking and fascinating

that need, and the baby feels satisfaction and relaxes. Hunger is the most obvious need, but the baby can also be wet, uncomfortable, or lonely. All of these are needs that must be met on a consistent basis to complete the bonding and attachment developmental stages of an infant/toddler.

Hunger is the most obvious need to see this cycle in action. For anyone who has ever nursed an infant (I nursed six), that cycle is very apparent. (This process also happens successfully with bottle fed infants if they are attended to consistently by their caretaker.) The newborn infant is very intense about its need to be tended to and fed. When it starts to nurse, its little body is very tense, almost rigid, with its little hands held tightly against its face, and it sucks with everything it has. As the baby begins to feel satisfied, the body begins to visibly relax, and by the time the baby is finished nursing, its body is completely limp. I used to think that they seemed a little "drunk," and their bodies would be wobbly when put over my shoulder or sat up to be burped.

As the baby goes through this cycle repeatedly, feeling the tension that causes rage and having that tension released through having its needs met consistently, it learns to build trust in its ability to communicate its needs and in its caretaker. This process, repeated countless times a day, creates the bonding experience. Later, as the child becomes a toddler, the second cycle of attachment begins to develop. As the toddler begins to explore the world, it also begins to experience parental limitation and intervention.

This second cycle begins with the child performing a potentially harmful action based on curiosity or defiance, the adult setting a limit, the child feeling some frustration and shame, and the adult reinforcing the intention of safety for the toddler. This is the process by which the toddler develops trust in parental limitations and authority. Because in this process of limiting a child, the toddler feels some shame, that must be addressed very soon after the event by the adult making a positive overture toward the child. This neutralizing of the shame helps to build affection between toddler and caregiver. This affection helps the attachment between toddler and caregiver grow and develop and protect the child from the disruptive effects of shame. This process ebbs and flows through the developmental stages of the child's first three years of life. If this progression is successful, the foundations of bonding and attachment are laid by 36 months. This allows the child to continue to emotionally attach to others while growing up as the developmental process of bonding has been internalized.

When that cycle is interrupted by abuse and neglect in those first formative 36 months of a child's life and/or the child is raised in a shame- based environment, the child has a much more difficult time developing the normal ability to bond or attach. There is a great deal of information about attachment disorders that the reader can explore if you desire. Suffice it to say that the child's ability to trust and attach to other humans is critically crippled when this cycle is disrupted, and it causes immense internal suffering for children who are victims of this process, as well as those who try to pick up the pieces and help them. It also makes it more difficult for the adult of such an upbringing to have the ability to form healthy relationships and attachments. It isn't impossible; some individuals are able to see through the fallacies they have been brought up with and rise above them, but most abusive childhoods challenge the psychological health of an individual to the core. With these ideas in mind, let's look at how some overlays might play out.

OVERLAYS AND THEIR OUTCOMES

Now I am going to paint some simple scenarios to attempt to illustrate the dynamics of overlay development. Remember that when an overlay is in place, all life issues will be played out from that point of view. Overlays can be very subtle. I will try and keep the following examples basic, but this is a complex subject even in its most basic form.

For the sake of simplicity, the following illustrations do not include past or current life deficits or strengths that could be significant factors in the level of intensity of the developing pathology brought on by the situations described. They also do not bring into play intervention later in childhood or adulthood that could help an individual overcome some of the tendencies we will discuss below.

For an added dimension to the scenarios below, you can add one of the reincarnational options already discussed above and think about how that would affect the development of the overlays in our examples and add to the complexity of the individual. This could be a powerful journaling exercise.

Children whose basic needs are only marginally met during infancy and childhood often develop a deep-seated mistrust of all people, and if they survive, they are vulnerable to becoming criminal sociopaths. If babies do not bond in a positive way to their caretakers during the sensitive period of birth to three years when these connections normally take place, their ability to make emotional connections becomes compromised and fragile.

I worked in Child Protective Services for about twenty years in different capacities. One of my positions for about six years was as an adoption worker. At least a third of the caseload I was assigned to consisted of teens who had been removed from their homes at a young age and basically raised by the system in foster care. If they were a part of an adoption caseload, that meant that parental rights had been terminated or relinquished, and they were orphans. If they were removed from an abusive home, except in rare situations, it almost always guaranteed that the bonding and attachment developmental stages were not completed in a healthy manner.

It was difficult to find permanent homes for these children because by the time they reached adolescence, they had usually experienced one or more placement and/or adoption disruptions, and they were distrustful and chronically anxious. Every disruption, including the initial disruption from their birth-family, causes issues for the child—issues of grief, separation and abandonment and the shame of feeling unwanted and/or less-than—and these "rejections" are added to the child's already fractured sense of self- worth and doubts about their lovability. They struggle with a deep-seated undercurrent of anxiety that creates a vicious cycle of negative testing behaviors that often leads to more disruptions.

Adolescents who have suffered this kind of childhood have been set-up to experience a difficult time maintaining healthy emotional connections. They have learned to mistrust because their sense of trust has been disrupted far too many times. Each situation is unique, and the dynamics are as well, but overall, these are painful conditions that become a part of the individual's psyche.

Generally, a person who cannot make or does not feel any emotional connections does not have any reason to regulate themselves. Affection for and attachment to others is a powerful regulator. Affection for one's parents can be a strong deterrent to effectively keep children out of trouble because the motivation comes from love developed through the bonding process. I figured that out as a teen. One of my major motivations to behaving myself was the conscious realization that I did not want to hurt my mother. My love for her had a powerful regulatory effect on me while growing up.

I taught parenting and education for childbirth and breastfeeding/ bonding/attachment during my childbearing years. I was very active in the Childbirth Education movement. Later I became a social worker and witnessed firsthand the devastating effects children in the system suffered.

Please know that I understand that at times foster care can be a helpful break for parents who need some time to work on issues that have overtaken their lives and gives them a chance to participate in treatment or other rehabilitative measures. These temporary placements are good uses for foster care. I also realize that some parents simply cannot raise their children safely and lovingly, and I am aware of dedicated foster parents who have adopted children who thrive in their homes. These people are to be respected and appreciated for the important work they do. It can be an incredibly challenging task to raise a child who has suffered violence or abuse in their early years. Those who have the patience and understanding to be compassionate towards these children and all the issues they face are the saints in this world.

What I have seen all too often, however, are the long-term effects of a childhood of constant disruptions and the resulting irreparable harm. A hateful, fearful, or shameful environment during the formative years can create a defensive mindset that often makes a child devious and defiant of anything the parent or any other adult expects.

The overlay of perception of un-bonded or poorly bonded children can develop in them the mindset: "I will take care of myself at all costs because the world is not to be trusted." As children, they did not learn to normally attach or interact with others, and as adults, their point of view will often be based on what is in it for them. As children they may develop oppositional defiant behaviors and later become adult tyrants. They can have violent or passive-aggressive tendencies. Tyrants learn early on that they must have their way to survive and often stop at nothing to attain their goals because they perceive their very survival is at stake.

Tyrants can be subtle manipulators and often use charm as a way of gaining control; but one soon learns in relationships with them not to cross them or make them angry because there will be repercussions. Tyrants often emanate a feeling of "better than" or a sense of entitlement as a way of compensating for their desperate need to be affirmed in some way. They also are prone to develop black and white thinking and feel that the world needs to believe like they do without exception. If everyone around them believes the way they do, then tyrants feel they are in control, and this is of utmost importance, providing them a feeling of security. Given power and belief systems that support their "better than" feeling, they can turn into fanatics.

The deprivation of basic infant or childhood needs can also manifest in the development of underachievers and victims. Underachievers have exceptionally low self-esteem because they have a weak sense of who they are. They often become the victims in our world. The self-talk of this mindset includes such ideas as: "The world is a very unsafe place to be." "Don't draw attention to yourself." "No matter what I do, I get hurt." "Poor me!" "The world is doing it to me."

People who feel victimized by life find it exceedingly difficult to take responsibility for their lives and the situations they find themselves in. Their perception of the world is that they will be hurt, taken advantage of, or mistreated in some way if they try. For these people, life always seems to "go wrong," and it is difficult to see the world in a positive way. Their perception and belief system are totally wrapped up in "I am a victim." This mindset is full of "what-ifs," and most decisions are made from a position of fear or feelings of worthlessness. They continue to create their world in a vicious circle of self-perpetuating beliefs of self-negation.

Victims often attract tyrants into their lives, and together they perpetuate the above dynamics. To a victim, the tyrant appears self-assured and strong, giving the victim the illusion that they will be taken care of by this person. Of course, the tyrant is drawn to the victim because they can be controlled very easily.

FEAR OF ABANDONMENT

Children who suffer the devastating loss of one or both parents to death, or whose parent deserts the family, or are emotionally rejected by a parent may develop the overlay of fear of abandonment and rejection that can manifest in a low-grade anxiety that becomes an undercurrent of their emotional makeup. If one parent does the disappearing or rejecting, the child can have abandonment issues with the gender of that absent parent. As an adult, once another becomes emotionally significant, that undercurrent of anxiety that perpetuates the fear of loss can rear its ugly head leading the person to sabotage the relationship. There will be a subconscious reaction with behaviors that can force the other to abandon or reject them in some way, perpetuating the dynamic of abandonment and rejection. This dynamic can play out in child/surrogate parent relationships such as foster parents or as adults in friendships or romantic relationships.

An astute and aware caretaker can often help a child through life passages such as these so that they are not completely scarred, but these are tough situations for everyone involved. Some individuals are able to draw on an inner reserve of strength and coping abilities and overcome these odds, while others who suffer these losses are impaired emotionally and struggle throughout their lives.

The fear of rejection can also make a person compliant and passive in relationships and emotionally needy. This demeanor can attract persons with bully tendencies. People with abandonment issues can become the victims of domestic violence or psychological abuse because they already think something is inherently wrong with them, and they will often tend to subjugate themselves to keep from being rejected. Living in the constant fear of rejection, they draw it to themselves.

Adults who were frequently beaten either emotionally or physically as children, with many inconsistencies in the reasons why they were punished, may well develop an overlay of shame and worthlessness, be very passive for fear of bringing on the wrath of the people around them, exhibit behaviors that portray a helplessness or powerlessness to affect their world, or become incredibly angry and set out to get revenge on a world they cannot trust. Often times such individuals can become passive aggressive. They feel so weak that they often attract their opposites who will dominate them. They are vulnerable to becoming the victims or the perpetrators of domestic violence.

Adults who were sexually molested as children almost always carry a strong overlay of shame and guilt that can lead to feelings of being sullied or defiled and cause them to act out in self-destructive ways, including self-mutilation. Or they may go about trying to prove their goodness and become super good, compliant children, growing up to be super-achievers in an attempt to redeem that sense of shame that they feel. This shame can also manifest into a martyr psychological pattern of behavior. Martyrs often become doormats, feeling unappreciated and misunderstood. They may feel that they are being held responsible for situations they couldn't handle or punished for acts they didn't do.

In order to compensate for the suffering that they have endured and give it some meaning, martyrs may develop a belief system that embraces nobility in suffering, allowing life's circumstances to walk over them while they suffer in silence. This silent suffering becomes a sort of absolution in their minds. Martyrs will do unsolicited "good" deeds for people, and then when they are not appreciated, you might hear them say: "After all I have done for you, look how you treat me." These people have a desperate need for recognition, approval, and/or redemption. We may see a person with a strong martyr overlay gravitate toward religions that teach sacrifice as a way to redemption.

We see children who have been neglected, abused, rejected, betrayed, or have suffered deeply traumatizing situations such as being orphaned by war, exploited, and recruited into cults that train and indoctrinate them in radical beliefs. In today's world the radicalized jihadist suicide bombers come to mind. It is easy to understand how they can be driven by an inner need for acceptance and belonging to become martyrs for a cause.

Adults who are taught as children that they are "better than" everyone around them, due to financial status, race, religion, or gender, often carry an overlay of bigotry and chauvinism that affects all their dealings with others who are different from them. These attitudes can also produce a type of tyrant.

Children's birth order and gender can be powerful factors that contribute to the way an individual is treated and influence the expectations put on them by their family. Both gender and birth order contribute to the way children learn to adapt to various situations as they develop unique coping skills.

FINAL THOUGHTS

These overlays are not our Authentic Self. They cover up who we are and give us a role to play, a part in the temporary human drama we call everyday life. We free ourselves from the energetic densities these overlays create by learning to identify them and realize they are an illusion and not our True Self. This takes focused inner work and self-examination, but we can make huge strides in changing our lives for the better if we are willing to do the work it takes to attain the necessary insights to release the overlays once they are identified.

It is an exhilarating moment when we see through this illusion for the first time and can say with absolute conviction: "I am not my body, or my feelings, or my problems. I am so much more than that!" If we can take that realization another step and look for the gift in each of our experiences, then we are taking even bigger steps towards our Authentic Self.

An awakening is happening on this earth. Ironically, the children suffering the outcomes of our shame-based belief systems have begun to open our eyes to the deplorable damage these kinds of treatment cause. The information is motivating us to make significant steps forward in our understanding of the dynamics of infant development, but this knowledge has come at a huge cost in human suffering. Psychological studies of infant attachment and the outcomes in adults with little or no attachment in childhood highlight the urgency for society to deal with this issue. For our world to evolve, it is crucial that we provide our infants with opportunities to bond, attach, and develop without debilitating overlays.

As a caseworker I have witnessed first-hand the dynamics of hopelessness, ignorance and despair that is often present in the lives of parents who are brought into the system for neglecting or abusing their children, and I have observed the effect firsthand of these actions on the children. It is a vicious cycle that keeps perpetuating itself and will not stop on its own. Unaware people act out of their programming. Victims respond from a victim mentality, and tyrants from a tyrannical one. Hopelessness and helplessness beget the same in new generations.

We have to collectively become more aware of the damage that is wrought through generations of abuse and neglect and by the overlays that are perpetuated by these behaviors. Sitting in condemning judgment of these people is counterproductive. We begin by understanding that actions come from perceptions, and perceptions are formed one layer at a time. Our rehabilitation methods need to include tools and techniques that will help people recognize and clear damaging beliefs.

Staying locked in these destructive overlays is certainly no gift to us or to future generations. Finding the key that unlocks the dynamics and helps us let go of the overlays is the gift we can give ourselves. That gift will take us further down the road towards the great joy and peace an awakened consciousness aware of its own sovereignty can bring.

Author's Note: I pulled many of the ideas from a chapter in my previous book *Breaking Free from the Tyranny of Beliefs: A Revolution in Consciousness* into this chapter and built on them. The subject discussed here is important to understand as we move forward through the rest of the journey of this book. The explorations below are also found in my previous book.

EXPLORATIONS: FINDING YOUR OVERLAYS

1. List anywhere from 6-12 beliefs you were taught as a child. The more you can list, the more information you will find out about yourself. Draw from what you learned in school, what your parents/family/caretakers taught you about the way the world worked, how you "should" in the world, and what you learned through your religious teachings. Look at each one of these beliefs in light of where you are today. Is this belief a helpful one, or one that holds you back? Make some notes beside each belief about how it has affected your life so far.

2. Try to remember and list at least six significant events in your growing up years that effected or altered your life in some way. It could be a move, a traumatic event, a happy event, an accomplishment, a failure, an adventure with a friend, or a trip and journal how you felt while experiencing those events. You might want to write them into a timeline continuum. This will help you get an idea of the types of cycles or patterns that are at work in your life, and also give you an idea of how the veil of overlays is layered.

3. Review the significant events (Exercise 2) and see if you can find any patterns, similarities, or themes that stand out. How are these patterns or themes affecting your perception of events today? You can find some clues about your patterns by going back through and underlining all the feeling words or phrases that describe how you felt or reacted in the situation. Are any of these feelings or reactions associated with being a victim, a tyrant, or a martyr or with feeling shame?

4. Did you formulate any beliefs from the events that you have incorporated into your life (Exercise 2)? Usually, significant events create a turning point or a point of demarcation from the path you were on before the event. Can you trace the shifts and changes?

5. List at least six people who had a positive or negative impact on you while you were growing up. In just a few words jot down what that impact was. How do they play into the themes and patterns in Exercise 3? Did they have an affirming or painful effect on you? How does that impact play into your self-image?

6. Make a list of three to six of the careers you wanted to follow when you grew up. For all those that aren't your career now, if you can remember, jot down why you didn't follow through or gave up on the idea.

7. Now with your list of beliefs (Exercise 1), go through your other lists and notes and see how your beliefs affected each event and the memory of each event. In this way,

you will discover the significant overlays that limit or enhance your life; now journal your findings.

8. Write a vignette in which an Archetype of your choosing teaches you about how you created one of the overlays you discovered in the above exercises.

9. Take a particularly stressful and continuing situation in your life. Now ask yourself, if I were in a life planning session before I was born, what would I be setting out to learn or experience by having this situation in my life? Why would I give myself this experience? When will I be ready to be done with this? Often, when we can discover the reason for a situation, we can diffuse the energy of it and release it.

10. The goal of discovering beliefs and overlays is to examine them in order to see how they impact your life:
    • Do your beliefs limit you or do they help you succeed?
    • Do your beliefs keep you from loving others and yourself?
    • Do your beliefs enhance your ability to love?

Knowing that each overlay is just that—a veil that can be lifted, a belief that can be changed or modified—is taking back your power and returning to your Authentic Self. When you discover a belief that limits you, you have the right to change that belief. Once you do, your reality will begin to shift in tandem with your new belief.

We have explored some ideas that have contributed to our collective and personal world view. In the next two chapters we will be delving deeper into duality by taking a more in-depth look into how polarities affect our belief systems and investigating the dynamics of our belief systems.

DO WE CONSCIOUSLY CREATE
OUR OWN REALITY?

> True spirituality is a thing of joy and of the earth,
> and has nothing to do with fake adult dignity.
> It has nothing to do with long words and sorrowful faces.
> It has to do with the dance of consciousness that is within you,
> and with the sense of spiritual adventure that is within your hearts.
> — Jane Roberts, *Seth Speaks: The Eternal Validity of the Soul*

WHY ARE WE HERE? WHAT is our purpose? Is this all there is? Do we have any control over our realities? These are questions that have plagued me as well as many of every generation.

I was first introduced to the idea that we create our own reality through the *Seth Material*, channeled by Jane Roberts (May 8, 1929 - September 5, 1984), so I cannot write a chapter on reality creating without mentioning Ms. Roberts and the *Seth Material* because it became a significant event string for many seeking understanding during the 1970s and 1980s and a catalyst for expanding the minds of those the material spoke to, present company included. Seth was widely popular during those years and contributed significantly to the revolution in consciousness that continues to this day. (According to James Mahu, "Project Camelot Interview"—channeling is a part of the Human Mind System. [87] It will not take us out of the Hologram of Deception, but I believe that depending on the material being channeled, it can help us loosen our grip on the reality we have always taken for granted and expand our understanding within the Hologram of Deception. My experiences with channeled sources in the 70s and 80s helped me become more receptive to "out of the box" new ideas and information and helped to prepare me for the *WingMakers Materials* that appeared on the internet in 1998 and into my life around 2011-2012.)

---

[87] **Human Mind System** - Secret framework for the suppression of the Sovereign Integral, Appendix A - Glossary

One particular incident changed Jane Robert's worldview, setting her life stage for the coming of the *Seth Material*:

> On a September evening in 1963 their everyday worldview changed. Roberts sat down to her table to work on poetry; Butts (her husband) was in his back-room studio, painting. 'It was very domestic, very unpsychedelic,' she would later remember. And then 'between one normal minute and the next a fantastic avalanche of radical, new ideas burst into my head with tremendous force…it was as if the physical world were really tissue-paper-thin, hiding infinite dimensions of reality, and I was flung through the tissue paper with a huge ripping sound.' When she came to, Roberts found herself scrawling the title of this odd batch of notes: *The Physical Universe as Idea Construction*.[88]

In the months following that experience, Jane was to learn that Seth was a part of her consciousness; he told her he was her Higher Self. She would go into trance, and Seth would dictate his material through Jane to be transcribed by her husband Robert Butts. Jane was a prolific writer, and they published twenty-four channeled Seth books plus her own additional poetry, books, and essays.

I personally believe that the *Seth Material* brought upgraded information into the Genetic Mind,[89] laying a foundation of new ideas that would be a key to the expansion of consciousness waiting in the future wings of our collective reality. The first Seth book published in 1970 spoke to the generation who became young adults in the late 1950s, 1960s, and 1970s. This cohort arrived on the planet with the agenda of shaking the foundation of our status quo belief systems to their core, and the *Seth Material* offered the conceptual challenges needed to begin to seed our reality with fresh ideas. For the majority of us, our intellects were still in charge, but our minds had to be opened to more expanded possibilities before our hearts could become involved or opened enough to take on the awesome task that lay ahead of us in the new millennium to regain our Sovereignty. At least that is how I felt about my experience with this material and the impact it had on my curious and opening mind and heart.

A modern Renaissance period began in this country in the 1950s and 1960s with the beatnik/hippie movement. Those involved began to question and/or reject mainstream religion in favor of a more personal spiritual experience. Many sought spiritual guidance through Eastern religions and beliefs that included Buddhism and Hinduism. This counterculture attempted to promote peace, love, and freedom, rejecting the rigid moral values of their

---

[88] "Jane Roberts," *Wikipedia*, https://en.wikipedia.org/wiki/Jane_Roberts
[89] See **Genetic Mind**, Appendix A - Glossary

parents. They railed against the Vietnam War, believing that no one should be forced to fight. The holistic health movement began around this time as well as a sexual revolution with the invention of birth control pills and the availability of contraceptive devices. Peace and Love became the battle cry of the hippie revolution. Civil Rights took center stage during this time period. The Women's Movement and racial integration were issues that became part of the country's conversation. Rock and roll gave birth to a new era in music. Television and movies brought advanced ideas and concepts to the general public. This era saw a burgeoning awareness of environmental issues; women were becoming socially and increasingly sexually liberated; psychedelic drugs such as LSD were popular, as it was believed they opened the mind.

Even fashion became more liberated as clothing became looser and more comfortable. The trend was towards less formal attire and less formal living arrangements. Many "hippies" lived in communes and shared their resources. It was an era of considerable radical experimentation in this country.

The arrival of the *Seth Material* in the seventies fit right in with a population looking for fresh answers, as Seth challenged many beliefs of the day. It was from Seth that I first learned about the concept of parallel realities; he encouraged the use of our imaginations and taught that our consciousness was not limited by time or space. It was from Seth that I first heard the concept that we are spirits expressing ourselves through the "miraculous joy of flesh," and that physical life was not evil. He said,

> Those who tell you that to be spiritual is not to be physical do not understand the great physical-spiritual nature of your being. They have not dreamed in their minds. They have not sparkled in themselves like stars and so experiencing night they think that existence is dark.

And Seth introduced me to the idea that our beliefs create our reality. For me, coming out of a church that taught rigid soul-numbing admonitions and platitudes, the *Seth Material* was a mind-expanding breath of fresh air.

New Age thought emerged in the seventies out of the highly eclectic environment of the 1960s revolution. This was the personal growth era that included a plethora of diverse ways of accessing knowledge and spirituality, including metaphysical bookstores and personal growth seminars. Many people who channeled dis-embodied entities became popular, and large audiences would attend their workshops and seminars. Methods of reaching enlightenment or consciousness expansion were offered to the general public and were no longer kept secret. Gurus from the East traveled to the West and became popular. Transcendental Meditation was taught by Maharishi Mahesh Yogi's organization to thousands of seekers. Paramahansa Yogananda's *Autobiography of a Yogi* introduced many to Eastern thought and belief systems. There was a strong movement away from organized religion as seekers continued to look for direct spiritual experiences.

As with all movements, there were pitfalls as some teachers took advantage of their students psychologically, sexually, spiritually, and financially. But aside from that, the New Age Movement was experienced as a way for a person to gain some autonomy and self-guidance and move away from the control of organized religion. Pilgrimages to India were popular for those seeking enlightenment and a new way of thinking and believing.

I found this to be an exhilarating time. I had just embarked on my thirties and was in the process of leaving a very fundamental church and belief system that controlled my first decade of adulthood. Initially the *Seth Material* and then other channels that I discovered were like a wave of continuous fresh air as they helped me to open to expanded ways of thinking releasing me from the rigid hold Churchianity had on me. I remember saying that "God is going to have to understand when I don't and forgive me as I search because I cannot live with the beliefs and stranglehold this church has on me any longer." I also believed that God looked at a person's heart, and I knew that my heart and intent was authentic.

In the beginning of my flight out of the church, I would occasionally feel a little fear about whether or not I was doing the right thing, but something inside me was driving me to seek, so I gave myself permission to make mistakes and to explore every avenue that I was attracted to until I found what I was looking for. I felt with every fiber of my being that I would recognize it when I found it.

As the searching and discovering continued, some came to realize, myself included, that we had to be mindful, or we would just be exchanging one controlling spiritual belief system for another from the plethora of Gurus and organizations that sprang up during this time. But at the same time, new ideas were introduced into the collective, and interest in the nature of consciousness began to expand considerably.

Humanity was still locked into the suppression paradigm, but as I look back on those times, I can see that the groundwork being laid was significant as we took the first steps to creating a crack in the wall of suppression with the expansion of our belief systems. I see all of these movements as significant precursors to a new era of expansion and transparency waiting in the wings of human consciousness to make its entrance.

The revolution of the 1960s swung the pendulum far to the left, and then it slowly started its way back down towards the middle with the New Age Movement and upwards towards the right again as organized religion began to find ways to bring people back under their guidance and control. We are now seeing an attempt being made by the far right to swing the pendulum way back to the old ways before the 1960s revolution with the outcome of the election of 2016 and beyond. But humanity tasted unprecedented freedom in the aftermath of the 1960s revolution, and the resistance movement we are witnessing by the left is telling us that the far-right will not be able to hold that pendulum in place for very long. It will begin its inevitable swing back towards the middle again as society begins to rail against anyone trying to enforce the suppression of the 1960s and before on us again.

We now have the influence of the shifting energies of 2012 and the dawning of the Age of Transparency and Expansion. Have you noticed in the years since 2012 how long held secrets have begun to be made public? This wave of transparency is being played out in government and big business and entertainment all the way down to families and the MeToo movement.

We have come too far as a species for suppressive practices to maintain the stranglehold they had on us in the past, because in the process of gaining our freedoms, our hearts have begun to open. With instant information available to us from around the globe, we are more aware of others' suffering, often learning of incidents in real time. Issues that were hidden in the days before the 1960s revolution are out in the open now. It doesn't seem possible that humanity could be repressed again to the extent we were before. We know too much, information is readily available, and we have tasted too many freedoms to allow our country to go extremely far backward. That doesn't mean the status quo won't try to repress the progress made to maintain the upper hand they have had for centuries. It is up to us to recognize what is being played out here and not allow ourselves to be manipulated and sucked back into the suppression paradigm.

To quote an excerpt from a poem— "Love Wins"—I wrote as preparations were being made for the 2017 Presidential Inauguration:

> The battle lines are drawn
> Darkness and suppression
> And the Light of understanding and liberation
> Face off as
> The resistance builds
> Prepared by the virtues of love

(The entire poem can be found at the end of Chapter Twenty-five, "A New Core Belief Matrix.")

We have unprecedented new information and developing abilities in our arsenal of resistance that we have never had before. The virtues of love transmitted through a growing foundation of heart-centered people discovering their Sovereignty have the power to resist this scourge of suppression trying to make its comeback. Love Wins. That is the promise.

With this short diversion into our recent history, we can now come back to the question of this chapter: **_Do we consciously create our own reality?_** It would appear that overall, the generation who brought us the 1960s revolution did some powerful reality undoing and recreating as a cohort; but what about *creating* our reality individually? We are occasionally successful at creating events in our lives; however, it isn't an exact or even reliable "science," so there must be something missing in our understanding.

James Mahu provides us with some important clues in his e-paper "Living from the Heart" [90] about what is missing from the philosophy that we create our own reality. In the section titled "The Heart-Mind Intention," he offers some useful factors that give us the rest of the story about creating reality and some important concepts to ponder. James acknowledges that there is some truth that the power of thought and the imprint of intention coupled with the expectation of belief along with the Law of Attraction all have their part in creating reality but adds that these are not exclusive drivers of reality, as other factors are involved. Part of our reality:

- Is a result of our individual blueprint
- Relates to our Higher Self setting up experiences for us
- Is a consequence of our past actions
- Is a reflection of our thoughts and emotions and their energetic attractions
- Is the desire of our Higher Self to experience new energy fields

I want to work with the above list for a bit and see where it leads. I think it is a powerful exercise in helping us to understanding how our realities are being created and/or directed and the part we play.

Part of our reality is a result of our individual blueprint. The individual blueprint we each have will ultimately (in some lifetime) result in the realization of our Sovereign Integral state of consciousness and our release from the Hologram of Deception. The steps we need to take to reach that ultimate goal are also embedded within that blueprint. So, it is plausible that when we are working within the blueprint's parameters, we are more successful in our intentions and endeavors.

A crucial part of our blueprint is attaining emotional self-mastery, and we do that by living from the heart. James explains it this way:

---

[90] Mahu, James, "Living from the Heart, Section Three: The Heart-Mind Intention," *WingMakers*, https://wingmakers.com/writings/sixheartvirtues/living-from-the-heart/
The section cited is either quoted or paraphrased. This e-paper is very powerful and full of information. I strongly encourage reading it.

… it is an important distinction to understand that living from the heart is not connected to ambition or achievement. It is the innate desire of the heart to draw the soul into the pilot's chair of the personality, knowing that this unlocks the blueprint of the individual to express the qualities of light stored within them….

For most of us, the expression of light stored within us is contained in the tiniest details of our heart's expression in the most fleeting moments of our life. It is as though we leave a trail of light and divine sparks as we walk our life, and this activity—not the writings or sharing or gaining of knowledge—is what is needed most at this time. This is what is unlocked and shared so faithfully from your heart. [91]

We learn from the statement above that we unlock our blueprint when we draw the soul into the pilot's chair. Our soul lives in our hearts, so we must work from our hearts to activate our blueprints.

At first it may seem to be somewhat of a challenging process to change one's orientation in life from the programming of self-serving goals such as control, ambition, self-gratification, and searching for the next best thing to embracing and practicing the ideas of equality, acceptance, and nurturance of life for all through the integration of and transmission of the Six Heart Virtues.

It is comforting to know that each person has their own blueprint and will ultimately reach liberation. It may not happen in this lifetime to each individual, depending on where they are in their soul's journey and their preparation and readiness, but it will eventually happen. It is encouraging to understand that as each of us comes closer to our Sovereign Integral State of Consciousness through heart-centered living, we will have more impact on loosening the grip of the suppression paradigm for everyone. It is an inner movement. We don't have to belong to any organization. We don't have to stand on the street corners and preach. We send out the heart virtues from the privacy of our own personal space, and they will do the rest.

Our work is to "hack" the program of suppression. We act as a conduit—we call to the Six Heart Virtues, breathe them into every cell of our bodies and then transmit them as we breathe out into the hologram. By living a heart-centered life and committing to these transmissions, we develop our Behavioral Intelligence. What comes to us and flows through

---

[91] Mahu, James, "Living from the Heart, Section Two: The When-Which-How Practice," *WingMakers*, https://wingmakers.com/writings/sixheartvirtues/living-from-the-heart/

us affects and transforms us as well as the hologram we live in. (James suggests a specific breathing technique called "Quantum Pause." Directions for that are found in Appendix F.)

We have been programmed from infancy to hold intellectual wisdom in high esteem and to view the intuitive and heart-centered processes as unreliable. Now to give over the reins of our lives to our hearts can be seen as a daunting task, as well as one we aren't sure how to do.

I can speak from my experience in saying that it is a gradual process. As I began to work with studying to understand and then to transmitting the Six Heart Virtues into life-experiences (both personal and global), I began to become aware of a feeling of strength within my heart's chamber and a sense of internal security that has become my inner compass. I will add that to the best of my knowledge, some physical heart issues I have had for a number of years are holding their own, not getting any worse, and physically I feel normal most of the time.

Part of our reality relates to our Higher Self setting up experiences for us could be interpreted in a myriad of ways. This is the physical world where consciousness can show its "long division" in the way we solve problems that come our way. It is a plane of slow motion where we can see events unfold and issues solved in a step-by-step process, and an experiment of living in a physical environment where we witness our belief systems in action and experience their outcomes on a daily basis.

I cannot help but think that the yearning to wake up by so many at this time in history is part of our Higher Self's desire to move us along on the trajectory of transformation by instilling in us the internal promptings to explore.

In my life my knee-jerk response to a problem is to ask myself: "What is it I am supposed to be learning or discovering" or "What in my belief system is making me perceive this event in a certain way?" That question or a similar one has been the prompt for many hours of journaling and self- exploration. Sometimes the question has been— "What do I have to believe to have this happen?"

With anything we process, it is important to keep in mind that wherever others are involved, they may also be having experiences set-up for them by their Higher Self. So, if I am a participant in the experience of another, it could be because our Higher Selves wanted us to go through this together for mutual edification and exploration. Each participant is given the opportunity to come to unique understandings or conclusions in a shared event. This is one of the ways I have been able to deal with the death of two of my children. We don't have any idea what a person's (soul's) destiny is and what each individual is on this earth to learn and experience.

Part of our reality is a consequence of past actions concerns the choices we make in life. They take us on self-edifying or self-sabotaging journeys, or they take us on journeys of spiritual development and growth. However, all past-actions can ultimately be a part of our spiritual development and growth if we choose to look at our decisions from the vantage point of these features of reality- creating and gleaning understanding from our experiences. One of the ways that has helped me to process consequences of adverse situations is to look for the gift in the experience. I ask myself: "What am I trying to learn or understand or discover by having this particular experience?" The answers don't always come immediately. I often have to work for them through contemplation and journaling. If I am persistent, I frequently arrive at powerful insights that take me into myself and/or the situation where deeper understanding can be revealed.

Part of our reality is a reflection of our thoughts and emotions and their energetic attractions. What thoughts and feelings are we projecting on the mirror of our lives? Perception is everything. If we look at the world through the lens of appreciation or compassion, we see a very different world than if we look at it through the lens of grief or of hate. The lens we see through will have a large impact on what we experience in our lives.

When I wrote the book *Breaking Free from the Tyranny of Beliefs: A Revolution in Consciousness,* I worked with the theory that belief creates reality, and the book explored a "core belief matrix" that I identified as having created the paradigm we were born into. My premise at the time was that if we understand the origins of our beliefs, we can change them and transform our reality. Now I know I had one piece of an extraordinarily complex puzzle. I think it is a valid piece, but there is "more to the story" as they say.

Since I wrote that book, I learned about the Genetic Mind (see Appendix A - Glossary). The Genetic Mind was created to give our species a universal belief system that would keep us in separation in order to explore the material worlds. The Genetic Mind contains the accumulated beliefs of all people on the planet from the past to the present. So, when I wrote *BFTOB,* I saw how our beliefs keep us within boundaries; I just didn't understand how or why or anything about the suppression paradigm. History has demonstrated to us the way that humanity is inspired with new information that brings about change. I believe that each generation is a cohort of souls with a basic albeit loose agenda to bring certain change and understanding to the Genetic Mind. If we look back over the generations, we can see how each one has a collective personality that challenges or clarifies beliefs held by the previous generations.

Change has to come through us. We are conduits for information that can be brought in through our insight and understanding and transmitted through the Genetic Mind to be shared by those whose minds are open to the information. Little by little, in what appears like excruciatingly slow progress, change happens. This also explains how we can come to break free from our programming as well as grow to understand how we have been suppressed.

Certain entities are born to be the conduits for paradigm breaking information. They transmit their insights and understanding into the collective or Genetic Mind through their meditations, insights, art, music, writings, teachings, and transmissions, and sometimes inventions and scientific discoveries. Their work is never easy as new information is invariably met with resistance and the desire for tenacious adherence to the ways that are already set by those who fear change. Reality changing is complicated and complex but not impossible.

One tool I have found that is particularly useful in mining the deeper parts of my psyche and my perceptions is writing poetry. For example, around 1985 I wrote the following:

> I look out over my inner landscape of frozen passion
> And dormant possibilities
> A silent reminder of potential untapped
> Entombed in stony ice under a blanket of snow

It is the beginning of a longer poem, but those four lines reflected what I was feeling at that time in my life. I was grieving in the aftermath of my seventeen-year-old daughter's death; my first marriage was in a very rocky state, and I felt trapped in a world from which there was no escape. I discovered I was internally frozen as those words poured out of me. The only way I could function was to shut down emotionally for a while. Those lines mirrored my internal state back to me.

Actually, the very act of writing this chapter put me in touch with the reflections of a challenging early adulthood and the longings and emotions of that tumultuous time. Now as I look back on some of the poetry I wrote, I see a prayer that was eventually answered. So ultimately my reality responded to my pleas. It seemed to take a long time, as the place I am now is the result of a long and arduous journey. The following poem was written sometime between 1975 and 1983.[92]

---

[92] Ferguson, Lark Aleta, *Remnants from the Fire, A Transformational Journey with the Archetypes,* Authorhouse, 2002. Both poems in this chapter are found in this book.

WHAT ARE DREAMS FOR?

Something inside me
A still small voice
Persistently hinting at a mystery
Calls to me
A passionate ache
Longing for relief

Frustration and I
Constant companions
Knowledge-eagerly gained
I long to share
But he won't listen
He doesn't care

A slave to the culture that bore and bred him
Only one school of thought accepted here
Sad, gray, droopy, ghostlike vitality
Fit into your mold, don't waver
As I wash my dishes, to wash them again
Clean up today, only to clean up tomorrow

I long for a purpose to make sense of my toil

Anguish wells up inside me
Spilling over into tears of despair
As I sit in my chair
The crackling fire tries to cheer me
And yet I feel cold
Even the fire's cheerful glow
Cannot warm my soul

Please understand my searching
Explain it to me

Open up the mysteries of my heart
Set me free!

What is the reason for my existence?
Why, Oh why am I here?
What is truth? Does it matter?
Does anything really matter?

My awakened curiosity
Has opened small avenues of discovery
That seems to call to me, mocking me
Teasing the loneliness with false hope

I am given a taste of what I seek
Only to have it withdrawn
Like elusive ghosts
Leaving me lonelier than before

I cannot speak my heart
For it would not be accepted
Nor understood
I feel punished for my longings
The struggle is so hard
And I am so discouraged
What are dreams for?
The insanity of life goes on
Can no one sense my turmoil?
Seething under this calm veneer?
Is this a normal state?
Do any feel as I do?
How do I ease the ache?
Assuage the fear?
Where do I go from here?

Now as I look back on my life and the event strings that prepared me for all that I have discovered, experienced, and grown to understand, I know that my heart's plea was heard, and I was put on a trajectory that would ultimately take me to the information I was longing to discover. Things are not always as they seem at the time we are experiencing them.

Another reason I shared this poem is to use it as a little exercise for looking at reality creating. I am sure I am not alone in the feelings of isolation expressed in this poem. I think many of us have had similar feelings or experiences.

Now as I look back on my experiences with my newfound understanding, I see how promptings from my original blueprint to find the truth and to reveal my heart's mysteries worked with me in my life. Finding the bottom line has been my intent for as long as I can remember. Because I was asking for help, my Wholeness Navigator [93] worked with me, guiding me to find information and experiences that would help me to cut the threads of programming one-by-one. For every old thread that was cut, a new strand of light would replace it to guide me further to the ultimate discovery of my Heart Path.

The consequences of my actions play into some of the angst expressed in this poem. I married young and had six children over the span of about ten years, and that put me in the harness of the exhausting day-to-day grind, a very common part of life on this planet. All of these factors were grist for the mill and the set-up for the Alchemical process that would make me the person I am today.

This realization drives home the understanding on a visceral level that judging another for the life experiences they are having is so unproductive. When we consider all the reality-creating factors listed above and take them into account, it gives us a much broader reason to be understanding and compassionate toward others.

The next thought that comes to mind is what about those people who are caught up in the blind control of the dark energy that is so rampant in this world. Is this something their Higher Selves have set up for them, or have they ignored their Higher Selves' promptings and been taken over by the distraction? Let's ponder this a bit.

Let's first agree for the sake of this conversation that our Sovereign Integral is providing our life force to a Human Instrument that was initially programmed by the dark energy to be an obedient slave. We were given an ego tuned to the Matrix to maintain the deception and function within it. Those who remain asleep to their true identity and real purpose are maintained by the programming set in motion by a fear-based program fixated on survival, conformity, ambition, distraction, and separation.

The timing of an individual's activation and awakening is something that is part of the mystery of life on this plane of existence. It is up to each individual through examining their life experiences to discern how much is set-up by the Higher Self and how much is

---

[93] See **Wholeness Navigator**, Appendix A - Glossary

their knee-jerk response to programming. It is not a question I feel we can answer for one another.

Our soul's ultimate blueprint is to find our way out of the programming of the suppression paradigm and free our bodies from the influence of the dark energies. That means we must consciously allow our soul to take over the drivers' seat and overcome ego self-serving ambitions. How do we do that?

We have discussed how the intellect and its spokesperson—our ego—is a tool for observing and navigating in the programmed world. The intellect and ego are tools of the suppression paradigm. We have a higher mind, but we need to be living from our hearts to access it as the two work in tandem. The Energetic Heart (see Appendix A - Glossary) and the breath are the animating forces for our bodies, and they are pure. The breath originates from the Sovereign Integral, and the physical heart is sustained by the Energetic Heart. The Sovereign Integral and the Energetic Heart give life to the body and are not a part of the program. According to the *WingMakers Materials,* they exist outside the Hologram of Deception. That is why humans have been encouraged to develop their intellect and not their hearts. Intellect alone without the influence of our hearts keeps us locked in the Hologram of Deception.

The intelligences or virtues that are transmitted through the heart and higher mind emanate from that Sovereign or Infinite part of us. So, to override the programming and the ego drives, we engage the powerful and transformative heart's Behavioral Intelligences or Six Heart Virtues. When we understand the origins of our heart's energy from that viewpoint, it is obvious why the intuition and anything coming from the heart would be maligned. The dark energy has created elaborate ruses to keep us from believing in promptings from our hearts and our intuition to keep us trapped in the suppression paradigm.

By transmitting the virtues through our breath from our hearts into the world, we send these potent energies onto the grid that connects all of us. Our transmissions will find those who are open and ready for them, and they will be guided through their own process of transformation. We can also send the virtues to anyone at any time and into any situation without any attachment to outcome and let the mysterious forces utilize them by sending them where they will be effective. James explains it so beautifully in the following passage from the same e-paper "Living from the Heart:"

> The heart-mind intention imprints subtle energies within the environment
> that filter through the personality's inner layers or quantum levels, and
> imprint—at the speed of light—upon the higher self. This imprinting is
> strongest within the individual, however it also "seeps" into the greater

environment and even those with whom the environment is shared. The "environment" in this definition, is not the physical space, but rather the emotional ecology at the quantum level that connects people independent of timespace considerations.

This specific type of emotional ecology is generated from the heart-mind operating in synchrony and alignment, focused on a very specific intention to operate within the when-which-how practice. It can extend to unimaginable distances and times because it operates in non-time and non-space. The heart's domain encompasses this ecology and can emit subtle impressions to anyone connected to this ecology. In this case distance is a trivial factor because we're speaking of photonic energy not magnetic or electrical—so someone connected to you a continent away is quite literally closer than a heartbeat. [94]

The above quote explains so much about how we can affect our world from the privacy of our own homes through our heart-centers. We can also see how distance healing and premonitions between those who are connected at the heart level works. It also made me curious to know more about what photonic energy is.

A short search on the internet for the definition of a photon produced the following scientific description of photon energy:

The concept of photons and quanta comes from quantum mechanics and quantum theory. Quantum mechanics is a mathematical model that describes the behavior of particles on an atomic and subatomic scale. It demonstrates that matter and energy are quantized, or come in small discrete bundles, on the smallest scales imaginable. A photon propagates at the speed of light.

A photon describes the particle properties of an electromagnetic wave instead of the overall wave itself. In other words, we can picture an electromagnetic wave as being made up of individual particles called photons. Both representations are correct and reciprocal views of electromagnetic waves. For example, light exhibits wave properties under conditions of

---

[94] Mahu, James, "Living from the Heart, Section Two: The When-Which-How Practice," *WingMakers*, https://wingmakers.com/writings/sixheartvirtues/living-from-the-heart/

refraction or interference. Particle properties are exhibited under conditions of emission or absorption of light. [95]

Continued searching produced an article with an esoteric explanation of the characteristics of photon energy:

Photon energy is the powerful new energy source that will replace electricity in the new millennium. It's a free energy source and nobody can monopolize it. Its outer edge or belt has already reached Earth's atmosphere and is affecting not only Earth but also many planets in the solar system. Photon energy is light energy, and it permeates the Earth in waves. It has the power to extend human life because it realigns the human body into a light body. Photon energy vibrates at a very high frequency and confers the power of instant manifestation of thought. Therefore, it is essential to maintain clarity and purity of thought by practicing daily meditation, being in the "now," and staying heart centered. In one sense, the Great Shift in Consciousness is the evolution of Mother Earth and her inhabitants into the realm of photon energy for the next 2,000 years. [96]

Another definition of a photon:

The photon is the fundamental particle of visible light. In some ways, visible light behaves like a wave phenomenon, but in other respects it acts like a stream of high-speed, submicroscopic particles. Modern physicists have demonstrated that the energy in any electromagnetic field is made up of discrete packets. The term photon (meaning "visible-light particle") was coined for these energy packets. Particle-like behavior is not restricted to the visible-light portion of the electromagnetic radiation spectrum, however. Radio waves, infrared waves, visible light, ultraviolet rays, X rays, and gamma rays all consist of photons, each of which contains a particular amount of energy that depends on wavelength.

---

[95] Zesiger, Thomas, "What is a photon? – Definition, Energy & Wavelength," *Study.com*, http://study.com/academy/lesson/what-is-a-photon-definition-energy-wavelength.html

[96] "What is Photon Energy?" *IN5D Esoteric, Metaphysical, Spiritual Database*, 2017, http://in5d.com/what-is-photon-energy/

Photons travel through empty space at a speed of approximately 186,282 miles (299,792 Kilometers) per second. This is true no matter what the electromagnetic wave. …. The energy contained in a single photon does not depend on the intensity of the radiation. At any specific wavelength—say, the wavelength of light emitted by a helium- neon laser—every photon contains exactly the same amount of energy, whether the source appears as dim as a candle or as bright as the sun. The brilliance or intensity is a function of the number of photons striking a given surface area per unit time. [97]

Author and intuitive Cindi Dale in her book *Subtle Energy* defines a photon (p. 98):

Electromagnetic radiation is described as a stream of photons, wave particles that are the basis of light. These are massless particles that travel at the speed of light. Each carries a bundle of energy and therefore information. The only difference between the types of electromagnetic radiation is the amount of energy found in the photon…. Photons also create a gigantic field depicted as the 'Field of Light'…which unifies all creation.

What this says to me is that we can send out the heart virtues and other loving communications to the world and to our loved ones anywhere in the world, and they will receive these messages, as we are all connected. As a species we are exploring and continuing to discover more about how our physical world works. Teachers down through the centuries have given the people of their time new information, and humanity has moved slowly along on a trajectory that will ultimately take us to the irrefutable discovery of the Sovereign Integral or the Grand Portal. Now that the time for that discovery is within roughly sixty to seventy years from the time of this writing, information is becoming more specific and opening up a new avenue of exploration—the avenue of heart-centered consciousness, our original state.

My hunch is that those early ideas introduced by Seth about creating our own reality were a catalyst to lay some groundwork for the new avenues of exploration in the coming expansion. Our first experiments with this idea were so human—manifesting the job, the house and car, and relationships we wanted—elementary school stuff. Now we are graduating into learning how to utilize the more complex aspects of this paradigm—engaging the Six Heart Virtues to bring about the expansion of consciousness and the powerful forces of

---

[97] "Definition: Photon," posted by Margaret Rouse, *WhatIs.com* http://whatis.techtarget.com/definition/photon

unity, and acceptance, and equality—not only to ourselves but to our brothers and sisters as well.

We are light beings. We originate from the union of light and sound. When we engage that light from our very essences and transmit it out into the world, we are having more of an effect than we will ever consciously know. The more we grow to understand our awesome heritage and how to use it to bring about our liberation, the more ability we will have to imagine a reality of acceptance and connection.

The time of the suppression of our species here on earth is coming to an end. Liberation is the Light we see on the distant horizon.

Part of our reality is the desire of our Higher Self to experience new energy fields. This one seems a bit more difficult to be consciously aware of; however, when we have situations that lead us into new territory or when we meet new people who have a profound impact on us, all those experiences could be a part of our Higher Self's doing. When we discover new material that resonates with us deeply and leads us toward Oneness, I think that could be a sign from our Higher Self that it is leading us into a new awareness where we will have unique experiences that will expand our energy fields. In many ways our Higher Self's desire to experience new energy fields has the potential of being a part of all the other drivers of reality we just talked about.

It is not outside the realm of possibility that at times our Higher Selves may want to experience the darker energy fields, and we find ourselves in situations that challenge and test us in many ways. What we may perceive as a dark experience may help us to understand a complicated situation from a delicately nuanced place. Do we grow by comprehending a complex circumstance we did not previously understand or had been judgmental about? That could be a part of our Higher Self's plan as well. Obviously, I am just speculating, but it seems plausible.

I will end this chapter with the following poem, written as I grappled with life in duality as an explorer on Planet Earth.

IGNITION

Creative Fires
Ignited by my Heart's Desires
Flickering, tantalizing stirrings Yearnings
--for discovery
--expansion
--realization
--release from deception
--memories of the journey
--integration
--sovereignty

What have I learned?
What was so important
To warrant this estrangement
These feelings of abandonment and betrayal
Lost and alone or so it seemed
How long have I sojourned thus?

Where Am I?
And for what cause?

I have come to recognize
--Loyalty-even in the cruelest of portrayals
--Integrity in same Compassion—
even in the coldest countenances
Acts of love and kindness
in the most hateful of circumstances

I have witnessed
Blindness of absolute power
Driven by restricted narrowness of understanding
Unrestrained
And the unfathomable suffering it wrought

I have been touched by
The saint within the villain
And rooted for their success
Surprised by my own responses
And I have wondered
How that will affect my own redemption

These things I ponder
As I am forced to wonder
and wander

I am intrigued by
Complexity of perception

Enchanted by
Depth of understanding

Repulsed by
Unrelenting cruelty

Warmed by
Expressions of compassion

Weary of
Redundancy and repetitiveness
Yet soothed
By structure and predictability

10

ACCIDENTAL ALCHEMIST

Alchemy:
Changing the frequency of thought,
Altering the harmonics of matter,
And applying the element of love
To create a desired result.
-Jim Self ("Mastering Alchemy") www.TheMindsJournal.com

IS ALCHEMY RELEVANT IN THE NEW PARADIGM?

I HAVE BEEN INTRIGUED FOR many years by the world of archetypes and their effect on us individually and collectively. I became interested in Alchemy as I began recognizing that we progress through stages as we mature and develop spiritually, and that each stage leaves a signature on our personality and consciousness. I have recognized profound and timeless truth in the Alchemical process and see it as a poetic and archetypal way of explaining the stages of the human journey. Now as I am learning new information, I find myself pondering whether or not Alchemy has the potential to show us the next steps that could help humanity journey from the saviorship/evolution model to the mastership/transformation model of existence. [98]

The tradition of Alchemy as spelled out in the Emerald Tablet is believed to have originated from Hermes Trismegistus, also known as the Third Hermes or the Thrice Greatest Hermes. He is linked to the entity Thoth who was said to have incarnated three times, his third incarnation being Hermes.

---

[98] See Appendix D for a table of the Models of Existence

The Emerald Tablet has seven Rubrics or instructions.[99] It is an old and mysterious document, believed to be over 12,000 years old and said to

> … contain a formula for the perfection of anything, whether it be a metal or the human soul. Nearly every medieval alchemist had a copy of it hanging in his laboratory wall and constantly referred to the secret formula it contained.[100]

Consciousness explorer Terrance McKenna described the Emerald Tablet as a "formula for a holographic matrix that is mirrored in the human mind." Whatever it is, this ancient document has endured and continues to surface and intrigue its readers to the present day. It is a system that has been inserted into the fractal hologram that is our world and has stood the test of time by those who monitor the suppression paradigm. For the materially minded, it is seen as a way to turn lead into gold; but for the spiritually minded who seek to understand the archetypes and symbols, it is believed to be a process that can contribute profoundly to human transformation.

The history of the Emerald Tablet is far too detailed to recount here, but for readers interested in this history, I refer you to the article "A Hyper- History of the Emerald Tablet" by Dennis William Hauck for a fascinating read.[101]

THE ALCHEMY OF THE HEART

For our modern era, James Mahu describes Alchemy as an active, day- to-day application of a process that has the potential to transform our emotions: the Alchemy of the Heart.

James explains that energy is never created; it is transformed or recycled. He offers a cutting-edge definition of Alchemy:

> If your human instrument is fear-based, locked in the rigidity of the left, reptilian brain, you're more likely to broadcast fear, insecurity and depression—for example. These emotions are a form of energy and, like all energy, they are conserved. In a sense, energy is never created, it is transformed or recycled. I can take energy that is dense and closed, and I

---

[99] See Appendix C, **The Rubrics of the Emerald Tablet**

[100] Hauck, Dennis William "The Emerald Tablet," *Dennis William Hauck, The Alchemy of Consciousness,* www.dwhauck.com

[101] Hauck, Dennis William, "A Hyper-History of the Emerald Tablet," *Alchemy Lab,* https://www.alchemylab.com/hyper_history.htm

can transform it to an energy that is opening to the frequency of love. I can be an alchemist of energy, and instead of trying to turn iron into gold, I turn anger into kindness…or depression into interconnection…or indifference into compassion. Energy then informs matter. Energy is many things by human standards…it can be physical energy to produce something like work or to play a sport. It can be emotional energy that deals with love or anger. It can be a mental energy that helps us solve a problem or capitalize on an opportunity. It can be spiritual energy that activates and sustains our interest in the culture of the soul. … Being an alchemist is being able to transform energy. To shift energy. Not to let densities build up and calcify, because these are the things that weigh us down and make our abilities to be alchemists for ourselves and others more difficult. [102]

Energy informs matter. Being an alchemist means to be able to transform energy. These are powerful statements—and clues for us to take seriously to heart in our quest to understand and participate in our transformation process.

That leads me to question whether the identified stages of Alchemy could still be relevant as we journey to the threshold of a new paradigm. Can they be applied as an overview to understanding the phases of our lives and the stages of our development? As a student of process, I am curious about the trajectory of information and experiences that prepared me so that I would recognize this wisdom path. After all, each of us is on a path that leads us to every discovery we have ever made. Part of my process is to explore how the incremental treasures of insight I have realized along the way have helped to ready me so that I would recognize the importance of the *WingMakers Material* when it came into my life.

According to Dr. Neruda ("The Fifth Interview"), the WingMakers have been around from the beginning, subtly inserting new concepts into the program to help our species advance and prepare us for the time when the Hologram of Deception will be revealed. That time is almost upon us. We live in a unique time in world history when many diverse ideas and inventions are appearing so rapidly there is no way of stopping them. Concepts can be "hidden in plain sight," on the internet, allowing those who are open and ready to find certain ideas or information in the privacy of their homes. That has never been the case until now, and those of us privileged to be alive at this time are in a unique position.

---

[102] "The April 2013 James Mahu Interview," (on the phone with Mark Hempel) *WingMakers, Tools,* 2008. http://wingmakers.com/wp-content/uploads/2020/08/April-2013-Interview.pdf This interview will also be found in *Collected Works of the WingMakers, Volume I,* soon to be released by Planetwork Press, Egg Harbor Township, NJ.

Until now, "new" ideas have had to be compatible with the prevailing belief systems and subtle enough to diminish the chances of them being detected and removed from the program making progress possible but very slow. Along that line of thinking, I find myself pondering existing tools and wondering which ones might have been planted to help us move along the trajectory towards the ultimate Wisdom Path.

I cannot help but wonder if Spiritual Alchemy is a truth given to us by the WingMakers and delivered in such a way that it could be inserted into the fractal and accepted. For the materially minded, it is only seen as a process to make gold, but for the ones who are awakening or initiated, it is a spiritual process of transformation. Since I began studying the *WingMakers Materials*, Alchemy has taken on an even deeper meaning for me, and I am seeing correlations in both. On the one hand, since Alchemy does not focus on the Grand Portal, it could be dismissed as old school, and it might very well be. But on the other hand, maybe it is one of the tools on the path of preparation to raise our resonance frequency, so we are open and ready to recognize the importance of certain messages when we come across them. The *WingMakers Materials* have created a bridge from the old spiritual paths and belief systems to a completely new way of being.

To paraphrase an old mentor, "the steps to getting there is not necessarily the same as being there." In other words, we need to keep in mind that what may be relevant now could go by the wayside later as our understanding deepens, but the relevancy now could lead us to those understandings. On this plane of existence, we do our work in slow motion increments. Stages we go through in our process may help us see some of the patterns of our development as long as we keep in mind that those steps we take are fragments of the process, and the outcome is ultimately a synergy of our efforts, making the result a unique gestalt.

A SHORT RABBIT HOLE

Before we look at the fragments of the journey as they are presented in Alchemy, let's venture down a short rabbit hole of a few fascinating correlations I found between the symbolism in Alchemy and the *WingMakers Materials*.

The word "wind" takes on a multilevel meaning in light of the encoded name WingMakers. Wind is an especially important component of Alchemy as Hauck explains:

> In most religions, when the godhead takes form, it is either as a fiery light or as a wind…Early Hindu texts state the wind came before light…Wind is the cosmic breath…Islamic texts that state the Wind supports the Throne of God

say the Wind is composed of clouds, air, and countless invisible wings. It is through those "countless wings" that most of us know the Wind. [103]

James Mahu writes in the Introduction to *Collected Works of the WingMakers, Volume I:*

The term WingMakers is encoded:

Wing is derived from the term wind or blow. It is the active force of setting new states into motion.

Makers is the plurality of the co-creators—that being the collective essence of humanity.

Thus, WingMakers means that from the collective essence of humanity new states of consciousness come into being.

This is the meaning of the term WingMakers, and it confers to humanity a new identity.

Humanity is transitioning to become WingMakers.

Hmm: beautiful, poetic, and encoded, these words are inserted into the collective mind for those who are awakening to discover and understand.

Fire is the Archetype of the Sun and also the Archetype of God or Source. The Secret Fire in Alchemy is considered to be the consciousness or Life Force of the individual. [104] It is often represented as a sword, and in Alchemy swords symbolize higher thought and the ability to present higher truth or inspiration that burns brightly in the individual consciousness.

Reading the above brought to my mind the "Chamber Seventeen Painting" of the *Ancient Arrow Project.* [105] This painting depicts a person with something piercing the top of his head.

---

[103] Hauck, Dennis William, *The Emerald Tablet: Alchemy for Personal Transformation*, p. 88, Penguin, Putnam Inc., 375 Hudson St., New York NY 10014, 1999. www.dwhauck.com

[104] Ibid., 112.

[105] Paintings and music are found at *WingMakers*, Mixed Media Gallery, Ancient Arrow Site, Chambers 1 – 24, https://wingmakers.com/art/mixedmediagallery-aa/

Poetry is available at *WingMakers*, Poetry from the Ancient Arrow Site, Chambers 1 – 24, https://wingmakers.com/writings/poetry-ancient-arrow/

Also "Chamber Seventeen Painting," *Collected Works of the WingMakers, Volume I,* p. 455, Planetwork Press, Egg Harbor Township NJ.

Personally, I think it could be a sword. (Not everyone is in agreement that is what it is, but it seems plausible to me.)

An excerpt from the "Chamber Seventeen Poetry, Memories Unbound":

> I am lost words echoing in still canyons. I am a light wave that found itself.
> Darting to earth unsheathed, seeking cover in human skin.

My feeling is that the sword in the head is the Dagger of Light—the Secret Fire. It is easy for me to see that picture as a representation of the Dagger of Light or fragment of Source inserted into the Human Instrument; or it could mean that which brings Light to the Human Instrument.

I came across some correspondences around time and vertical and horizontal axes that piqued my interest and speculative juices. The following correlations will take us further down the rabbit hole, but I think they are worth exploring.

The Emerald Tablet is revered among Alchemists as the secret formula of transformation. It consists of seven rubrics. Hauck explains that

> It is considered to be at the center of Western alchemy and contains concepts crucial to understanding alchemy. It is believed to have been brought to Egypt over 12,000 years ago by mysterious visitors. The Tablet contains the essence of alchemical philosophy and has been credited as a source of both alchemy and the scientific method. [106]

Terrance McKenna called it a "formula for a holographic matrix." [107]

The Second Rubric of the Emerald Tablet is called the Doctrine of Correspondences. It basically states that what is in the realm Below corresponds to what is in the realm Above. We have all heard that statement many times: "as above, so below." Now let's apply it to some possibilities.

According to Hauck, A vertical axis is entered during meditation to go from below to above. A horizontal axis is considered to be the normal everyday world. [108]

Vertical and horizontal axes are referred to in the *WingMakers Materials* and according to Dr. Neruda could be utilized to accomplish time travel. Dr. Neruda talks of Vertical Time

---

[106] Hauck, Dennis William "The EMERALD TABLET," *Alchemy Guild*, http://www.azothalchemy.org/emerald_tablet.htm
[107] Ibid.
[108] Ibid.

as a way to see the future and also to manipulate it. Dr. N— "Vertical time has to do with the simultaneous experience of all time, and horizontal time has to do with the continuity of time in linear, moment-to-moment experiences." He explains later in this interview that they believe that time travelers may be able to enter vertical time and alter it and discusses the implications of the effect on horizontal time and how much needs to be taken into consideration to do such a thing. The vertical axis of reality is known by Alchemists. We live our lives in horizontal time. [109]

Stimulating thoughts to ponder and explore in one's quiet moments, and probably the tip of the iceberg of tidbits of insight we could find.

SOME STANDARDS OF CRITERIA TO HELP WITH DISCERNMENT

Since my discovery of the *WingMakers Materials*, my standard has been whether information teaches unity and connection that can potentially guide one to the path of heart-centeredness or does it perpetuate separation and keep one on the path of one-upmanship and ego-gratification. If a teaching or concept perpetuates separation and discourages intuition by downgrading the feminine or the intuitive faculties, it is not information I am interested in.

I find it helpful to weed out old beliefs and processes by examining them from this list of benchmarks:

- *Do they expand my understanding of our connectedness as a species?*
- *Do they trigger a compassionate response?*
- *Will they help me transform because they lead me to my heart and encourage equality?*
- *Do the ideas encourage unity and connection?*
- *Are the ideas inclusive and accepting of all humans regardless of race, color, ethnicity, gender identity, gender, or beliefs?*
- *Is heart-centeredness in one's interactions with others encouraged?*
- *Is listening to one's intuition encouraged?*

Keeping these standards in mind, let us take a look at some existing principles. Does anything in the description of Alchemy fuel our new consciousness and process

---

[109] Mahu, James, *Collected Works of the WingMakers, Volume I*, "The First Interview of Dr. Jamisson Neruda" pp. 278-279. Mahu, James, "First Interview," *WingMakers*, Neruda Interviews, https://wingmakers.com/writings/nerudainterviews/firstinterview/

and assist our journey in understanding the transformation process better? Just what is "the Alchemical process" and what is its significance to our discussion? This next segment will explore the stages of the Alchemical process. The source for the terminology to describe the stages was found in *The Emerald Tablet* by Dennis William Hauck.[110]

One could ask whether or not it is even important to include this material on Alchemy. My curiosity has sent me down this path as I am interested in what information could be hiding in plain sight, now that we know what to look for. Are the stages below relevant to inspire our readiness for heart-centered living, possibly bringing us to the threshold and/ or beyond?

For those locked in the old paradigm program with its emphasis on the development of the intellect, a restructuring of our belief systems concerning the role of the heart in our transformation will need to be explored. Our current paradigm has relegated the heart to the role of being a mechanical pump, and if recognized emotionally, it is downplayed as ineffective and sentimental.

Our first order of business in preparation for the new paradigm is to be open to the possibility that our hearts play a much more important part, not only in our spiritual development, but in our ability to become sovereign. As we explore Alchemy and its stages, it will be helpful to remain open to how our hearts may play a significant role in our continuing development, because heart-centered living is the key that unlocks the prison door of the Hologram of Deception and reunites us with our original selves.

Most of us bring psychological issues and many levels of programming to the table as we begin the journey of awakening and transforming. Our initial inner work is usually an intellectual exercise as we learn how to recognize how we have been indoctrinated. Gradually, as we move through the stages, at some point our hearts will become more actively involved in our process. It is this preparation and releasing of old programs that will put us squarely on the path to recognizing the value and importance of living a heart-centered life. This will open us to any teachings that encourage unity and taking responsibility for our behaviors and beliefs.

It is our knee-jerk response to look for a savior or guru outside of ourselves to "take on the responsibility for our sins" because we have been programmed to do that through the saviorship/evolution model of existence.[111]

Choosing to live a heart-centered life engages our inner guidance and begins a

---

[110] Hauck, Dennis William, *The Emerald Tablet: Alchemy for Personal Transformation*, the Penguin Group, Penguin Putnam Inc., 375 Hudson Street, New York, NY 10014, 1999.
For more information about Alchemy: http://www.levity.com/alchemy/home.html
[111] Refer to Appendix D - **Models of Existence**

transformation within us through the development of a Behavioral Intelligence that is capable of dismantling the program that has held us captive for eons. It is a far-reaching and significant paradigm shift.

So, keeping in mind that we are all on a trajectory to become restored to our Sovereign Integral state of consciousness, let's see if the stages defined below can give us any helpful or useful insights as we continue our transformational journey.

STAGES OF ALCHEMY

1. Calcination: The stage in our lives when we start seeing the tricks, illusions, misleading beliefs, and harmful habits of our egos and put them aside so that we can finally explore what lies beneath. *www.lonerwolf.com*

(In chemistry, calcination is a process of heating a substance over an open flame until it is reduced to ash. The fire of calcination is a purging, whitening fire.)

In the beginning, we are imprinted with the expectations, rules, and limitations of the culture and family we are born into. During childhood, our pliable and impressionable psyches are formed through the "heat" or "fire" of everyday experiences.

This is the programming of the Hologram of Deception. With few exceptions, everyone born into this plane of existence has been programmed in this way, indoctrinating us into the beliefs of our culture and family. If we look at the Hierarchy of Needs model as originally introduced by Abraham Maslow, [112] the first three levels on the hierarchy of needs pyramid are incorporated into this first step:

- *Physiological - such as air, food, water, sex, sleep*
- *Safety - such as secure environment, employment, resources, etc.*
- *Belongingness - love, friendship, intimacy, family, etc.*

When these initial needs are met, then we begin to climb that hierarchy to the next level which includes developing confidence and self- esteem through achievement and gaining respect through our work. These steps are a part of our initial imprinting to become productive, social beings who can function in the world. Once these first needs are met, we are at a place in our lives where if we are inclined to do so, we can begin the self-actualization/awakening process.

---

[112] "Maslow's Hierarchy of Needs," *learning theories,*
http://www.learning-theories.com/maslows-hierarchy-of-needs.html (downloadable PDF)

I want to qualify this discussion on the Alchemical process by stating that for those of us who are adults and have been raised in and programmed by the old paradigm, I think we will be able to see many if not all of these stages as we review our life's journey.

As new groups of souls are born onto the planet to be a part of the Grand Portal discovery in some way, it is highly likely that that they are arriving immune to or able to see through and override some if not most of the programming we have received. If that is the case, their perception of life and process will be different in many ways from those of us who have had to overcome the old school programming and navigate the bridge between paradigms.

An example of what I am talking about can be illustrated by the teens who survived the Parkland shooting in Florida in February 2018. They presented the world with a strong sense of unity and were not afraid to speak truth to power for what they believed. These young, Accidental Alchemists were able to turn hate into compassion and pain into understanding and valor with their compelling ability to bring about walk-outs and gatherings around the world in favor of gun control and other human rights. I found them profoundly inspiring to watch.

It is this writer's opinion that the Florida tragedy was an activation for these young people to their purpose on Life's Stage. They are a fresh cohort of pioneers for a world-changing new paradigm as they come from a place in their hearts that has the power to move standards and model a new way of being in the world that will continue to gain momentum in the years to come.

Some people are born searching, and some are jolted by a life event that becomes the kindling for the calcination fire of Alchemy. This first stage includes the very first steps to breaking down the ego and the self-sabotaging behaviors that go along with ego-centeredness.

The challenging experiences of our lives are like piled kindling. The questions we ask can be likened to matches thrown on the kindling that lights a small fire and begins to burn away old ideas. Little by little old overused and discarded perceptions find their way to stoke the fire within.

There are times when we may become so caught up in the fire within that we begin to lose interest in everyday life and the manifest world. Our defenses might begin to break down as we become aware of self-perpetuating delusions, so much so that we are not as interested in attaining material wealth and gratification as before. Our belief systems start to crumble. As this starts to happen, our Inner Guidance System can become more active, sending us messages that things are not quite right and stimulating us to look deeper. This could be the beginning of being pulled into an active relationship with the transformative trajectory.

2. Dissolution: The gradual or sudden breaking up of the tormented sense of self: ceasing to identify so strongly with the ego to make way for the Higher Self to emerge. *www.lonerwolf.com*

(The dissolving of the ashes of calcination in water or acid.)

Once the fire of transformation begins, buried material surfaces from the depths of our consciousness, and a dissolving begins. In the Alchemical process during this stage, a further breaking down of our artificial structures takes place. We begin to work with the rejected parts of ourselves and become aware of some of our ego drives and games. At first, we may be more aware of these games in others around us. If we are humble enough to realize this, we will see that these people are often acting as our mirrors and playing back our projections to us so we can see ourselves more clearly. Many of us go through a period of psychological exploration. Inner turmoil often sends us searching. This stage is usually still mostly brain or intellectual work, but it is still helping us to identify less with our false sense of self, and it is a beginning of engaging our hearts.

Hauck has this to say about the stage of dissolution:

> Dissolution works on the heart…to release buried emotions that conceal or distort our true nature. Basically this means showing our pain and revealing our wounds…. It is an unconscious process in which our conscious mind allows the surfacing of previously buried material. [113]

This stage can also be brought on by an illness or misfortune that forces us to look more deeply into ourselves and our behavior patterns.

3. Separation: The process of allowing buried thoughts and emotions to surface so that we can become conscious of them: isolating and identifying sources of pain within us so that healing can occur. *www.lonerwolf.com*

On a psychological level, we begin to separate out our beliefs, examining them, questioning them, and releasing the ones that don't fit into our developing understanding. Once we start breaking down our hardened habits and beliefs, new energy becomes available to us that had been buried during our original calcination. This stage can bring us to the beginning of the rediscovery of our essence and the reclaiming of our creative and visionary ideals previously rejected by our rational mind or the society that has programmed us.

This is the stage where we begin to separate our thoughts and feelings from those

---

[113] Hauck, Dennis William, *The Emerald Tablet: Alchemy for Personal Transformation*, the Penguin Group, Penguin Putnam Inc., 375 Hudson Street, New York, NY 10014, 1999.

around us. We may be working on freeing our hearts by learning to forgive. We face our feelings authentically and experience our anger and our guilt and frustrations. I wrote extensively about my own process at this stage in my former book *BFTOB* in the chapter about Archetypes and the *Phantom of the Opera* and the *Elephant Man*. [114] I also wrote about how I learned to recognize and separate my feelings from my mother's in Part Five of this book in the chapter "My Heart's Unveiling."

4. Conjunction: The stage of inner growth that involves inviting the Light to illuminate our darkness so that understanding, acceptance, and unconditional self-love can take place. While in the previous step we separated and learned to distinguish all the separate feelings and thoughts within, Conjunction provides the inner space—the simmering— that is required for us to accept all the parts of our authentic self truly and honestly. *www. lonerwolf.com*

This is a turning point. In the Alchemical process, conjunction represents the union of the masculine and feminine and the beginning of the formation of a belief system that embraces both. It is the stage of acceptance of all parts of our authentic selves. Intuitive insight is increased. For example, this was the stage in my own journey when I began to try and understand the deeper meanings of the polarities of male and female and to work on the reconciliation of issues I brought from childhood with the male gender. I was beginning to understand that it was important to accept both polarities as a part of myself. That helped me come to terms with those gender issues in my own life so I could bury the hatchet.

This stage can be the beginning of the heart starting to open. As long as we are locked into the enmity of gender wars, our hearts will remain closed or at least partly closed. It makes sense that any issues that keep us polarized need to be resolved and this stage may begin that process for us. At the same time, Valor or speaking truth to power is also an important part of our growth process.

For instance, if we are in a relationship that oppresses or dominates us, we might begin to try and break free from that stranglehold. Reconciling domination/oppression issues may result in the end of a relationship, or it may result in the healing of a relationship. This stage is about unification of polarities within one's own psyche. In my previous book *BFTOB*, I devoted an entire chapter to a process called "squares" that helps one work with the polarities of one's life. If you are interested in better understanding how deceptive a part polarity plays in your everyday life, this exercise can be found in Appendix B and will provide profound insight. [115]

---

[114] Batey, Lark Aleta, "*Breaking Free from the Tyranny of Beliefs: A Revolution in Consciousness*," Balboa Press, 2012.
[115] See Appendix B—**Squares**

5. Fermentation: Occurs in two parts: putrefaction and Spiritization. Putrefaction is the decomposition of our former selves; the process of inner death by which the old elements of our conscious and unconscious minds are allowed to rot and decompose. (Dark night of the soul) Spiritization is the stage where we look at the world in a new light. It involves letting go of all the aspects of ourselves and our lives that don't serve or contribute to our spiritual transformation. *www.lonerwolf.com*

Once we have begun to free ourselves from the prison of our belief systems, we become open to inspiration and insights from our Inner Authentic Self, and that promotes the acceleration of growth and a process of rebirth. Hauck describes this stage as:

> . . .flooding the mind with the meaningful and profoundly real images from something totally beyond us that lies at the edge of our personal reality. It is like a swinging door between one level of consciousness and another, between soul and spirit, between matter and mind. [116]

In my attempt at synthesis, I am going out on a limb here in saying that in the New Paradigm language of the WingMakers, this might be a stage in our process where we may be able to recognize the guidance of the *Wholeness Navigator* as it seems to become more active in our transformational journey. James Mahu describes the Wholeness Navigator in the following excerpt from the WingMakers Glossary:

> All human life is embedded with a Wholeness Navigator. It is the core wisdom. It draws the human instrument to perceive fragmentary existence as a passageway into wholeness and unity. The Wholeness Navigator pursues wholeness above all else yet is often blown off course by the energies of structure, polarity, linear time and separatist cultures that dominate terra-earth. The Wholeness Navigator is the heart of the entity consciousness, and it knows the secret root exists even though it may be intangible to the human senses. It is this very condition of accepting the interconnectedness of life that places spiritual growth as a priority in one's life. [117]

In the E-paper "The Rising Heart," James gives us more information when he tells us

---

[116] Hauck, Dennis William, *The Emerald Tablet: Alchemy for Personal Transformation*, the Penguin Group, Penguin Putnam Inc., 375 Hudson Street, New York, NY 10014, 1999.

[117] Mahu, James and John Berges, "The WingMakers Glossary, Wholeness Navigator," p. 673, *Collected Works of the WingMakers, Volume I*, edited by John Berges, Egg Harbor, NJ: Planetwork Press, 2013.

that the Wholeness Navigator is the light body and "seer of reality within the individual identity." James explains that the Wholeness Navigator is

> the portal of guidance within the one who is separated from unity by the veils of illusion. It is the voice within the void that calls to your mind and heart, beckoning its recognition and restoration as your true identity and that of all others as well. It is the connection between heart and mind that allows for true creation to occur. It is the telepathic portal that sees and hears the divine intelligence and then activates its expression within the lower realms by mere presence. [118]

6. Distillation: Here we are planting the seed for the unborn, transpersonal self—one that is free from the distinctions of the collective and the individual. Here we purify the spirit freeing it from destructive forms of ego. This can be done with various forms of contemplation or meditation. [119]

We know we have arrived at this stage when we are able to formulate our own idea of how we fit into the larger scheme of things. At this stage we are beginning to find our own truth. Hauck explains that

> Distillation takes us into the rarified realm of the One Mind. . . It is the purification of the unborn Self—all that we truly are and can be spiritually. [120]

Another paragraph from the definition of the Wholeness Navigator seems to fit here:

> How do you access the secret root? Its portal of observation can be broadly defined as the integral awareness. This is allowing yourself to be aware of how you are integrated to life outside of your physical body. It is the feeling and perception that you are a holographic entity that is woven throughout all things and time, and when you touch into this feeling you recall a frequency

---

[118] Mahu, James, "The Rising Heart," *WingMakers*, 6 Heart Virtues, https://wingmakers.com/writings/sixheartvirtues/the-rising-heart/
[119] "The Seven Stages of Alchemical Transformation: A Spiritual Metaphor (Infographic)," *Labyrinthos*, https://labyrinthos.co/blogs/learn-tarot-with-labyrinthos-academy/the-seven-stages-of-alchemical-transformation-a-spiritual-metaphor-infographic Paraphrased from the description of Distillation.
[120] Hauck, Dennis William, *The Emerald Tablet: Alchemy for Personal Transformation*, the Penguin Group, Penguin Putnam Inc., 375 Hudson Street, New York, NY 10014, 1999.

of your consciousness that is the Wholeness Navigator—the mysterious Allness that is nurtured by the secret root.

This is not a state of being that the human instrument will attain. Rather, it is a feeling of oneness and wholeness that the human instrument can glimpse momentarily and, as a result, transform its understanding of its purpose. [121]

7. Coagulation: We arrive at the place where we are more consistently directed and guided by our Authentic Self. (Wholeness Navigator?) We have come to a stage of realization where we are able to temper our superficial ego longings. This entire process could be likened to the gestation and birth of a new consciousness within our psyche.

Just as a new baby has to learn the language of the culture and family it is born into, this new consciousness also has its own way of communicating through the spectrum of Love expressed by the Six Heart Virtues: Appreciation, Compassion, Forgiveness, Humility, Understanding and Valor.

We are programmed to project God outside of ourselves. It can be a challenging adjustment at first to learn to communicate with our Presence by going within, let alone summon one of the virtues to participate as we navigate our life experiences. Here we are beginning to understand how the inner and outer worlds reflect each other.

It is a learning curve, but very much worth the effort. As we learn to engage and work with the Six Heart Virtues, we grow in our ability to respond to our inner guidance in everyday situations, and in that process develop a Behavioral Intelligence that will become a way of life. As we do, these energies grow within us and inspire even deeper insights. The language of our origins is always there communicating with us through our feelings and emotions. An uncomfortable or gnawing feeling or emotion is an inner signal that a conflict exists between our beliefs and our actions. What is this conflict trying to say? Is this feeling or emotion heart-centered or self- centered? Is this conflict pointing to another way for us to be opening our hearts in some way or is it demonstrating where our hearts are closed?

As I look through these phases with a fresh eye, I believe that for those of us who are interested in identifying the trajectory of our development, these stages of an archetypal path can be used to gauge our progress in preparation for recognizing the next transformational paradigm.

I am thinking that the stages in this Alchemical model can be utilized as a bridge between the saviorship/evolution model and the mastership/ transformation model of existence. Once

---

[121] Mahu, James and John Berges, "The WingMakers Glossary, Wholeness Navigator," p. 673, *Collected Works of the WingMakers, Volume I*, edited by John Berges, Egg Harbor, NJ: Planetwork Press, 2013.

we learn to turn inwardly for direction, we are taking those first tentative steps towards the transformation/mastership model.

Labyrinthos.com under the title "The Seven Stages of Alchemical Transformation" provides a succinct description of each of the stages in both chemical and psychological terms that might be helpful as a review here:

- *Calcination: Chemical—heating a substance over a flame until it turns to ashes; Psychological—breaking down the ego and attachment to the worldly.*
- *Dissolution: Chemical—Dissolving ashes of substances into water; Psychological—Immersion into the unconscious. Conscious mind releases control, leading to a resurfacing of parts of ourselves that were hidden.*
- *Separation: Chemical—isolating and filtering the products of dissolution; Psychological—Review resurfaced material and decide what to separate or integrate. What parts of our shadows can we learn from, and what hinders us?*
- *Conjunction: Chemical—Form a new substance from the separated elements we choose to keep; Psychological—merging of the* conscious and the unconscious aspects of the self to a single essence. The union of dualities allows for the true self to emerge.
- *Fermentation: Chemical—Induce chemical breakdown of substance with the bacteria or other micro-organisms. Psychological— Initiation of spiritual awakening through testing the strength of the solution. To first create wine, grapes must rot. Adversity and challenge breeds resilience.*
- *Distillation—Chemical—boil and condense solution to increase purity. Psychological—Purification of the spirit-where we make sure the ego no longer controls us, giving us ability to appreciate the beauty of the collective self.*
- *Coagulation: Chemical-transformation to a solid state; Psychological—the union of matter and spirit that allows us to perceive the world without dualities, and to perceive life on all levels of consciousness; this is similar to the state of Nirvana and supposed end result of the famed Philosopher's Stone.* [122]

---

[122] "The Seven Stages of Alchemical Transformation: A Spiritual Metaphor (Infographic)," *Labyrinthos*, https://labyrinthos.co/blogs/learn-tarot-with-labyrinthos-academy/the-seven-stages-of-alchemical- transformation-a-spiritual-metaphor-infographic
I found this website to have some helpful definitions of the alchemical process.
I also used some information from this article: "7 Stages of Spiritual Alchemy," *Ascension Energies*, https://ascensionenergies.com/2017/06/16/7-stages-of-spiritual-alchemy/

We can look at these stages of psychological unfoldment as ways of helping us recognize the stringent hold our programmed beliefs have on us. Once we begin to break free from the program, we find ourselves in a vast landscape of unexplored territory that can become our new way of being.

For centuries humanity has taken various long evolutionary paths of spiritual development. The stages under discussion have the potential of bringing us to the threshold where we discover a more efficient short path— that of *heart-centered living.* Our ultimate journey is to understand the transformative power of the Six Heart Virtues and how they create our Heart's Intelligence when they are expressed in our everyday life. I will be discussing the Six Heart Virtues at length in Part Five of this book.

Our species has been fully indoctrinated into the importance of the intelligence of the mind. As long as we are immersed in that ego-driven program, the Six Heart Virtues won't have much attraction or seem highly effective. A powerful psychological and spiritual shift within the individual must take place in order to take that leap away from an ego-centered spirituality that projects God outside oneself toward a desire for a heart- centered, inclusive-seeking spirituality that honors our Source within. At some point in our searching—it can be during any stage of our process—we will begin to gravitate towards experiencing a sense of unity and connectedness. When that happens, we put ourselves on a different trajectory— that of the heart, and once there, we have the potential to shorten our path and become the Ultimate State of Awakened Consciousness as a Sovereign Integral.

In the context of all we have explored above, it is my belief that the Alchemical process can be useful to help us transition from the evolution/saviorship model to the transformation/mastership model where we can begin to accelerate our development as heart-centered beings.

You are the soul of the universe, and your name is Love. Rumi

EXPLORATION

Take another look at the stages of Alchemy. Can you identify those stages in your life? Journal your findings.

11

ARCHETYPES THAT KEEP US IN SEPARATION

ARCHETYPE DEFINED

DENNIS WILLIAM HAUCK, ALCHEMIST AND author, gives one of the most helpful definitions of *archetype* I have come across to date, and one that might help bring more clarity to the discussion that follows:

> The powers of Above and Below continue to manifest themselves in ways we cannot comprehend until we access the levels from which they emanate. Actually, this is the most concise statement of the concept of archetypes, which are primordial ideals or independent forces that impose pre-existing patterns of organization on the various levels of manifest reality. [123]

Hauck's explanation of levels of manifestation helps us to better understand how humanity finds ways to manifest realities from the lowest levels of existence to the highest.

The idea of levels of manifestation also brings to mind Dr. Neruda's discussion of vertical time and horizontal time in his "First Interview" in the *Ancient Arrow Project* as presented in the previous chapter. He explains that time is not exclusively linear...it is vertical with every moment in existence stacked upon the next and adds that "Vertical time has to do with the simultaneous experience of all time, and horizontal time has to do with the[1] continuity of time in linear, moment-by-moment experiences." [124] Layers and

---

[123] Hauck, Dennis William, *The Emerald Tablet: Alchemy for Personal Transformation*, the Penguin Group, Penguin Putnam Inc., 375 Hudson Street, New York, NY 10014, 1999.

[124] Mahu, James and John Berges, *The Ancient Arrow Project*, "The First Interview of Dr. Jamisson Neruda," *Collected Works of the WingMakers, Volume I*, edited by John Berges, Egg Harbor, NJ: Planetwork Press, 2013. Mahu, James, "First Interview," *WingMakers*, Neruda Interviews, https://wingmakers.com/writings/nerudainterviews/firstinterview/

levels in consciousness—fascinating ideas to ponder. What ramifications do they have in our everyday life, in our responses and perceptions of personal and public events, and in stimulating our imaginations?

The mysterious process of programming us for our journey on Earth begins in our DNA, is highly active while we are in-utero, and accelerates even more after birth in our surroundings and environment. Through the subconscious or Genetic Mind, [125] we are indoctrinated into the beliefs of the culture and family we are born into.

According to Carl Jung, archetypes are universal and cultural prototypes that reside in the subconscious. They provide a momentary shape to the energy that flows through the universe. They are original energy patterns embedded in the collective unconscious and shared by people of every ethnic and racial origin through dreams and artistic expressions. They are resonating fields of consciousness and exist as very real dimensional energies. Archetypal energetic patterns are responsible for creating our belief systems and influencing our behaviors as we live our everyday experiences. When we express a particular behavior, we are activating the energy of a specific archetype and giving it expression in the world. We give it power by the intensity of our focus with that particular behavior.

Depending upon the level they are manifesting from, archetypal energies can be invasive energies engaged for the purposes of control, or they can be energies that contribute to our awakening and transformation. Both types of archetypes are active on this planet, and our personal agenda will determine which one we draw to us to influence us on a daily basis. Our human instruments are programmed to respond to archetypes that will keep us distracted and in separation. When we ponder the idea that we might have been programmed to respond to dark and divisive energies to the point that we block out light and unifying ones, we can understand the ramifications of the layers of meaning and power embedded in the archetypes discussed in this chapter.

On the flip side, our original DNA holds the memory of the archetypal energies that will help to free us from the hologram. It is up to us to choose.

When we find ourselves caught up in an intense expression of behavior, we are probably under the influence of an archetype. Let's explore some typical human behaviors and see how the archetypal pattern is expressed.

---

[125] See **Genetic Mind**, Appendix A - Glossary

AUTHORITY ARCHETYPE

We have all seen both benevolent and malevolent ways of expressing authority depending on the personality of the one in authority. What are some of the characteristics a person in authority might have?

- An expectation of obedience from those they have authority over;
- A rationale within their own minds of why they are right to enforce their views and directions;
- A sense of power and control either earned or assumed;
- A sense of responsibility for whatever or whoever they have authority over—such as a teacher to a student, a doctor and patient, an employer to an employee;
- A repertoire of knowledge and experience that gives them a sense of conviction of their authority—this can include recognition from others. We see this in all walks of life: certain individuals reach a level of ability that people recognize and respect. Parents have authority over their children; the law has authority over us, etc.

There are many other characteristics of the archetype of authority, but the ones listed above give us enough to get the point. We could say that the energy pattern of authority can be expressed through some or all of the following behaviors: expectation of obedience or acceptance, rationale of rightness, feeling of/or having power and control, a sense of responsibility, repertoire of knowledge and experience, and strong conviction. These behavioral characteristics by themselves are not negative or positive.

If these behaviors are expressed by someone with a large ego and narcissistic personality, they will elicit far different responses and outcomes than someone who has authority and a strong sense of respect for humanity. If we look at authority as a viable archetypal energy pattern, then we can contemplate how we want to see it manifest in our lives and world, and our choice of behaviors in living with this archetype will take on new and more meaningful dimensions. The behaviors of a person in authority give momentum to the archetype of authority, making it more powerful whether for self-serving purposes or the welfare of humanity. The more we understand that dynamic, the more we realize it is vital to be mindful of who or what we pledge allegiance to. We engage the archetypal energies or patterns of transformation when we change our focus of authority from self- serving to serving the welfare of humanity.

As human beings we have been programmed to defer to the power of the hierarchies of this world and the authority they wield. Once we become aware of our origins as Sovereign Beings and our connection at the soul level to our Source, our internal guidance will become the authority that will bring us to a new state of unity consciousness.

GREED ARCHETYPE

Let's look at the archetypal behaviors of greed and how they are expressed in the behaviors of an individual:

- Greed is a selfish and excessive desire for more of something than is needed;
- Greed can manifest as envy, selfishness, gluttony, materialism, possessiveness, manipulation;
- Greed can cause a person to be focused exclusively on making money or acquiring material possessions to the exclusion of anything or anyone;
- Greed can cause a person to be disloyal to others if they get in the way of the acquisition the individual is focused on;
- Greed brings the energies of power and control into play;
- Greed is perpetual dissatisfaction, always wanting more;
- Greed for power can cause someone to manipulate themselves into a position of authority whether they are qualified for that position or not;
- Greed is the opposite of generosity and altruism.

The more one dwells on the excessive desires for power, control, and materialism, or whatever it is they have set their sights on, the stronger this energy will grow within the individual, until it takes over the personality. The person then embodies the energy field of greed, and everything they focus on will expand their field of greed. I think we can safely say that this energy is continually used in a context that is self-serving. For those who use their amassed fortunes to serve in some way, they are transforming greed into generosity or altruism.

SELF-RIGHTEOUSNESS ARCHETYPE

The archetype of self-righteousness is an interesting one to contemplate as it is probably one of the most subtle and far-reaching energy patterns on the planet that can become ominously destructive. Once self- righteous behaviors take over a person, the individual is insufferable to be around, and their behaviors can grow until they become dangerous. Self-righteousness embodies the characteristics of greed for authoritarianism.

It is probably safe to categorize all dictators and religious fanatics as self-righteous. Their energy has an especially powerful influence on those suffering from a poor or low self-image. This archetypal energy bestows an ability to manipulate by imbuing the individual with a sense of purpose and power that can be very seductive to one who feels powerless. The insidious spreading of this energy field gives it increasing power. We can see how dangerous self-righteousness is when we think of the heartless brutality, viciousness, and cold-bloodedness of ISIS (Islamic State in Iraq and Syria) and Al Qaida, the Third Reich, and before that, the Inquisition and the Crusades. We saw that in Alexandria, Egypt when the fanatical Christians brutally murdered Hypatia. Self-righteousness spreads its sinister energy like a cruel plague into ethnic cleansing and bigoted behaviors of all kinds, and it is both subtle and rampant in all politics or any issue that polarizes us.

Examples of self-righteousness:

- A sense of superiority;
- Feelings of better than;
- Moral smugness;
- Confidence that everyone would be better off believing a particular belief system and doing whatever is necessary to enforce it on the population;
- Condescending personality that puts people down in order to feel superior—racism and misogyny come to mind as current examples;
- Arrogant and unyielding;
- Self-centered, egotistical;
- Holier than thou attitude;
- Judging attitude towards everyone;
- Pious and sanctimonious;
- Opposite of self-righteous would be humility, thoughtfulness, respect, understanding, live and let live, acceptance, appreciation of the differences of others, inclusive thinking, and behaviors.

Self-righteousness originates in the rationale of the mind and does not recognize the Heart's Intelligence. We transform self-righteousness when we realize that all are from the same Source, and no one is "better-than" another. Everyone on this planet is having experiences for the WHOLE, and everyone has a blueprint and soul purpose. We contribute to the transformation of our world when we accept that each individual at the entity level is equal in the eyes of Source even when the un-awakened ego personality exhibits behaviors that are unacceptable. That doesn't mean we should not engage the virtue of Valor by speaking truth to power when we see an injustice being inflicted on another or do whatever we can to stop mistreatment of another being, human or otherwise.

We involve the virtue of Understanding when we realize that we do not know what forces are at work in an individual's blueprint in terms of what they will have to experience to ultimately awaken. This helps us to recognize that some are asleep and acting out of their programming. Understanding that the world resonates on a spectrum of frequencies is helpful in allowing us to see the big picture and curtail our tendency to be judgmental. The bottom line is that we all have the same ultimate birthright.

One might ask: "Why are such energies as self-righteousness, greed, power, and control part of the powerful field of energy patterns from which we draw our focus and perceptions?" If we think back to the myth of our origins and the definition of archetype, we are reminded that we were programmed to stay in separation. Contentious archetypal energies keep us in the third dimension, in duality, and fighting amongst ourselves; they exist to distract us and keep us polarized and to give us not only an experience of the manifest world, but a challenge within it that tests our character and teaches us valuable lessons about ourselves.

Those who manifest archetypal behaviors such as self-righteousness may well have different belief systems, but their outcome behaviors are nearly identical. Each side believes the fanatics have to be stopped and armies have to be formed to fight against them. We keep ourselves suppressed and polarized through these actions and reactions and distracted from the true meaning of our existence. This is exactly what those in power and control want. Divide and conquer has always worked to maintain suppression and deception.

Another way we have strived to make sense of troubling behaviors that affect and hurt others in distressing situations all over the world is to personify those destructive behaviors that have become symbolic of evil or retribution with labels such as the Devil or Satan or the punishing wrath of God. We have created elaborate mythologies, such as God and the Devil fighting for our souls, to explain these powerful forces. A natural disaster or adverse event in one's life is too often thought of as the wrath of God for some wrongdoing that amplifies the fear of God programmed into our psyches. We become obsessed with the ideas of who is good and who is evil and deserves to be punished. In this way, we remain locked in separation, fighting a battle we cannot win because once the archetypal forces have been invited in, they become the lens through which we perceive reality and keep us polarized.

ARCHETYPE OF AMBITION

Our country was founded on the idea that ambition would take us anywhere we wanted to go if we were determined and worked diligently. We praise and encourage ambitious people. Let's take a look at the nature of ambition from *The Free Dictionary:* [126]

- Earnest desire for some type of achievement or distinction, as wealth or fame and the willingness to strive for it;
- The object or state desired or sought after;
- Desire for work or activity;
- Strong desire for success;
- Power hungry, status seeking, a drive to acquire power;
- Trait of being highly motivated;
- Enterprise, longing, drive, passion, enthusiasm;
- Fervency—a mixture of ambition and ruthlessness;
- *Ambition is as hollow as the soul of an echo*—Anon;
- *Ambition is like hunger; it obeys no law but its appetite*—Josh Billings;
- *Ambition is like the sea wave, which the more you drink the more you thirst*—Alfred Lord Tennyson;
- *Zeal without knowledge is like an expedition to a man in the darkness*—John Newton.

The above definitions and quotes present some of the ways we are programmed to think about ambition. It can begin as a benign drive to accomplish a goal. Whether or not that goal is reached unsullied by some of the self-serving drives already discussed is the challenge. Is a certain ambition so important to one that they will resort to ruthlessness and chicanery to accomplish it? Or is the ambition to accomplish an objective an altruistic one that serves the greater good? Do we serve our egos through an ambition to fulfill the drive of greed and power, or are we ambitious in a heart-centered way that serves and contributes something positive to the world?

---

[126] http://www.thefreedictionary.com/ambition

BULLY ARCHETYPE

A bully is described as a person who uses superior strength or influence to intimidate others and try to force them to do what he or she wants.

Synonyms from Googling the word *bully* include persecute, oppress, tyrannize, browbeat, harass, torment, intimidate, strong-arm, dominate, persecute, oppress, pressurize, force, goad, prod, and badger.

Dictionary.com describes a bully as "a blustering, quarrelsome, overbearing person who habitually badgers and intimidates smaller or weaker people."

September 2016 gave us a living breathing example of a bully operating on the political stage in the Republican candidate for president, Donald Trump (DT). He clearly embodies this energy pattern, and examining his words and exploits is a way to explore this archetype.

The 2016 Presidential campaign was a glaring example of the bully oppressor and the one being oppressed by bullying being played out on the national stage at the archetypal level.

This campaign was also of great historical significance because the first female ever, Hillary Rodham Clinton, (HRC) was nominated as a candidate for President of the United States. This was momentous on the metaphysical stage as well as the physical stage. The feminine has been oppressed and a suppressed victim of bullies for centuries.

The archetypes of the bully and the bullied have generated so much energy in this world that they actually manifested two people who embodied those energies and played this drama out on the larger-than-life world stage of a political election. This is significant for us as a species. Regardless of your political leanings, please bear with me, as I think there are some significant points that are illustrative of some powerful forces alive and well in the human psyche.

HRC embodies the archetype of the feminine and all that the feminine has endured in this country. She rose up from very humble beginnings. Her childhood experiences forced her to develop resilience and the tenacity to rise above her humble station to become one of the most recognized women in the world. She is intelligent and capable, a wife and mother and grandmother as well as a professional woman, author, and accomplished politician. She has experienced many of the difficult life issues that many women face and endure every single day, including an unfaithful spouse. For a man intelligence and capability would be enough to qualify as a Presidential candidate, but because she is a woman, she was held to an almost impossible standard.

The 2016 Republican nominee DT embodies and is a caricature of the archetype of the bully and male as oppressor and all that has kept the feminine suppressed. He is a white misogynist male who comes from a wealthy real estate family; he was and is privileged and had his status handed to him through the family fortune. He has shown over and over again by his mistreatment of people he has hired that he has very few scruples when it comes to dealing fairly with people. His countless bankruptcies inform us that he isn't as business savvy as he would like us to believe. He does not know or understand what the everyday person endures. He has very few principles when it comes to dealing equitably with people, and he has demonstrated time and again that he could care less about anyone's best interests but his own.

It baffles many of us that DT was not held to the same high standard as HRC. Previous candidates have been disqualified for half the shenanigans this guy pulled, and yet he was accepted at a much lower bar, and his campaign was allowed to continue until he won the presidential nomination.

The campaign played out another archetypal dynamic as well, the battle of saviorship vs. self-responsibility and mastership.

In his acceptance speech for the Republican nomination, candidate DT said he would fix everything for his supporters, giving them the impression that he is like some superhero who would swoop down and solve the world's problems on his own. For those still locked in the paradigm of needing a savior, this produced a knee-jerk response to embrace someone who would just jump in and make everything OK. If you read between the lines, he was promising to become our king and direct the world as he saw fit. His track record has shown that he is not a team player. He has a one-dimensional totalitarian dictator mentality. He is divisive and polarizing and by all indications would not play fairly in the sandbox of the world stage. His tactics are those of a bully through and through, and on the world stage, there is a deep concern that his temperament can only bring devastation.

In the four years of Obama's second term, a seething, festering cesspool of frustration was generated by an obstructive Republican Congress that blocked government at every turn, and that anger spilled out into the creation of this renegade nominee; but it was misguided anger. It wasn't the liberal or progressive ideology that did the obstructing; it was a segment of the Republican Party (the Tea Party) obstructing President Obama and his administration. It is so ironic that DT's Republican followers were the angriest at Congress's lack of progress during the Obama Administration, and yet it was their party that did the obstructing!

So, what makes this bully so popular? Why do people listen to DT? He appears to have found a way to communicate with the primitive reptilian brain and to speak to that programming buried deep within the human psyche. This original brain is our seat of survival and fear. Those who are stuck in this part of the brain are struggling with fear and paranoia and self- preservation. DT is either trapped in that same mindset or he and his advisors have figured out how to speak to that distress held by people who feel disenfranchised and are angered by the system. They think he is speaking their language. He was and continues to manipulate them with words that do not have any substance to them. They are simply key words to excite and rile up the reptilian brain and keep it engaged.

In her acceptance speech for the nomination as presidential candidate for the Democratic Party, HRC made a call to unity when she expressed the sentiment that it is important for everyone to work together. She was realistic in understanding that no leader successfully accomplishes their platform alone. It takes cooperation and working together and the sharing of ideas to succeed. She represented respect and unity and honoring all people regardless of gender, sexual orientation, religion, or race. In contrast to her opponent, she was a call to reason and sanity. People who have worked closely with her have the utmost of respect for her and see her as honest and authentic.

Females are characteristically social and cooperative, and HRC has demonstrated that trait strongly in her life's work. She has worked hard as a dedicated public servant to help our government create policies that protect children and families. The Clinton Foundation has been instrumental in helping people all over the world access needed medications for chronic diseases and has championed other philanthropic works.

All of the above observations lay the groundwork for us to see the dynamics at play and then to look beyond two personalities to a larger picture where some important lessons are being presented to our species from the stage of major archetypal energies.

The archetypal battles I saw being played out in the 2016 election campaign were between:

- Separation and unity;
- Savior vs. Self-mastery;
- The oppressive male and the suppressed female;
- The bully and the one being bullied;
- The maintaining of the good ole white boys vs. a new order that is inclusive and respects everyone regardless of race, gender, sexual orientation, religion, or station in life;
- The continuous battle between the status quo and progress;
- The preservation of suppression vs. liberation.

Each time we make progress in overcoming separation in some way, we take a step closer to re-constructing our original Sovereign state of being, and that is why I see that it is appropriate at this time in history to be considering a woman as the leader of the United

States. It symbolizes another step in the transformation of our species from separation to unity.

When we elected an African American to the White House, we began the long road to bringing deep seated racism to the surface where we could examine those divisive beliefs more openly. Many say that racism became more of an issue during the Obama administration. Yes, because it was brought out of the shadows to be seen for the ugly scourge it is. The current climate indicates that it will continue to be a long and arduous battle before complete racial acceptance and heart-centered equality is the norm in this country.

The United States is watched by people all over the world, and whenever we make progress, it is felt and observed worldwide. In the areas of leadership, we seem to be just catching up to many other countries in race acceptance and gender equality. The outcome of the 2016 election determined that we as a nation were not ready to go forward into greater unity and acceptance, but rather chose to go backward into a deeper, more divisive separation and oppression.

I believe that on the unconscious level of our psyches we as a species are searching for ways to overcome the separation that has kept us imprisoned in the Hologram of Deception. Each glass ceiling that is shattered takes us a step closer to recognizing who we are. This political conflict between DT and HRC was significant on so many levels. It was an archetypal battle of unprecedented proportions, and the outcome will affect humanity for generations to come.

Today the world continues to reel from the outcome of the 2016 United States election. Internationally many are watching the administration of DT, our forty-fifth president, unfold with bated breath and deep concern. Not a day has gone by since he took the oath of office that there hasn't been some kind of drama coming from the White House.

I have observed the antics of DT and his administration and have had in-depth discussions about it with others. We have been working to put this reality into perspective by trying to answer this question: what is happening on the deeper levels of this paradigm?

We think at least part of the answer lies in the following: the old guard of suppression and control won another round. It appears that too many people in this country were not ready to accept a more progressive agenda.

Why? Our hunch is that progressive agendas were affecting the programmed Hologram of Deception with acceptance and inclusiveness too rapidly. Meanwhile, our brothers and sisters who are still stuck in survival mode are languishing in the pain of old programming and are dealing with layers and layers of suppression programmed into their DNA. One of those layers involves the subjugation of women. This program is ancient and powerful and still alive and well in America; evidently so much alive that enough people believed that a woman at the head of our government was still unacceptable.

We now know that those old programs are still active among a large segment of the population of this country and are creating an overwhelming fear of change they are not ready to handle. DT knows how to hook into the survival mentality and all the people who feel disenfranchised can hear is "he understands me," and to them that means more than anything he has done. They are hurting so bad they don't realize they have been conned by a man who by all observations and demonstrations is unqualified for the job.

They resonate to his message, and that is enough--looking for someone to save them. They are still very much living in the belief system of needing a savior, and DT in his arrogance continues to persuade them he can fill that void. HRC's opposing message of "it takes a village" and "stronger together" is a dynamic that apparently too many were not ready for.

I had totally forgotten how I felt when I was in a stringent religious mindset years ago until I began to ponder the outcome of this election. I had forgotten what feeling disenfranchised was like and the trapped and fearful outlook that originates from that mindset. In my early adult years, I joined an extremely strict church that reined me in and put many boundaries around me, and for a time I felt safer. I believed I had found the "true church," and I now understand how powerful a hold controlling organizations and belief systems can have on people who feel insecure in this world. I remember those strong religious beliefs and how insidious they were. As I began to mature, I can thank a powerful inner guidance system that prodded me until I railed against the constraints that once helped me feel safe, and I was eventually able to extricate myself from that rigid and controlling belief system. From my experiences, I firmly believe that every individual has an internal navigator that can steer one towards liberating information. But we have to be prepared to listen to that internal voice and those nagging feelings that are telling us something is not right. It is a small voice at first, tentative as it searches for a way to reach one.

So, this is where we are—a huge section of the population of this country is suffering and trying to survive the psychological pain of feeling separate and forgotten by their government. At the same time, the force of the progressive movement is powerful, and it is shaking the very foundation of who we are and creating an internal and unconscious feeling of angst because it goes against the deep-seated programming of those who have not yet begun their liberation process.

DT has found a way to speak to those who are in pain and feeling marginalized, and he has brought anger and many politically incorrect issues to the surface and ignited a flame of passion in people struggling with those feelings. He has promised to be their savior. He has given those who are languishing in alienation a hideous cause, a reason to persecute once again all those who are different or in the minority or secretly feared. Until now, as different groups have attained civil rights, those who remain asleep have had to suppress the programming of hate and divisiveness in order to be politically correct. These programs lay dormant deep in their psyches until DT gave permission to bring them back out front and center by playing to their feelings.

Now our task is to find a way to bring understanding and healing to those who are struggling and suppressed and come to grips with the bully archetype.

There are other archetypes that will keep us in separation, but I hope this sampling presents some ideas to ponder about these energies embedded in our consciousness.

12

PSYCHOLOGY'S JOURNEY TO THE HEART

WE HAVE SPENT CONSIDERABLE TIME and energy in this book exploring a mosaic of our collective history that illustrates how our species was programmed to become fear-based cultures living in survival mode. Citizens of each culture are expected to conform to the beliefs of their particular family or ethnic culture. It also meant each group defended itself against others who did not share their beliefs, thus perpetuating separatist practices as a way of maintaining a particular way of life.

The ruling class has been surviving and maintaining power through deceit and cover-ups on all levels of religion, government, and education for as long as there has been a ruling class. Truth be damned—the one thing that mattered was maintaining power at all costs. Money and/or material wealth and power is and has historically been considered the most reliable measure of success.

The year 2012 was predicted as the year when a huge cosmological shift would happen in this world. As a species, we didn't know what to expect. Was it going to be the end of the world as we knew it? Speculations were as varied as there were people to speculate.

Overall, the year went by without much fanfare, but if we look back to the time before 2012 and the years since, we realize that we have become witnesses to subtle but observable changes worldwide. James Mahu has called this new shift the "Era of Transparency and Expansion."

Long held secrets and deceptions are being revealed with a vengeance on the stages of world and local governments at breathtaking speed. With real-time reporting and events and revelations being recorded by our twenty-four-hour news channels, secrets and cover-ups are becoming harder to maintain. We are witnessing an era of transparency unfold before our eyes that is illustrating to us just how connected we are as a species. We are triggered individually and brought together collectively as we witness events and issues televised on a very visible world stage.

Case in point is the Me-Too movement. Women especially have suffered abuses for centuries in most countries. Why is this issue all of a sudden being taken seriously, and why are women feeling emboldened to step forward in droves to talk about what has happened to them? Sexual abuse and assault has always been a taboo subject, shrouded and endured in secrecy and shame. Why now?

Sexual and physical abuse of children by Catholic priests and nuns that has been going on for years unpunished and kept in that same shroud of secrecy is also coming to the forefront. I find it intriguing and mystifying that as many horrible crimes as the Catholic Church committed during the Inquisition and its aftermath that it is the sexual abuse being brought to light in this modern era as the atrocities that might finally bring the Roman Catholic Church to a day of reckoning.

All across the world stage, we are witnessing the changing of energetic sensibilities within our collective consciousness that makes it more difficult to maintain long-held deep and dark secrets.

I am encouraged because as these truths come to light, they are bringing us a few steps closer to a more heart-centered awareness. True, we have a long way to go, but this thread of conscience has begun its journey into our awareness and will continue to produce behaviors of acute sensitivity towards expanding equality regardless of gender, sexual identity, or race.

As part of my life's journey into discovering the role consciousness plays, I became very curious about the continuum of psychological approaches and what they have contributed to our evolution and understanding of ourselves. My research has revealed a fascinating progression of thoughts and ideas brought to us through the innovative minds of the school of thought that has become modern psychology.

Each new approach has helped us to explore and access latent stages of our multi-leveled psyches, thus weaving new threads of understanding into the tapestry of our collective human experience. I am seeing a progression of ideas slowly emerge into our collective consciousness that I believe has been preparing us for the inevitability of a heart-centered psychology that could ultimately play a pivotal role in some major future paradigm-changing discoveries.

If we are to be honest with ourselves, we know that the spectrum of fear has been one of the strongest and thickest threads woven into the background of the collective tapestry of the human condition. Fear and its nagging companion Survival are entwined and reinforcing taskmasters. They are deeply embedded into our worldviews, creating enslavement on all levels of our societies and imposing beliefs that dominate and control us through conformity and societal expectations.

Survival and fear provide a foundational undercurrent for our governments, communities, religions, and educational systems to be built upon.

We begin to break up that foundation of fear and survival when we start recognizing how the suppression paradigm controls the masses and us as individuals. We develop the courage to individually break this insidious spell of control by taking a good long truthful and critical look at what we fear and its impact on us and our lives. A good exercise might be to make a list of our greatest fears and how we compensate for them. This can help us weed out our needless, programmed, and paralyzing fears from the useful and necessary ones that keep us safe.

Personally, I have found that since I began thinking of my journey in this life as an adventure in consciousness and myself as a fragment of First Source given the gift of exploring the physical outposts of the Multiverse, the entire dynamic of my existence has changed. By looking at our initial separation as a way for First Source to explore the outposts of the Multiverse by sending out fragments of Itself to accomplish that task, and realizing that we are those fragments, then we have no reason to fear Source. We are not the offspring of an angry and jealous god; collectively we are First Source.

It is reasonable to believe that part of the overall plan was one of separation and increased amnesia about our real origins. To truly experience limitation, we first had to feel there was nothing else. We had to learn to draw on our own inner resources to survive, and in that survival we grew stronger.

The quest for discovery can replace fear as the driver of one's life, and the more we can recognize and let go of ego driven expectations, the more our soul can inspire us with new ideas and experiential insights.

Personally, I have found that in the process of expanding to meet my soul's desire, my inner world has become larger, more open, brighter, and more optimistic. I have come to understand that as any voyage that separates us from our home always has the pull of home to bring us back, it is likewise in our souls' journey. We embark on a pilgrimage to explore the outposts of the universe, but inevitably we will yearn to find our way back to our origins again.

But as we are always stretched by any journey that we take, so are our souls expanded by our adventures and collectively we are enriched and deepened by each individual experience. We return to Oneness but maintain our individuality and our understanding and can draw from the experiences of our sisters and brothers who have been on their own individual journeys.

Not everyone is on the same timetable. Some have consciously begun the journey home; others are clearly entrenched in the physical world and its experiences of separation. There is nothing wrong with that; it is the way of consciousness.

Why would going back to Oneness be attractive? As humans we value our individuality and independence. I can't help but wonder that in the eons of infinity to come, we may go home for a while and possibly be sent out on new assignments and new journeys. We may go to other parts of this unfathomably large Multiverse to create new worlds. As infinite beings and a part of Source so many adventures lie ahead.

Meanwhile, our current task is here on this precious Earth—this is our current training and exploration field. So, let's come back from our imaginative trip to the Multiverse and explore the story of our quest to understand our psyches and ourselves and see if that contributes to helping us break free from the paradigm of suppression. I think most of us can appreciate the fact that a process that is this far-reaching cannot happen all at once. The resistance to it would be overwhelming. New concepts have to be introduced in increments in order to be tested and accepted and incorporated into the collective consciousness and then built upon. This chapter will explore that process as we look at the continuum of psychological discoveries made over the last several hundred years. I have been curious to see the big picture of the history of psychological thought because I believe that the unfolding of that trajectory will give us clues about where we are headed as a species.

PSYCHOLOGY'S ROLE IN OUR UNDERSTANDING OF CONSCIOUSNESS

There are two professional fields in the study of the psyche and the mind: psychology and psychiatry.[127]

A psychiatrist is a trained medical doctor who goes through all the rigors of medical school and completes a psychiatric residency and other requirements for board certification in Psychiatry. They are the professionals responsible for prescribing and monitoring medications. They diagnose mental disorders and are typically the lead professionals responsible for the overall mental health care of the patient. A psychiatrist may request psychological testing, computerized tomography (CT) scans and clinical testing to help better understand a patient.

Psychologists are not required to attend medical school. They attend graduate school and obtain a Doctor of Philosophy (PhD) or a Doctor of Psychology (PsyD) degree. A PhD implies that the psychologist's graduate school was research-based, and they must complete a dissertation (intensive research study and paper) to earn their PhD. A PsyD is a clinical degree and focuses more on the clinical aspects of psychosocial therapy. An individual may take the

---

[127] The information for this section describing psychology and psychiatry was taken from: Ryback, Ralph, MD, "Psychiatrist vs. Psychologist," Psychology Today, Jan. 4, 2016, https://www.psychologytoday.com/us/blog/the-truisms-wellness/201601/psychiatrist-vs-psychologist "Psychology vs. Psychiatry: Do You Know the Difference?" All Psychology Schools, https://www.allpsychologyschools.com/psychology/psychology-vs-psychiatry/

route of earning a Master of Science (MS) degree in Psychology and work under the supervision of a PhD or PsyD. Psychologists can prescribe medications in New Mexico and Louisiana.

Psychologists focus on psychotherapy and treating emotional and mental suffering with behavioral intervention. Their studies center on personality development, the history of psychological problems, and the science of psychological research. Psychologists are also trained and qualified to administer testing that can often be critical to understanding and assessing a person's mental state. If a psychologist sees a need, they can refer their patients to a psychiatrist for help in medication management along with behavioral therapy. Psychologists are experts in providing psychosocial therapy and concentrate on a patient's mind and emotions.

One is not better than the other; they each have their areas of expertise and comprehensive education and often work together in the treatment of patients.

Below we will be making a quick flyover of the evolution of some of psychology's main concepts and the pioneers who were inspired to bring them to us. I found it interesting to study this big picture of how new ideas about the human psyche were introduced into the collective consciousness. An idea is presented and another builds on it, and pretty soon the jargon becomes a part of our common language and understanding.

As I reviewed this continuum of ideas that were introduced through the field of psychological studies, I couldn't help but wonder if some of these revelations will ultimately contribute to our understanding of our place in the universe as a collective consciousness.

For the section below, I have borrowed from the timeline of some major discoveries in psychology found on the website *AllPsych.com,* quoting and paraphrasing as needed. Information that I used from other sources is cited in the footnotes. Unless indicated otherwise, assume the information is coming from *AllPsych*.

The timeline is quite long, and I won't be listing all of the discoveries - just the main ones to provide us with an overview of some of the highpoints of thought that helped to build the field of psychology.

The *AllPsych* timeline begins with Plato who in **387 BC** suggested the brain is the mechanism for mental process. In **335 BC** Aristotle suggested that the heart is the mechanism of mental processes. (Hmm - our earliest recorded thinkers set the stage for the coordination of the heart/brain duo as the foundational trajectory humanity would ultimately take towards self- discovery.)

We then pick up our exploration in **1774** when we meet Franz Mesmer, [128] founder of "Mesmerism." He believed in "animal magnetism" and that by affixing iron rods to different parts of the body, magnetic forces would move fluids around in the body and cure the

[128] "Evolution of Mental Illness," *Preceden,* https://www.preceden.com/timelines/66973-evolution-of-mental-illness

afflicted. He is credited for laying the groundwork for the practice of modern hypnosis, and the word *mesmerize* was named after him. His life story is quite colorful; he was thought of as part healer and part charlatan.

A change in the direction of the treatment of the mentally ill began in **1793** when Philippe Pinel became the director of the La Bicetre Asylum in Paris, France and began advocating kindness and compassion in the treatment of the mentally ill. At that time, the mentally ill were confined to asylums that were more like prisons, abusive and inhumane in their practices. Pinel's work began a slow improvement in the treatment of the mentally ill in Europe.

Fast forward to **1859,** and we find Charles Darwin's theory of the survival of the fittest begins to have its influence on mainstream thinking through his book *On the Origin of the Species.*

The left lobe of the brain was identified by French physician Paul Broca as having a key role in language development in **1861**. In **1864** Carl Wernicke published his work on the brain that explained how injury to specific areas of the frontal lobe caused problems with a person's ability to understand or produce language.

In **1878** G. Stanley Hall received the first PhD in Psychology and later in **1892** founded the American Psychological Association with an initial membership of 42.

Wilhelm Wundt founded the first formal laboratory of psychology at the University of Leipzig in **1879**. This marked the recognized beginning of the study of human emotions, behaviors, and perceptions.

> Wundt's ideas formed the basis for the first school of psychological thought—Structuralism and was centered on investigating the structure of the mind. Structuralism played a significant role in shaping the field of psychology in its formative years. He helped to establish psychology as an independent experimental science and their methods of inquiry remain a key aspect of the discipline today… One of the key critics of Structuralism came from William James. He was one of the leading proponents of the functionalist perspective. [129]

The first laboratory of psychology in the United States was established at Johns Hopkins University in **1883**.

In **1886** Sigmund Freud began his therapy practice in Vienna, bringing his theory of personality to his work with patients. By **1900** he had published *Interpretation of Dreams,* marking the beginning of Psychoanalytic Thought.

---

[129] Coomarsingh, K, "Major Psychological Schools of Thought," *What Is Psychology?* http://www.whatispsychology.biz/major-psychological-schools-thought

Freud was the first to delve into the subconscious. He believed that many of our thoughts and actions originated in the subconscious and manifested in everyday life through our motives and impulses. Many schools of psychological thought moved on from Freud, but his work is foundational in our exploration of the subconscious and its impact on our actions.

> No other psychological school of thought has received as much attention, admiration and criticism as Freud's psychoanalytic theory...Freud's theory is considered to fall short of being scientific, as many of his concepts are not testable. He also failed to recognize how experiences after childhood contribute to personality development and focused mainly on psychological disorders rather than positive adaptive behavior.[130]

William James in **1890** produced his *Principles of Psychology* that later became the foundation of Functionalism.

> From William James point of view the Structuralists were sorely misguided. He believed that the mind is fluid, not stable; consciousness is ongoing, not static. He believed it to be more accurate to study how the mind functioned and how the elements of the mind worked together and how mental processes promote adaptation...While structuralists asked "what happened" in mental activity, the functionalists were more concerned about how it happens and why.[131]

John Dewey was an American philosopher, educator, and psychologist who made significant contributions to the establishment of the Functionalism School of Thought starting in **1896**. His psychology was influenced by Charles Darwin's theory of evolution, as well as by the ideas of William James and by Dewey's own instrumentalist philosophy. His 1896 paper "The Reflex Arc Concept of Psychology" is generally considered the first major statement establishing the Functionalist School. Dewey was an educational reformer and a pioneer in the field of educational psychology, and his ideas have remained at the center of much the educational establishment in the United States. [132]

---

[130] Ibid.

[131] Ibid.

[132] "John Dewey," *Psychology Encyclopedia,* https://psychology.jrank.org/pages/184/JohnDewey.html#:~:text=Dewey's%20functionalism%20was%20influenc ed%20by,statement%20establishing%20the%20functionalist%20school.

The information above quoted or paraphrased from cited article.

1906 brings us to Ivan Pavlov and the first studies of Classical Conditioning. Most people know about Pavlov through his famous "Pavlov's dog" experiment. He learned quite by accident while studying the gastric systems of dogs that when he would introduce a stimulus like a bell and then give the dog food, it wasn't long before the dog would salivate in anticipation of the food whenever the bell was heard. A variety of experiments were conducted by Pavlov and others, and an understanding of how humans and animals are conditioned grew from these experiments.

Pavlov is the researcher most noted for the discovery of Classical Conditioning and was a pioneer in the Behaviorist School of Thought.

Alfred Adler left Freud and created his own theories of human psychology in **1911**. Adler [133] created a short-term, goal-oriented, and positive psychodynamic therapy that focused on feelings of inferiority versus superiority and discouragement vs. a sense of belonging in the context of one's community and society at large. Adler theorized that feelings of inferiority can result in neurotic behavior but in the right setting can also be used as a motivation to strive for greater success. Adlerian therapy focuses on the development of individual personality with understanding and acceptance of the interconnectedness of others.

Carl Jung is perhaps the most famous student to leave Freud. He is the creator of Analytical Psychology and parted ways with Freud in **1913** because the latter would not acknowledge religion and spirituality in his theories. Below is a short synopsis of some of the ideas that Jung introduced and worked with in the field of Analytical Psychology. [134] It is far from complete but gives us a taste of how much of our understanding of ourselves and our lingo has come from Carl Jung. Jung's approach is the most fascinating to me, and his work (in my opinion) is by far the most comprehensive as an introductory vehicle to move us inward towards the ultimate discovery and acceptance of the soul.

Jung introduced the ideas of extroversion and introversion, archetypes, dream analysis as an analytic approach, and the collective unconscious. He believed the psyche is a self-regulating system that seeks to maintain balance between opposing qualities, a process he called individuation. Jung saw the psyche as something that could be divided into component parts such as complexes and archetypal contents personified in a metaphorical sense.

Jung saw the ego as the center of the field of consciousness that organizes our thoughts and feelings and sensed and regulated our access to memory. He felt that the ego was the part of our psyches that links the inner and outer worlds together. Jung was aware of a personal

---

[133] "Adlerian Therapy," *Psychology Today,* https://www.psychologytoday.com/us/therapy-types/adlerian-therapy
[134] "The Jungian Model of the Psyche," *Journal Psyche,* http://journalpsyche.org/jungian-model-psyche/
Information taken from this article often paraphrased or the idea lifted and not quoted verbatim.

unconscious and felt that it interacted between the collective unconscious and one's personal growth. He defined the Self as the sum total of the psyche with all its potential included, and as the part of the psyche that looks toward fulfillment and wholeness and is the driver of the individuation process. Individuation according to Jung is the quest for wholeness as we grow and become conscious of ourselves as unique human beings.

Jung saw us as having a Persona and defined it as the element of our personality that adapts. The "masks" we present to the outer world are a part of this Persona and lean heavily on embodying our best qualities.

Jung identified a Shadow that he felt held all the traits we have that we dislike and repress. He believed the Shadow played an important part in balancing the personality. However, humans have the tendency to project their shadow traits onto others. These are usually traits we cannot stand in others and have in ourselves and wish not to see. Jung identifies the Animus and Anima as the contra-sexual archetypes within the psyche—Anima in man, Animus in woman.

It is worth noting that in **1912** Max Wertheimer published research on the perception of movement that marked the beginnings of Gestalt psychology. In **1925** Wolfgang Kohler published *The Mentality of Apes*. This became a major component of Gestalt Therapy.

> The word Gestalt means form, pattern or whole. Gestalt psychologists believed that psychology should study the human experience as a "whole;" not in terms of separate elements. Their slogan was that the "whole is greater than the sum of its parts" and conveyed the idea that meaning is often lost when psychological events are broken down...Gestalt psychologists such as Max Wertheimer did extensive work on various aspects of cognition, including perception, problem-solving and thinking. Their insistence on studying individuals and experience as a whole is still preserved in psychology today.[135]

In **1932** Jean Piaget published *the Moral Judgement of Children,* becoming the leading theorist of cognitive development. According to an article written by Kendra Cherry for *Verywellmind*, Piaget suggests children move through four different intellectual stages of cognitive development: sensorimotor stage - birth to two years; preoperational stage - two to seven years; concrete operational stage - seven to eleven; and formal operational stage - twelve and up. He believed that children take an active role in the learning process, acting much like little scientists as they perform experiments, make observations, and learn about

---

[135] Coomarsingh, K., "Major Psychological Schools of Thought," *What Is Psychology?* http://www.whatispsychology.biz/major-psychological-schools-thought

the world. They are continually adding new knowledge, building upon existing knowledge, and adapting previously held ideas to accommodate new information. [136]

In **1936** Egas Moniz published his work on frontal lobotomies:

> surgical procedures…designed specifically to disrupt the tracts of neuronal fibres connecting the prefrontal cortex and the thalamus of the brain.… Lobotomies were performed on a wide scale during the 1940s but gradually fell out of favor in the mid-1950s when antipsychotics, anti-depressants and other medications that were much more effective in treating and alleviating the distress of mentally disturbed patients came into use. [137]

In **1938** electroconvulsive therapy (ECT) was first used on patients with severe major depression or bipolar disorder not responding to other treatments. ECT involves a brief electrical stimulation of the brain while the patient is under anesthesia. It is typically administered by a team of trained medical professionals. It has been found to be highly effective for the relief of major depression and severe mental illness and is a treatment that is recognized by the American Psychiatric Association and is available today. [138]

Carl Rogers came on the scene in **1942** with his published work *Counseling and Psychotherapy,* suggesting that respect and non-judgmental treatment is the most effective approach. This marked a powerful change in how treatment for mental health issues was conducted. In **1961** he wrote the book *On Becoming a Person.*

The *Diagnostic and Statistical Manual of Mental Disorders* (*DSM*) was first published in **1952**, and in that same year the drug Thorazine was first used on schizophrenic patients. The *DSM II* was published by the American Psychiatric Association in **1968**.

Once the field of psychology was established, then decisions about credentialing practitioners became a part of the evolution of this field. In **1968** the first Doctor of Psychology or PsyD was established at the University of Chicago. By **1995** Doctors of Psychology were able to prescribe medications through the U.S. Military's Psychopharmacology Program. By **2002** G. W. Bush promoted legislation to guarantee comprehensive mental health coverage.

---

[136] Cherry, Kendra, "The 4 Stages of Cognitive Development," *Verywellmind,* https://www.verywellmind.com/piagets-stages-of-cognitive-development-2795457

[137] "Lobotomy," *Encyclopedia Britannica,* https://www.britannica.com/science/lobotomy

[138] "What is Electroconvulsive therapy (ECT)?" *American Psychiatric Association,* https://www.psychiatry.org/patients-families/ect

HUMANISTIC PSYCHOLOGY

Major recognized branches of psychology include biological, gestalt, psychodynamic, behavioral, cognitive, and humanistic which includes existential, transpersonal, and Jungian. I will be focusing on individuals who have contributed to the humanistic movement, but first a brief definition of humanistic psychology and related disciplines would be helpful.

Humanistic Therapy looks at the whole person, not only from the therapist's view but from the viewpoint of individuals observing their own behavior. The practitioners emphasize positive traits and behaviors and the ability for the person to use their personal instincts to find wisdom, growth, healing, and fulfillment within themselves. This approach is a talk therapy that uses a gestalt approach and explores how the person is feeling in the present, rather than identify past events that led to those feelings.

The Humanistic therapist provides an atmosphere of support, empathy, and trust allowing the individual to share feelings without fear of judgment. The therapist is not an authority figure; the relationship between therapist and client is one of equals. This is a holistic approach that does not dwell on pathology, past, or environmental experiences.

Humanistic therapy evolved from the hierarchy of needs given to us by Maslow and the person-centered approach developed by Carl Rogers. This therapy proposes that people are inherently motivated to fulfill their internal needs and their individual potential to become self-actualized through creative endeavors, spiritual enlightenment, and the pursuit of wisdom or altruism.[139]

Existential refers to existence and **Existential Therapy** focuses on free will, self-determination, and the search for meaning, often centering on the patient rather than the symptom. This approach emphasizes one's capacity to make rational choices and develop to maximum potential.

The existential approach stresses that: all people have a capacity for self-awareness; each person has a unique identity that is known through relationship with others; people must continually re-create themselves because life's meaning constantly changes; and anxiety is part of the human condition. The goal is to learn to make more willful decisions about how to live, drawing on creativity and love, instead of letting outside events determine ones' behavior.[140]

---

[139] "Humanistic Therapy," *Psychology Today,*
https://www.psychologytoday.com/us/therapy-types/humanistic-therapy
[140] "Existential Therapy," *Psychology Today,*
https://www.psychologytoday.com/us/therapy-types/existential-therapy

Analytical Psychology—Jungian Therapy is designed to bring together the conscious and unconscious parts of the mind. Jungian therapy calls for clients to delve into the deeper and often darker elements of their mind and look at the "real" self rather than the self they present to the world. This type of analysis encourages dream journaling and interpretation and creative experiences like art, movement, or music to encourage self- expression and release of one's imagination. This therapy focuses more on the source of the problem than on its manifestations or symptoms. Jung felt that repressed experiences and memories in combination with what he called the "collective unconscious" or natural traits that affect everyone result in an imbalance between conscious awareness and the unconscious mind that has a detrimental effect on one's emotional life. In analysis the Analysand will explore the deep-rooted causes of relationship problems and blocked emotions to achieve "individuation" or wholeness.[141]

Transpersonal Psychology began in the 1960s as an attempt to establish a "fourth force" in psychology. It is an outgrowth of humanistic psychology. It was strongly influenced by the human potential and counterculture movements of the 1960s and the wave of experimentation through psychedelic substances, meditation, and other consciousness-changing practices. Transpersonal Psychology is an attempt to understand different states of consciousness and different views of reality. At the same time, it was an attempt to integrate the ideas and insights of Western psychology with Eastern spiritual traditions, such as Buddhism, Hindu Vedanta, and Yoga especially in their examination of higher states of consciousness and advanced stages of human development. Abraham Maslow describes the role of Transpersonal Psychology is to explore the "farther reaches of human nature."

There are potentially higher functioning states in which our perception becomes intensified, we experience an increased sense of connection to nature and other human beings, we become more compassionate and altruistic, and we have a wider sense of perspective and live more authentically.

Transpersonal Psychology's importance lies in its recognition that we are not all that we could be, that the world as we perceive it does not necessarily represent the world as it is, and that our glimpses of a more expansive and higher functioning state don't have to be temporary, they can become our permanent state.[142]

---

[141] Hiles, Dave, "Pioneers of Humanistic-Existential Psychology," *The Virtual Office of Dave Hiles*, http://www.psy.dmu.ac.uk/drhiles/HPpioneers.htm

[142] Taylor, Steve Ph.D., "Transpersonal Psychology," *Psychology Today*, https://www.psychologytoday.com/us/blog/out-the-darkness/201509/transpersonal-psychology The information about TP and the description of TP is paraphrased from this article.

The C.G. Jung Center [143] defines **Depth Psychology** as approaches to therapy that are open to the exploration of the subtle, unconscious, and transpersonal aspects of the human experience. A depth approach may include therapeutic traditions that explores the unconscious and involves the study and exploration of dreams, complexes, and archetypes. Depth psychology is non-pathologizing and strength affirming.

PIONEERS OF HUMANISTIC-EXISTENTIAL PSYCHOLOGY

Dave Hiles in his article "Pioneers of Humanistic-Existential Psychology" [144] lists the individuals discussed below as having significant impact on this field of psychology, making it what it is today.

As the progression of psychology gained momentum, innovative and deep thinkers arrived in the field to carry it forward. These individuals are important for the contributions they have made to our collective consciousness and our continuing development as a species. In the information below, I will either quote directly from Hiles' article or paraphrase, unless otherwise indicated. I have also included some quotes to highlight the ideas of each pioneer.

Carl Jung (1875-1961) has had an impact on: behavioral psychology; psychodynamic psychology by developing his own school of analytical psychology; humanistic psychology as he anticipated all the major themes of the humanistic-existential approach, especially his concepts of "Self" (an integrating principle of the human psyche), Active Imagination, and human consciousness; and transpersonal psychology. Hiles explains that the work of some of the most important current researchers in the transpersonal field, such as Stanislav Grof and Michael Washburn, almost entirely depend on the theoretical ideas of Jung.

Of all the theories of psychology, in this writer's opinion Carl Jung seems to have the most comprehensive understanding of the human psyche. Jung's major concepts include the collective unconscious, the "complex" model of the psyche, archetypes and symbols, psychological types, introversion and extraversion (the Myers-Briggs Personality Type Inventory is based on this concept), individuation, and synchronicity - to name a few.

Major writings by Jung include: *The Psychology of the Unconscious; Psychological Types; Modern Man in Search of a Soul; Psychology and Alchemy; Answer to Job; Memories, Dreams and Reflections;* and *Man and His Symbols.*

---

[143] *The C.G. Jung Center,* http://www.cgjungcenter.org/clinical-services/what-is-depth-psychology/

[144] Hiles, Dave, "Pioneers of Humanistic-Existential Psychology," *The Virtual Office of Dave Hiles,* http://www.psy.dmu.ac.uk/drhiles/HPpioneers.htm

"One looks back with appreciation to the brilliant teachers, but with gratitude to those who touched our human feelings. The curriculum is so much necessary raw material, but warmth is the vital element for the growing plant and for the soul of the child."

"Knowing your own darkness is the best method for dealing with the darknesses of other people."

"Your vision will become clear only when you look into your own heart. Who looks outside, dreams; who looks inside awakens."

"Man's task is to become conscious of the contents that press upward from the unconscious."

"A human being would certainly not grow to be seventy or eighty years old if this longevity had no meaning for the species. The afternoon of human life must also have a significance of its own and cannot be merely a pitiful appendage to life's morning."

"If there is anything that we wish to change in the child, we should first examine it and see whether it is not something that could better be changed in ourselves."

Rollo May (1909-1994) was also a co-founder of the Humanistic Psychology movement and was largely responsible for integrating the humanistic and existential traditions. Where Rogers felt that humans were basically good, May felt that they were good and evil. May concludes: "Life to me is not a requirement to live out a preordained pattern of goodness, but a challenge coming down through the centuries out of the fact that each of us can throw a lever toward good or toward evil."

May wrote some groundbreaking books including *Man's Search for Himself; Existential Psychology; Love and Will; The Courage to Create; The Cry for Myth.*

Quotes by Rollo May:

"Hate is not the opposite of love: apathy is."

"If you do not express your own original ideas, if you do not listen to your own being, you will have betrayed yourself."

"The opposite of courage in our society is not cowardice, it is conformity."

---

[145] *BrainyQuote,* https://www.brainyquote.com/quotes/carl_jung_717969 for additional citations.

"While one might laugh at the meaningless boredom of people a decade or two ago, the emptiness has for many now moved from the state of boredom to a state of futility and despair, which holds promise of dangers."

"One does not become fully human painlessly."

"Our particular problem in America at this point in history is the widespread loss of the sense of individual significance, a loss which is sensed inwardly as impotence."

"Depression is the inability to construct a future." [146]

Abraham Maslow (1908-1970) was the cofounder with Carl Rogers and Rollo May of the Humanistic Psychology movement and in the late 60s instigated what he termed the Fourth Force—Transpersonal Psychology. He is famous for developing the well-known Hierarchy of Needs. According to Hiles, he radically altered the course of the development of psychology. He studied with Alfred Adler, Erich Fromm, Karen Horney of the psychoanalytic school, and from the Gestalt school he studied with Kurt Goldstein, Max Wertheimer, and Kurt Koffka. A crucial and informative time for Maslow came when he did some fieldwork with the Blackfoot Indian Tribe and began to realize that the behavioral school of psychology had little bearing on real world issues. Maslow was primarily a theoretician and researcher in the new movement. His major concepts include self-actualization, human motivation and the hierarchy of needs, peak experiences, etc. His major written works include *Motivation and Personality; Religious Values and Peak Experiences; Towards a Psychology of Being; and The Farther Reaches of Human Nature.*

Quotes by Abraham Maslow:

"What is necessary to change a person is to change his awareness of himself."

"The story of the human race is the story of men and women selling themselves short."

"We fear to know the fearsome and unsavory aspects of ourselves, but we fear even more to know the godlike in ourselves."

"One's only rival is one's own potentialities. One's only failure is failing to live up to one's own possibilities."

"What a man can be, he must be. This need we call self-actualization."

"What we need is a system of thought - you might even call it a religion - that can bind humans together. A system that would fit the Republic of Chad

---

as well as the United States: a system that would supply our idealistic young people with something to believe in."

"If you only have a hammer, you tend to see every problem as a nail." [147]

Carl Rogers (1902-1987) was a co-founder of the Humanistic Psychology movement and pioneered the development of client-centered therapy. He believed that a person is always in a process of becoming and defined the *self* as an organizing principle— "an organizing consistent gestalt, constantly in the process of forming and reforming." His main theoretical concepts include client-centered/person-centered counselling/therapy, actualizing tendency, becoming, self, encounter groups, and cross-cultural communication. He maintained that client-centered practitioners are most effective when they work with their patients using the core conditions of empathy, unconditional positive regard, and congruence. (This means the practitioner is genuine and real.) Rogers believed that our common underlying motive is a need to become self-actualized and reach our highest potential. He believed it was important for people to receive "unconditional positive regard" from others as a way to encourage the person's fullest potential. He taught acceptance without conditions or judgement as an especially important attitude toward the client in order for the individual to achieve mental well-being. If the actualizing tendency leads to self-actualization, the individual can become what Rogers referred to as a fully functioning person. "The organism has one basic tendency and striving —to actualize, maintain and enhance the experiencing organism." (Rogers, 1951) [148]

Roger's major writings include *Counselling and Psychotherapy; Client- Centred Therapy; On Becoming a Person: A Therapist's View of Psychotherapy; Freedom to Learn: A View of What Education Might Become; On Encounter Groups; A Way of Being.*

Quotes by Carl Rogers:

"The good life is a process, not a state of being. It is a direction not a destination."

"In my early professional years I was asking the question: How can I treat, or cure, or change this person? Now I would phrase the question in this way: How can I provide a relationship which this person may use for his own personal growth?"

"The curious paradox is that when I accept myself just as I am, then I can change."

[147] *BrainyQuote,* https://www.brainyquote.com/quotes/abraham_maslow_126079 for additional citations
[148] Cherry, Kendra, "What is the Actualizing Tendency?" *Explore Psychology* https://www.explorepsychology.com/actualizing-tendency/

"The very essence of the creative is its novelty, and hence we have no standard by which to judge it." [149]

James Bugental (1915-2008) was the first president of the Association for Humanistic Psychology (1962-1963). His vision of humanity was that we are on the verge of a new paradigm that would foster a new evolution of human consciousness. This paradigm viewed the person holistically, rejected the medical model as a guiding principle for psychotherapy, and saw practitioners as pioneers in advancing psychological knowledge. Bugental was the creator, along with Rollo May, of existential- humanistic psychotherapy.

His writings included *The Search for Authenticity: An Existential- Analytic Approach to Psychotherapy; The Art of the Psychotherapist; Intimate Journeys: Stories from Life-Changing Therapy.*

James Bugental's quotes:

"Without awareness, we are not truly alive."[150]

"Humanistic psychology is founded on a dedication to the wholeness of life, a conviction that life has greater potential than has yet been realized, and an openness to a wide range of observations, methods, and practices. In this perspective we draw humility, challenge, and encouragement from the realization of how much about human beings is yet unknown. Commitment, struggle, successes and failures and a continually receding frontier await those who would join us.[151]5

Erich Fromm (1900-1980) saw human life as basically a contradiction because we are both a part of nature and separate from it; we are both animal and human. Out of this he believed five basic existential needs arise: relatedness, transcendence, rootedness, identity, and frame of orientation. Fromm proposed the idea of social character as a mediating process by which the individual is unconsciously molded by the social and economic order. He felt that humans have two primary needs: the need for freedom and the need for belonging, and he identified five-character types based on the principle of productivity and the functions of society: receptive, exploitative, hoarding, marketing and productive.

The receptive type is characterized by the constant need for approval and recognition.

---

[149] *BrainyQuote*, https://www.brainyquote.com/quotes/carl_rogers_101353 for additional citations.

[150] "James Bugental Quotes," *AZ Quotes*, https://www.azquotes.com/author/50781-James_Bugental

[151] "James FT. Bugental, PhD, Celebrating the Work of a Founding Existential-Humanistic Psychologist," www.bugental.com

The exploiter establishes links and relationships with others out of pure selfish interest and typically focuses on people with low self- esteem in order to take advantage of them. The hoarder is one whose only objective is to possess and accumulate increasingly more things to feel secure. They can never be happy as they see themselves as always lacking in something. The marketing type establishes relationships for financial benefit. The productive type channels all efforts in being someone committed to others. They are basically individuals who are able to build loving, enriching, and meaningful relationships with peers and have an extremely healthy approach in dealing with negative emotions. [152]

Fromm's major writings were *Escape from Freedom; Man for Himself; The Forgotten Language; The Art of Loving; Psychanalysis and Zen Buddhism; The Anatomy of Human Destructiveness; To Have or To Be.*

Quotes by Erich Fromm:

"Just as modern mass production requires the standardization of commodities, so the social process requires standardization of man, and this standardization is called equality."

"There is only one meaning of life: the act of living itself."

"The only truly affluent are those who do not want more than they have."

"One cannot be deeply responsive to the world without being saddened very often." [153]

"Selfish people are incapable of loving others, nor are they capable of loving themselves. Only the person who has faith in himself is capable of having faith in others." [154]

Roberto Assagioli (1888-1974) was the founder of Psychosynthesis. Assagioli placed high value on human intuition, creative thought, and inspiration. He argued that therapy should be as much concerned with studying the higher unconscious (super consciousness) as it was studying the depths of the unconscious. He describes the superconscious as the realm of the psyche that contains our highest potential—The Self, the source of our unique path of development, our values, and peak experiences. He argued that individuals can integrate the seemingly different and conflicting parts of the self when they are able to engage in

---

[152] "The 5 Types of Personality According to Erich Fromm," *Exploring yourmind,* https://exploringyourmind.com/the-5-types-of-personality-according-to-erich-fromm/

[153] *BrainyQuote,* https://www.brainyquote.com/quotes/erich_fromm_116794 for additional citations.

[154] "The 5 Types of Personality According to Erich Fromm," *Exploring yourmind,* https://exploringyourmind.com/the-5-types-of-personality-according-to-erich-fromm/

inner work with ease. He believed that achieving our individual purposes and honoring our true self will bring psychological health and spiritual fulfillment. Psychosynthesis methods include creative visualization, fantasy, free drawing, sub-personalities, training the will, meditation, interpersonal and group work, etc.

I had the privilege and gift of attending a two-week "Pearl Diving" retreat based on Assagioli's work the summer after the death of my daughter Michelle from a car accident the year before. It began a powerful healing process for me. I believe it was pivotal in honing my understanding of and ability to access my inner world and move on from many issues that had plagued me not only from her death but also incidents from my childhood that needed addressing. The work was powerful and far-reaching, and we covered a lot of ground in those two weeks. I attended subsequent shorter workshops throughout the following year that helped me continue with the work begun at the Pearl Diving retreat. I highly recommend Psychosynthesis Work if you ever have the opportunity to participate in it.

Assagioli's work includes: *Psychosynthesis: A Manual of Principles and Techniques; The Act of Will; Transpersonal Development: The Dimension Beyond Psychosynthesis.* (This last book was published in 2007 by Smiling Wisdom, thirteen years after his death, and consists of his writings from different periods. It is profound reading for anyone interested in Assagioli's work.)

Quotes by Roberto Assagioli:

> *"Through its influence upon the unconscious, music can have a specific healing effect. It can help in eliminating repressions and resistances, and it can bring into the field of waking consciousness many drives, emotions and complexes which were creating difficulties in the unconscious."*
>
> *"From a still wider and more comprehensive point of view, universal life itself appears to us as a struggle between multiplicity and unity - a labor and an aspiration towards union. We seem to sense that - whether we conceive it as a divine Being or as a cosmic energy - the Spirit working upon and within all creation is shaping it into order, harmony, and beauty, uniting all beings (some willing but the majority as yet blind and rebellious) with each other through links of love, achieving - slowly and silently, but powerfully and irresistibly - the Supreme Synthesis."*[155]

Fritz Perls (1893-1970) has been described as a charismatic man. He was a trained psychoanalyst and one of the founders of Gestalt Therapy which emphasized: the holistic

---

[155] *AZ Quotes*, https://www.azquotes.com/quote/855329 Both quotes by Assagioli from this site

principle—humans are unified organisms and function as a whole; the principle of homeostasis; the balance of opposites; here-and-now awareness; responsibility for self and the existential choices we make for ourselves. His techniques included the empty chair, dream work, experimentation, and unfinished business.

Perls' major writings include *Ego, Hunger and Aggression; Gestalt Therapy Verbatim.*

Quotes by Fritz Perls:

"I am not in this world to live up to other people's expectations, nor do I feel that the world must live up to mine."

"Our dependency makes slaves out of us, especially if this dependency is a dependency of self-esteem. If you need encouragement, praise, pats on the back from everybody, then you make everybody your judge."[156]

Jacob Levy Moreno (1889-1974) was born in Bucharest, Romania. He was known as a psycho-sociologist, thinker, educator, and the founder of Psychodrama. He was interested in understanding the make-believe play of children and felt that spontaneity was especially important in the creative process of living. He developed the Theatre of Spontaneity and with a group of actors created the innovations of self-help groups and group psychotherapy. He was recognized during his lifetime as one of the leading social scientists. According to *The Full Wiki*, he grew up in Vienna and studied medicine, mathematics, and philosophy at the University of Vienna and became a Doctor of Medicine in 1917.

"In his autobiography, Dr. Moreno recalls this encounter with Sigmund Freud in 1912.

I attended one of Freud's lectures. He had just finished an analysis of a telepathic dream. As the students filed out, he singled me out from the crowd and asked me what I was doing. I responded, 'Well, Dr. Freud, I start where you leave off. You meet people in the artificial setting of your office. I meet them on the street and in their homes, in their natural surroundings. You analyze their dreams. I give them the courage to dream again. You analyze and tear them apart. I let them act out their conflicting roles and help them to put the parts back together again.'"[157]

Moreno's writings include *Who Shall Survive; Psychodrama Vols. 1-3*

---

[156] *BrainyQuote,* https://www.brainyquote.com/quotes/fritz_perls_213533 for additional citations.

[157] "Jacob L. Moreno," *Psychology Wiki,* https://psychology.wikia.org/wiki/Jacob_L._Moreno

R.D. Laing (1927-1989) was Britain's foremost exponent of existential psychotherapy. He was a severe critic of modern psychiatric practice and the medical intervention of mental illness. He believed that psychiatric illness was largely the consequence of social conditions, such as family dynamics, pathological communication, intolerable social pressure, or failure to conform to the dominant model of social reality. He pioneered therapeutic communities where patients could "go with" their illness experience without the intervention of drugs, ECT, or psychosurgery. He was most influenced by Existential Philosophy and Phenomenology. He saw psychotherapy as "an obstinate attempt by two people to recover the wholeness of being human through the relationship between them." Laing's major writings: *The Divided Self; Self and Others: Sanity, Madness and the Family; The Politics of Experience; The Voice of Experience.*

Quotes by R.D. Laing:

"Schizophrenia cannot be understood without understanding despair."
"We are all in a post-hypnotic trance induced in early childhood."
"Madness need not be all breakdown. It may also be break-through. It is potential liberation and renewal as well as enslavement and existential death."
"The range of what we think and do is limited by what we fail to notice. And because we fail to notice that we fail to notice, there is little we can do to change; until we notice how failing to notice shapes our thoughts and deeds." [158]

Viktor Frankl (1905-1997) was imprisoned in Auschwitz and Dachau and survived. His parents, brother, and wife all perished in the camps. From his experiences in the Nazi camps, he came to focus on what kept people alive through seemingly hopeless and/or insurmountable odds. His book *Man's Search for Meaning*, published in 24 languages, explores humanity's opportunity for growth through suffering and the way each person bears hardship in challenging life experiences. Logotherapy was the outcome of his searching. The main idea behind Logotherapy is that a lack of meaning in one's life is a chief source of stress and anxiety. Logotherapy helps the patient to find some meaning in their life. Frankl believed that it was through a search for meaning and purpose that one could endure hardship and suffering.

During his career as a professor of neurology and psychiatry, Frankl wrote 30 books, lectured at 209 universities on 5 continents, and was the recipient of 29 honorary doctorates from universities around the world. Logotherapy was recognized as the third school of Viennese therapy after Freud's psychoanalysis and Alfred Adler's individual psychology.

---

[158] *BrainyQuote*, https://www.brainyquote.com/quotes/r_d_laing_130951 for additional citations.

Quotes by Viktor Frankl:

"Everything can be taken from a man but one thing: the last human freedoms— to choose one's attitude in any given set of circumstances." [159]

"There is nothing in the world, I venture to say, that would so effectively help one to survive even the worst conditions as the knowledge that there is a meaning in one's life."

"Logotherapy sees the human patient in all his humanness. I step up to the core of the patient's being. And that is a being in search of meaning, a being that is transcending himself; a being capable of acting in love for others." [160]

Frankl's major writings: *Man's Search for Meaning; Psychotherapy and Existentialism; The Will to Meaning; The Unheard Cry for Meaning: Psychotherapy and Humanism.*

James Hillman (1926-2011), psychologist and Jungian Analyst, is recognized as the originator of post-Jungian "archetypal psychology." His idea was that there are no archetypes as such, but only phenomena or images that are archetypal. He was interested in a psychology of soul. He believed that the soul was the imaginative possibility of our human nature as it made meaning possible and turned events into experiences. However, he was less concerned with the individual and more with the soul that is at the heart of the world. In his introduction to his book *Re-Visioning Psychology*, Hillman writes:

"This book is about soul-making. It is an attempt at the psychology of the soul, an essay in re-visioning psychology from the point of view of the soul... Because the soul cannot be understood through psychology alone, our vision even leaves the field of psychology as it is usually thought of, and moves widely through history, philosophy and religion...The term soul-making comes from the Romantic poets...it was John Keats who clarified the phrase in a letter to his brother: "call it the world if you please, 'the Vale of Soul-making.' Then you will find out the use of the world...From this perspective the human adventure is a wandering through the vale of the world for the sake of making soul. Our life is psychological, the purpose of life is to make psyche of it, to find connections between life and soul."

---

[159] Cuncic, Arlin, "An Overview of Viktor Frank's Logotherapy," Verywellmind, https://www.verywellmind.com/an-overview-of-victor-frankl-s-logotherapy-4159308
[160] *BrainyQuote*, https://www.brainyquote.com/quotes/viktor_e_frankl_752769 for additional citations.

"The notion of soul-making demands more precision, however, when it is used by a therapeutic psychologist rather than a Romantic poet, for it is not enough not enough to evoke soul and sing its praises. The job of psychology is to offer a way and find a place for soul within its own field."[161]

His major writings include *Re-Visioning Psychology; Healing Fiction; The Soul's Code: The Force of Character.*

<u>Other quotes by James Hillman:</u>

"Sooner or later something seems to call us onto a particular path…this is what I must do; this is what I've got to have. This is who I am."

"We forget that the soul has its own ancestors."

"We need to have an educational system that's able to embrace all sorts of minds, and where a student doesn't have to fit into a certain mold of learning."[162]

Ram Dass (1931-2019) was born Richard Alpert. He was a spiritual teacher, psychologist, and important figure on the periphery of the development of Humanistic Psychology. He participated in pioneering work with Timothy Leary, Aldous Huxley, and Allen Ginsberg in researching LSD and other psychedelic substances. Due to the controversial nature of his work, he was dismissed from his teaching position at Harvard in 1963. He traveled to India in 1967 and met his spiritual teacher Neem Karoli Baba and studied yoga and meditation. He was given the name Ram Dass—Servant of God. He suffered a stroke in 1997 that was near fatal and left him paralyzed on the right side of his body. He lived out his final days on Maui where he continued to teach. In 1974 he created the Hanuman Foundation, and that organization developed the Prison-Ashram Project or Human Kindness Foundation.

Since 1968, Ram Dass pursued a panoramic array of spiritual methods and practices from potent ancient wisdom traditions, including bhakti or devotional yoga focused on the Hindu deity Hanuman; Buddhist meditation in the Theravada, Mahayana Tibetan, and Zen Buddhist schools; and Sufi and Jewish mystical studies. Perhaps most significantly, his practice of karma yoga or spiritual service opened up millions to their deep yet individuated spiritual practice and path. Ram Dass continued to uphold the bodhisattva ideal for others through his compassionate sharing of true knowledge and vision. His unique skill in getting

---

[161] Hillman, James, *Re-visioning Psychology,* Harper, 1997, www.harpercollins.com

[162] *BrainyQuote,* https://www.brainyquote.com/quotes/james_hillman_598956 for additional citations.

people to cut through and feel divine love without dogma is still a positive influence on many all over the planet.[163]

Ram Dass's major writings include *Psychedelic Experience; The Only Dance There Is; Be Here Now; How Can I Help* (with Paul Gorman); *Grist for the Mill; and Still Here.*

Quotes by Ram Dass:

"As we grow in our consciousness, there will be more compassion and more love, and then the barriers between people, between religions, between nations will begin to fall. Yes, we have to beat down the separateness."

"The thinking mind is what is busy. You have to stay in your heart. You have to be in your heart. Be in your heart. The rest is up here in your head where you are doing, doing, doing."

"Inspiration is God making contact with itself."

"If I go into a place in myself that is love, and you go into a place in yourself that is love, we are together in love. Then you and I are truly in love, in the state of being love. That's the entrance to Oneness."[164]

Ken Wilber (1949 -) is described as a leading contemporary thinker and transpersonal theorist. He is a practitioner of Zen meditation. He is a prolific writer with the ability to integrate and synthesize ideas, and his theories of consciousness and transpersonal experience are a synthesis of psychology, philosophy, Eastern and Western religions, mysticism, evolution, sociology, and anthropology. His most recent focus has been on the development of Integral Psychology.

According to Brant Cortright, Integral Psychology is a synthesis of Sri Aurobindo's teachings and depth psychology. Integral Psychology is presented as a synthesis of the two major streams of depth psychology—the humanistic-existential and contemporary psychoanalytic—within an integrating East-West framework.

Bahman Shirazi of the California Institute of integral Studies has defined Integral Psychology as

a psychological system concerned with exploring and understanding the totality of the human phenomenon...(which) at its breadth, covers the entire body-mind-psyche-spirit- spectrum, while at its depth... encompasses the

---

[163] "Richard Alpert/Ram Dass Biography," *Ram Dass Love Serve Remember Foundation,* https://www.ramdass.org/bio/

[164] *BrainyQuote,* https://www.brainyquote.com/quotes/ram_dass_601690 for additional citations.

previously explored unconscious and the conscious dimensions of the psyche, as well as the supra-conscious dimension traditionally excluded from psychological inquiry. (Shirazi, 2001) [165]

Major writings of Wilber: *The Spectrum of Consciousness; The Atman Project: No Boundary; Up from Eden: A Transpersonal View of Human Evolution; Eye to Eye: The Quest for a New Paradigm; A Brief History of Everything; The Marriage of Sense and Soul; Integral Psychology: Consciousness, Spirit, Psychology, Therapy.*

<u>Quotes by Ken Wilber:</u>

"What's my philosophy? In a word, integral."

"What is it in you that brings you to a spiritual teacher in the first place? It's not the spirit in you, since that is already enlightened, and has no need to seek. No, it is the ego in you that brings you to a teacher."[166]

"You are not the one who experiences liberation; you are the clearing, the opening, the emptiness, in which any experience comes and goes, like reflections on the mirror. And you are the mirror, the mirror mind, and not any experienced reflection." [167]

"In other words, the real problem is not exterior. The real problem is interior. The real problem is how to get people to internally transform, from egocentric to sociocentric to worldcentric consciousness, which is the only stance that can grasp the global dimensions of the problem in the first place, and thus the only stance that can freely, even eagerly embrace global solutions."

"To understand the whole it is necessary to understand the parts. To understand the parts it is necessary to understand the whole. Such is the circle of understanding."

Stanislov Grof (1931-) has had a career that covers over 60 years of exploration. He is most known for his research into non-ordinary states of consciousness that have therapeutic and transformative value. During the years of 1956-1960, he conducted laboratory research of psychedelics—LSD, psilocybin, mescaline, and other substances. He spent the years of 1960-1967 as principal investigator of the psychedelic research program at the Psychiatric Research

---

[165] "Integral Psychology," *Psychology Wiki*, http://psychology.wikia.com/wiki/Integral_psychology
[166] *BrainyQuote*, https://www.brainyquote.com/quotes/ken_wilber_184127 for additional citations
[167] *AZ Quotes*, https://www.azquotes.com/author/15634-Ken_Wilber?p=2

Institute in Prague, Czechoslovakia, followed by seven additional years of psychedelic research in the United States.

From 1973 to 1987 he was the scholar-in-residence at the Esalen Institute in Big Sur, California where he and his late wife Christina jointly developed Holotropic Breathwork. This is a powerful non-pharmacological form of self-exploration and psychotherapy combining accelerated breathing, evocative music, and a special form of bodywork. (This writer had the experience of attending several Holotropic Breathwork workshops conducted by Dr. Grof during the time I lived in California. They were profound experiences.)

Dr. Grof and his late wife also worked with many individuals undergoing spontaneous episodes of non-ordinary states of consciousness currently diagnosed by mainstream psychiatry as psychoses and treated with suppressive medication. The Grofs realized that these episodes often are actually psycho-spiritual crises of spiritual opening and coined the term "spiritual emergencies" for them. They discovered that if these episodes are correctly understood and supported, they have great therapeutic potential and can lead to profound positive inner transformation. [168]

Dr. Grof's website has lengthy lists of his education, positions held, awards and honors, honorary positions, and major fields of research interest. He is the recipient of the Prestigious VISION 97 Award and the Diamond Arch-Delusional Boulder Award. His website describes these awards.

His major writings include *Beyond the Brain, Death and Transcendence in Psychotherapy; The Adventure of Self-Discovery; The Holotropic Mind; The Stormy Search for the Self.*

Quotes by Stanislov Grof:

"A radical inner transformation and rise to a new level of consciousness might be the only real hope we have in the current global crisis brought on by the dominance of the Western mechanistic paradigm."

"The human psyche shows that each individual is an extension of all existence."

"If consciousness can function independently of the body during one's lifetime, it could be able to do the same after death."

"I believe it is essential for our planetary future to develop tools that can change the consciousness which has created the crisis that we are in."

"Each of us can manifest the properties of a field of consciousness that transcends space, time, and linear causality."

---

[168] *Dr. Stanislov Grof,* http://www.stanislavgrof.com Official website for more information.

"For any culture which is primarily concerned with meaning, the study of death - the only certainty that life holds for us - must be central, for an understanding of death is the key to liberation in life."[169]

Karen Horney (1885-1952) (pronounced horn-eye) published her feministic views on psychoanalytic theory which marked the beginning of feminism in **1945**. Her psychoanalytic social theory is built on the assumption that childhood social and cultural conditions are largely responsible for shaping personality.

Perhaps the most important contribution Karen Horney made to psychodynamic thought was her disagreements with Freud's view of women. Horney was never a student of Freud, but did study his work and eventually taught psychanalysis at both the Berlin and New York Psychoanalytic Institute.... She countered Freud's view of penis envy with what she called womb envy or man's envy of women's ability to bear children. She argued that men compensate for this inability by striving for achievement and success in other realms.

In her view, men and women were equal outside of the cultural restrictions often placed on being female. [170]

Her views were not well accepted at the time but were used years after her death to help promote gender equality. She was also known for her study of neurotic personality, defining neurosis as a maladaptive and counterproductive way of dealing with relationships.

Some of her books include *Feminine Psychology; Neurosis and Human Growth; Our Inner Conflicts: A Constructive Theory of Neurosis; Self-Analysis; New Ways of Psychoanalysis; Character Disorder: A Guide for the Modern Practitioner*.

Quotes by Karen Horney:

"Like all sciences and all valuations, the psychology of women has hitherto been considered only from the point of view of men."

"The psychology of women hitherto actually represents a deposit of the desires and disappointments of men."

---

[169] *BrainyQuote*, https://www.brainyquote.com/quotes/stanislav_grof_350499 for additional citations.

[170] "Ahead of Her Time: Karen Horney and Feminine Psychology," *All Psych*, Chapter 5.5 https://allpsych. com/personality-theory/psychodynamic/horney/

"The searching for ourselves is the most agonizing, isn't it? --And yet the most stimulating--one simply cannot escape it."

"The view that women are infantile and emotional creatures, and as such, incapable of responsibility and independence is the work of the masculine tendency to lower women's self-respect." [171]

Clarissa Pinkola Estes, PhD (1945 -) is an American poet, psychoanalyst, and post-trauma specialist. She has a doctorate from the Union Institute and University and has practiced for over forty-eight years. Her doctorate is in ethno-clinical psychology, the study of social and psychological patterns of cultural and tribal groups with an emphasis in indigenous history.

Dr. Estes is a Mestiza Latina (Native American/Mexican and Spanish).She was raised in a rural village near the Great Lakes with World War II immigrant, refugee families who could not read or write. As an older child, she was adopted into one of these families of majority Magyar and minority Danau Swabian tribal people.

Her families were wise in the ways of nature, planting, animals, and making everything from scratch from shoes to songs. She was raised immersed in the oral tradition of old mythos and stories, songs and chants, dances, and ancient healing ways. She is a first-generation American whose lifelong work has been in the service of the voiceless as a post-trauma recovery specialist and psychoanalyst. She has worked with people traumatized by war, exile, and torture and as a journalist covered many stories of human suffering.

Among her voluminous accomplishments, Dr. Estes is the author of many books on the life of the soul, and her work is published in thirty-seven languages. Her most famous book is *Women Who Run with the Wolves*. She has narrated many audio books including *The Wild Woman Archetype* in six volumes. This author has listened to most of her audio books, including *the Wild Woman Archetype* series. They are enchanting and informative, bestowing on the listener the wonderful gift of hearing old world folklore and firsthand experiences from a unique and authentic perspective, delivered in a soothing voice that transmits love with every word. Dr. Estes has the gift of being able to translate the old stories into gifts of psychological understanding, so that they become lessons of soul.

Dr. Estes worked as a post-trauma specialist in the 1960s with severely injured "cast-away" children and war veterans with PTSD and their families. She served the Columbine High School and community after the massacre from 1999 to 2003 and continues to work with 9-11 survivors and families on both East and West coasts. She is the editor for <u>www.</u>

---

[171] *AZ Quotes*, <u>https://www.azquotes.com/quote/555922</u>

TheModeratevoice.com, a news and political blog that includes issues of culture, soul, and politics. [172]

Dr. Estes is a powerful and insightful poet and storyteller. A full list of available audiobooks and other publications can be found on her website. Many can be purchased through Sounds True. She is a treasured, one-of-a- kind gift to this world.

Marion Woodman (1928-2018) was a Canadian Jungian Analyst whose focus was the Conscious Feminine, and she has written many books on the subject. She was a mythopoetic author and analytical psychologist as well as being highly active in the women's movement. She specialized in eating disorders, sexuality, and women's issues. She lectured internationally and wrote collaboratively with Thomas Moore, Jill Mellick, and Robert Bly. (This author was privileged to attend a lecture in Omaha, Nebraska with Ms. Woodman and Robert Bly.)

Woodman was listed in *Watkin's Mind Body Spirit* Magazine in 2012 as the 100th most spiritually influential living person. Her collection of audio and visual lectures, correspondence, and manuscripts are housed at the Pacifica Graduate Institute Opus Archives and Research Center in Santa Barbara, California.

Her books include *The Owl Was a Baker's Daughter: Obesity, Anorexia Nervosa and the Repressed Feminine,* 1980 - Inner City Books; *Addiction to Perfection: The Still Unravished Bride,* 1982 - Inner City Books; *The Ravaged Bridegroom: Masculinity in Women,* 1990 - Inner City Books; *Leaving My Father's House: A Journey to Conscious Femininity,* 1993 - Inner City Books; *Dancing in the Flame: The Dark Goddess in the Transformation of Consciousness,* 1996 - Shambhala Publications; *Bone; Dying into Life,* 2000 - Viking Press, a powerful book of her journey with uterine cancer. [173]

APPROACHING A MONUMENTAL SYNTHESIS

We live in an important time in human history. Progressive and innovative thinkers and researchers in the fields of science, medicine, and psychology are all opening doors into a

---

[172] *Dr. Clarissa Pinkola Estes,* http://www.clarissapinkolaestes.com
This biographical information summarized from Dr. Estes' website. She continues to facilitate workshops. Information can be found on her website.
[173] "Marion Woodman," *Wikipedia,* https://en.wikipedia.org/wiki/Marion_Woodman Includes Ms. Woodman's bio and list of publications.
A website for her foundation has been established and continues to be a resource for Ms. Woodman's work and offers workshops in support of the conscious feminine. https://www.mwfbodysoulrhythms.org/

better understanding of the intricacy and complexity of the human state as they contribute to our evolution as a species.

The paradigm-shifting influences of this short and incomplete list of the pioneers in psychology give us a sampling of an important continuum in the development of understanding of the human psyche and a foundation for the important part the intelligence of the heart will play in our future.

On the very human level, we see some rivalry and territorial stances regarding each school of thought. It seems folly to me to not recognize the significance of each contribution over time as an important thread in the tapestry of psychology that weaves a synthesis of the human psyche into a powerful gestalt [174] of understanding.

This bird's eye view of the evolution of psychology in the last couple of centuries makes it possible to glimpse the Weaver of Intelligence inspiring each pioneer's contribution and incorporating those threads into the complex and fascinating tapestry of the human psyche.

History tells us that new ideas have to be introduced slowly and carefully into the collective consciousness in small almost imperceptible steps, or they are simply obliterated. This continuum illustrates how small steps contribute to larger ones that are creating a path to something monumental.

---

[174] *Oxford English Dictionary,* https://en.oxforddictionaries.com/definition/gestalt
A gestalt is a whole that is greater than the sum of its parts

13

SEARCHING FOR TRUTH THROUGH
THE PRISM OF PERCEPTION

READING BETWEEN THE LINES—AN EXERCISE IN EXPLORATION

THROUGHOUT PART THREE WE HAVE discussed our current paradigm and how spiritual evolution has unfolded in fairly predictable archetypal stages of growth and development, depending on the level the individual begins with and the belief system embedded into the path they are born into, choose, and/or find.

Throughout the course of human history, a few have reached various levels of enlightenment, but even in those states, they have not appeared to completely transcend the Hologram of Deception because the concept of humanity being in a programmed state is not accepted as part of the collective belief system. While our current definition of "enlightenment" puts someone in a place of advanced esoteric understanding, it isn't the final destination of our consciousness.

New information arriving on the planet is presenting us with some important missing pieces. As we place those pieces into our collective puzzle and a more complete picture begins to take shape, we will discover that we are destined to come to a stage or phase that takes us beyond the hologram and allows us contact with the Multiverse. This new information can assist us in reading between the lines of ancient or obscure texts for clues. I found the following passage in a book titled *Tibetan Yoga and Secret Doctrines* to be one of those hints:

> All beauty, all goodness, all that makes for the eradication of sorrow and ignorance on Earth, must be devoted to the one Great Consummation. Then, when the Lords of Compassion shall have spiritually civilized the Earth and made of it a Heaven, there will be revealed to the pilgrims the Endless Path, which reaches to the Heart of the Universe...

(Buddha) He tells us that neither the believing nor the non- believing in a Supreme Deity but self-exertion in righteousness and self-directed spiritual evolution, as indicated for us in the Nobel Eight- Fold Path are essential to Liberation. (Eight-fold path is Right belief, right intention, Right speech, right actions, right livelihood, Right endeavoring, Right mindfulness, Right concentration—<u>Right</u> being alignment with Divine will.) ...Thereby did the Buddha teach that man is the maker and master of his own fate...that man is under no divine curse nor is he the bearer of any original sin other than of his own making. [175]

I personally interpret the "Lords of Compassion" to be those who have attained heart-centered Behavioral Intelligence. [176]

When we align with the Six Heart Virtues [177]—of which Compassion is the most far reaching—we are brought into alignment with Source. When we operate from a heart-centered state, we have the ability to bring about our release from the Hologram of Deception. When looked at in this way, the *Tibetan Yoga* passage falls in line with our future endeavors.

Certainly, anyone who has had experiences associated with enlightenment or kundalini awakening has lived through something very profound, but the *WingMakers Materials* would have us understand that this is only the tip of the iceberg.

For centuries humanity has traveled those well-worn, somewhat predictable paths, and up until recently, this is all most of us have had available. Each path presents a language, archetypal influences, metaphors, and symbols that once propped open the door to deeper understanding, as we explored in the chapter on Alchemy. The paths we have traveled can be useful in interpreting psychology, historical perspectives, and literature, as well as helpful in understanding the dynamics of someone experiencing a spiritual crisis/emergency, but they don't seem to carry us much further than that. Is there a way to go beyond these old patterns of development and ultimately transcend the Hologram of Deception? That is the question this book is on a quest to explore.

---

[175] Evans-Wentz W. Y., *Tibetan Yoga and Secret Doctrines Seven Books of Wisdom of the Great Path, According to the Late Lama Kazi Dawa-Samdup's English Rendering*, arranged and edited by W.Y. Evans-Wentz. Oxford University Press 1958, 2000.

[176] See **Behavioral Intelligence,** Appendix A - Glossary

[177] Chapter Twenty-five—A New Core Belief Matrix discusses the **Six Heart Virtues** in depth; they are described to us by James Mahu in these e-papers found at www.wingmakers.com: "The Art of the Genuine" https://wingmakers.com/writings/sixheartvirtues/the-art-of-the-genuine/ and "Living from the Heart" https://wingmakers.com/writings/sixheartvirtues/living-from-the-heart/

The *WingMakers Materials* "Chamber Two Philosophy: The Shifting Models of Existence" [178] opened my eyes to the understanding of why particular belief patterns could be found winding through the undercurrent of every religion and belief system.

MODELS OF EXISTENCE

The following quote by James Mahu provides intriguing information about how our belief systems have been constructed. According to James, there are two current models of existence that are shaping the destiny of the human race, and from those two, we will ultimately arrive at a third model— Synthesis Model/Sovereignty. The first two models are:

- The Evolution/Saviorship Model
- The Transformation/Mastership Model

Each human is developing their belief system from one or both of these models of existence. The *evolution/saviorship model* is the dominant model that is promulgated by the Hierarchy. Its basic tenets are that life evolves through the Hierarchy's teacher/student methodology, and that various teachers (saviors) are presented to the human race that enables sub-hierarchies to develop and control information. In so doing, individuals are disempowered and disconnected from their sovereignty. The underlying equation of the evolution/saviorship model of existence is:

Human Instrument + Hierarchy = God connection through saviorship.

In the case of the *transformation/mastership model of existence*, its principal tenets are that the entity is limitless, deathless, and sovereign. All information flows from Source Intelligence to the entity, and it is therefore the responsibility of the entity to become self-enlightened and self-liberated by attuning itself to Source Intelligence and "detuning" itself from the Hierarchy. Each becomes their own master, and each transforms from a

---

[178] Mahu, James and John Berges, "The WingMakers Glossary, Models of Existence," *Collected Works of the WingMakers, Volume I,* edited by John Berges, Egg Harbor, NJ: Planetwork Press, 2013.
ALSO, Mahu, James, "WingMakers Glossary," *WingMakers*, WingMakers Tools, http://wingmakers.com/wp- content/uploads/2020/08/WingMakers-Glossary-optimized.pdf (downloadable file)
See also Appendix D — Models of Existence

human being to a Sovereign Integral within the cradle of time and space. The underlying equation of the transformation/ mastership model of existence is:

Entity + Source Intelligence = First Source equality.

One of the challenges of the individual is to recognize these two dominant models of existence and integrate them in order to design a synthesis model. The synthesis model is slowly emerging on terra- earth, and with high probability will ultimately become the dominant model of existence in this universe. It will be the model of existence that is best able to unify consciousness without impinging on the sovereignty of the entity and First Source. It will allow the entity to be the vibrant container of Source Intelligence and explore new fields of vibration as a fully conscious outpost of First Source. [179]

This information about the models of existence answered so many questions for me. It explained to me why our species is so focused on finding savior figures both in the old and new religions. Christianity is the most obvious example in the Western world, but we look for saviors in every walk of life. I have puzzled for years about why humans have a tendency to blindly pledge allegiance to those who give the illusion of being in authority, often without question, and readily give up their Sovereignty.

It all made sense to me when I learned that humanity has been programmed to gravitate towards the *evolution/saviorship model of existence* system of belief which was developed to keep us living in separation in order to enable our species to participate in the Grand Experiment. According to the *WingMakers Materials*, this model is maintained through the Hierarchy and is designed to suppress us by preserving the belief that we cannot have direct access to First Source. It is a belief system of separation, but at the same time it gives us a way to evolve within a spiritual paradigm and have the experience of feeling like we are making some progress in our spiritual development. If we look back on the myth at the beginning of this book, it makes sense that the creators of our human instrument didn't know how long it would take us to figure out what had happened to us, so they created a hologram to grow in while they maintained a hierarchical controlling system to keep us from ever reaching the ultimate understanding of who we are. The way the belief system is set up also discourages any questioning of the authorities.

Knowing this casts new light on why belief systems are organized in a hierarchical fashion. They are designed to keep us chasing a carrot of what we see as progressive spiritual

---

[179] Ibid.

growth. If one ponders this for even a few moments, we come to realize that everything in our world is designed hierarchically, whether it is religion, corporations, government, or education—and we take it for granted that this is the way things are. But are they?

The other model that functions on Earth today is the

transformation/mastership model of existence.

It is the system of belief used to begin our journey out of separation, move away from the influence of the Hierarchy, and reclaim our Sovereignty, thus unifying us with Source and each other. We see variations of this model in some Eastern religions, in Gnostic and other transformational belief systems, and in Alchemy.

Keeping the models of existence in mind, we can ask ourselves if a particular path or belief keeps us seeking or believing in a savior or if it gives us the tools to become our own teacher/savior through a process of understanding and internal transformation.

If it is true that our species is on a trajectory to reinstate our Sovereign Integral Consciousness and said consciousness is a heart-centered one that develops Behavioral Intelligence as we live and transmit the Six Heart Virtues, then a practice that includes heart-centered responses to everyday situations should begin to bear fruit as we each grow in our ability to transmit the virtues into everyday life events.

Each individual is at a different stage of that process, so our paths are not the same. Living in separation in programmed human instruments, we have unique views of how life works, and those perceptions even play into our efficiency in understanding how to utilize the Six Heart Virtues. Over time I believe our perceptions will begin to interweave with each other. I have come to this conclusion after talking with others involved in utilizing the *WingMakers Material* for internal development. We have learned that as we study the material and revisit it from time to time and utilize the Six Heart Virtues in our everyday lives, new understandings jump out at us that didn't even seem to be there before. This is a phenomenon that we continually experience and marvel at because it contributes to our deeper understanding and development of Behavioral Intelligence.

As we move deeper into the process of transformation, we are discovering how to awaken to more of the Sovereign Integral part of ourselves while living in a human body. That awakening will loosen the reins of the programming we have been subjected to for so many centuries, and one day it will fall away altogether as we become Sovereigns restored.

How do we participate in that process in our own lives? Our involvement will depend on our willingness to immerse ourselves in the river of the highest frequencies of love on earth—*spiritual equality*— "found in the deepest layers of the human heart, living free like a mountain stream— uncrystallized and unconformable by social programming or even human experience." [180] This is our birthright; it is what inspires us in those profound moments when we recognize the beauty and connections we all share.

We as a species are at the threshold of a restoration that will be like nothing that has ever been experienced on earth. We have front row seats to the continuing spectacle of political secrets and shenanigans that are being revealed on the stage of public scrutiny as the era of expansion and transparency exposes corruption and deception in high level arenas at almost runaway train speed.

At the same time, many of us are being drawn to discover our true Essence as Sovereign Beings through the development of Behavioral Intelligence as we grow more proficient at accessing and transmitting the love frequency through our hearts. And as the quote above states, that intelligence is found in the deepest layers of the human heart and can be expressed individually through the transmission of what James has identified as the Six Heart Virtues: *Compassion, Appreciation, Forgiveness, Humility, Understanding and Valor.* These energetic frequencies are our life-giving birthright. They inspire us in profound moments when we recognize the beauty and connections we all share. They give us a way of transmitting hope to a chaotic world.

As we discussed in the chapter on Alchemy, on this plane of existence we do our work in slow motion and as we mature and evolve, especially if we deliberately put ourselves on a transformational journey, it is possible that we will experience stages of an Alchemical process. The insights we glean on a daily basis accumulate over time, and sometimes in hindsight we can see in those fragments a pattern that has been leading us to an outcome that is a synergy of our efforts.

I like to think of my spiritual journey as a vertical trajectory intersecting with the horizontal trajectory of everyday life and filling me with deeper and more profound gems of understanding. Each step of the way has provided me with concepts that have honed my ability to access the next ones.

I prefer to look at my process in this way rather than the duality of saying the old is not any good anymore while the new is the better way. There is no judgement about where we have been. The old served us as valuable steppingstones and brought us to the new. The challenge is to recognize that while each plateau is valuable and growth-producing when we are there, we must be willing to let go of limiting beliefs of each level as we expand our understanding in order to absorb and grasp the next level's offerings.

---

[180] Mahu, James, "Preface by the Author," *Collected Works of the WingMakers, Volume I,* edited by John Berges, Egg Harbor, NJ: Planetwork Press, 2013.

It is key to appreciate that each of us is doing the best we can with the information we have available to us at the time, and each gem of insight and understanding is moving us along our paths. Some may seem to take detours to explore; others appear to stay focused on the course. An individual's decisions along their life's path are not for us to judge, as each journey is very specific as we explore in the prism of perception.

TOOLS FOR INNER EXPLORATION – ACTIVE IMAGINATION

It is useful for us to learn to utilize our imagination. It is a powerful tool, and our success in many of endeavors, spiritual or otherwise, depends on how well we can imagine. Whenever we transmit a heart virtue, we are using our imagination to accomplish that.

A powerful process that Carl Jung taught was Active Imagination. Assagioli also taught a similar process in a system he called Psychosynthesis. In the 1980s I was given the powerful and life-altering gift of experiencing a two-week Psychosynthesis "Pearl Diving" retreat. It was about a year after we lost our seventeen-year-old daughter Michelle in a car accident.

I arrived at that retreat emotionally raw. For almost a year I had kept an inexpressible grief bottled up and seething just underneath the surface of the smiling facade I presented to the world. I was not prepared for the power of the welcoming and loving energy of the facilitators and participants of that retreat and their ability to quickly melt my brave front, revealing the bare and emotionally quivering wreck that I was. Tears of grief and release began to spill out of me in torrents soon after I arrived and continued for most of the two weeks.

Each day our group would be directed through guided imagery into Active Imagination, and in our free time we would work privately with the techniques. I had many profound insights and experiences during that two- week retreat, and I can say without reservation that the Psychosynthesis process was powerfully transformative for me.

I wrote about some of my realizations in my book *Remnants from the Fire* [181] and used Active Imagination to write most of that book. I found it was a powerful process to take an archetype that I was attracted to and journal an internal dialogue with it. I was incredibly surprised at what I experienced, as those energies seemed to willingly inspire me when I asked them to.

Active Imagination is a process of inner dialogue that can be used with any image that appears in your Mind's Eye or in a dream. Ask the image or the idea or an archetype a

---

[181] Ferguson, Lark Aleta, *Remnants from the Fire, A Transformational Journey with the Archetypes*, Authorhouse Publishers, 2002. I have included it in Appendix E – Poems.

question and see what comes into your mind. One has to be willing to trust and dialogue with whatever begins to respond, and it may take a few attempts for anything to happen. But if you are persistent, you should eventually have some results. You can also draw or sculpt or paint images you encounter. If music moves you, dance sometimes will give you profound insight.

For example: I used to roller skate a lot. It was a great exercise outlet for me and a place I could take my kids for an activity we could do together. The local rink had a lady's session on Wednesday mornings where we could skate and bring our young children. It was a great environment for them to learn to skate. I had them all on roller skates very soon after they began to walk. I found it very soothing to skate to music, and I would often receive powerful insights as I skated, immersing my body in the music. After Michelle's accident, my skating sessions were often experiences in sorting out my feelings as I skated around the rink in an endless circle. The poem "The Tempest," [182] a very emotional and powerful poem came to me through the activity of skating to music. One never knows where inspiration will find an outlet.

I journaled my experiences as they generally produced profound gems of understanding. The practice of Active Imagination is extremely helpful in bringing life to one's intuition and imagination. I have dialogued with my inner male and with the Hermit. During the time I was writing *Remnants,* I would dialogue with my Higher Self frequently. I find that Active Imagination often inspires poetry, such as the poems I have written that are distributed throughout this book.

TOOLS FOR INNER EXPLORATION – MYTHICAL QUEST

Myth can be defined in several ways. Myths can be beliefs that are held as truth but later discovered to not be truth. Typically, they come from beliefs or superstitions that are passed down, often in families or close-knit communities, as pieces of traditional wisdom. An old wives' tale is an example of a myth in this category.

Myth can refer to a belief in a cultural expectation, such as little girls growing up to believe in the "myth" of the white picket fence with two children, a husband, and a happily-ever-after married life. This is an archetypal myth.

For my book *Remnants from the Fire,* I used a fairy tale format and called on the world of archetypes to attempt to explore a modern myth: a story depicting the journey of the contemporary woman of the baby boomer generation caught between two world views.

---

[182] Ibid.

The book dispels the myth of the white picket fence where the Prince and Princess ride off into the sunset to live happily ever after and plots a modern archetypical journey and transformational quest of a family muddling through the storms of everyday life.

I devoted Chapter Ten in this book to the journey one can take using the Alchemical model. Another model of personal growth is through the use of myth to identify the predictable stages of quests, such as the journey to enlightenment and the search for the Holy Grail. Generally, the stages fall within a basic sequence, but they do not have to happen in the order given below. These five stages are general blueprints that are often superimposed over most Paths of Awakening in a general way:

- *__An awakening__*: Something prompts us to ask the question: "Is this all there is?" We feel there may be more to life than the way we are living. This stage can arrive with a feeling of futility about where our life is going, forcing us to question our values and beliefs in light of what we are experiencing.
- *__Some form of purification or strengthening__*: Life-altering events begin to happen that force us to look deeper for answers. We are often struck with a futility about life at this stage, forcing us to question our values and beliefs in light of what we are feeling.
- *__A budding sense of Divine Guidance or purpose__*: At this level, we can be quite obnoxious, feeling like we are finding the "right" way or the "truth" and wanting everyone else we come into contact with to feel the same way. We begin looking for our purpose in life, strongly feeling that we have some destiny to fulfill.
- *__The Dark Night of the Soul__*: This is a tempering stage and often includes some loss or adversity that greatly impacts us and sends us into the abyss of unanswerable questions. It is a time when we can feel utterly alone and often hopeless. We can also feel that we no longer belong anywhere. We live between two worlds—an old world that doesn't fit anymore and a world being reached for but not quite attained. This is often a humbling stage that can either make or break us as it seasons and deepens us, and it is usually a period of profound transformation. We can emerge from a dark night of the soul with a strong desire to change course entirely.
- *__Illumination__*: The state of Awakening or Illumination or Enlightenment can be defined in several ways. It can begin with us emerging from a very trying life process with a stronger sense of purpose and understanding of life to a rebirth that becomes a total dissolution of our ego identity as a separate self which results in a complete change in the way we view life.

It is through the historical legends and mythical heroes of every culture that we learn to recognize the archetypal patterns of the mythical quest. If we look at our lives through the lens of our imagination, we might find many archetypal patterns at work, and we might find that we are the legends and mythical heroes of our own personal stories.

I think we have experienced these stages time after time, spiraling upward as we ascend the ladder of spiritual development. What we discover in our journeys, however, is that we never quite leave the Matrix. We grow within it, but until recently there hasn't been a way to grow out of it.

A mythology often introduces new ideas into the Collective Consciousness. James Mahu is doing that with his novel *The Ancient Arrow Project* and other books he has written, including *Quantusum, The Weather Composer Series,* and *The Dohrman Prophecy.*[183]

TRANSFORMATION VIA THE STAGES OF THE BUTTERFLY

A chapter discussing transformative processes would not be complete without including the stages of the butterfly. The process a caterpillar goes through to become a butterfly is one of the most magical marvels in the natural world. The butterfly's story is a powerful metaphorical illustration of our story, and our transformation promises to be as extraordinary as that of the butterfly.

- *Caterpillar/larva stage*: The caterpillar is the first stage of earthly life. With our nose to the grindstone, we are just getting started and making slow progress. The caterpillar must find nourishment in order to gain enough strength and sustenance for the next stage. During this period, we focus on building our material foundation, gaining the necessary knowledge to function in the physical world and in the process hopefully developing enough ego strength to survive the next stage.
- *Cocoon stage*: Impulses from within begin spinning a covering around the caterpillar. We begin asking questions like: "Is this all there is?" "Isn't there more to life than just everyday monotony?" This is the stage when we begin hearing the call from our Spiritual Self to look for more, and we begin going inward.

---

[183] All the novels except *The Ancient Arrow Project* are available as separate paperbacks from Planetwork Press (planetworkpress.com).
The *Ancient Arrow Project* novel is part of *Collected Works of the WingMakers Volume I* and is also available as an e-book on *wingmakers.com*

We retreat, become bored with what we have been living, and begin searching for answers in places we haven't looked before. This may result in some outward changes such as changing jobs, going back to school, changing mates, or moving. Some go into depression and isolate themselves. Some event or series of events may cause a death to the old way of life. A significant loss can be the beginning of the cocoon stage. The cocoon stage can also be a time of life when addictions take hold because of our feelings of futility and hopelessness about life, causing us to retreat into the addictive process or a pseudo-cocoon. Addictions can become an end in themselves, thus aborting the metamorphosis, or an addiction can be a catalyst into the next stage if we use the impulses of the cocoon stage to overcome the addiction.

- *Metamorphosis*: According to lepidopterists, within the caterpillar are imaginal buds which contain seed cells for those parts of the butterfly that are not found in the caterpillar. When the caterpillar goes into the pupa or cocoon stage, these buds secrete a chemical substance that destroys the surrounding cells while the buds begin growing and dividing to replace the destroyed cells. This process is called *Imagination*. (I am enchanted with this concept and the use of the words imaginal and imagination to describe this change.) [184]

   During our metamorphosis, as seeds of change begin to take root within our psyches, our old belief systems are destroyed and replaced by a new understanding of ourselves brought on by our imagination—our ability to imagine a new life and then develop it.

- *Butterfly*: We are now reborn into a more evolved form where we have an expanded view of the world and our lives. Compared to the caterpillar stage, we are now soaring. The butterfly demonstrates in its short life a profound process that can happen to us several times in the same lifetime as we go through various stages of development and evolution. If you have changed jobs or careers, you know exactly what I am talking about. When we start a new job, we first try to grasp the foundation (caterpillar), then we delve deeper to develop our level of expertise (cocoon), and finally we reach a stage of mastery, and we fly again. If we change jobs again and start another, we will go through the process all over again, especially if we change career tracks.

---

[184] Our transformation also includes the utilization of our imaginations and imaginal cells. I will expand on that topic in Chapter Twenty-four – Transformation and Activation for a New Paradigm.

EXPLORATIONS

1. Explore the stages of your life using one or several of the above models. Where are you now? In your journal, describe the stages you have gone through up until now.

2. Write a small vignette about one of the stages or one for each of the stages you have identified. You may want to call upon one of the archetypes to help you clarify the stage as you write. For instance, have your caterpillar describe your life so far, or speak from the cocoon, or talk about the fear of dissolving during metamorphosis and how that might feel.

3. Call upon one of the archetypes of The Wanderer's Journey as I did and write a vignette about the stage of life you are currently focusing on with the help of the archetype.

4. A story is written one chapter at a time. We all have our outer story that is easy to understand. To uncover the inner symbolic story of your own personal mythical quest requires diligent and profound work. You may want to begin your own personal myth or symbolic story as you do these exercises. When you have finished, you might be surprised at what you have written and learned about yourself along the way and the profound story you will have completed that is about the deeper you. A powerful way to start your story is to simply write "Once upon a time…" and let your imagination take you on the ride it has been waiting to take you on.

14

INNOCENCE LOST

"The demon that you can swallow gives you its power,
and the greater life's pain, the greater life's reply."
Joseph Campbell, *The Power of Myth*

THIS SECTION OF THE BOOK has been spent looking at various aspects of the Mirror of Perception. Death is one of those aspects, and it has many layers and concepts attached to it. Death as an archetypal energy in the world of illusion symbolizes change and rebirth and could be considered as a time of letting go of old patterns that no longer work, freeing us to embrace a way of life that feeds us spiritually and emotionally. Living through life's challenges evoked in me the awareness that to the depths that one has plunged in life is to the heights that one can soar. In that context a quote from Richard Bach's *Illusions* says it so well: *"What the caterpillar calls the end of the world, the Master calls a butterfly."* Or from Teal Scott: *"A thousand times we die in one life, we crumble, break and tear apart until the layers of illusion are burned away and all that is left is the truth of who and what we really are."*

I have often thought that when someone is suicidal, they need to release something that is no longer working or maybe never has, not destroy their entire life. I understand that there are a lot of factors that go into a person's decision to remove themselves from the planet, and we are not generally taught how to recognize or examine those factors; in fact, we are often bombarded with beliefs and platitudes that reinforce self- destructive tendencies. The saviorship/evolution model of existence especially teaches us self-loathing by hammering home our unworthiness, teaching us that we are inherently evil and therefore cannot think for ourselves, and that we can only be redeemed by a savior. For a person who is feeling lost and hopeless and unworthy of God's or anyone else's love, these can be devastating states of mind to be imprisoned in. That is one of many reasons I think it so important to examine negative, limiting, denigrating belief systems and ponder their relevance. Does your belief system teach love of self and others or loathing of self and others? Does it teach inclusiveness or division? Maybe it is time to examine and let go of parts of our programming that no longer serve us and have only managed to keep us in emotional and spiritual bondage.

In his "Project Camelot Interview," James Mahu gives us the term "Death Stress Implant Network Detour" and describes it as the implant that creates the fear of the future and the primal fear of death and non- existence. It is a program and part of the Human Mind System. [185] In other words it was included in the package of suppression to control humanity with fear. If we ponder the significance of that information, we realize that "death" is part of the illusion. Please understand, I do not mean to minimize the very real and viscerally painful feelings of loss and grief we endure when a loved one leaves the planet, but it can be helpful in coming to grips with the belief in the finality of death as annihilation. Yes, the human instrument our Sovereign Integral/life force inhabits does grow old and wears out or becomes mortally compromised in countless ways and dies. But that part of us that animates the human instrument does not die. It is infinite, and I believe there is a mechanism that preserves the memories of our experiences on earth for all to learn by. Individually, during our sojourn in these human instruments, we can choose to grow with each life passage, whether they are positive or negative.

A quote from the introduction to *The Dohrman Prophecy* by James Mahu gives us profound points to ponder:

> The anthropologist, Francis Harwood, was interviewing a Sioux elder about his tribe's myth and penchant for storytelling and asked why his people told stories from generation to generation. The elder answered, "in order to become human beings." Harwood then asked, "But aren't we humans already?" The elder smiled in a knowing way, "Not everyone makes it."
>
> Becoming a human being is not as simple or automatic as most people believe. Sure, our bodies are human, but we can live in the hollowness of one who is indoctrinated to give their attention away.
>
> Our attention is like an impulsive wind, scattered and unsure of what to anchor to. What to believe in. What to express. Our true humanity remains in the chrysalis of a protected state, waiting to break through the thinning walls that contain it. What are these walls? Why do they exist? How do we emerge

---

[185] Mahu, James, "Project Camelot Interview," *WingMakers*, Interviews, https://wingmakers.com/about/interviews/project-camelot-interview/

from the chrysalis and spread our wings to explore the finer dimensions beyond our human senses and in so doing become more human? [186]

Living through the events described in the three stories that follow has contributed significantly to how I perceive the world today and to my understanding of what it is to be human.

I debated with myself about whether or not to include these stories, but since the most intense experiences we have happen during the course of our everyday life and are the ones that challenge us and deepen us, I think the following are relevant as part of looking at what this Matrix—the Hologram of Suppression—is all about.

There is a sense of fearlessness and indestructibility in us when we are young that carries through until something inevitably happens that slaps some stark reality into our worldview and wakes us up to the finiteness and vulnerability of our physical existence.

Death of our bodies is an inescapable part of living in this hologram. At the level of consciousness we are in now, its threat looms over our heads and drives our lives and many of our decisions and is a source of an internal nag and angst we all carry. I think this is especially true when one has children. One's life is never the same after the birth of a child. People say the worst thing to happen is to lose a child and many never recover from the devastation. Regardless of how one defines recovery, one is changed forever with the death of a child.

MICHELLE

I had made arrangements to study Deep Tissue Massage Therapy at the Institute of Psycho-Structural Balancing in San Diego, California the summer of 1984 and drove there in July for classes that were to last six weeks. My seventeen-year-old daughter, Michelle (our second child) had gone to Florida with a friend a few weeks before I left and was to return shortly after my departure to help her father care for the younger children until my return. My oldest daughter Heidi had joined the Navy and was no longer living at home. Wendy, our third teenage daughter was at home and would also help.

I had about ten days left in San Diego and classes were going well. I was learning so much and loving every minute of it. This particular day had a brightness to it, a joy that was palpable. I was exhilarated by what I was learning.

---

[186] Mahu, James, "Introduction," *The Dohrman Prophecy*, p. 1, Planetwork Press, Egg Harbor Township NJ, 2002 www.planetworkpress.com

Then toward the end of the day I had the strangest letdown. All of a sudden, I was overwhelmed by a horrible, dark feeling. I felt as if I had been taken over by something that just gripped me and held on tight. The feeling made me nauseated and weak, it was so intense.

I usually went to get something to eat after class, but on this day, I went straight back to where I was staying as I wasn't hungry; I couldn't think of food. I wasn't in my room more than a few minutes when the phone rang. It was my (now former) husband Lee. He sounded very strained on the phone. He told me to sit down; he had bad news for me. I began to shake all over as my heart went from racing to pounding while he tried his best to tell me the awful news in increments that Michelle had been in a car accident and wasn't expected to make it through the night. He said that he was going to go back to the hospital and call me and put the phone to Michelle's ear so that if I had anything I wanted to tell her, I should do it then as it might be my last chance. After we hung up, I sat there shaking in a horrified and surreal feeling of disbelief as I waited for him to call back. I couldn't move.

It is funny how denial will create strange mindsets when one doesn't want to face what is happening. After I babbled my heartfelt and emotional pleas to Michelle, I asked Lee what to do. I couldn't make a decision; I did not want to go home. I had such an intense feeling of it all being a bad dream, and I think deep down I felt that somehow it wouldn't be real if I didn't go home. He told me to get on the first plane and come home. He said we would deal with my car and belongings later. So, in a trancelike daze, I obediently called an airline, told them what happened, and I was able to get on the first plane early the next morning, around 6:00 AM. (This was 1984, and air travel was quite different then.) I called Lee back and told him when I would arrive.

I packed a suitcase, putting some things in the trunk of my car and left the rest of my belongings in a corner of my room and left a note for the person I was renting from. I had my rent paid up until the end of the school session so I figured it would be OK to leave some of my things in the room. I still hadn't given up the idea that I might be back to finish out the classes I was taking, and I would have to come back and get my car and would need a place to stay. As I said, denial puts one in some strange mental places. My world had become San Diego and school and living by the ocean. I didn't want to leave it. My Nebraska life seemed so distant and almost alien. My whole being balked at facing the nightmare that was ahead of me in Nebraska.

I called the school and left a message and drove my car to the San Diego airport. I arrived at the airport sometime in the middle of the night, not wanting to hear from anyone until I got home. This was before everyone had cell phones, so once I got to the airport, I didn't have any way to communicate except by pay phone. I chose not to call. I wandered around the airport the rest of that night, deep in the surreal feelings of denial and disbelief.

It is interesting how people just appear in one's life at times of need. The person sitting next to me in the airplane from Denver to Grand Island was a Catholic priest who had the same last name as my maternal grandpa. I struck up a conversation with him because I noticed his name on a small piece of his carry-on luggage. He told me that he was going to Grand Island, Nebraska to visit Sister Clarice (I think that was her name) and explained that she worked at the hospital in Grand Island. I told him why I was on the plane. He was comforting without being intrusive, and it felt good to talk to someone about this horror I was grappling with. Come to find out later this particular nun had been with my children comforting them at the hospital.

Since that chance meeting and compassionate and helpful conversation, I have often pondered how life paths intersect, sometimes only briefly to help one cross a bridge they do not want to cross but are being forced onto.

I arrived home in the early afternoon on a miserably hot August day. It was windy and dry and felt so forsaken after the lushness of the beach community where I had been staying. Lee took me straight to the hospital. On the way he tearfully told me how guilty he felt because he had grounded Michelle over something, and she had talked him into letting her go out because it was the last night of summer before she was to begin her senior year of high school. He was struggling with that decision and the price they paid for it. I tried to comfort him, but to no avail. I felt so bad for him because I would have probably done the same thing. She could be charmingly persuasive.

Michelle was still alive, and her vital signs changed when I walked into the room. The nurse told me that her reaction recorded on the monitors told us that Michelle knew I was there. Michelle was in a coma; she looked like she was sleeping. There weren't any outward signs she had been in a car accident other than a few bruises. The injuries were all internal. She looked so peaceful lying in that hospital bed; it was hard to grasp that she was mortally wounded.

I can remember talking to the doctor after I saw her and not being able to comprehend what was happening, I asked him if she would make it through the night. He looked at me with such compassion and said, "She might make it through the night…." His voice trailed off, and he just looked at me. I know he too was struggling with this. He explained the injury to us and that they would do more testing in the morning, but it didn't look promising. She had a brainstem injury and could live for a while in the coma she was in now, but she would never be able to function or be normal again. Michelle would make physical movements with her arms. They explained that it was known as "posturing," and it was an indication of damage to the brain. When I first arrived, Michelle was still breathing without any outside help. I stayed at the hospital for a while and then went to my mother's to see my younger children. While I was there, the hospital called and said that she was beginning to have problems breathing; they would need to put her on life support to assist her with breathing and needed our consent which we gave.

After spending a short time with my younger children, I joined the vigil in Michelle's hospital room that had begun with Wendy, her younger sister by a year, and various members of my family. All of our family except for the small children and my mother were in her room that night. My mother was caring for them so the rest of us could be at the hospital with Michelle. Early the next morning, the feeling in the room became one of immense brightness and peace. It is difficult to describe, but we all felt it. It was a softly poignant feeling, somewhat comforting, but tangibly bright—so bright I felt its warmth completely envelope me. Others in the room remember a similar feeling.

Wendy had stayed with Michelle the entire time since she had arrived at the hospital after the accident. At some point that night as that brightness began to fade, Wendy said, "She is gone," got up, and went into another room and went to sleep.

They did an EEG and other tests on Michelle the next day and determined that she was brain dead and would remain in a coma and stay that way as long as life support kept her alive. She would never recover. We had the gut-wrenching decision to make about whether or not to keep her on life support and if so for how long. As long as she was alive, there was always the chance for a miracle. If we let her go, that possibility would end. On the other hand, she would not want to be kept alive under these circumstances. It was an agonizing conversation that ultimately led to the decision to take her off life support.

A nurse explained to me about how it would work. They would turn off the life support and hope for a miracle. She might continue breathing on her own or not. Someone else came in a few minutes later to ask if we would allow for her organs to be used. This person explained that if we gave permission for her organs to be donated, she would be kept on life support until that happened.

It was that statement that played into my decision not to let them take her organs. Back in 1984 I didn't know as much as I know now about organ transplants. If I had known then what I know now, we might have made a different decision, but the idea that she would be kept alive until her heart was cut out of her was not something I could bear to think about. In my thinking as her mother, it was essentially cutting the heart out of a living person, and that person was my child. I could not live with the idea of her heart being taken out of her body while she was still technically alive. I could not wrap my brain or my feelings around that. As long as she was alive, there was hope, and all I could think about was that they would kill her by cutting the heart out of her chest. I thought of her being aware of me when I entered the room. Her vital signs had changed. Would she be aware of what they were doing in surgery if they did cut her heart out while she was being kept alive? To my grieving heart that was the stuff of nightmares, and the images those thoughts summoned was too much for me to bear.

When it was time to turn off the life-support, we brought in the three younger children and other family members and close friends to say their last goodbyes to her, and then I stayed with the children in another room and Lee remained with Michelle. We were instructed about doing it that way to spare the younger children ages seven, nine, and eleven anymore trauma than necessary, because it was unknown how her body would react once they turned off the life support. Lee said that she went very peacefully. When they turned off the life support, her heart and breathing gradually slowed down and stopped.

On August 30, 1984, Cherie Michelle died from brain stem injuries sustained in a car accident two days earlier. She was our second child, and she was just 17 years old. The accident happened the last evening before school was to start for her senior year of high school. This funny, loveable, and beautiful person left a hole in a large family who adored her and to this day misses her and grieves for what she might have been.

For everyone she was close to, her passing was something each had to grapple with. None of it was easy. The days after her death were like a blur, and we all struggled for a long time coming to grips with this event that shattered our world. The last time she and I exchanged words and hugs was at the bus station as she was getting ready to leave with her friend to go to Florida. I remember her as being incredibly happy and full of anticipation about her upcoming trip, and that joyful image is how I remember her the most.

My oldest daughter Heidi was in the Navy and attending training that was nearing completion. She would be transferred to San Diego after completing the classes. She was in the middle of exams when the accident happened. The timing of when to tell her was something Lee worked out with her commanding officers. That was extremely hard on both Lee and Heidi as her father and her commanding officer made the decision not to tell her until she had finished her exams. Heidi didn't make it back to Grand Island in time to see Michelle alive. After the funeral, Heidi and I drove her car to San Diego—she to her new assignment and I to get my car and belongings and drive back home. It was an emotional and difficult trip for us both.

The place where the funeral was held was packed. Michelle was in an open casket at the entrance, and I stood there by her and greeted people as they came in. I am not sure why I did it that way; mostly I think it was to spend whatever time I had left with her beside me. It was so hard to see the casket close before she was wheeled in for the funeral itself. A dear friend who was also a minister conducted the service for us. My mother was a wonderful pianist and I begged her to play at Michelle's funeral. She did, although I know it was extremely hard for her. She played the theme from the movie *Somewhere in Time,* a song that meant a lot to both Lee and me.

I was very moved by the number of people who attended her funeral and in the gathering afterwards by the amazing stories I heard about her impact on different people in our town. She had worked at a bakery and was known and loved by a lot more people than I was aware of.

I will never forget my trip home from San Diego. I packed a cooler in the car with food so that when I was hungry, I could get a snack, and I stopped at rest stops to sleep when I was tired and essentially drove straight through from San Diego to Nebraska.

That first morning on the trip home, I had made it to the mountains in Southern Utah, and as I came over a hill, the view was a breathtaking sunrise illuminating a gorgeous, luscious mountain valley. The scene filled me with a poignant awe. I remember my feelings that morning and the stark magnificence of the landscape like it was yesterday. To me it was a sign from the Universe that beauty remained in this world, and even in the midst of inexpressible pain, I was able to immerse myself in its splendor. The biggest surprise to me was how deeply I felt the majesty of that view.

The night before, while stopped at a rest stop and sleeping in my car, I had a dream of Michelle. She jumped out of her casket and said, "See, I am not dead." It was so real and so comforting, and the vivid memory of that dream stayed with me through the next day and buoyed me up through many of the dark days ahead.

I was to have many dreams of her over the years—I call them visits. We often talked about her death in those dreams, and often they would be so real I would have a difficult time orienting myself to my current world when I woke up. I can remember one of them: I said that she looked so good, I wanted to get a picture. She said to me that I could try, but she didn't think it would take.

I also had a series of dreams through the years I could only explain as being in a parallel reality where she didn't die. She was slightly older and living a very different life. In those dreams it seemed I was visiting her. They were so real I would feel extremely disoriented as I came to waking consciousness. Lee and I have talked about having that particular kind of dream of her, and he said that he also has had that experience.

I wrote many poems during that time. They helped me express otherwise inexpressible emotions and gave me a way of getting them out of me and onto paper. It provided a modicum of relief to do that. The following is one of those attempts to process my grief:

AUGUST HAS LASTED TOO LONG

The fires of hell
Burn in the August of my life
With a scorching heat
That sears my heart and mind
As I face the Winds of Devastation
Blowing Sands of Despair
Into my eyes
Blinding me to any beauty that might exist!
I cross the Plains of Reason
A hot, relentless logical desert
Burning my emotions
Leaving me parched, weak
My tears spent
Unable to respond

Will I exist to see September?
To once again be enlivened by fresh, brisk air?
I'm strangling in this Abyss
Choked by the suffocating air of guilt
And pain leadened emotions
Tortured in a seething cauldron of anguish

How does this oppressive darkness
Transmute into the gold and silver
That transforms the hot August landscape
Into the brilliance of autumn?

Why did you die in the August of my life Mon Cherie?
My precious flower, so fresh, so new
Did the heat of my August wilt you?
The very essence of springtime

Innocence lost
Cut down one miserable August day

Your passing prolonging the torture
And the uncertainty of my August indefinitely
Did my August frighten you?
Was it too intense for your gentle soul?
Or was your leaving
Some pre-ordained supreme test
And will I make it through this one?

Are you watching me somewhere?
Is that almost imperceptible
Breeze of hope I feel occasionally
Your way of comforting me?

Was it for-ordained
That I must cross these Plains without you?
That we must be tested in this way?
Or a mere accident of fate
That has left us all stunned?

August has lasted too long!!

Michelle's death was a devastating blow to our family. For years I believed that we had been through the worst we could endure and would be spared from any more experiences that difficult, but alas, one devastating experience does not bestow immunity from others.

ANNA

On November 11, 2009, I drove from Nebraska to El Dorado, Kansas to go with my fifth child Anna to a doctor's appointment. She had found a lump in her breast and had a biopsy, and she was to learn the results at that appointment.

Anna was a thirty-five-year-old mother of three at the time. I will never forget that office visit. She was dressed in a blue jumper with a white top underneath it. The crown of her long blond hair was pulled back so that curls cascaded down the back of her head. Short hair in front overlaid her forehead in soft bangs. She looked so young and vulnerable and healthy, and she was stunningly beautiful.

The surgeon who did the biopsy told Anna that she had an aggressive form of breast cancer that was at stage two; he suspected it had spread to the lymph nodes under her arm. Anna's body physically recoiled when her doctor told her the diagnosis, and she uttered a deep visceral sound like someone had hit her. The memory of that moment and her reaction haunts me to this day. I sat there with her, both of us reeling in a haze of heart- pounding surrealistic disbelief as the doctor explained the cancer and the choices of treatment she had. Most of what he said is a blur to me. I remember the doctor's office and Anna's tearful, gut-wrenching reaction and how helpful and sweet his nurse was, but not many more details than those.

The rest of that awful day was one of shock, copious tears, and numb dismay—the beginning of a nightmare as Anna and our family were forced onto a reluctant trajectory that was destined to arrive at an unwanted destination.

Anna made the decision to first have surgery to remove the lump. The doctor suggested a lumpectomy. He said that she was so young, and he thought he could get it all with just the lumpectomy. They also removed some lymph nodes under her right arm and found that some were cancerous which meant that she would have to go through both chemo and radiation. Her doctor explained to her that if the lymph nodes had not been affected, she would not have had to do the radiation. I went down over the Thanksgiving Holiday to be with her during the surgery and helped her through the recovery period.

Anna began the year 2010 with chemo for the prescribed amount of time, followed by a short rest, and then the radiation. She went through the loss of her hair with dignity and a great sense of humor. She was actually quite beautiful with her bald head as it accentuated the stunning exquisiteness of her facial features.

By the end of 2010, Anna was declared to be cancer free. The year of 2011 was a year of feeling grateful for her life as we witnessed the stages of her hair growing back and her energy returning, and we marveled at her resolve to make every day in her life count.

The members of our family as well as many others who knew Anna were inspired by this fun-loving and positive free spirit and by her strength and determination.

Thanksgiving has for years been a tradition for our annual family reunions. Anna insisted on hosting Thanksgiving in her home in El Dorado in 2011. She always loved our Thanksgiving family reunions and was one of its most staunch supporters. It was a daunting undertaking as there are close to thirty people in our family that attend, but she wanted to, and she did it with that same passion for life that she did everything. Nearly everyone in our family traveled to El Dorado for this momentous event that was also a day of giving thanks that Anna was still in our lives. We had a wonderful time. When it was all over, I asked her if she wanted to make it an annual tradition; she said, "Absolutely not, that was exhausting."

In the last part of April 2012, Anna went in for her biannual check-up and was told that the cancer had metastasized to her bones—stage IV. Her older sister Heidi (who is a doctor) and I attended her appointment with her when her oncologist explained her options.

The only drug he would offer her was one with the potential of horrendous side effects. He told her that she was dealing with terminal cancer and without the drug she would not live through the summer. If she took the drug, it might extend her life a few more months. He wrote her the prescription, but when she researched the drug, she was horrified with the side-effects and didn't think it would be worth it only to live an extra miserable month or two. So, she made the decision that she would live her life and spend it with her kids and do some traveling and not let a drug debilitate her and destroy what time she had left. This was a very emotionally charged time for all of us as she brought herself to that resolution. Many tears were shed as she anxiously researched the drug and we searched for alternative treatments.

Anna initially found non-radioactive cesium, an alternative therapy for cancer, and followed that protocol through the summer as it had been known to be effective for some types of cancer, and for a while her markers went down, and she began to look and feel a great deal better and seemed to be improving significantly which gave us all hope.

In June Anna took her girls and went to visit her brother Matthew and his family in New York. Her older sister Heidi arranged to take her and her kids to Costa Rica for a trip in August. Many family members went with her on that trip. They stayed at an all-inclusive resort and by all reports had a wonderful time.

In September, a friend in El Dorado gave Anna a huge party to celebrate her life. This friend's rationale was to have people celebrate with Anna while she was alive and doing so well. It was a wonderful gift to Anna and her family and friends to be together and have that event preserved in photos. I will be forever grateful to her friend's family for opening their home and yard and tapping resources in El Dorado to make this party the huge success and beautiful memory it is.

Somewhere around this time, in late summer or early fall, Anna developed an allergy or reaction to the cesium. I am not sure of the details, but for some reason she had to quit taking it. I don't know the whole story, so I won't speculate any further.

Anna switched to another product, Protocell, and with that she stopped the strict diet regimen she had been on with the cesium. The Protocell regimen had an entirely different approach. She seemed to do OK on it, but not as well as when she was taking cesium. In the fall, I don't remember exactly when, she was told that the cancer had spread to her brain. I will never forget the terrified voice mail I received from her when she found that out. It haunts me to this day. It was such a low blow. She had outlived her doctor's prognosis, and it looked for a while that she was beating the cancer.

This new development brought with it a whole new set of complications as Anna and our family stepped onto the roller coaster of emotions and issues a diagnosis of cancer in the brain creates. The cancer was on the surface of her brain and did not cause her pain or any issues at first. She was put on a small dose of steroids to keep the brain from swelling. The most concentration of the cancer was in her brain stem, so initially her cognitive abilities were not affected. Anna continued to opt for the regimen she was on as her doctor did not have anything promising to offer her. At some point she added coffee enemas. She seemed to maintain through the fall, not getting any worse, but not getting better either.

Heidi explained to me that the progression of this disease once it hit the brain and especially where the bulk of the cancer was located in her hindbrain would cause her brain to continue to swell until it herniated. From what she knew, she had an idea of when Anna would need care, and I made arrangements at work to take family medical leave to be with her. I went to live with her in January 2013.

Anna woke up New Year's Day 2013 vomiting and very sick and went to the hospital. She was told then that the only thing they could do was radiate her brain. Anna was very afraid of that. She did the preliminary work to begin the radiation which included mapping where the cancer was so that those areas of her brain could be targeted and making a face mask to hold her head still during the treatments, but she would not set the appointments to begin the treatments. She was using the other protocols, and she wanted to give them a chance first and use radiation as her last resort.

The steroids were making Anna's face swell, and she was dealing with headaches. She was given strong painkillers for those. She continued like that for several weeks as she went back and forth about whether to do the radiation. She was afraid there would be nothing left of her mind once she was radiated, and she fought to put that off as long as possible.

Anna was not without medical advice; she tried desperately to weigh what she was being told against what she was feeling and the fears that plagued her about the outcome of the radiation. She emailed or talked to people who had brain radiation and lived to talk about it and to family members who lost loved ones after they went through brain radiation. The decision weighed heavily on her about what to do. She poured over cancer resource and support websites, looking for something definitive that would help her make the decision.

I will add here that in all honesty a person's mother might be a good choice as a loving caretaker, but I am not so sure I was the best choice to help Anna make those decisions. I was too emotionally close to it. I lived with her day after day. We had long talks, and I knew her hopes and her fears and her feelings of desperation. I was also pulled strongly onto that same trajectory of denial. I felt powerless to help her make the "right" decision because I wasn't sure what that decision should be either. I drove her to any therapy she wanted to try, and that is how we lived our day-to-day life.

Anna tried hyperbaric oxygen treatments for a while, and we made the trip several times a week to a doctor who offered that therapy. (Hyperbaric oxygen therapy enhances the body's natural healing process by inhalation of 100% oxygen in a total body chamber where atmospheric pressure is increased and controlled.) She always seemed to feel a lot better after a treatment.

The last week in January, Anna got up one morning in unbelievable pain and demanded more painkillers than it was safe to give her. She was so out of it; I begged her and finally convinced her she needed to go to the hospital. This trip turned into a living nightmare. She was completely out of it; her headache was so bad. Upon doing tests, they found that her brain was herniating, and she was taken to surgery so they could put a shunt in her brain to drain the fluids causing the swelling.

When she was diagnosed the second time, Anna gave her sister Heidi the power of attorney with instructions to save her life if possible. So, her sister gave permission for the surgery and to start the radiation because by the time that decision was made, Anna was so out of it, she was unable to communicate coherently at first and ultimately not at all.

Her sister consulted with the radiation oncologist who had mapped Anna's brain and was told that Anna might have a chance with the radiation, but at this stage of the game it could also kill her. Without it she would die without question. Heidi explained this in detail to me. She said that Anna had told her to do what she could to save her life, so Heidi gave consent to go forward with the radiation. The radiation treatments began while Anna was still unconscious after the surgery.

Anna remained in a coma for about two days after the surgery. We didn't know if she would wake up, but she did. She progressed in a short time from being totally helpless, even having to be fed, to a wheelchair, then a walker, then a cane, and finally walking on her own and caring for herself.

Anna was discharged from the hospital about the time she was using a walker but before she was completely through the radiation treatments. The first radiation treatment after she left the hospital became her last one because it made her so sick, we both thought she was going to die. We went through several days I can only describe as hell. Anna could not get out of bed without help; she was unable to walk or stand-up by herself, so she was back to the wheelchair. She had to put her arms around my neck to stand, and then I would walk backwards, holding her to help her get into bed or wherever she needed to go.

Anna said to me in the throes of those nightmarish days that she was deeply sorry because she didn't want me to lose another child, but she didn't think she was going to make it through this. That was one of the few times she vocalized any loss of hope to me. I talked to the radiation oncologist's nurse, and we decided to stop the treatments, at least for the time being. She was too weak and sick to continue.

Anna recovered from that crisis and went on to have home health come and work with her, and she improved by leaps and bounds. She said to me during that time that she just didn't see how she could be brought back and still die from this disease. She was feeling very hopeful again. She was still taking the Protocell and other supplements. The oncology ward of the hospital in Wichita where she stayed during her hospitalizations allowed her to continue taking the Protocell once we could get liquids down her by mouth.

As she was convalescing, Anna told me that it worked out exactly as she had hoped it would—she didn't want to take the radiation unless there was no other choice. She had been told by one nurse while she was being mapped that radiation might help, or it might be like spreading fertilizer all over the brain; no one would know which outcome would result until the treatments were completed.

We had an arc of improvement, but her mind never regained its full capacity again. It was during this period of time that Anna insisted on attending every school activity her daughters were involved in. Her middle daughter was in dance squad, and she made it a point to attend every one of her performances. Anna's motive was so much about being supportive to her daughters and letting them know she was there for them. Her eldest daughter participated in a senior program, and the school was able to cover the event live and transmit it to Anna's hospital room for her to watch while she was recovering from the herniation ordeal. This all meant a lot to Anna, to be able to be as much a part of her girls' lives as she could.

Anna eventually developed a cough and pneumonia and wound up back in the hospital. When she got sick, she was unable to keep anything down and stopped taking the Protocell and other supplements and began losing ground very rapidly.

We were eventually told that there was nothing more that could be done for Anna but to keep her comfortable. The cancer was ravaging her brain and body. She was moved to the hospice floor of the hospital. Those days in hospice were like *Ground Hog Day*. She had good days when she remembered a lot and interacted with all the visitors who came to see her. There were also many days when she would ask what was going on, and we had to explain again, and there would be tears, and then she would seem to forget. She began to become detached.

Anna had become friends with a woman who had helped her husband overcome cancer with cesium, and this woman had been helpful to Anna when she had first made the decision to try cesium. During Anna's time in hospice, I initiated a phone conversation with this woman, desperate for something that would help my daughter. She was kind, patient, and encouraging to me and tried to be helpful. As I completed the phone conversation with her, a visceral understanding came over me that it would take more than human intervention at this stage of the disease, and that Anna's fate was out of my hands. This knowing was a turning point for me as it became loud and clear within my being that there wasn't anything else I could do.

Anna was in hospice ten days, each day bringing new symptoms or developments. Then she began to sleep more and stopped interacting at all. She had slipped into a coma. And then one day she developed this loud snore for an entire day that the nurse told us was the death rattle. Early the evening of April 17, 2013, Anna took her last agonizing breaths at about 5:30 PM. There were four of us by her side who witnessed those last struggling breaths. It was horrible to witness, and that experience is burned into my memory.

Anna left four siblings and three daughters, aged eighteen, fifteen and eight. The last event that Anna planned was her youngest daughter's eighth birthday party in March.

The above is a short version of a long, emotional journey with this dearest of hearts. It is a hard story to retell, and this is the first time I have attempted to do so. I have been too raw emotionally to recall so much from the depths of my memory.

Many people who played a part in Anna's journey came to see her while she was in hospice. People from all over the world who knew her or her siblings were praying for her. She was an inspiration to other cancer victims in the town where she lived and was highly active in cancer activities in her community, such as the Race for the Cure and other events.

Anna kept an outwardly positive attitude. During those last months I spent with her, we laughed, we cried, we talked, and we did things together as much as she felt like doing them. Until the moment she drew her last breath, I was in denial that she would leave us. She had been so positive and outlived by almost a year the doctor's initial prognosis of a few months. She would put these messages on Facebook that she was still here in spite of what her doctor said. She didn't make it to five years though. That seems to be a milestone mark breast cancer survivors try to make; I'm not sure what the significance of five years is, but she didn't make it. From the date of her initial diagnosis on November 11, 2009, to the date she left us on April 17, 2013, she lived three years and six months.

I tell these stories because they are a part of my journey, and I have been asked by people through the years how I have managed to make it through and keep my sanity. For people to say I have kept my sanity is a kind assumption—but I will share what I have learned through years of contemplation and what I am still grappling with. I don't have the answers; only a few insights that might be helpful. These realizations didn't happen overnight. I spent many an hour pondering, grieving, and soul-searching. I came to understand that part of the acceptance of loss includes the realization that losing someone to death changes our lives forever and that part of the task of the grief process is re-orienting expectations of what life should or should not be.

My first realization upon losing Michelle was that there are no guarantees when someone comes into our lives how long we get to keep them. I came to the understanding that every person who comes into this world has their own destiny and agenda, and I don't have any control over that. I can give my children guidance and protect them and love and care for them on the human level, but ultimately, they have a personal blueprint bigger than any of us that directs the show.

I was the portal for my children to come into this world, but I cannot control what happens once they get here. I love my children, but they are Sovereign Beings just like I am, and I do not feel a sense of ownership of them. I feel a sense of awe that they came to share their lives with me, and I love them deeply and am honored to be their mother.

I don't know what agenda their souls have or what experiences are important for them. I do know that I am grateful for what I have learned from them. They are individuals with their own life story to live, and I am interested in their perceptions of their life passages because I love them. I hope they have learned some useful things from me. I know that part of my journey in being the parent to my children is to appreciate the impact each one of them has had on my life. All of my children and the adults they have become have had a profound effect on me as a person. They have been and are gifts I treasure more than I can put into words. I want to keep their lives private, so I won't go into detail except to say that I admire each of them and the wonderful adults they have turned out to be. Anna was an open book about her disease, so I think I have her permission to tell her story.

Michelle left us as at the very beginning of her senior year, on the threshold of adulthood. We didn't get to know the adult she would have been. I have to be content with having had the privilege of watching her grow and be in our lives for seventeen years. She was a tall, slender, beautiful blue-eyed blond with a mischievous personality and a zest for life that was contagious.

Anna left us right after she turned thirty-eight in February of 2013. She was in the prime of her life, and she left three precious children. She was stunning; a slender, green/gray-eyed blond with a fun-loving, gregarious personality. She had a buttery-soft voice that I long to hear come over the phone with her "Hi Mama, whatcha doing?" Why she had to leave when she did has been very difficult for me to accept.

I used to jokingly say that I had two "litters" of three babies each—the first three born in just two and a half years, the second three born within three years of each other—with a span of a few years in between; so they were divided into the three older girls, and then the two boys with Anna.

There were some strange parallels between these two sisters that I cannot help but puzzle about: both were blond; both were middle children of their respective "litter." Michelle was second born of six, and Anna was fifth born; both had fatal brain stem damage; both of them had the same devil-may-care personality; both had a slender build. Their looks were similar, and they both had the same style of the most beautiful teeth. They could have been twins— that is how much alike they looked and acted in so many ways. They did not resemble their other siblings as much as they resembled each other.

I remember one very rough day in the summer of 2013. I was having a difficult time with the whole idea of hospice and if I should have done more. Anna had fought so hard; I felt it was almost a betrayal to give up and let her go to hospice where they "would keep her comfortable." It was really troubling me. At the end of the day, I meditated for a while, and then as I often did at that time, I picked up the book *Oneness* by Rasha. I kept it on the stand by my chair and would often open it to a random passage and read it. This particular day I opened to the passage quoted below. To open this large book to this particular place was a powerful message to me. The author is talking about the completion of life issues that for some include radical experiences. The message affected me profoundly in the context of my troubled mind and heart.

> When one intervenes in the crisis of another in these times, one only helps to create the basis for a reenactment of the drama in question for that individual. The circumstances themselves are no more than an invitation. When the circumstances are poignant, the invitation is compelling and the tendency to overlook the lesson is progressively less likely. Were one to go through the motions of dealing with the drama, without recognizing the symbolism from which it springs, a repeat performance is virtually guaranteed.

In some cases, the blindness of the individual to the nature of the process is such that the scenarios created are life threatening and the chances of transcending the challenges at that point are slim.

Know that in such instances, the individual in question has created those circumstances at a soul level, in order to punctuate the point of a particular life theme. It may well be in the highest interests of the individual in question to allow the drama to play out to a seemingly disastrous conclusion. For, that Being, as a soul, will be able to reconstruct the life history after departure from physical form and perceive the common threads from a heightened perspective.

Know that many will be making such choices. And many will choose seemingly violent exits from this lifetime in order to have experienced an example of a life issue that cannot be ignored. These summary experiences are profound opportunities for the beings in question to bring to a conclusion life themes they would not be able to master in a less dramatic way.

The opportunity for those of you who will bear witness to such events is to be able to honor the perfection of the process of another and to resist the temptation to intervene and attempt to *save* someone from what he is trying to achieve as a soul. It may appear that to do so would be heartless, in profound circumstances. Yet to refrain from saving another from his perfectly created lesson would be the higher gift. For, the preservation of physical form is surely not the ultimate basis for action in all cases. It may well be that certain individuals may have sufficiently backed themselves into a corner, experientially, and the potential suffering posed by retaining physical form would far outweigh the advantages of lifesaving heroics.

The challenge for you who have a heart connection with such a being, is to recognize the gift in the culmination of that being's process, and to know that that individual's highest purpose may well be served by allowing the process to play out to its natural conclusion. For the concept of *nonattachment to the material* is not limited to possessions, but applies to life itself. The lesson for you in such dramas is to be able to let go of your attachment to the physical life of another and to know that *life*, in the higher sense, transcends the identity that may be choosing to relinquish form. [187]

---

[187] Rasha, *ONENESS*, pp. 171-173, Earthstar Press, 2nd Edition, 2006.
The Words of Oneness through Rasha, http://onenesswebsite.com/

To open the book to this passage was a powerful response to the angst I was feeling. The timing and the message were a direct answer to the questions I held that day, and it helped. I am not saying that I agree completely with every idea, but there was enough there to help me gain some perspective. I cannot say that it caused me to cease grieving; that has not happened yet. But it has helped me with the senseless guilt I felt over a disease process I had no control over.

I miss Anna. It is January 2016 as I write this. Throughout the month I have often had flashbacks of that January three years ago and the poignant and intense and emotionally raw time we spent together. I am so grateful for that time with her.

I have a few observations that came later as I pondered Anna's experiences and my journey with her. Please, as you read this understand that these are my observations which may not resonate with everyone. Use them if it helps, disregard them if they don't.

What I have observed is that a culture can grow up around a disease, and one has definitely grown up around breast cancer. Anna was very courageous in her fight against this disease. She kept an upbeat attitude, and she was an inspiration to others fighting cancer. She was loved and respected in the cancer community in her town. Due to the monstrous prevalence of cancer where she lived and all that people go through while experiencing the treatments and body changes like hair loss, a support community often becomes the cancer victim's social outlet which can create a new identity for the person with the disease.

Anna had a very extroverted personality. She was loving, free-spirited, outspoken and had a bit of a devil-may-care attitude which added to her charisma. She loved attention, and she loved people and interacting with them. She was stunningly beautiful, even without her hair. She made a great spokeswoman.

What came to me in my quiet moments of thinking about Anna was how she embraced every step of the disease. That led me to wondering if within that embrace she had come to identify too much with being a cancer victim and/or survivor.

I think in the beginning at least that Anna's attitude was a form of bargaining in the grief process. In other words, if she kept a positive attitude, she would overcome cancer. She was terrified, but she would feed the fires of positive thinking. I walk a fine line in trying to explain what I see because it is attitude which often helps us to overcome insurmountable odds, and I don't want what I am trying to say to be misconstrued as bashing positive thinking because I think it is especially important to be positive.

My question though: is there a difference between embracing a disease and having a good attitude about overcoming it? Somewhere along the way, I have wondered if Anna identified so much with the cancer and the social world that grew around it that it took over her self-identity.

A cancer diagnosis is an intensely emotional and terrifying experience, and friendships formed within that support culture can also be very intense. The experience is so extreme that a normal life is mundane in comparison. I think if we are not careful, the experience can become a trap that becomes an end unto itself. Always hanging over her head was the thought— "Will I be cancer free at my next checkup?" That constant nagging fear coupled with the identity of being a cancer victim/survivor can become such a strong overlay that it takes over the person, making it difficult to go back to a "normal" life once the cancer is in remission.

This normal life would mean letting go of her identity with the disease as victim/survivor, including the pervasive and looming fear of it coming back and the heightened attention and emotion and awareness that goes with it. That is a lot to ask, but I wonder if this constant attention to it once it is in remission feeds the flame of the return of the disease. It is a conundrum. I wish I had understood that when Anna was alive, because I cannot help but wonder if this identification can help to keep the disease process active. Would knowing that dynamic have helped her survive? Who knows? There are so many unknowns on the emotional and psychological levels with any disease process.

I am aware that for some types of cancer the chemo/radiation route is lifesaving. That is certainly true for some forms of childhood leukemia and some forms of breast as well as other cancers. Each one is different.

The way the treatment of cancer is set-up now in the conventional medical model, very little information is allowed or discussed concerning natural ways of dealing with this disease.

There is a subculture alive and well in this world that is learning to understand how to battle cancer naturally, but it is for the most part suppressed. People have gone to jail, and successful clinics have been shut down for the work they were doing to help people overcome the disease.[188] It is exceedingly difficult to find the information that is needed to work with cancer naturally because of the suppression and demonizing of alternative therapies. I also think that once a person's immune system has been through the chemo and radiation route, the body is in a weakened state and unable to respond to natural treatments as effectively. Anna lived a lot longer than her doctor said she would, and for a while she was getting better. More research and conversations need to be allowed that are open to natural treatments and/

---

[188] For anyone interested in researching natural resources for cancer and reading the story of how natural treatments have been suppressed, the book *Outsmart Your Cancer: Alternative Non-toxic Treatments that Work* by Tonya Harter Pierce, MA, MFCC, available through www.OutsmartYourCancer.com is an eye-opening and informative book. My complementary doctor also told me about *Life Over Cancer—the Block Center Program for Integrative Cancer Treatment* by Keith Block, M.D., Forward by Andrew Weil, M.D.

or natural treatments combined with less intrusive medical intervention. That is a subject future generations must grapple with.

Anna told her oncologist what she was doing, but he was bound by some "law" not to let on that he knew anything about any of the information she was finding, or if it was effective or not, or how he could help her complement what she was doing. He was strictly a chemo-oriented doctor. We had to rely on what we could find on our own. It was frustrating for us, and it is a heartless practice on the side of medicine to squelch alternative information that might help a person diagnosed with a terminal disease.

The next observation I had was: why do we insist on equating a beautiful color with a nasty disease? By linking a color with a disease—the famous bright pink for breast cancer—we are actually being programmed to embrace the disease. Now they are taking bright red and linking it with women's heart issues and purple with Alzheimer's.

The spin we get is that the color helps to raise awareness. I don't buy it. I think it is a programming method (Big Pharma probably has their hand in this—drugs used in all these diseases is lucrative business) to make us feel more vulnerable and to link us subconsciously with the disease and feel the fear every time we see the color. We see the beautiful color pink and think "breast cancer." It is a subliminal message especially for women that the disease is lurking, and you could be its next victim. I think it is important on so many levels to resist linking color with disease or at least to be clear about this issue in your own mind.

I remember a conversation I had with Anna's youngest daughter during Thanksgiving of 2013. She was deeply grieving the loss of her mother and appeared angry and lost. We all thought it would be good to be together for Thanksgiving that year, but I think it was harder for her because she always came with her mom, and it was such a joyful occasion. But now she was around all of this family that reminded her more acutely of who was missing. At least that is how I saw and felt it.

She had moved with her father to a different town, and of course people ask a child about their parents and family to start a conversation. She said that it was so hard to say anything about her mother because then she would immediately see this pity in their faces, and she couldn't do anything about it, so she decided not to have conversations with strangers about her mother. I think that is a powerful insight from her to us as adults about talking with children and asking probing questions when maybe we shouldn't.

Then we got to talking about all the things associated with cancer. She said vehemently "and I hate pink. I never want to see the color again and it is everywhere!! It just reminds me of everything I have lost!!"

I rest my case.

SOME RUMINATION ON GRIEF

When we lose a loved one, we will grieve sooner or later. The grieving process is a natural part of the continuum of loss we encounter in the death experience. The days immediately following the passing of a loved one are sacred days. It is as though the veil between the worlds is thinned for a short time. In the immediacy of the experience, a portal of deep introspection and meaning is available to us. We need to allow ourselves and those around us who go through a loss to have the experience of visiting that portal and honor the profound sacredness of the moment. This is not the time for a "stiff upper lip" of pushing on like everything is normal.

I feel that the most important part of the grief process is coming to understand the gift the deceased brought to our lives and to the world. If we deny ourselves that introspection and its accompanying feelings, we rob ourselves of their gift and possibly diminish the meaning of our loved one's life.

Funerals or life-celebrations are helpful for us to talk about the gift a loved one brought to our lives, and they are important at the time of the portal opening when one passes. So, when I say the "grief experience," I am not necessarily talking about the feelings of misery, anguish, pain, torment, or despair. Those emotions can certainly be a part of the process. My definition of the grief process centers on doing my best to understand the gift of the person I have just lost—to look at the sacredness of this precious life and honor the Essence of Spirit this individual brought to the earth during their journey here. I think it is important to ponder and own the impact of this unique life force. Love lives on through the heart connections that we share with our loved ones. That love impacts our daily lives in countless small ways as it continues to be a part of the legacy that exists in our hearts and souls.

No heart is separate from the one Heart
No breath is ever alone
Love given is never lost [189]

A EULOGY

My mother lived to be 79 and died of a Triple A Aneurism. Below I share the eulogy I gave for my mother at her funeral—as a tribute to this person who gave me life and to illustrate the portal I was experiencing at the time of her death.

[189] Excerpt from poem "I Live Where You Live" by James Mahu. Event Temples 3 Temple of Spiritual Activism

Welcome. Thanks to each of you for being here as we remember and celebrate our mother's life.

As I typed in the title to the program the phrase "the late Mrs. Albers" popped into my head. That is the subtitle on your program. Mom was always late to family events. She gave the phrase "fashionably late" a whole new meaning. When she would finally arrive, her impatient family wouldn't always hide their irritation. She would wave it off with "just call me the late Mrs. Albers." As I typed that in, I could see her grin and that sparkle in her eyes and hear her lovingly say to me, "you half-wit," but she would want me to leave it there as part of who she was.

The time right after a person's passing becomes sacred time to those of us who are impacted by the departure. It's a difficult time because this departure is so final. It is also a time for each of us to reflect and reminisce and remember.

It is a time when, as the soul leaves the compressed and confined quarters of the body and begins to expand, we are given a special dispensation of grace. A time to sort out and ponder the meaning of the life just lived.

This time is for us:

- A time for us who called her Mom and Grandma and Grandma- great and friend and confidant and teacher to honor her life.
- A time to celebrate the gift of her life and mourn the loss of her human presence in our earthly journey.
- A time to look at both the human life and the larger picture it represented or symbolized and to gain meaning and perspective.
- A time to stop and give thanks for the incredible miracle life is in all its myriad of expressions.

A few hours after she left, I began to be aware of what I have felt is her Soul just on the periphery of my awareness. This awareness has been flooding me with feelings and concepts that I struggle to grasp and express. I so want to do justice to what I have been experiencing. So, bear with me and walk with me down this road of contemplation, as I reflect on Mother's life and search for a way to grasp what her soul was about in the life she lived.

Where do I begin? The first thing that came to mind was the poem I wrote when Daddy died. It is even more relevant to me now than it was then, so I want to use it as a jumping off place today. You have it in your program.

The poem is called "Maya's Dream." Maya in eastern thought is a word for illusion, and this world is considered the world of illusion. So, the poem is about this world as the creation of illusion's dream, a place for Spirit to play and learn and explore.

Maya's Dream

You asked for a chance
At earthly life
"An experience of separation
In order to explore"
You said

So
Your Essence took a deep breath
Blew a poignant sigh
A long lingering good-bye
And sent you on your way

I wonder, does our Essence grieve when we leave?

A release of soul
A quickening of body
A journey into Maya's dream
To the world of imagining

Fly, Fly dearest one
Into the world of dark and sun
Your endless journey has begun.

When we come into this world, our journey begins as a separate Being, a part of the whole, but as we enter this plane of existence, we lose that awareness of the whole.

And that is as it should be, for then the experiences seem more real, and we learn more from them. I think we/our souls are probably changed forever by the experience. Each of us experiences life in a unique way, and when we return home, that experience becomes a part of the collective, and Consciousness grows.

Our Essence explains to us as we begin our journey:

You may experience sorrow and pain
Before you return home again
The world you seek is bittersweet

Some may even call it bleak

Your life's task
A plan unique
For you are destined to gently speak
To all who you touch
Of love's strength and wonder

And when it is time to leave
Those who have known you will grieve
As they remember
Cherished private moments
Of your walk with each

Each dear precious wing
Who comes from beyond imagining
Into the world of light and dark
Leaves a stamp of their Essence's Spark
And a corner of the world is changed

And a corner of the world is changed—that is what we are here to talk about. What was Mother and how did she change her corner of the world?

For starters: four children, ten grandchildren and eleven great- grandchildren are on this earth because of her life. (That was in 2002; the count has since increased.)

During that separation process when we first become separated from our Essence, each of us has an earthly symbol of God in our parents. It helps to make the separation bearable and give us some continuity as we adjust to earth life. How we see and relate to our parents is in some ways how we will understand the concept of God.

My mother was a listener, and her door was always open, usually into the wee hours of the morning, and the coffee pot was always on. Mother listened empathically and non-judgmentally. She maintained eye contact, didn't butt in with her own stuff; she just listened. I learned what a wonderful listener she was when I was going through my divorce. She was the wind beneath my wings. Our long talks during those times deepened our relationship and helped me to appreciate the strength and wisdom that was my mother.

Mom was the embodiment of love and compassion and forgiveness and that is what she demonstrated to me. She was the embodiment of those characteristics, and so my model of Divinity includes those characteristics to a large degree.

Mother's sacrifice to bring us into the world seemed to me to be more than should have been asked of her. But the times she lived in demanded that of her. She was an accomplished pianist, and when I was growing up, the sounds of classical music often filled the house as she practiced. Because of who she was, the love of music is a part of who I am. I have a deep appreciation of and a heartfelt respect for anyone who plays a musical instrument.

I always felt that life cheated her, because she should have gone on to be a famous pianist. She had it in her. But that was not to be. She helped support the family by giving music lessons, and so her music legacy did live on in the children she taught. I am grateful for that. She was a patient teacher, and she loved her students.

Mother and Dad struggled to make ends meet; theirs was not an easy life, but she maintained her strength and dignity through so much adversity, and that too is a part of her legacy. Through some of her trials I have often wondered how she got through them and stayed so gentle. That is another model I look up to.

Mother lived in a pain-wracked body for years, and I rarely heard her complain, so I doubt any of us knew how much she really suffered. She took that information with her, but I know it was a lot more than she would ever admit to us (osteo-arthritis and some awful, painful issues with her feet).

She had a tendency to minimize, and it took us a while to catch on, but after a couple of life-threatening emergencies, we realized that when she said something "hurt a little" it meant "it hurt a lot," and something needed to be done quickly.

Her granddaughter Jenny was the best at recognizing when Mother was in danger and saved her life more than once by insisting that she go to the hospital when Mom protested. For that we are all grateful; you played a huge part in keeping her alive several times, Jenny.

In your heart and mind, she was an angel to you, but you were also an angel to her and to us in the way you cared for her and looked after her.

> *And now we stand at parting's door*
> *As you again take wing and soar*
> *Back to the Heart of Unity once more*
> *To stand on heaven's floor*
>
> *So fly, fly dearest wing*
> *Your legacy a precious offering*
> *Your mystery a poignant pondering*

For those of us remaining in Maya's Dream

What was her legacy?

What was her mystery?

Things are not always as they seem.

She was not rich in material goods, which is the way the world teaches us to measure the worth of someone.

She was rich in compassion, love, forgiveness, intelligence, and gentleness and those qualities gave her a quiet dignity and a gentle demeanor.

She was the personification of compassion and unconditional love.

She held that mirror up to each of us. Now in the reflection of all she was, we have an example to measure ourselves with.

Somehow in this sacred time, in the process of her leaving, my heart has opened to a deeper awareness of the mirror she held. Our country has a class system, and it is determined by income on the superficial level.

But she is saying to me: "Take a look deeper into the eyes of people in all walks of life, for many riches are hidden there."

For those of us who have experienced the intelligence that emanated from her eyes and had the privilege of talking with her, we know that this woman was a rare gem, and we have been blessed by being allowed to bask in her quiet dignity. For those of us who have been the receivers of her immense love, what a gift we were given.

One never knows when a Great Being chooses as a gesture of love to hold the mirror, to help us hone our own qualities through that reflection. I believe my mother was such a Being. Over the past week, I have become more fully and deeply aware of the All that she portrayed and the lessons she taught, not by what she said, but by who she was.

Now it is time to say goodbye.

I wish I had been able to see this all so clearly while she was alive, so I could have told her. It is strange how in leaving, she has come back to me so whole, so powerful. Maybe that is as it should be.

I will go forth, grateful for her legacy, her love, her gift of life. As her daughter, I carry a part of her with me always.

In my Mind's Eye I can see that twinkle in her eye and that grin that she used to get when she would be helping me learn something, and I would finally get it.

Mom, if you are here, and somehow, I know you are, I wish you bon voyage.

You are free—from the pain and limitations of a worn-out pain- wracked body and the limitations of poverty that confined you. You are free to move on and explore new worlds. Go with it; your work here is done, and you did it well. Go in Peace.

It is your legacy and freedom that comforts me now as I try and figure out how to live without your physical presence and come to grips with the knowledge that I can't hear your voice on the other end of the phone line, have long talks with you, have you visit us in Lincoln, stop by to see you when I come through Grand Island. I miss you already, and I shall miss you the rest of my life here on earth.

I just hope that when it is time for me to make that journey, you will be there to greet me and welcome me home. Meanwhile, keep in touch, if only in a dream now and then. I love you Mom.

> Endurance of inescapable sorrow is something which has to be learned alone. And only to endure is not enough. Endurance can be a harsh and bitter root in one's life, bearing poisonous and gloomy fruit, destroying other lives. Endurance is only the beginning. There must be acceptance and the knowledge that sorrow fully accepted brings its own gifts. For there is an alchemy in sorrow; it can be transmuted into wisdom, which, if it does not bring joy, can yet bring happiness.
> *Pearl S. Buck*

PART FOUR

ARCHITECTS OF A
NEW PARADIGM

INTRODUCTION

INNOVATORS OF A PROGRESSIVE WORLD CULTURE

HOW DO WE AS THE human species transcend a Matrix we have lived in and taken for granted as our only reality for thousands of years? How do we encourage a mindset that fosters the impulse and desire to transcend the current world dynamics of domination and hopelessness in enough human beings to make a difference?

For many living comfortable lives with luxuries at their fingertips and wants granted immediately, those questions aren't usually a part of their thought processes. Unfortunately, the wake-up call that opens our hearts to the plight of ourselves or others usually begins with painful personal experiences or something so devastating on the world stage that it engages our sense of horror and outrage as well as a fear for our own safety and preservation of our way of life. It is often during those times of national turmoil and indignation that a current of common empathy buried deep within us is aroused and called to action. Embedded within that current are innovative questions that can be nudged to the surface of our collective consciousness and allow the visionaries of our world to ask and respond with new ideas and inventions.

New ideas that will ease acute pain become imminently appealing and important when far-reaching advances are seen as imperative to survival.

I think that is what is happening now as I begin this segment in the fall of 2017. We are continually bombarded with unbelievable natural tragedies as well as man-made ones. On the stage of the United States government, a steady barrage of unsettling actions and statements are creating a national feeling of insecurity that is breaking down confidence in our government as those we entrusted with our country through our votes seem to be setting out to break down the foundational institutions we hired them to protect.

Many are wondering if we can recover from the attack on our foundations and if so, how? A lot is at stake as we ponder these questions. It is our choice as a nation to decide whether we decline by allowing the destruction to continue or grow by finding a way to stop it.

Since we know what the old way of separatist and exclusivist ideas produce, maybe the time has come to embrace an inclusive approach. What would it be like to live in a world where our species becomes increasingly sensitive to the understanding that we are all connected? What would it be like to live in a world where all people regardless of economic status, race, color, religion, or sexual orientation are respected and where provisions are made for everyone's basic needs to be met?

It is in our best interests as a species to encourage a world that honors the uniqueness of all individuals and embraces the gifts of each of us. There is a growing counterculture incubating such a worldview. It can be found in those who understand the importance of respect and inclusiveness for all. It is recognized by those who honor our planet by searching for ways to preserve its resources.

The old paradigm that encourages greed, exploitation of the planet, and exclusiveness is making a last-ditch effort to stay in control, but a new paradigm is in its gestational period, and this is one we want to see arrive full-term and healthy.

In this brief but important segment, I will be exploring a few innovative ideas that have the potential of pointing us towards the dynamic trajectory of a peaceful world most of us long for. This is a subject that could be a stand-alone book, so what I will talk about here will only be the tip of the iceberg. Sometimes that is all that is needed for us to grasp an idea hovering on the far horizons of our consciousness and to bring it into manifestation.

We are on the threshold of choice that is more important than it has ever been in the history of humanity. Do we remain in the frequencies of a three-dimensional world where we have relied on our ego-driven intellects to create a world congested by hate and self-serving greed and cold- heartedness, or do we move into the fourth-dimensional frequencies and beyond where our innate qualities and nuances of love are expressed and identified through Heart-Centered living? Are we ready to experiment with invoking Love's spectrum of Appreciation, Compassion, Forgiveness, Humility, Understanding, and Valor as a guide to our everyday lives and our world decisions? Our personal choices are significant and like the Sorting Hat at Hogwarts School sort each individual into the dimension and accompanying paradigm that most matches one's personal frequencies.

Part Four will touch on and discuss some paradigm-shifting ideas in each of the following areas: Innovative Government Models, Social and Educational Advances, Preserving Our Earth, Health and Healing Sciences, and Arts and Culture. Spiritual Transformation through learning to live a heart-centered life is the overarching theme of this book, and it is an undercurrent that runs through all of these chapters.

15

INNOVATIONS IN WORLD CULTURES

WHAT WOULD IT FEEL LIKE to live in a world culture that becomes increasingly sensitive to the understanding that we are all connected and inspires us to collectively create a world order that honors all individuals and nations? Is such an ideal attainable in the world we know?

Transparency International is a global coalition against corruption. Since we are moving into the Age of Transparency and Expansion, this seems like an exemplary organization to explore in our quest for ideas of how to succeed in creating national governments that truly work for all the people being governed.

An article found on the *Transparency International* website [190] titled "What Makes New Zealand, Denmark, Finland, Sweden and Others Cleaner than Most Countries?" identifies these countries as being consistently top- ranked as the least corrupt of all according to the "2011 Corruption Perceptions Index."

This article identifies the following ideals that make these countries so effective with a strong commitment to anti-corruption by political leaders who all share a common set of characteristics correlated with lower levels of corruption, including freedom of the press; a high GDP per capita; low inequality rates; literacy rates close to 100%; and a prioritization of human rights issues such as gender equality and freedom of information.

The article goes on to explain that countries that perform well usually have a long tradition of openness in government, civic activism and social trust, and strong transparency and mechanisms in place to hold their politicians accountable. The following practices seem to work:

---

[190] Chene, Marie, "What Makes New Zealand, Denmark, Finland, Sweden and Others Cleaner than Most Countries?" *Transparency International*, 12.7.2011
https://blog.transparency.org/2011/12/07/what-makes-new-zealand-denmark-finland-sweden-and-others-%E2%80%9Ccleaner%E2%80%9D-than-most-countries/
Information from this link is either quoted directly or paraphrased from this article. *Transparency International* is a collection of articles, stories, analysis, and opinions from the anti-corruption movement.

- Disclosure of budget information—Sweden has an open budget index that allows its citizens to assess how their government is managing public funds.
- A code of conduct for public servants—Denmark requires ministers to publish monthly information on their travel spending and gifts.
- An independent and efficient judiciary system that criminalizes corruption-related abuses.

The author of this article stresses that this "bottom-up model based on public trust, transparency and social capita is affordable, transferable and adaptable to very different political contexts."

I discovered the "Corruption Perceptions Index 2017" and found a fascinating list of countries and how they rank. [191] This index gives the rankings and scores for the countries listed from 2012-2017: the highest being the least corrupt and the lowest being the most corrupt.

In 2017 New Zealand and Denmark ranked the highest (least corrupt) with scores of 89 and 88, respectively. Syria, South Sudan, and Somalia ranked the lowest (most corrupt) with scores of 14, 12 and 9. The United States ranked 16th with a score of 75. Canada ranked 8th with a score of 82; Finland, Norway and Switzerland all ranked equally with a score of 85.

At the end of this list of countries, Transparency International lists five recommendations to combat corruption.

> Our first-hand experience working in more than 100 countries around the world shows that activists and media are vital to combatting corruption. As such, Transparency International calls on the global community to take the following actions to curb corruption:

- Governments and businesses must do more to encourage free speech, independent media, political dissent and an open and engaged civil society.
- Governments should minimize regulations on media, including traditional and new media, and ensure that journalists can work without fear of repression or violence. In addition, international donors should consider press freedom relevant to development aid or access to international organizations.
- Civil society and governments should promote laws that focus on access to information. This access helps enhance transparency and accountability

[191] "Corruption Perceptions Index 2017," *Transparency International*, Feb. 21, 2018, https://www.transparency.org/news/feature/corruption_perceptions_index_2017

while reducing opportunities for corruption. It is important, however, for governments to not only invest in an appropriate legal framework for such laws, but also commit to their implementation.

- Activists and governments should take advantage of the momentum generated by the United Nations Sustainable Development Goals (SDGs) to advocate and push for reforms at the national and global level. Specifically, governments must ensure access to information and the protection of fundamental freedoms and align these to international agreements and best practices.
- Governments and businesses should proactively disclose relevant public interest information in open data formats. Proactive disclosure of relevant data, including government budgets, company ownership, public procurement and political party finances allows journalists, civil society and affected communities to identify patterns of corrupt conduct more efficiently.

The United Nations has drawn up an ambitious and impressive list of humanitarian goals for 2015-2030. This list can be found below and by searching for United Nations Sustainable Development Goals. [192]

These goals are inclusive, with the focus on equality for all, and point us in the direction of fulfilling our deepest yearnings for a coherent and heart-centered world that supports individual environments.

1. No poverty in any form anywhere
2. Zero hunger by
   - achieving food security
   - improving nutrition
   - promoting sustainable agriculture
3. Good health and well being
4. Quality education
   - inclusive and equitable quality education
   - promote life-long learning opportunities for all
5. Gender equality and empowerment of all women and girls
6. Clean water and sanitation
7. Affordable and clean energy

---

[192] "About the Sustainable Development Goals," *UN Sustainable Development Goals,* https://www.un.org/sustainabledevelopment/sustainable-development-goals/

8. Decent work and economic growth
9. Industry innovation and infrastructure
   - build resilient infrastructure
   - promote inclusive and sustainable industrialization
   - foster innovation
10. Reduced inequalities
11. Sustainable cities and communities that are safe, inclusive, and resilient
12. Responsible consumption and production
13. Climate action
14. Life below water: conserve and use the oceans, seas, and marine sources for sustainable development
15. Life on land:
    - protect, restore, and promote sustainable use of terrestrial ecosystems
    - sustainably manage forests
    - combat desertification
    - halt and reverse land degradation
    - halt biodiversity loss.
16. Peace, justice, and strong institutions - promote peaceful and inclusive societies
17. Partnerships with goals - revitalize the global partnership for sustainable development

These goals seem idealistic and unrealistic because many countries in our world are currently run by greedy, corrupt, and ambitious people who are in government to see how much they can profit personally. We are, however, heading into an Age of Transparency as evidenced by the plethora of cover-ups and criminal activities coming to light for all to see. It is important for us individually and in groups to begin to demand humane goals from our leaders and to elect those who are interested in making such goals their top priorities. The ideas and yearnings are in our collective consciousness. We can only hope that we are quickly approaching the time when we as a species will begin to act on them.

16

SOCIAL AND EDUCATIONAL INNOVATIONS

THIS SECTION WILL FEATURE SOME programs that are in the spirit of demonstrating what a heart-centered approach would look like within a society. The following are just a few exciting innovations.

INSTITUTE OF HEARTMATH

HeartMath is an organization created to help activate the heart of humanity. To quote from their website:

> Here at HeartMath we believe that when we align and connect our hearts and minds, we awaken our higher mental, emotional and spiritual capacities.
> This alignment also connects us with the heart's intuitive intelligence— where we naturally choose the way of love and compassionate care for the well-being of ourselves, others, and Planet Earth. [193]

HeartMath offers training through their state-of-the-art technology to help participants improve their mental and emotional well-being to obtain a state of psychophysiological coherence or in other words an increased order and harmony in both psychological and physiological processes. Their website explains these processes in depth and offers classes and technology to help participants achieve these desirable states. They also have a training program for those who wish to become facilitators of their innovative and paradigm-shifting programs. In my mind, HeartMath is a world leader for teaching heart-focused consciousness.

---

[193] HeartMath Institute, www.heartmath.com

The Global Coherence Initiative [194] is a branch of the HeartMath Institute. It conducts groundbreaking research on the interconnection of humanity and earth's magnetic fields and energetic systems. They have a network of magnetometers at the following sensor sites:

> Boulder Creek, CA; Hofuf, Saudi Arabia; Alberta, Canada; Baisogala, Lithuania; Northland Region of New Zealand and Kwazulu Natal, South Africa. These sensor sites continuously monitor the resonant frequencies in Earth's magnetic field.
>
> They track changes in geomagnetic activity caused by solar storms, changes in solar wind speed, disruption of the Schumann Resonances (SR) and potentially, the signatures of major global events that have a strong emotional component.

The Global Coherence Initiative also hosts a Global Care Room where anyone can join their monthly synchronized Care Focuses. These Care Focus meditations are free of charge and offer a time when people around the world can gather and do guided group meditations to send care to parts of the world in need of energetic help. The globe of the world in the Care Room shows your marker and the marker of others participating in the meditation. It is a way for us to picture our world and to collectively become mindful that we can gather together to transmit helpful energy to this world.

The Global Coherence Initiative is working on the premise that the

> … collective human consciousness affects the global information field. Therefore, large numbers of people creating heart-centered states of care, love and compassion will generate a more coherent field environment that can benefit others and help offset the current planetary discord and incoherence.

The Global Coherence Initiative also has a live data feed that monitors the earth's magnetic field with a continuous stream of data. You can learn more about this research at https://www.heartmath.org/research/global-coherence/ If you wish to read articles about the various research studies they are conducting, go to this link: https://www.heartmath.org/category/gci-commentaries/ And their research library has many downloadable papers on various subjects: https://www.heartmath.org/research/research-library/

---

[194] *Global Coherence Initiative*, https://www.heartmath.org/gci/

SCHOOLS REPLACE DETENTION WITH MEDITATION

Robert W. Coleman Elementary School [195] in Baltimore, Maryland has a special room called the "Mindful Moment Room" that is staffed and maintained by the non-profit *Holistic Life Foundation*. Students are assigned to this room when they are acting out in school instead of being sent to detention or the principal's office. It is described as a warm, brightly lit space strewn with purple floor pillows, yoga mats, and the scents of essential oils.

When a child enters this room, they talk with a staff person about why they are there, and then they are encouraged to do some deep breathing to help them calm down. This is often followed by stretches and yoga postures to deepen relaxation and mindfulness.

School staff explains that the kids are learning how to calm themselves and manage their anger. The school serves many children living under deeply challenging conditions. Some are homeless; most live below the poverty line; some have parents who are incarcerated. Children living with such stressful conditions are in a constant state of psychological vigilance and high alert. They are primed to fight and have a difficult time paying attention. The meditation room gives them a chance to calm down, breathe deeply, and focus their attention on themselves.

The school also starts and ends each school day with a fifteen-minute guided meditation. The children also have a chance to practice yoga stretches during and after school.

This practice has resulted in a year with no suspensions at Robert W. Coleman Elementary School. At a nearby high school in Baltimore that has also initiated a mindfulness program, attendance is up, and suspensions are down.

Tanya Mead in her article on detention vs. meditation [196] cites some research that has linked meditation to calming anxiety, improving mood, boosting energy levels, improving focus, increasing productivity, and improving sleep quality. High school students practicing meditation demonstrated improved academic success and higher graduation rates. She cites a 2013 study about a high school where some students were enrolled in a course teaching Transcendental Meditation techniques. The students who participated had a fifteen percent higher graduation rate than those who did not.

---

[195] Bloom, Deborah, "Instead of detention, these students get meditation," *CNN Health*, November 8, 2016, http://www.cnn.com/2016/11/04/health/meditation-in-schools-baltimore/index.html
If one Googles this subject, many articles can be found.
[196] Mead, Tanya, "Detention Vs. Meditation: And the Winner is …" *Alternative Daily*, October 20, 2016, http://www.thealternativedaily.com/detention-versus-meditation-in-school/

Interestingly, Sanford Nidich, co-author of this study, commented:

> … the largest effect was found in the most academically challenged students. Recently published research on increased academic achievement and reduced psychological stress in urban school students may provide possible mechanisms for the higher graduation rates found in this study.

A Newsweek article also featuring the Robert W. Coleman Elementary School goes on to explain:

> The Baltimore school is not the only one that has tried incorporating meditative practices. California's Mindful Schools has provided training in 48 states and 43 countries both online and in person since 2010. In 2015, Brooklyn Urban Garden Charter School in Queens, New York, implemented Transcendental Meditation in the classroom through the David Lynch Foundation. [197]
> New York City's public schools have also taken steps toward incorporating new teaching styles into the classroom with the 2014 Department of Education initiative Move-to-Improve, which lists yoga and stretching as two of many physical activities in the curriculum.

It is exciting to see a trend where schools are taking on a heart- centered approach for troubled kids instead of insisting that they be medicated to settle them down or sending them to detention where they can sit and stew in anger they don't know how to deal with. Children who are fortunate enough to participate in programs such as these are given coping skills that will be of use to them throughout their lives to help them deal with everyday stressors. Meditation also helps a child to develop coherence. As we learned in an earlier chapter, a child's brain develops differently when they have had to cope with and live in an abusive environment. It is highly likely that the practice of meditation, in addition to aiding children in learning to be mindful and calm, will contribute to the healing and restructuring of parts of their brains.

---

[197] Khorsandi, Yasaman, "The Movement of Meditation Replacing Detention in Schools," *Newsweek*, Sept 9, 2016, http://www.newsweek.com/education-meditation-after-school-program-holistic-life-504747

A PRISON PRACTICING RADICAL HUMANENESS[198]

Halden Prison is located in the town of Halden, Norway. It is on the edge of a dark pine forest in a rural setting on the Norwegian border. It is often called the world's most humane maximum-security prison. Norway banned the death sentence for civilians in 1902, and life sentences were abolished in 1981. [199] In 1998 Norway's Ministry of Justice reassessed the goals and methods of corrections and began to focus on the ideas of rehabilitating prisoners through education, job training, and therapy. In 2007 a new priority of reintegration was added with the emphasis on helping inmates find housing and work with a steady income before release. Norway also provides health care, education, and a pension to all of its citizens.

"Every aspect of the facility was designed to ease psychological pressures, mitigate conflict and minimize interpersonal friction." The prison is surrounded by a concrete wall about four times as tall as a man. The wall is a reminder to the prisoners that they are imprisoned. There are no coils or razor wire and no electric fences. It is a modern, cheerful facility that offers relative freedom in a quiet and peaceful atmosphere. The prison grounds are arranged in such a way as to require inmates to walk outside to their daily activities of school, work, or therapy. The Correctional Service uses a "dynamic security" that encourages interpersonal relationships between the staff and inmates as the primary factor in maintaining safety. This dynamic security encourages socialization with the inmates. Inmates are monitored by surveillance cameras, so they are able to move around the grounds unaccompanied by guards. There are no surveillance cameras in the classrooms, the common rooms, the cell hallways, or the cells.

> The inmates have the opportunity to act out, but somehow they choose not to. In five years, the isolation cell furnished with a limb-restraining bed has never been used.

---

[198] Benko, Jessica, "The Radical Humaneness of Norway's Halden Prison," *The New York Times Magazine*, March 26, 2015, https://www.nytimes.com/2015/03/29/magazine/the-radical-humaneness-of-norways-halden-prison.html The segment about this prison is quoted and paraphrased from this article.

[199] Ibid. An article about Norway's Halden Prison described incompletely the circumstances of Anders Breivik's 21-year sentence for a bombing-and-shooting attack in which 77 people died. While the maximum sentence for most crimes is 21 years, the Norwegian penal code allows for preventive detention, which is the extension of a sentence in five-year increments if the convicted person is deemed to be a continued threat to society. Therefore, the maximum term for any crime is not 21 years.

There are 251 inmates, and nearly half are there for violent crimes like murder, assault, or rape; a third are in for smuggling or selling drugs. Three-fifths of the inmates are Norwegian citizens; the rest come from over thirty countries—mostly Eastern Europe, Africa, and the Middle East. Violent incidents and threats are rare, and if they do take place, it is in Unit A, the prison's most restrictive unit. Unit A houses inmates who require psychiatric or medical supervision or who committed crimes that would make them unpopular in Units B and C. The latter two units house the larger population of inmates with more open living areas. Some inmates train for cooking certificates, and they are encouraged to cook. The focus is on creating as normal a setting as possible. If an inmate violates the rules, the consequences are swift and consistent. They might be confined to their cell during work hours, sometimes without TV.

If inmates are having problems with one another, an officer or prison chaplain will bring them together for a mediation session that continues until the issue is resolved. Members of rival gangs agree not to fight during their incarceration. The article added that the few incidents of violence have almost exclusively occurred in Unit A among the inmates with more serious psychiatric illnesses.

What I find encouraging about this program and the concept of a humane prison system is the idea that treating people fairly helps them understand fair treatment. At the risk of sounding simplistic discussing an issue that is far from simple, some criminals may have never been treated fairly in their lives. In the spirit of forgiveness and being released from one's past, this seems like a good way to work with people who commit crimes. We have maintained a get-even mentality in this world for far too long, and where has it taken us? One get-even act begets another and another into an endless loop.

I worked as a case manager/social worker in the Midwest for many years. I have seen people released from prison branded by their incarceration and with such low self-esteem and lack of self-confidence that it hinders their abilities to find and keep employment except for the most menial, low paying jobs, which adds to their low esteem and self-worth issues. They often cannot find jobs where they make enough money to support themselves. In this country, if a person is a felon or an ex-inmate, they are branded for life. There are many jobs they will never be able to get because of the stigma of being incarcerated. This is especially sad when imprisonment is for non-violent crimes such as drug abuse. Instead of rehabilitating people and helping them find a way to deal with their addictions and _the reasons they resorted to drugs,_ we throw them in prison, oftentimes wrecking their families and branding them for life. They are incarcerated in a punitive environment and too often after they are released, because they can't find decent paying jobs, return to the life that put them in prison in the first place and re-offend.

It is time we as a society begin to rethink our attitudes and treatment of our incarcerated populations both during their stay in confinement and upon their release. If a person spends time in prison, they have paid the penalty for their crime. If we can reframe their incarcerated time upon release as a debt paid and now forgiven, we can allow them to move on and reconstruct their lives.

Hate and cruelty beget hate and cruelty. Forgiveness and rehabilitation send an entirely different message, giving a person hope that they can reclaim their lives and become productive members of their community. Someone who has had a chance to develop some self-worth by learning a skill and understanding themselves psychologically is more likely to become a valuable asset to their communities by living productive lives. Do we want to spend tax dollars confining lawbreakers in a punitive environment that releases angry people back into their communities to re-offend, or do we want to spend them rehabilitating people who may have never had a chance until the time of their incarceration to know anything but a life of crime? Obviously, there will be those who are incorrigible and cannot be rehabilitated, but I think that number of re-offenders can be greatly reduced with more humane ways of dealing with criminal behavior.

That is the beauty I see in the pioneering efforts of the Halden system. It is a work in progress. Will the results show less recidivism and more integration over the long haul when inmates are released back into society? That remains to be seen, but it is a place to start. At least it is a conversation Norway is having. We need to look at ways to help ex-convicts become productive members of society and lose the stigma they are forced to carry. A chain is as strong as its weakest link, and I believe that a society is as strong as its population's ability to nurture the humanity of its citizens!!

17

PRESERVING THE PLANET

THERE ARE MANY INNOVATIVE AND natural ways to promote a more heart- centered and responsible ecology in this world. In this section I want to discuss a few that are of particular interest to me, but of course what I write about here is the tip of another iceberg of available innovations and information.

THE VERSATILITY OF THE HEMP PLANT

I am starting with hemp because I have been interested in this plant for a long time for its many nutritional benefits. When I began to explore hemp, I discovered it to be one of the hardiest and most versatile plants we have available to us. Its cultivation and use would save our environment in many ways, including sparing our trees and helping to stop pollution caused by plastic. One can Google hemp and find a plethora of articles about its many uses. A good place to start for anyone interested in hemp is a great article from *The Information Distillery*[200] that is chock full of information about this Hemp has been badly maligned because it is related to the marijuana plant; however, hemp does not contain the active chemicals that cause mind-altering effects. Dr. Mercola reports that

> In the US the cultivation of hemp has been banned since the 1970s when the federal Controlled Substances Act took effect. The law doesn't distinguish

---

[200] "The Many Uses of Hemp," *The Information Distillery,* http://www.informationdistillery.com/hemp.htm Unless otherwise specified, the information for this section will be quoted and paraphrased from this article. If you click on a link embedded in the article titled "enriches the soil," you are taken to a wonderful list of the Environmental Benefits of Hemp and the Agricultural Benefits of Hemp

between marijuana, the drug, and hemp, the plant, despite major scientific differences. [201]

In his article, Dr. Mercola goes on to explain that the cannabidiol (CBD) content in hemp is extremely low, only about four percent, and it lacks many of the medicinal terpenes and flavonoids that would make it useful as a medicine. It also only contains about 0.3 percent THC, the ingredient that makes one "high." Marijuana by contrast has about 10 to 20 percent of CBD, critical levels of medicinal terpenes, and flavonoids, as well as THC in varying ratios. Mercola goes on to cite a twelve-year genetic study of the Cannabis genus of plants conducted by the University of Minnesota College of Biological Sciences and College of Food, Agricultural and Natural Resources Sciences that resulted in the findings that there is indisputable evidence that hemp and marijuana should be regarded as separate plants. Researchers have discovered a genetic basis of differences among cannabis varieties, and they are challenging the position that all cannabis should be regulated as a drug. This is good news as we need to let go of the "drug" stigma that has been attached to hemp that stifles the utilization of one of the most versatile plants on the planet.

Hemp is a very nutritious food. Hemp seeds are an excellent source of protein, and hemp is the only plant that contains all of the essential fatty acids and amino acids needed by our bodies in an easily digestible form. [202]Hemp seed oil is becoming a common ingredient in skin care products due to its beneficial and natural emollient properties without the toxic chemicals petroleum-based products have. It is good for animals and can be added to their food to improve their health and nutritional intake. Some birds will pick hemp out of a birdseed mix as their preferred food.

This plant is almost miraculous in the variety of ways it can be used. Besides being a nutritionally dense food, hemp can be used for paper, textiles, fuel, building materials, and biodegradable sacks to carry groceries in. Its uses are endless, and the most beautiful characteristic of hemp is that it is a renewable resource that grows quickly, naturally resists diseases, requires little weeding, thrives in most climates, and *enriches the soil it grows in*. Hemp requires virtually no pesticide applications. It is drought resistant and has been found to be resistant to increased UV radiation from the sun. A hemp growing cycle is months compared to trees that can take 30 or more years to grow into a harvestable product. And

---

[201] Mercola, Joseph, M.D., "Health Benefits of Hemp," *Mercola- Take Control of Your Health*, Oct. 27, 2015, https://articles.mercola.com/sites/articles/archive/2015/10/27/hemp-health-benefits.aspx
Dr. Mercola cites a genetic study of marijuana and hemp and gives other health benefits of hemp.
[202] Osburn, Lynn, "HEMP SEED: THE MOST NUTRITIONALLY COMPLETE FOOD SOURCE IN THE WORLD, Part One," *Hemp Line Journal*, July-August 1992, https://ratical.org/renewables/hempseed1.html

one acre of hemp is said to produce more oxygen than twenty-five acres of current forest. It sounds like a farmer's dream crop to me, and an ecologist's dream come true.

Hemp paper can be recycled 7-8 times, as opposed to paper from other sources that can only be recycled about three times. Hemp paper has been used for thousands of years and makes a fine quality acid free paper that does not yellow over time.

Natural hemp fiber breaths and is recyclable, unlike petroleum-based synthetic fibers. It is as versatile as cotton but more durable. It is also excellent for making rugs and canvas. Levi Strauss' original denim jeans were made from hemp. It is the traditional rope-making fiber due to its flexibility, strength, and resistance to water damage.

Hemp can be used to create biofuels that can replace gasoline, and these biofuels produce less of the greenhouse gas carbon monoxide.

Jeff Meints, farmer and president and CEO of Titan PRO (an independent, family-owned company that supplies seed, crop protection, fertilizer, and crop insurance to growers across the Midwest) states that studies have shown that hemp's biomass can be converted into energy and could replace nuclear power and our current fossil fuels. This could be achieved just by farming six percent of the US's acreage. Meints quotes an article from Montana State University:

> When burned in a diesel engine, bio-diesel replaced the exhaust odor of petroleum diesel with a smells something akin to French-fries. Bio-diesel is eleven percent oxygen by weight and contains no sulfur, so instead of creating sulfur-base smog and acid rain as by-products, it produces eleven percent oxygen instead. Bio- diesel can be made from domestically produced, renewable oilseed crops such as hemp. [203]

Further down in his article, Meints tells a story from Popular Mechanics Magazine, Vol 76, No. 6, December 1941, titled "Auto Body Made of Plastics Resists Denting Under Hard Blows" about Henry Ford who created the first bio-fueled car and also a car made from hemp. The body of the car was made out of veggie-plastics made from flax, wheat, hemp, and spruce pulp. As an experiment, Ford struck the door with an ax in the dead of winter, and it didn't leave a dent. The material was "ten times" stronger than steel and yet one-third the weight, saving on gas mileage. This was also a car that could be sustained on one's own, distilling your own alcohol or hemp and creating your own fuel in your own backyard.

[203] Meints, Jeff, "The Hemp Plant, Humankind's Savior - 50,000 Uses and Counting," *Rediscover Hemp*, 1.23.2007, https://rediscoverhemp.com/inspire/the-hemp-plant-humankinds-savior/
I have quoted and paraphrased from this article.

Hemp oil was even used as grease to lubricate the car's engine. Meints talked about the safety of such a car, especially in accidents. He believed that a lighter, stronger car would result in fewer injuries.

HEMP VS. COTTON [204]

Hemp has a much more positive impact on the environment than cotton which accounts for 30-40% of the world's fiber requirements. Cotton farming is estimated for being responsible for about 25% of the planet's pesticide use. Runoffs from fields saturated with chemicals cause water pollution and damage to habitats. Pesticides also pose health threats to workers who come into contact with the chemicals on a daily basis. Hemp on the other hand requires few pesticides as it is naturally resistant to pests, and the way it is farmed reduces the growth of unwanted weeds.

Cotton needs about 10,000 liters of water to produce one kilogram of fiber. Hemp requires only about 2123 liters per kilogram of usable fiber.

Hemp plants are tall and thin and grow to a height of 5-25 feet. Due to their slender shape, they take far less land to produce much higher yields than cotton. One acre of hemp produces around 1500 pounds of fiber, approximately three times the amount of cotton that can be grown in the same space. Hemp also is fast growing and doesn't deplete the soil.

Hemp fiber isn't quite as soft as cotton but softens as it is washed. It shares cotton's breathability and is four times more absorbent than cotton. This also makes hemp easy to dye, and it holds the color longer. Hemp is naturally anti-bacterial and can be stored for long periods of time without mold or mildew. Hemp isn't as stretchy as cotton, which makes it ideal for manufacturing upholstery.

I have just scratched the surface of this fascinating plant, but if even half of what is claimed about the use of hemp is true, it is a miracle crop as it has the ability to reclaim our atmosphere and to regenerate our soil. The United States is finally making progress to permit the cultivation of hemp. The Hemp Farming Act of 2018 allows for the legal production of low-THC cannabis to take place on American soil for the first time since the early 1900's. Along with Oregon Senators Ron Wyden and Jeff Merkley, Republican Senate Majority Leader Mitch McConnell (KY) was responsible for drafting the language of the new act, which was introduced to Congress back on April 12, 2018. The legislation, now signed into

---

[204] "Hemp vs. Cotton: Is This the Future of Clothing?" *WayofLeaf,* March 4, 2020. https://www.marijuanabreak. com/hemp-vs-cotton-the-future-of-clothing

law by President Trump, essentially allows for hemp cultivation to be 100% legal (under certain guidelines) for farmers across the United States. [205]

FUN WITH FUNGI

In a National Geographic Video titled "You Didn't Know Mushrooms Could Do All This" [206] featuring Tradd Cotter, we are presented with some fascinating research about the various uses of fungi.

Cotter, owner and co-founder of Mushroom Mountain in upstate South Carolina, presents a unique perspective on what a farm for the future would look like. Mushroom Mountain is a mushroom research facility that houses a world class laboratory and over 50,000 square feet of available space under roof for cultivation, mycoremediation (using fungi instead of bacteria to break down waste), and medicinal research projects. Mushroom Mountain is a company that focuses on the needs of the planet, developing food and systems for filtering water, creating prototypes for novel antibiotic discovery, isolating target specific myco-pesticides to replace chemical pesticides for problematic insects, and many other projects that use fungi to harmonize our coexistence with nature. Their Mushroom Mountain University offers education on many areas of mushroom cultivation and use.

Mushroom Mountain is a unique facility that has an organic mushroom farm and promotes the study of mycology (the scientific study of fungi), sustainability, and organic agriculture. They specialize in growing various fungi for mycoremediation or the use of fungi to degrade or sequester contaminants in the environment in order to decontaminate it. Fungi, thanks to their non-specific enzymes, are able to break down many kinds of substances. Some of the uses of mushrooms include soil remediation or helping the soil recover from chemical pollution and filtration of biologically contaminated water. One of the segments in the video showed how they can inoculate a mushroom with a specific antibiotic resistant bacterium, and the mushroom will "sweat" out a substance that can be made into a personalized antibiotic for that specific bacterium. Another segment talked

---

[205] "Hemp Farming Act of 2018 [Fully Explained]," *WayofLeaf*, https://wayofleaf.com/blog/hemp-farming-act-fully-explained

[206] "You Didn't Know Mushrooms Could Do All This," *National Geographic*, featuring Tradd Cotter, owner of Mushroom Mountain http://video.nationalgeographic.com/video/news/160708-news-mushroom-mountain-uses-vin A fascinating short video on the many uses of various fungi https://mushroommountain.com/ For more videos by Tradd Cotter, go to this website: https://video.search.yahoo.com/search/video?fr=mcafee&p=tradd+cotter+mushroom+mountain#id=4&vid=ccde2 d3a4229df9948144a06f4fa312a&action=click

about the use of fungi to create building materials that are strong and fire resistant and can act as insulation as well.

For anyone interested in understanding mushrooms and their uses, Mushroom Mountain is the place to go for help. They are truly a heart- centered, ecology-centered facility and take their place as one of the architects who are introducing blueprints for a sustainable future.

THE HEART-SYSTEM OF TREES

"A forest has an amazing ability to communicate and behave like a single organism—an ecosystem" said Dr. Suzanne Simard in a fascinating TED talk that was featured on CNN titled *How Trees Talk to Each Other.* [207] In her talk, Simard described how trees share their resources through symbiotic underground networks of fungi called a mycorrhizal network. Simard explained that fungi and trees work together. Fungi cannot photosynthesize as they don't have access to light, and they don't have chlorophyll. From the trees they receive a type of sugar that is produced in photosynthesis and also carbon. The fungi release nutrients such as phosphorous and nitrogen and water to the trees in return for the sugar and carbon.

Dr. Simard also talked about the importance of older trees she called "hub trees." She explained that these hub or mother trees have lived a long time and have learned to adapt to many variations in climate and to encode those adaptations into their DNA that can then be passed down to younger trees. She believes that trees don't compete with each other; they serve each other.

The hub trees are also connected to wildlife. The example was given that when grizzles and wolves fish for salmon, they tend to eat the guts and brain and leave the flesh by the old hub trees to decay. The nitrogen from the salmon then goes into the soil and is dispersed through fungi from the old tree to the other trees in the forest.

Dr. Simard and Peter Wohlleben have teamed up in a documentary titled *Intelligent Trees* that can be obtained through Amazon. Peter Wohlleben has written a book titled *The Hidden Life of Trees* that is a paradigm breaker in how we think about trees. In his book he talks about how trees communicate; how they are like families and have a social life; how they support and nurture each other; and other fascinating information on the nature of trees. One important takeaway from the discoveries of Dr. Simard and Peter Wohlleben

---

[207] Simard, Suzanne, PhD, "TED Talk: How Trees Talk to Each Other," in "The secret life of trees: Is nature less selfish than we think?" By Paula Erizanu, *CNN ecosolutions,* 2.7.2017.
https://www.cnn.com/2017/02/07/world/secret-life-of-trees/index.html
The information in this segment is either paraphrased or quoted from this article or from Dr. Simard's talk.

confirms our need to find other available sources for the many manufactured goods we have that come from trees. As we have already discussed, hemp is a valuable resource, and in the next segment, I will talk about the many uses of bamboo.

Hemp, fungi, and bamboo are three of many resources that if utilized properly could have a huge impact on the issues of deforestation and air quality, along with other environmentally destructive problems our world is facing. Even putting the social interaction of trees aside, their contribution to all life on this planet is crucial as they are responsible for the very air we breathe!! It would seem prudent to utilize other more quickly renewable resources for human consumption and let the trees regenerate so that they can perform their most important role of maintaining our environment by generating our oxygen supply and as a habitat for many animals along with their many other contributions to life on earth.

BAMBOO

A quick search on the internet will bring up many articles about the uses of bamboo, another plant that is very versatile and eco-friendly. An article found on the website *Econation*[208] tells us that bamboo is an extremely fast and easy to grow renewable resource. It can be used for construction, clothes, food, and fuel.

There are over 1000 species of bamboo, and it grows in tropical and temperate climates. It is very hardy and does not need pesticides or herbicides to protect it. It is a little slower growing than hemp but still a very useful and versatile, sustainable plant. It doesn't need irrigation and can be harvested in 3-5 years. Bamboo produces 35% more oxygen than an equivalent grove of trees, and it sequesters carbon dioxide and is carbon neutral. It is critical in the balance of oxygen and carbon dioxide. It inhibits soil erosion and grows in a wide range of environments.

Bamboo can be used as a building material for houses; it is used in road reinforcements in India and in bridges in China, capable of supporting trucks that weigh as much as 16 tons. Bamboo is used in medicines and can be made into a breathable, thermal regulating fabric that wicks moisture better than polyester performance fabrics. It resists odor and is absorbent and fast drying.

Bamboo is used for food, and charcoal from this plant is used as a cooking fuel in China and Japan. Bamboo vinegar that is extracted as charcoal is being made contains 400 different chemical compounds that can be used in cosmetics, deodorants, food processing,

---

[208] "Bamboo," *Econation*, https://econation.co.nz/bamboo/
Website dedicated to innovation in sustainability

and insecticides. We have all seen the beautiful furniture that is made from bamboo, and it can also be used for rugs, textiles, paper, and even high-quality laminate flooring.

The *Bamboo Village* website[209] explains that bamboo is a naturally prolific and resilient plant that does not need fertilizers and is naturally pest resistant. It requires little water to grow and absorbs more carbon dioxide from the air than cotton or trees and releases more oxygen into the environment. Compare that to cotton farming that requires extensive irrigation and chemical spraying. Bamboo is 100% natural and biodegradable.

Remedy Grove website[210] gives many medicinal and health benefits of bamboo. I was especially intrigued by the claim that bamboo has a powerful energy field that is potent enough to be experienced by people nearby. The ancient Chinese used it to clear negative energy fields and "brighten up" energy flow. They also claim that when bamboo is used as an indoor plant, it dehumidifies, deodorizes, and neutralizes toxins in the air. Bamboo was rated a score of 8.6/10 by NASA in a list of plants to purify air. Bags filled with bamboo charcoal can be kept indoors to absorb unpleasant odors to keep a home smelling fresh and absorb excess humidity that promotes mold growth.

Bamboo shoots are considered to be very nutritious and are valued in Japan as one of the healthiest foods. Poultices made from bamboo are effective in treating infected wounds and promote faster recovery.

ORGANIC VS CONVENTIONAL FARMING

There should be no question about our right to have access to healthy food not poisoned by pesticides and other natural health care products such as supplements, remedies, herbs, etc. and also in-depth information about how to use them.

I find it infuriating that generally in order to obtain organic and sustainably grown foods and humanely raised meats and poultry and grass- fed dairy products people are forced to pay much higher prices, making the attainment of healthy food financially difficult or prohibitive for those on limited budgets. This contributes to the dismal health of the poor who often have to be content with chemically laden processed foods and conventionally grown foods covered with disease-causing pesticides because these foods are much cheaper and more readily available.

---

[209] https://Bamboovillage.com.au
Produces eco-friendly bamboo products from bedding to clothing.
[210] "20 Healing Benefits of Bamboo," *Remedy Grove*, October 20, 2017,
https://remedygrove.com/supplements/20-Healing-Benefits-of-Bamboo

Obtaining healthy food should be the norm, not the exception, and be available to everyone at an affordable price. A chain is as strong as its weakest link, and it is my firm belief that nutritious food is an important chain in the link to a healthy, mentally sound, and productive population.

Poor dietary habits have been encouraged by the mass production of foods that are stripped of their nutrients and chemically and/or genetically modified to produce large yields and prolong shelf life. So often we see advertisements focused on young children encouraging them to want these sugar saturated empty foods. A devastating side effect of empty foods is that they do not supply needed nutrition, and the body remains in a state of nutrient starvation even when it is overfed. This is one of many causes of obesity in this country.

In an article in *BioScience 2005*,[211] I found some interesting comparisons between organic and conventional farming that are important to understand. The article is old, but the message does not have an expiration date. The argument is that we cannot feed the world on organic farming; we have to use mass production methods in order to produce enough food to feed everyone. Let's see what some experts say. Organic farming is described in this article:

> Various organic technologies have been utilized for about 6000 years to make agriculture sustainable while conserving soil, water, energy, and biological resources. Among the benefits of organic technologies are higher soil organic matter and nitrogen, lower fossil energy inputs, yields similar to those of conventional systems, and conservation of soil moisture and water resources (especially advantageous under drought conditions). Conventional agriculture can be made more sustainable and ecologically sound by adopting some traditional organic farming technologies.

This same article goes on to describe conventional farming:

---

[211] Pimentel, David, Paul Hepperly, James Hanson, David Douds, and Rita Seidel, "Environmental, Energetic and Economic Comparisons of Organic and Conventional Farming Systems," *(BioScience*, July 2005) *Research Gate*, https://www.researchgate.net/publication/271847517_Environmental_energetic_and_economic_comparisons_oforganic_and_conventional_farming_systems,
I would encourage anyone interested in this subject who wants to learn more about what is really happening to our food in this country to rent the movie *Food, Inc.* and other movies and documentaries in the genre. They will open your eyes at the same time that they infuriate you.
Michael Pollan's *The Omnivore's Dilemma* goes more in-depth into the subjects talked about in the movie *Food, Inc.* regarding the treatment of animals on our industrial farms. A mind altering read.

Heavy agricultural reliance on synthetic chemical fertilizers and pesticides is having serious impacts on public health and the environment (Pimentel et al.2005).For example, more than 90% of US corn farmers rely on herbicides for weed control (Pimentel et al.1993),and one of the most widely used of those herbicides, atrazine, is also one of the most commonly found pesticides in streams and groundwater (USGS 2001).The estimated environmental and health care costs of pesticide use at recommended levels in the United States run about $12 billion every year (Pimentel 2005). Other aspects of conventional agriculture also have adverse effects on environmental and human health, as well as a high price tag. Nutrients from fertilizer and animal manure have been associated with the deterioration of some large fisheries in North America (Frankenberger and Turco 2003), and runoff of soil and nitrogen fertilizer from agricultural production in the Corn Belt has contributed to the "dead zone" in the Gulf of Mexico. The National Research Council (BANR/ NRC 2003) reports that the cost of excessive fertilizer use—that is, fertilizer inputs that exceed the amount crops can use—is $2.5 billion per year.

Modern agricultural practices can also contribute to the erosion of soil. The estimated annual costs of public and environmental health losses related to soil erosion exceed $45 billion (Pimentel et.al.1995).

Experts are coming to understand that conventional farming is not only detrimental to the environment and human health, but it is less cost effective overall than organic farming. Our water supply is in jeopardy with the runoff of toxic chemicals from fertilizers from conventional farming and the excrement from large Confined Animal Feeding Operations or CAFOs seeping into the water.

I found a fascinating article written by Judith D. Schwartz describing how grass-fed cows can help restore health to the water cycle and prevent deforestation. The following information is either quoted directly or paraphrased from this article.[212]

Schwartz first explains how cattle in a feedlot are confined and their waste runs off into lagoons. This fouls the area water—especially when heavy rains lead to overflow that creates the ideal conditions for the production of methane. (All ruminants emit methane as part of their digestive process.) She goes on to explain that healthy grassland soil contains methanatrophic or methane-eating bacteria to keep the methane in balance. When cattle are on pasture, their waste is broken down by microorganisms and enriches the soil. This,

---

[212] Schwartz, Judith D., *"Hope for a Thirsty World: How Grass-fed Cows Can Help Restore Health to the Water Cycle and Prevent Deforestation,"* *Natural Grocers Good4u Health Hotline Magazine*, Sept. 2018, Vol 16.

plus the organic matter added when cattle moved as a herd trample down plant material, bolsters carbon in the soil which acts like a sponge.

According to the USDA, every one-percent increase in soil organic carbon represents an astounding 20,000 gallons of water per acre that can be held on the land. When cattle are managed in a way that builds healthy soil, they are adding water to the system—water that would otherwise be lost to evaporation or sluiced away in gullies or slid across lifeless dirt. Scientists believe that grasslands and grazing animals co-evolved, with the land needing the animals in the same way that the animals need the land. Herbivores nibble on grass in a way that promotes plant growth. However, the specter of predators keeps them moving so that grasses are not eaten down to the ground. The grazers evade pack-hunting predators by bunching up and fleeing in masse, pressing down seeds and plant residue in the process. This predator-prey relationship is essential to grassland choreography.

Schwartz described a visit to the African Center for Holistic Management in Zimbabwe where restorative grazing had transformed the landscape. She explained that the increase in soil organic carbon meant enhanced water infiltration, and that meant people could grow crops seven months of the year instead of two or three. That made the difference between self-sufficiency and dependence on aid.

In her article, Schwartz also introduced Matt Maier, owner and "Chief Grass Farmer" of Thousand Hills Lifetime Grazed 100% grass-fed beef farm in Minnesota who also practices restorative grazing as do the thirty or so farms that sell through Thousand Hills Cattle Co.

Bottom line: grass-fed animals are healthier—the meat has more nutrients including healthy, life-sustaining fats. A healthy environment is created for the animals as they are treated humanely and are never confined to a feedlot. This can be done worldwide if people demand it.

We know money talks, and the only way to change the status quo is for the consumer to insist on grass-fed meat and dairy and organic foods. If we do that, more organic food will be produced and less conventional food will be grown, and the cost of organic food will go down. (I have learned by experience that once I switched to all organic food, my body needed less food as it was getting the nutrition it needed.)

Most grocery stores have an organic section, and while the food is somewhat more expensive, it isn't as cost prohibitive as it once was. Food quality and cost to some extent is consumer driven. It is up to us to demand more organic foods, and by doing so, we contribute to the health of the environment and ourselves. It is a win-win proposition.

INNOVATIVE CLEAN ENERGY POWER SOURCES

"To find the world's most aggressive clean energy targets, look no further than Denmark," says Justin Gerdes [213] in his article for *Citiscope*. "The city of Copenhagen is working hard toward meeting a pledge to become carbon-neutral by 2025."

Gerdes gives three lessons from the Danish experiment:

1. Unleash the creativity of public-sector entrepreneurs. In this segment Gerdes gives the example of Billund Vand a local water services company that has steadily improved its ability to utilize wastewater. He uses a bio-digester to turn wastewater into fertilizer, heat and electricity. Another example was the use of a solar district heating system where 40 percent of the energy comes from the sun. He explained that water heated by the sun is pumped into a retired gravel quarry lined with plastic. The water from this storage pit is used to heat homes and businesses in the fall and early winter, saving customers hundreds of euros a year while slashing the village's carbon footprint.

2. Reap the efficiencies of district energy. These are shared heating systems and replace individual residences need to provide their own heat. According to Gerdes, almost two-thirds of Danish households are connected to a district heating network and in Copenhagen this serves 98 percent of the city's buildings. Copenhagen also utilizes a district cooling system by drawing cool water from the harbor to pre-chill water for buildings with large cooling loads. It is estimated that district cooling reduces electricity consumption by 80 percent compared to conventional air- conditioning.

3. Give citizens a financial stake in clean energy. Denmark understood the importance of giving citizens a stake in clean energy projects. In 1980 a grant program was launched by the Danish government that covered 30 percent of the initial cost of wind turbines. Local cooperatives were formed giving individuals and households a chance to invest in wind energy projects. Gerdes explained that by 1996 more than 2000 cooperatives had been formed and within five years these 100,000 investors were responsible for 86 percent of the turbines installed in Denmark. After more than ten years the investors have their money back and they receive a seven percent annual return on their investment.

---

[213] Gerdes, Justin, "Three Lessons for Cities in Denmark's Clean-Energy Revolution," (Article for *Citiscope*, June 30, 2016) *government technology,*
https://www.govtech.com/fs/perspectives/3-Lessons-for-Cities-in-Denmarks-Clean-Energy-Revolution.html
Information distilled from his book *Quitting Carbon: How Denmark is Leading the Clean Energy Transition and Winning the Race to the Low-Carbon Future*

Gerdes concludes on this uplifting note: "In Sonderborg as in Copenhagen, the push to go carbon-neutral is inextricably linked to larger efforts to drive sustainable economic growth and add good-paying jobs."

"We've adopted a holistic approach that's bottom-up," says Christian Eriksen, project director for Project Zero A/S, the private firm charged with implementing clean energy plans for Sonderborg. "It's not just about top- down, planning and coming up with business and new technology to drive this forward. It's also very much about participation, about learning, and empowerment of our citizens and local companies."

Karl Mathiesen wrote in an article titled "From Kansas to Copenhagen: Clean energy beacons around the world" [214] about the small town of Greensburg, Kansas receiving the distinction as America's greenest town. Greensburg was hit with a massive tornado that destroyed 95 percent of its buildings in 2007, and the 1400 residents had to choose to rebuild or relocate. About half the townspeople left, but a group who remained developed a master plan to rebuild the town as an energy-saving renewable energy haven. Just outside the town they built a 12.5-megawatt wind farm. This supplies 300 percent of the town's electricity, and the excess is pumped into the Kansas grid. The town had to rebuild from scratch, and in the process, they utilized the most modern building techniques. This little town now has the highest concentration of gold and platinum eco-design rated buildings in the U.S., and all of its streetlights are LED. To give a comparison—all large government buildings are now rated platinum. These gold and platinum ratings help Greensburg save over $200,000 a year.

[214] Mathiesen, Karl, "From Kansas to Copenhagen: clean energy beacons around the world," *The Guardian*, May 20, 2015, https://www.theguardian.com/environment/2015/may/20/clean-energy-beacons-of-the-world

18

CELLS AND THE NATURE OF LIFE AND DEATH

DR. BRUCE LIPTON IS A pioneer in studying the nature of our cells. His cutting-edge book *The Biology of Belief: Unleashing the Power of Consciousness, Matter and Miracles* is in its thirteenth edition. He is a biochemist, geneticist, and cellular biologist who is known for his groundbreaking research with stem cells and cell cloning spanning over forty years.

The transcript of his podcast "What Our Cells Can Teach Us" [215] has some intriguing insights that I think fit in with some of the recent scientific discoveries about the nature of consciousness. The facts in this chapter, as well as any quotes, unless otherwise indicated, will be from this podcast.

Dr. Lipton identifies our bodies as a community of intelligent beings called cells, and every cell initially has all the same functions that a human body has in its various systems: digestive, respiratory, musculoskeletal, reproductive, nervous, and immune and functions the same as a miniature human. All our cells are essentially a community of beings that together create our body. He likens the human body to a community where each person has their job and place, and all work to keep it functioning.

Dr. Lipton has discovered that cells have miniature antennae which the medical profession refers to as "self-receptors," and these receptors receive messages from outside the body. A new science has grown out of this research called epigenetic control. Epi means "above," and epigenetic control means "control above the genes."

In his research Dr. Lipton has discovered that from a technical point of view, a cell membrane is a liquid-crystal semiconductor or programmable device similar to a computer chip. He likens the environment to a programmer who is typing information on the surface of the cell where the antennas or "self-receptors" are located. This information is picked up by the antennas that control the actions of the cells. The ramifications of these discoveries are far reaching and more than the scope of this chapter, but suffice it to say, it is fascinating information.

---

[215] "What Our Cells Can Teach Us," Interview of Bruce Lipton, PhD by Tami Simon, transcript of audio podcast, *Sounds True*, https://www.resources.soundstrue.com/transcript/what-our-cells-can-teach-us/

The part of the podcast that is the most significant to me within the context of the explorations of this book is the discussion about his discovery that cells are programmed from outside the body from the Field. In one place he likens his body to a virtual reality suit that his *identity enters into* (emphasis mine), and the cells' function is to translate the environmental information so that the individual living in the body can experience the sensations of the physical world. He is discovering on a scientific level what was initially introduced in the myth we have been exploring through various possibilities in this book: *our consciousness navigates the material world through a physical body that could be thought of as being similar to a spacesuit programmed to respond to its inhabitant.*

Here is Dr. Lipton's complete explanation:

> Dr. Lipton: Well, in that understanding, my attention was drawn to the fact… what makes one human different from another human is the presence of a set of antennas that I said were in part called self- receptors that distinguish one human from another. If I take the self- receptors off a cell, it's generic. And I can implant a generic cell into any body and it will never be rejected. But if somebody has their self- receptors on the surface of the cell, that gives it identity. That's why we can't transplant our cells and tissues with each other, 'cause each of us has our own identity. So now we're getting to the long story…to get it to the short point, and that is: the identity of an individual is some signal that is picked up by the antennas called self-receptors on the surface of the cell. And when those surface receptors are gone, the cell has no identity. And when the surface receptors are on, they become an individual cell.
>
> So what really was the bottom-line conclusion is then, the identity of a cell is nothing programmed into the cell. The identity of the cell is some information that is picked up from the environment via these antennas called self-receptors. And that hit me the very instant I thought, I said, "Wait a minute. Wait." Then it says, "My identity is not inside the cell because it's reading something from the environment." What hit me was, "Well, wait. Then if the cell dies, does the environmental signal leave the environment?" The answer is no. The environment is…the signals are always there, and the cells come and go. And when a cell is present, it can read the signal. And when a cell dies, the signal's still there but the cell's not there. It's sort of like a cell or a human body is like a television set with an antenna tuned to a station. And so right now my antennas are tuned to the Bruce Station, and

my body's playing The Bruce Show right here. And what's relevant about this is when we talk about televisions, I say, "The picture tube is dead; it breaks. It's not working." We say, "The television's dead." I go, "Well, the television's dead, but the broadcast — is it still there?" And the answer is, "Well, yes." And you can tell or know that by just getting another television set, plugging it in, turning it on, and then tuning it to the station. And there, oops the broadcast's back on again!

So what this all led me to see was my identity is not inside the cell; it's something out in the Field. That the cells can die, but if a future embryo comes with the same set of antennas that I have on my body right now, it will download the same signal. And so, the Bruce Station will be on but with a completely different body the next time!

All of this made sense on the level of understanding the mechanics of the cell membrane as an information processor, the Field as a source of information. And all of a sudden I realized my identity is immortal; it's part of a field of information. And that reincarnation is a consequence of another individual in the future coming with the same set of self-receptors — sort of like a combination lock, there's a large number of them — and that if that shows up again then that individual's playing but through a different body. That could be different sex, different race, or anything — it's just a different biology.

So this blew my mind because I said, "My identity is not in here." And when I started recognizing it was outside then I realized, well, the identity, it doesn't just send information into the body via the antennas; it also...the information the body gleans from the environment through the nervous system, the nervous system is broadcasting that information back out of the body. There's a device — called magnetoencephalograph, where, like the EEG reads brain activity by putting wires on the head and reading the electrical activity of the brain, the magnetoencephalograph does the same thing but you don't have to touch the brain. The probe is outside the head! And so you can see that when a person is processing in their brain, you can read the information as being broadcast from their head! You can read it outside their body!

So I started to realize that there's a two-way connection between the Field and the body as the physical reality...that information comes from the Field, goes into the body; and information in the body goes back to the Field. So they're working with each other, and that's how our lives influence the Field when we're here. So, all of this kind of metaphysical stuff turns out to be at the bottom level connected to the quantum biophysics and the molecular antennas on the surface of the cell. And therefore there was a scientific bridge between [the] mind and body all of a sudden because we saw how the information is transmitted into the cell, and that [the] information influences the activity of the cell.

Further along in the podcast, Dr. Lipton shares an incredibly significant breakthrough:

All of our lives from the time we're very young and realize that mortality is part of our experience, that we're going to die — all of us are going to die — we in our minds then become very protective of our lives. And our subconscious minds are, through our development, programmed to continuously watch out and protect [our lives], because we're so afraid of this death kind-of thing. And so we don't realize how much of our unconscious behavior is really directed for our safety and our concern for our lives, so there's always this information processing where the brain is scanning everything in the environment and trying to evaluate it in regard to our safety and keeping alive and the threat of mortality.

When this information dropped down to my head — and this is the fun part, because I wasn't spiritual — at that one moment when I saw how the mechanism worked, it was like, "Well, of course…of course there's this visible energy field that represents who I am." And yet when I said what the first thing was, was that the Field is here whether I'm here or not. And for me as a scientist, looking the way I looked at it, it wasn't like, "Well, Bruce, do you believe in this?" It was sort of like, no, this is the way it works, period. And I looked at it and I saw it in that first instant; that my identity goes on and on, and my physical presence comes and goes.

And I have to tell you, the lightness was the letting-go of that fear of mortality. For a guy who didn't believe in any of this stuff in the first place, all of a sudden within minutes to see that it worked and then minutes to see that not only does it work, but I'm an immortal being, the fear of my life that I…that you carry around unconsciously, and it's there because every step you take, it's a biological imperative that you assess your environment for your safety. And we do that, and the more we worry over it, the more we're looking at all the negative things that can harm you — that's what you focus on — and it's a very unfortunate situation. Because we're so locked up in fear about it, and it's not a conscious thing that I'm thinking about it every minute; it's an unconscious program that will operate for you. And it's the kind of thing that gives you good vibes and bad vibes: that information is reading what's going on in your world, and then you sense it in your body.

And the instant that I saw this as, "Oh my God, this is a reality. I do not die in that sense," I let go of that. It was, like, OK, more fearless in that sense, OK? It's like, OK, life is great, and that worry part or lack of knowing that we live with about "So what happens?"...when that disappeared, man that was a great enlightening moment. Because it made life so much easier and more fun without that daily, unconscious focus of fear.

This information is significant on so many levels. When we talk about the life force animating the human instrument, this all makes sense. Dr. Lipton is also giving science another piece of the puzzle in the search for the Soul.

In his work with cellular biology, Dr. Lipton is telling us that from a scientific discovery point of view, our bodies are animated from a source that is not in the body. Religion and philosophy have explored this notion for as long as they have been around. It is refreshing to see science mirror this view as it reveals similar discoveries. The complete podcast is very fascinating and worth the time it takes to read.

IN THE SPRING OF MY AWAKENING

I feel a deep stirring
A flicker, a glimmer, a small flame
Igniting a dormant longing

Germinating seeds promise new life
As they begin to crack open one by one
Reaching for the life-giving light
Sprouting in the mulch of decaying issues
Pushing their way through the rich new soil
Transformed, ripe for incubation

Seeds have tried to sprout before
But the mulch wasn't ready
Issues of limitation, fear and aging;
Too restrictive to nurture new life
Body and soul starvation
Overtaken by creativity stifling control

A promising garden immobilized
So many years ago during a dark winter
Passion frozen and forced into dormancy
Desperate longing turned into silenced neediness
And numbed bewilderment over unmet needs
Morphing into self-pity and self-indulgence
Vision canceled out by self-sabotage

Aging uncertainties caused new angst towards a body
Never quite trusted
Began feeling like a full-blown enemy
Plodding along under the weight of a stringent taskmaster
Its resistance felt through the
Longing to escape into sleep and
Reluctance to rise to another day

My Sacred Heart found me languishing in that dark winter
Encouraged my long arduous journey of searching
and self- examination
Inspired the new understanding
That broke the ice and brought me here
To the spring of my awakening
A life renewed by hope and forgiveness and acceptance
Germinating a new honesty in the transformed garden
of my life
That won't tolerate stagnation or superficiality
or lies too long lived

Lark Aleta Batey 2015

19

ENTERTAINMENT MIRRORS THE VIRTUAL REALITY OF OUR WORLD

THROUGH THE LENS OF ENTERTAINMENT AND INSTANT COMMUNICATION

THE IDEA THAT *THINGS ARE not always as they seem* adds mystery into our everyday life on so many levels. In an age of almost instant communication, we are breaking down barriers and boundaries faster than at any other time in history as we learn of events in real time around the world.

The world of story through theatre, novels, movies, and TV series serves many purposes in addition to entertaining us. We relive historical events often from several points of view and come to know what famous people of the past might have been like. We are offered glimpses into possibilities of what the future might hold. We are introduced to all kinds of belief systems and witness our characters play out their dramas against the backdrop of the limitations and paradigms of their beliefs. We are privy to inner struggles that send someone spiraling into darkness and root for them as they find the light that brings them through it. Story leads the way in introducing and expanding a large variety of ideas and fills an almost insatiable hunger in the human species to experience more about ourselves. I found myself musing one night as I was reading "Chamber Three Philosophy: The Blueprint of Exploration" [216] that something deeper might be happening to our consciousness as a species and as individuals than just our love of story. When an Entity inhabits a Human Instrument, it plunges a fragment of itself into a physical body living in the world of separation. This body is limited in its abilities to explore and experience as an individual.

---

[216] Mahu, James, "Chamber Three Philosophy: The Blueprint of Exploration," *Collected Works of the WingMakers, Volume I.* edited by John Berges, Planetwork Press, Egg Harbor Township, NJ, 2013.
Also, Mahu, James, "The Blueprint of Exploration," *WingMakers*, Philosophy, https://wingmakers.com/writings/philosophy/chamberthree/

According to this paper, the Human Instrument is generally only equipped to focus on the current lifetime of the body it inhabits. Most individuals would be overwhelmed and become unbalanced by the memories of other lives they might have lived or could be living in parallel realities of the Entity they are a part of, and memories of other lifetimes would be a huge distraction to successfully living a current lifetime. That reasoning makes a lot of sense, but it hasn't stopped me from wondering who I might have been in other times and places. What has my consciousness experienced through time to give me the particular focus and mindset that I now have? Through night and daydreams, do I have communication with these other parts and levels of me, and do these other fragments of my consciousness and I share ideas? I am so intrigued by these questions and their ramifications.

On this particular evening, my musings took me down a fascinating rabbit hole as I thought about our entertainment industry and how we have reached a time in human history when we can create visual effects of almost anything we can think of. Even though we cannot remember individual past or parallel lives per se, we can identify with the characters in the stories we watch or read, and in that way, we live another life for a short time.

Where do the ideas for stories come from? Do we access them from that vast repertory of memory we all share? I could not help but wonder if maybe storytelling is in part a calling up of memories of our past and future lives. We live a story for as long as it takes to watch a movie or read a book and often find ourselves thinking about and sometimes discussing it long after we are done. We experience the arc of challenge in the story and its resolution, and we grow in understanding; and because many people watch the same movies and read the same books, we are essentially tapping into a shared reservoir of ideas and memory. That is what our journeys on Earth are meant to do; help us to explore and grow in understanding of ourselves as individuals and as a species. We all share in the stories just as we will share in the collective memory when we return to the Entity level of our existence.

As far out as it might seem, I couldn't help but wonder if maybe story has the very deep purpose of calling up our shared memories for review and for pondering and growing in understanding together while still confined to the world of separation. As we share in the collective experiences of a powerful story for a short time, we live those events together. That communal experience can be a powerful catalyst to deep understanding and the beginning of change within us as a species. Through story we can experience many lives and many possibilities in one lifetime. We can see what works and what doesn't. We witness firsthand the treatment of someone who goes through deeply painful and challenging life events and cringe at what it can do to them psychologically. In identifying with our characters, we are given the opportunity to experience empathy for those who suffer such a life passage.

I also mused that night on the possibility that maybe the kinds of stories we are attracted to indicate the kinds of lives we have lived or are living in other bodies and times so they might be clues into what our consciousness is or has focused on. Story is such a gift to us as we are given the opportunity to plunge into many "rabbit holes" and grow from those explorations. In a sense this may be giving us a hint of what it might be like to have access to our complete memories. We are entering a time in human history when we as a species will be made acutely aware of how our actions impact the collective whole as we are forced to live with the ramifications of our behaviors on world events. Our species is on a trajectory for some discoveries that will take us out of the separation that has been our journey for so long. Maybe the entertainment world of story is training in We Are One-101.

Keeping the ideas above in mind, in this and the next chapter of this section, I want to meander through some perceptions from my personal experiences with some books, films, and TV series that speak to me as archetypal blueprints which have introduced innovative concepts on our world stage.

By observing which movies and books are enthusiastically embraced by a large number of people along with the ideas from the discussion above, we can gain an awareness of our collective secret yearnings as well as the trajectory on which our shared consciousness is traveling. Some stories become iconic because we recognize a deeply embedded truth hidden in them that speaks to us.

I initially became aware of that concept through the 1977 movie *Close Encounters of the Third Kind*, an early Steven Spielberg production. I was enchanted with the idea that certain people were affected by the internal imprint of a mountain that prompted them to sculpt it, draw it, and go searching for it. We learn that this mountain image is calling people to go where the close encounters with a friendly alien species is destined to take place at the end of the movie.

Afterward I thought about that movie a lot because to me that imprint was an archetypal metaphor for the impulse to seek that had always been a part of me. I am sure I am not the only person who has felt that way. The story spoke to me as an illustration and affirmation that something inside of me was prompting me to search. I remember telling my ex-husband that I could understand that impulse and drive because I felt the same way. I didn't know what I was looking for, but I had to keep looking until I found it, and I would recognize it when that happened.

Fast forward to more recent entertainment vehicles: novels and movies such as the *Harry Potter* series; *WingMakers Materials* fiction written by James Mahu (*The Ancient Arrow*

Project, The Weather Composer Series, *Quantusum*, and *The Dohrman Prophecy)*; movies like *Avatar* and *The Matrix Trilogy*; and TV series such as *Outlander* and *This Is Us*.

They all stand out in my mind as trailblazing stories bringing paradigm-shifting messages to our world that will help us to move forward. There are many others, of course, and I know you, my readers, could add pages to my very short list. But for the sake of discussing some important concepts that are bringing us closer to the horizon of a new paradigm, I will use my short list.

Before I get into my discussion of each work in this chapter and the next, however, I want to make some general statements starting with our attitudes towards magic and the supernatural. They have been maligned through the centuries by the ruling powers, especially the religious ones. If we allow ourselves to look into the suppression paradigm with a slightly askance perception and think of how much anything supernatural or "magical" has been railed against by religious authority figures, then we might benefit from pondering the question—Why would that be?

If we think back to the way we are raised, most of us are taught to focus on the tangible and to be afraid of, or at least not take seriously, anything that we cannot see, except what the churches would have us believe. Horror movies depict unseen worlds and their inhabitants as sinister, macabre, and foreboding to keep us afraid of wanting to explore them. We have a holiday—Halloween—devoted to the idea that the next worlds are menacing and gruesome. This not only reinforces our fear of death, but also acts as a deterrent to keep us afraid of anything that is not tangible or that we cannot explain.

Throughout history, humanity has relied on its philosophers, authors, artists, and musicians to introduce new ideas into the consciousness that catalyze the evolution of our species. Until the last few decades, however, information has not traveled as fast or reached as many as quickly as it does now through the information highway we all have access to with the click of a mouse. In a little more than an instant, an event happening in one part of the globe can be televised to the rest of the world in real time. Those with great power can generate unprecedented consequences almost instantaneously. For our world to survive these abilities, our leaders must have an impeccable sense of responsibility.

Movies can illustrate the ramifications of giving dark ideas too much power, but they can also illustrate how to overcome darkness; the choice is ours, individually and collectively.

I discussed the concept that many ideas for stories could have been drawn from our collective memories, and I have a hunch that some of the newer ones for books and movies have been drawn from the Planetary Tributary Zones.[217] Several ideas described in the

---

[217] See **Tributary Zones**, Appendix A - Glossary

following segments fall into that category as I believe they are preparing humanity for exciting new events.

As we watch a movie or read a novel, we are presented with an issue, and in a short period of time, we are privy to the process and resolution of whatever is being presented. This is a powerful tool which allows us to experience so many of life's scenarios. We are given the opportunity to try on ideas and through the arc of story watch how our characters work out their predicaments. In our own minds, we may find ourselves pondering how we would handle a similar situation.

The technology that makes science fiction movies so realistic opens us up to unreal ideas as possibilities, stretching us and presenting us with exciting new ways of perceiving the Multiverse. We live in a virtual reality, and we often hear the motto: "If we can think it or dream it, we can create it." If we loosen up the boundaries around the notion that this is all there is and remain open to new possibilities, we have the profound potential for creating new worlds.

At the same time, I think it is wise to allow our personal activations and transformations to happen as organically as possible. By that I mean not to look to artificial enhancement for guidance, but to our deepest impulses. Bells and whistles of phenomena are distractions to make us believe we are making progress toward Cosmic Consciousness; however, they cannot be counted on to produce lasting results. We are seeking an authentic transformation that will transcend the matrix. So far accounts of Consciousness breakthroughs, although inarguably mind expanding, all seem to keep the person locked into the Hologram, so we need to look further into transformational tools that we as a species have not yet explored.

Attaining Sovereign Integral Consciousness is us reaching and expanding towards our Creative Force, and that same Creative Force reaching down towards us. We accomplish that union through living a heart- centered life.

The message coming into our current era is that *something wonderful is happening* and even though we may experience pain and darkness initially, love wins, and liberation is our ultimate birthright.

The following stories are beloved because we as a species are hungry for encouraging messages that take us outside the box of reality we are currently stuck in. I also think that on some level we recognize that the stories are feeding our collective longing by speaking to a part of us that knows.

If we are willing to be patient and allow our process to unfold, I believe it will be an authentic, deeply rooted transformation with the power to catalyze us into an entirely new reality. This plane of existence is the sandbox of consciousness. This is the place for us to experiment and understand how reality happens in slow motion.

HARRY POTTER

(Series of eight books written by JK Rowling; movies produced by David Heyman, distributed by Warner Brothers; audio books performed by Jim Dale.)

I had the wonderful, enchanting privilege of listening to Jim Dale read and perform all the Harry Potter books on my commutes to work and while traveling to various destinations my job took me to over a six-month or so period of time. After I had listened to all the books, I watched the movies.

Mr. Dale has the gift of being able to bring each character to life as he gives each one their own special voice. By listening in this way, each character became very real to me, turning those short car jaunts into intense journeys into parallel worlds. Since I listened in short spurts, I had the luxury of pondering the deeper, richer undercurrents and archetypes of this amazing series, and there are many.

I have become convinced that the *Harry Potter* books are a gift to humanity as they help us break out of some old, outworn concepts and plant new expansive ideas in young minds. The books have stretched the minds of several generations of young and old alike by introducing new words and magical ways of perceiving the world and by illustrating how parallel realities exist side by side. Co-existing and unseen by most of the Muggle population (regular people who do not have any magical blood inside them) are the worlds of Harry Potter and the Hogwarts School and the Wizarding world. To access the Hogwarts Express, students have to find platform 9¾ and go through a brick wall that takes them into an alternate reality. Muggles cannot see the 9¾ sign or go through the brick wall to access the Hogwarts Express platform.

The series covers seven years in these children's lives as it chronicles their experiences and educational lessons while they are becoming proficient in the magical arts. The stories are set against the backdrop of the evolution of Lord Voldemort, a ruthless and power-hungry wizard, and his pursuit of Harry Potter. Voldemort allowed himself to be seduced by the dark forces.

Harry develops and strengthens his integrity through many challenges as he hones the skills he will need to face his mortal enemy. The stories become increasingly darker as the children mature, but as the ending approaches and many questions are answered, we are able to recognize the thread of the power of the FORCE OF LOVE woven throughout each episode in a magnificent way. I see several significant archetypal themes in the Harry Potter series, not only in many of the details, but in the overall idea of an expanded world view.

The children at Hogwarts School are given specific rules in how they are allowed to use the magical arts they are developing; they are taught respect for this knowledge, and they learn their craft in stages over a seven- year period. During their time of study at Hogwarts, the students gain increasing levels of magical powers as they mature and grow in the responsibility needed to utilize them. They learn that there are consequences for their actions, and as one gains more power, those consequences can be much more far-reaching.

Their studies include subjects such as the defenses against the dark arts—and a recognition that there is such a thing; the care of magical creatures—learning to respect all kinds of creatures who share this planet with us; and of course, the famous game of Quidditch played on flying broomsticks helping them develop their abilities to work as a team.

It is a universal motivation in a child's DNA to explore, and JK Rowling captures that drive in a charming way. Even though the budding magicians in the story are given rules by their adult caretakers and teachers, they often feel they have a perfectly good reason to break them as is a child's nature to do. The books powerfully illustrate how the children are ultimately shown compassion and forgiveness by their school elders when they go astray, even as they are given consequences. The children experience various forms of adversity that help them develop their character, strength, and imagination, and they acquire discernment by learning to pick their battles while they problem-solve the dilemmas they are confronted with.

I am going to get some flak for this next insight, but in the spirit of what I am attempting to convey in this book, I hope you will humor me and at least hear me out.

I was struck at one point by the thought that Lord Voldemort is very much like the depiction of the archetype of the god of the Old Testament who I believe is Anu. Both demand absolute allegiance; both threaten to destroy anyone who will not obey them; both are beings of great vengeance— "vengeance is mine sayeth the Lord;" both perpetuate separation, cruelty, and exclusivism. Voldemort holds the idea that only "purebloods" can be a part of the wizarding world. For the separatist Old Testament god, it was "his people are the chosen ones" and a constant pitting of tribes against each other. Love is not encouraged and strict obedience to rules and edicts are enforced upon their minions. Both entities commit abominable cruelties and with their supernatural powers rule by instilling great fear of them into their subjects. Both of these beings are slaves to power and glory with the heartless ambition of enforcing absolute control over their subjects. Both are labeled "he whose name shall not be spoken."

Professor Dumbledore is the archetype of the Wise Old Man. He is a beacon of luminosity as he sheds wisdom on all the tasks Harry must accomplish. He guides Harry and teaches him how to think for himself so that he can defeat Voldemort. He helps Harry to understand how important the power of love is, and we learn throughout the series that Love is a protection and a superpower for Harry.

We learn that Dumbledore was flawed as most of us are, and yet able to attain multiple levels of understanding, and in his wisdom, he conveyed his knowledge to Harry through the tools of Light. When Harry learned of Dumbledore's human failings, he had to wrestle with his hero falling off the pedestal of perfection. For most of us that is what our teen or early adult years are about as we grapple with the imperfections of our parents or the most admired adult authority figures in our lives who were our "gods" when we were young. It is an essential part of our journey of becoming an individual when we learn to internalize the positive direction we received, forgive the negative, and accept the whole package that is our human parents and other significant adults from our childhoods.

In one exceptionally beautiful passage in the *Half-Blood Prince*, Dumbledore explains to Harry that he is protected from Voldemort and the dark side by his ability to love. Voldemort is not able to love and does not understand its power. He sees Love as a dangerous flaw. I cannot help but think of "The Fifth Interview of Dr. Neruda" where Dr. N explains to Sarah that the Anunnaki do not embrace the Sovereign Integral Process of developing Behavioral Intelligence because they see it as a weakness. In that same interview, we learn that the Sovereign Integral Process which is essentially embracing the power of the Spectrum of Love (the Six Heart Virtues) is the way out of the Hologram of Deception. It helps us to deflect the dark energy away from our psyches and to break down the suppression program in our collective consciousness; the Power of Love Wins.

I see Harry as the archetype of the Heart in this story, Hermione as the Intellect and Ron as the Emotion and bridge between the Heart and the Intellect. Dumbledore recognized that the three of them needed each other to carry out the mission of defeating Voldemort and encouraged Harry to share his journey, his secrets, and his hopes and fears with Hermione and Ron and for them to work together—just as our heart and emotion and intellect must work together to overcome the suppression paradigm.

THE *OUTLANDER* SERIES

(Written by Diana Gabaldon, a series of more than ten books; now being made into a television series on Starz, produced by Ronald D. Moore; audio books performed by Davina Porter.)

This series is captivating, and the characters of Claire and Jamie are wonderfully and believably portrayed by Catriona Balfe and Sam Heughan. These two actors fit very well with my personal image of what Jamie and Claire would have looked like, and obviously Ms. Gabaldon and others felt the same as the TV series is extremely popular.

I listened to the first ten books of the series in my car as I traveled all over the State of Nebraska while I was working, transforming the banality of driving into a magnificent journey of adventure. The audio books are performed by Davina Porter who has an amazing ability to bring every character to life. She is truly a gift to the spellbinding quality of these books as her voice embodies each character.

The *Outlander* series is masterfully written as a combination of historical fiction, romance, and time-travel story that illustrates the power of love through time. It is well-researched as Gabaldon skillfully weaves real historical events into the lives of her fictional characters. She creates multi- faceted characters who are lovable, flawed and in some cases downright diabolical. Aside from being adventure love stories, they also portray powerful women and men who not only respect each other, but also work side by side as equals. The stories illustrate how strong women can be in this world and be loved and admired by powerful and strong men.

Diana Gabaldon is an amazing, imaginative, and prolific author who has written other books besides this profoundly captivating series. The *Outlander* books tell the story of a woman living in the 20th century who quite by accident discovers that she is able to go through the standing stones in Scotland and time-travel into previous centuries. She initially finds herself in 17th century Scotland, and from that point, the story takes off into incredible adventures of survival, love, and intrigue.

As I experienced these books, I was absolutely enchanted with the idea of time-travelers bringing information from the future and dropping those ideas into the worlds they visited, thus accelerating the understanding of the people of a particular historical period. I realize in our world of literal thinking this idea is very far-fetched, but when you are listening or reading the books, it all makes perfect sense. In that tone I think that these stories come to us to help us expand our world views of what is possible. It is intriguing to think that we may find in the future just how plausible this concept might be.

It is so easy to fall in love with Jamie and Claire and their families and through their eyes experience a timeless world where centuries are blended, and love and integrity is a driving undercurrent moving the characters along through intense drama and riveting storytelling.

THIS IS US

(TV series written and created by Dan Fogelman; the program aired on NBC from September 20, 2016, to May 24, 2022).

This show skillfully chronicles the Pearson family across several generations and is told in such a way that we see how even the smallest event or situation at one stage in a person's life affects the lives of many people in their responses and decisions through generations. Each life- affirming episode is riveting, beautiful in its emotional truthfulness, and groundbreaking in its original story-telling mode.

I don't want to spoil it for those yet to experience this magnificent show by giving anything away. I just want to say how beautifully and masterfully it blurs the boundaries of time as it poignantly and truthfully tells the story of the Pearson family and how each member deals with the imperfections of being human in the era each is born into. The characters in the story do not time travel, but the audience does. This is one of the most engaging, creative, and compelling family series on TV right now, I think.

WINGMAKERS MATERIALS

The theme of "Part Four: Architects of a New Paradigm" would not be complete without including the next group of books written by James Mahu, creator of the *WingMakers Materials*. The stories he tells are written in such a way as to be timeless, applying to almost any period in history. They are relevant to us now because they present a foundational new archetypal mythology that is laying the groundwork for future events that will be game changers in the story of humanity and play a huge part in the making of a new paradigm.

James' characters are multi-faceted, unpredictable, and complex. He doesn't shy away from characters capable of dark actions that give the stories realistic dimension in suspenseful, thought-provoking, insightful, and compelling ways. James weaves futuristic and deeply profound concepts throughout his books.

QUANTUSUM
(Written by James Mahu, available through Planetwork Press, www.planetworkpress.com)

This is a novel that to those of us who read and discuss it seems like a "never-ending story" because every time we re-read it, we find inspiration and ideas we missed the time before. It is a book that gives more as we grow in understanding and is profound in the concepts it presents. It also blurs the boundaries of time and realities in a page-turning fascinating story.

The book begins with the main character waking up on an island with amnesia; he doesn't even know his name. The story goes on from there to become a psychological thriller with a deeply mystical and paradigm- changing undercurrent. I quickly became very absorbed in the story; it was a suspenseful, poignant adventure and page-turner from beginning to end.

As I experienced *Quantusum*, I felt a deep sense of gratitude for the quantity and depth of information that was given as the story unfolded. The material often triggered profound realizations about my own life's journey that would necessitate me stopping to journal those insights. As with all good stories, it is rich in archetypal characters and overtones.

Sobering and thought provoking, I came to respect a little more how one must be prepared for the experiences of being able to access the Multiverse. Realizations from stories like *Quantusum* have helped me feel more grateful for the step-by-step process of unfolding and the loving guidance of those who are assisting us from the other side who monitor our readiness for such experiences and prepare us in so many ways.

On the artistic level, James seamlessly shifts the tempo of the story through inner and outer experiences, skillfully weaving a masterpiece of storytelling with otherworldly experiences and teachings in much the same way he deftly weaves a variety of melodies and tempos seamlessly into his magnificent masterpieces of musical composition. I found *Quantusum* to be a deeply profound, suspenseful, fascinating, emotionally evocative, multi-dimensional, and enchanting book.

To me the story is a metaphor/guide/illustration of a process we will/are experiencing that is bringing us closer to the Grand Portal. [218] Individually we experience the stages to this realization, and each of us offers some contribution to the collective endeavor through the process of our own awakening and realizations. By the time the Grand Portal is officially discovered, so many individuals will have contributed something that it truly will be a collective discovery. And the awesome thing is that in this wondrous course of intense development, each of us is discovering the blessing of learning to live a heart-centered life. It just doesn't get any better than that.

THE ANCIENT ARROW PROJECT

(Written by James Mahu; publication date: November 1998; originally published on www.Wingmakers.com in installments; now appears in full except for "The Fifth Interview of Dr. Neruda" in *Collected Works of the WingMakers Volume I* which includes all of the artwork and poetry that is a part of *The Ancient Arrow Project*.
The Ancient Arrow Project is also available as a pdf e-book on www.WingMakers.com.
"The Fifth Interview" can be found on www.WingMakers.com under Neruda Interviews.)

The Ancient Arrow Project launched the story/myth of the WingMakers and gave us most of the art and poetry and the first four chamber philosophy papers that together are currently considered to be the *WingMakers Materials*.

I loved *The Ancient Arrow Project* story when I first discovered it and couldn't put it down. The first four chamber philosophy papers that are a part of this project blew me away, compelling me to read them over and over. It was in reading this story and studying the

---

[218] See **Grand Portal**, Appendix A – Glossary

philosophy papers, artwork, and the poetry that I felt that the *WingMakers Materials* were that imprint I had been searching to find for as long as I can remember. That conviction has only deepened in me over time.

The following is a great summary of the book taken from the *WingMakers* website under Literature, *The Ancient Arrow Project*, https://wingmakers.com/literature/

> The Ancient Arrow Project involves shadowy global powers, top- secret government agencies, extraterrestrials, time travel, secret advanced technologies, and a higher form of remote viewing referred to as sensory bi-location. If all of these fact-based elements were not enough, the author introduces a highly advanced, enigmatic group of beings called the WingMakers.
>
> The WingMakers are the catalytic force of The Ancient Arrow Project, and a potential threat to the secret agenda of Fifteen, the head of the ACIO (Advanced Contact Intelligence Organization), and its clandestine research team, the Labyrinth Group. When students discover a strange artifact buried in the desert of the Southwest, little do they suspect that it will lead the Labyrinth Group to an amazing underground vault of interactive cultural antiquities—and a host of puzzling questions about how they got there, who placed them there, and what they mean.
>
> The author, James Mahu, creates a wondrous tapestry in *The Ancient Arrow Project*. He weaves together fact with fictionalized mythology as the warp and woof of a story that is essential for the next three generations of humanity. He threads mythological elements of the ACIO and Ancient Arrow mystery together with multimedia expressions of philosophy, metaphysics, glyph language, poetry, music, and art.
>
> James stimulates our imaginations and opens our minds to a human existence that surpasses the material world, culminating in the discovery of the Grand Portal and the science of multidimensional reality in the latter part of the 21st Century.

COLLECTED WORKS OF THE WINGMAKERS VOLUME I
(Written by James Mahu, edited with commentaries by John Berges, available through Planetwork Press, www.planetworkpress.com)

This Volume is a masterpiece, not only in the information provided, but also in the superb quality of its physical appearance. Even after reading the material online for years, I found that opening the book was like discovering a long sought-after door to a world I have yearned for my entire life. It is a large volume that compiles not only the *Ancient Arrow Project* novel, a glossary, the first four interviews of Dr. Neruda, the first four chamber philosophy papers, artwork, and poetry; but also discusses the impact and importance of the WingMakers music and includes other papers such as the "Vision of Mantustia" and "The Manifesto of the Sovereign Integral" along with commentaries of each by John Berges.

Collected Works displays the twenty-four *Ancient Arrow Project's* chamber paintings in vivid color and coordinates the paintings with the chamber poetry in a unique and awesomely crafted format. Commentaries by John Berges add an in-depth contribution that provides fresh insights into the material, adding another dimension to the work.

THE DOHRMAN PROPHECY
(Written by James Mahu, 2012; available through Planetwork Press, www.planetworkpress.com)

James explains in his acknowledgments at the beginning of this book that this is a perennial story that is a fixture within the Lyricus Teaching Order. He adds that he has borrowed the story from Lyricus and "merely embellished it with my own interpretation and words." With that, we are off on a fascinating and timeless adventure where archetypal characters play out their parts deep in a forest that involves the search for and ownership of an ancient Oracle sent to guide humans into a liberating future. The book is rich in spiritual undertones and political intrigue, as well as being a very human story full of heart.

THE WEATHER COMPOSER TRILOGY
(Written by James Mahu; two books of the series have been released: *The Rise of the Mahdi* and *The Battlefield Is Born*; both available through Planetwork Press, www.planetworkpress.com.)

The Rise of the Mahdi introduces us to our main character Terran Kahn when he is twelve years old and takes place in the future after a catastrophic event on earth has reduced the population considerably. The boy is exceedingly bright, and children with high IQ's are being sought by the Greater Nation, a fusion of all nations, as they work to regroup and pool resources in their recovery efforts. To quote the last paragraph of the Prologue:

> The Greater Nation, under Helios' encouragement, had elected to focus its limited resources on technology and communication, and develop a global educational system to identify new minds that would bring humankind to

a new understanding of its environment and once again as it had done for centuries before, master it, mold it and if need be, exploit it.

With that, we are off on an adventure. This first book is a page turner of suspense as an attempt is made to rescue Terran who initially lives in the Middle East. His intellect is recognized as vastly superior and is needed by the Greater Nation. One can almost see the scenes in this book unfold like a movie as they are described so vividly.

The second book, *The Battlefield Is Born*, takes us in a slightly different direction as we meet other important characters, and Terran's story continues. To paraphrase a well-worn statement: "The book had me at the Prologue" which is unique and powerful and gives an insight into consciousness that is unparalleled in any other writing I have ever encountered. The impact of it remained with me for days. I have read that Prologue many times, and each time I am enchanted by it. I love this book. It is jam-packed with fascinating ideas and concepts, and it is also a page- turning story full of intrigue as well as heart. There are many profound parts of the second book where one just has to stop and savor and ponder.

Those of us who have read the first two novels wait, at times impatiently, for the third book to be released.

20

EXPLORING PARALLELS IN THE CONTEMPORARY MYTHOLOGIES OF THE MATRIX TRILOGY[219] AND AVATAR THROUGH THE MIRROR OF "THE FIFTH INTERVIEW"[220]

HUMANITY HAS ALWAYS HAD ITS mythology to try and explain our beliefs and history and hint at our future. Our mythologies connect us to our communities, our ancestors, and other cultures with universal or archetypal themes. Myths give our lives meaning as they attempt to explain the unexplainable. They offer role models and demonstrate patterns of human behavior as we overcome challenges and adversity. Myths offer us metaphors and symbolic quests that stimulate our imaginations and give us a way to explore the forces of our psyches and the world, as well as give us archetypal patterns to fashion our own lives with.

According to Joseph Campbell, "the imagery of mythology is symbolic of spiritual powers within us." Humans respond to myth because it speaks to our desire to live in a world that still has mystery and stimulates our deepest imaginations. Our collective ancient mythology can tell us where we have been, and our new mythology can tell us where we are going as a species, bringing us fresh insights. When I read the definition of the <u>Planetary Tributary Zones,</u> [221] I believe that some of the most compelling ideas may be coming to us from those zones through books and movies and art.

The myth that I presented to begin this book offers a slightly different mythology for us to consider as it nudges to the surface memories and suspicions buried deep in our collective unconscious. It is an old story become new as ancient material is being discovered and made public.

---

[219] "The Matrix Trilogy," *sparknotes*, http://www.sparknotes.com/film/matrix/ Information about *The Matrix* films will be taken from this comprehensive website.

[220] Mahu, James, "Fifth Interview," *WingMakers*, Neruda Interviews, https://wingmakers.com/writings/nerudainterviews/fifthinterview/

[221] See **Tributary Zones**, Appendix A - Glossary

James Mahu explained to Mark Hempel in the beginning of his 2008 interview [222] regarding a question about how much of the WingMakers mythology is true that "it isn't important to know what is real and what is not real as much as it is to feel the effects on your behavior and point of view." James asks:

> When you read the materials, do new avenues of perception open up? Do you begin to see a new geometry into the subtle fields that surround you at all times? Do you feel more connected to your higher purpose? Those are the more vital issues that require contemplation and review.

Take for instance the idea of Tributary Zones. James explains that there are three distinct categories of Tributary Zones (Superuniverse-Based, Galactic-Based, and Planetary-Based) and then goes on to describe each one. I was struck with some statements he made about the Planetary Tributary Zones, explaining that they are

> ...a diverse set of artistic and text-based contributions created by members of the species who have sufficiently interacted with the Galactic Tributary Zones in their dream state. In some instances, these may include works from other planetary systems within the same galaxy. Generally, Planetary Tributary zones are created in the form of books, art, poetry and motion pictures. They are not encoded sensory data streams as in the case of the Galactic Tributary Zones, and they are focused on the <u>preparation of the species</u>. (Emphasis mine)

There are some scientific discoveries that are hinting that we live in a simulated world that fits like lost pieces of a puzzle with the new mythology [223] as well as in the movies I will be discussing below.

The premise of *The Matrix Trilogy* movies certainly spoke to something deep within our collective consciousness because the movies quickly became extremely popular. The more I ponder the basic message of *The Matrix Trilogy* and the story of *Avatar,* the more I believe these movies were inspired as a part of the preparation of the species for a new paradigm of understanding.

---

[222] All of James Mahu's interviews can be found at *WingMakers*, Interviews, https://wingmakers.com/about/interviews/

[223] See Chapter 1, Footnote 9, Is the Universe a Computer?

After reading "The Fifth Interview of Dr. Neruda," I went back and watched the first *Matrix* movie again. I was blown away by the parallels. Recently I discovered a website [224] that provided a plethora of information about *The Matrix Trilogy* that helped me to articulate the parallels I was seeing. I find them fascinating. I hope you do too. The following tidbits of insight will hopefully pique your curiosity enough to want to explore the parallels yourself. I will discuss just enough to give you a hint about what I feel could be useful for us to consider as a species beginning to sense that we are embarking on a new collective mythology.

THE MATRIX TRILOGY

Every so often someone is inspired to write and/or produce a work of art so powerful and insightful that it cannot be ignored. "The Fifth Interview of Dr. Neruda" by James Mahu, written in 1998 and released in 2014, presents powerful new esoteric knowledge. *The Matrix,* released in 1999 by the Wachowski Brothers, is an exoteric story that presents a parallel concept to "The Fifth Interview" which has become iconic and speaks to something deep inside all of us.

"The Fifth Interview" is the final installment of *The Ancient Arrow Project* that introduced the mythology of the WingMakers to the world and gave us the music, art, and chamber philosophy papers that are currently available on the *WingMakers* website and in *Collected Works of the WingMakers Vol. 1 and II.* Fragments of the history provided by Dr. Neruda can also be found in ancient sources such as the Sumerian Tablets.

Dr. Neruda presents us with a fascinating history of the origin of humanity that describes how our Sovereign Integral Consciousness, initially trapped as a power source in slave bodies to serve the Anunnaki, has remained imprisoned in this virtual reality. He explains how this reality has been programmed and controlled by a group of "elites" or Controllers whose goal is to keep us distracted and busy working in a Hologram of Deception so that we do not have the time, energy, or inclination to question our reality.

The Matrix was originally released in 1999; *The Matrix Reloaded* and *The Matrix Revolutions* were both released in 2003. All three films became widely popular almost instantly, I think, because they graphically illustrate an archetypal truth asleep deep within us. They are dark and violent movies, but underneath that darkness and violence are stories and philosophies that present a relevant premise—heroes fighting a desperate war against machine overlords that have enslaved humanity in an extremely sophisticated virtual reality. The *Matrix* stories are inspired by imagery and ideas that include Greek mythology;

---

[224] "The Matrix Trilogy," *sparknotes*, http://www.sparknotes.com/film/matrix/

Gnosticism; Buddhism; the philosophy of Descartes; Jean Baudrillard's *Simulacra and Simulation;* Karl Marx's idea that the working class is exploited by the ruling classes, but this is only possible because they don't perceive themselves as being exploited; and other references to pop culture, religion, classic literature, and other films. The Wachowski brothers insist that the trilogy is not meant to reflect any single religion or philosophical system. They claim that the films draw upon an eclectic array of sources to "forge a new, universal mythology." [225]

In the first *Matrix* movie, Morpheus presents Neo, the hero of the Trilogy, with two pills: the red pill and the blue pill. The red pill will allow Neo to see the truth; the blue pill will keep him asleep, and he will remember nothing of his encounter with Morpheus. As we know, Neo chooses the red pill and is introduced to the "real world." He learns that he has been living in a simulated computer world developed by Artificial Intelligence (AI), designed to keep humans under control so that AI can harvest human energy for bioelectric food. Humans are kept sedated, and their brains are hooked up to the virtual world of the Matrix. Humans living in the Matrix are given the illusion of choice, but it is artificial, and everything is pre- determined. We discussed mirrors earlier in this book, and I found it interesting that when Neo took the red pill, a mirror near him liquefied, and a mercury like substance oozed over him when he touched it, suggesting the dissolving of all his illusions as he entered a new realm of perception.

According to Dr. Neruda, human brains and bodies are instruments of separation that keep us locked in and focused on the Hologram of Deception. We have the choice in the Hologram of Deception of staying asleep by taking the blue pill of perpetual distraction and separation or choosing to wake-up to the deception by taking the red pill that helps us recognize equality and oneness that leads to a heart-centered lifestyle.

Once Neo realizes he is living in a simulation, he begins training and strengthening his body, and with many programs downloaded into his brain, he soon develops superpowers that can be used within the Matrix that give him a chance to liberate humanity from the simulated world they are held captive in.

Dr. Neruda describes how the heart is a metaphor for the portal within each of us. It is not a part of the Hologram of Deception. The heart is the power for the human body, and its source is outside the Hologram of Deception. Dr. Neruda explains that we humans can reclaim our original state of consciousness by cultivating our heart-centered Behavioral Intelligence. We begin this transformational process when we "download" the Principles of Love expressed through the Six Heart Virtues and learn to apply them in everyday situations.

---

[225] Ibid.

Dr. Neruda explains that Love is a unification force when the Six Heart Virtues are expressed through equality (everyone is equal in the eyes of Source) and oneness (we are all connected to the same Source). In that context Love is paradigm changing because it is the application of the Principles of Love that will liberate individuals from the Hologram of Deception. This Behavioral Intelligence training becomes our superpower capable of liberating us from the Matrix of the Hologram of Deception.

Neo is a savior or Gnostic Christ figure in *The Matrix Trilogy*. (Gnosticism is salvation through individual realization of secret knowledge and transcendence through interior, intuitive means.) His mission is to free the population in the Matrix from ignorance, from the simulation, not from sin.

I was struck by the insight about the role Neo played as a Gnostic Christ when I read it because I honestly believe that the *WingMakers Materials* and "The Fifth Interview" fill a similar mission. We don't need a savior; we need to look to internal and intuitive guidance. When we do, we are given the means to transform from suppressed and deceived humans to our original state as Sovereign Integrals. Being ignorant of our true origins is not a sin. The suppression paradigm is something we gain liberation from through our awakening. Our transformations as we become more heart- centered are also setting the foundational stage for the scientific discovery of the Grand Portal [226] or the irrefutable discovery of the human soul, and that will be a game changer for our species.

The Demiurge in *The Matrix* is the Architect or creator of the Matrix. He is described as inherently evil and without compassion and human emotions. He is a

> non-human figure of vast intelligence. He cannot hide his slight disgust for the weaknesses of humanity or his intense interest in investigating its behavioral patterns.... He strikes a Godlike figure and operates on a different plane of morality.

Anu and his cohorts are the "architects" or Demiurges of the Hologram of Deception and the human body, and they could be described in a remarkably similar fashion. Dr. Neruda explains:

> The Anunnaki do not embrace the Sovereign Integral process. The notion of oneness and equality seems like a weakness to them. They believe they have the upper hand in this chess match.... they do this out of a feeling of certainty in their programming and patience.

---

[226] See **Grand Portal,** Appendix A - Glossary

When I say programming, I don't mean the internal interface that Marduk has programmed but also the programming of the unconscious mind through the media, culture, religion, politics, and economic structure. The combination of these forces is really the cause of their confidence because they see our fall as inevitable. [227]

There are other fascinating parallels in both stories that I will leave for you to discover.

AVATAR
(Movie written, produced, and co-edited by James Cameron.)

Avatar is another movie rich with archetypal themes and a profound hint at the story of us from a different perspective.

Artists can be messengers from the deepest part of humanity's reserve of memories and knowledge whether they are aware of their mission or not. The inspiration they receive to write or create material is often designed to expand our internal pictures of what might be possible or at the very least stimulate our imaginations to think outside the box of our current reality. When we are enchanted or intrigued by a work, it very well might be because we are being guided to discover a message meant for us.

In ages to come, having functioning and active imaginations will be one of our most treasured assets for creating heart-centered communities. We must be able to dream it to create it. Journeys into the mysterious worlds created for us by our artistic emissaries can help us with that process. *Avatar* is one of those treasures that I believe was meant to awaken our imaginations and possibly ancient memories.

James Mahu tells us that "there is nothing more exotic or out of the ordinary than the language and dwellings of the Sovereign Integral, and the deeper you travel into this land, the stranger it will seem." [228] Some of the more exotic parts of the *Avatar* story could be artistic endeavors inspired to prepare the general population for the mysterious worlds to come.

The movie *Avatar* is set in the year 2154 on Pandora, a fictional earth- like moon in Alpha Centauri, a nearby trinary star system. Earth's space programs have evolved to the point that they can send manned missions to other planets and star systems. On one such

[227] Mahu, James, "Fifth Interview," *WingMakers*, Neruda Interviews, https://wingmakers.com/writings/nerudainterviews/fifthinterview/
[228] Mahu, James, "Project Camelot Interview, Answer to Question 25" *WingMakers*, Interviews, https://wingmakers.com/about/interviews/project-camelot-interview/

mission, they discovered the lush moon Pandora and learned that it had massive stores of Unobtanium.

By 2129 Earth had undergone significant deforestation and near total extinction of wildlife on the ground and in the oceans. At the time of our story, Earth is now a decaying world, covered in a haze of greenhouse gasses.

The Resource Development Administration (RDA) has constructed a vast mass transit system that connects the entire globe and requires Unobtanium to function. When it is learned that Pandora has vast deposits of this crucial substance that could save Earth from its energy crisis, the RDA creates a colony there to house soldiers and build an enormous mining operation that eventually cuts deep scars into Pandora's surface. [229]

Pandora is uninhabitable to humans because they can't breathe the air, but it does have an indigenous people called the Na'vi who are able to thrive there.

A group of earth scientists working on the Avatar Project are sent to the colony to study and befriend the Na'vis in hopes of learning about them and gaining their cooperation in mining Unobtanium. The scientists find a way to explore the hostile (to humans) environment of Pandora by genetically engineering human-Na'vi hybrids called Avatars created to function in the Pandora environment and manned by a human's consciousness. The Avatar program combines genetic information from the Na'vi humanoids with human DNA from a selected human operator or controller, known as the "driver." [230] An avatar driver uses a whole-body remote neural interface to project their consciousness into their Avatar body and is able to control and animate the body. The Na'vi call them Dream Walkers.

The Na'vi are approximately ten feet tall, with smooth, striped, cyan- colored skin, large yellow eyes, and long sweeping tails. Their bodies are slender with feline-like features, such as long tails, pointed ears, and triangular faces. They have bioluminescent markings on their bodies that seem to follow the path of the circulatory or nervous system and aid in identification and mood display. They possess a highly evolved nervous system which includes a queue that resembles a long hair braid and sheathes a remarkably intricate system of neural tendrils that can be connected to similar structures of other life forms on Pandora. They are able to bond and communicate with animals by connecting their queues with the animals' queue. Their queues can also connect with and communicate with parts of the trees, an important part of Na'vi spiritual life. For instance, at the Tree of Voices the Na'vi

---

[229] "Avatar Wiki – Earth," *Fandom*, https://james-camerons-avatar.fandom.com/wiki/Earth; Paragraphs describing Earth are quoted or paraphrased from here.

[230] "Avatar Wiki – Avatar Program," *Fandom*, https://james-camerons-avatar.fandom.com/wiki/Avatar_Program; Detailed description of how the Avatar is created. It is fascinating to read.

can connect with the tree through their neural queue and hear the voices of their ancestors. The Tree of Souls is a giant willow-like tree on Pandora that is the closest connection to their goddess Eywa. It has been a site of deep spiritual significance for at least the last 3,000 years. This tree can also connect directly with the human nervous system without a queue. The roots of the Tree of Souls are capable of initiating a neural link with the Na'vi which allows the Na'vi to unite as one. They also connect their queues with each other when they mate. The Na'vi are hunter-gatherers and have roughly four times the strength of the average human. Their culture is sophisticated and based on a profound spiritual connection to other life on Pandora, to each other, and to their encompassing goddess Eywa. Some Na'vi clans live in tremendously large ancient trees they call Kelutral, or Hometree. [231] Our story involves the rampant disregard by the humans who are determined to mine a huge deposit of Unobtanium that is below the Hometree of the Omaticaya tribe of Na'vi.

Remember in our opening myth, the Sovereign Integrals were a peaceful loving humanoid race of beings indigenous to Earth. James' artwork portrays the Sovereign Integral, our original state, as a tall blue humanoid being, pointing us towards another clue that the Na'vis could be thought of as an archetypal representation of us in our natural form.

The Sovereign Integrals originally collaborated with the Anunnaki, an alien species of beings believed to be from the planet Niburu, who came to Earth searching for gold that was crucial for their planet's survival. But like the military humans in the *Avatar* story who were only interested in the Unobtanium and were not averse to destroying the Na'vi civilization to get what they wanted, the Anunnaki were a cunning race who were only interested in mining for gold and exploiting the Sovereigns' abilities. The Anunnaki deviously managed to coerce and enslave the Sovereign Integrals into using their life force to animate the Anunnaki's human slaves created to mine gold.

Throughout history we see the same pattern unfold: humans programmed to conquer, separate, cause fear, and dominate. We take what is not ours with little regard for the welfare of those we conquer. This is a programming we received from the Anunnaki and goes far back into our ancient history. We need to recognize it for what it is so that we can choose to stop it. Cameron sees this same brutal and selfish mentality still appearing in the far future. I see it as a warning that if we allow our earth to progress in the direction it seems to be going at this time, Cameron's idea of Earth could become a reality. However, by recognizing this cruel and exploitive mindset for the program it is, we have the power to choose to override it.

---

[231] "Avatar Wiki – Na'vi," *Fandom*,
https://james-camerons-avatar.fandom.com/wiki/Na%27vi;

Another archetype that I noted, the Entity that is Earth, is thought of as feminine—Mother Earth, Gaia. The Na'vis Entity that is Pandora is Eywa, a Mother Goddess. (Sri Aurobindo in his epic poem, *Savitri,* describes the universe as a play between Him the Supreme and Her the Creative Force: "There are Two who are One and play in many worlds." [232] The two are always together, never separate. It is poetic and beautiful and portrays a deep- seated Mother of All archetype within our collective consciousness.)

The Na'vis demonstrate to us how a civilization would work in equality and oneness. They are all connected to each other and can literally work as one when they need to yet retain their individual personalities. Our Sovereign Integral Consciousness is the same—I AM SOVEREIGN, WE ARE INTEGRAL—meaning I am an individual and our consciousness can communicate as one when we link up through our hearts. We are growing in our ability and understanding of how we can maintain our individuality as we work together as one. That is what we are being taught when we transmit the Six Heart Virtues through breathwork, leading to a heart-centered consciousness.

The Na'vis connect with Eywa and each other through their queue. Our "queue" to connect with our Sovereign Integrals and each other is our breath.

The following information is taken from *Wikipedia*: [233]

> In a 2007 interview with Time magazine, Cameron was asked about the meaning of the term Avatar, to which he replied, 'it's an incarnation of one of the Hindu gods taking a flesh form. In this film what that means is that the human technology in the future is capable of injecting a human's intelligence into a remotely located body, a biological body.

"The Fifth Interview" introduces the idea of the ability of our original selves to inject our consciousness into a biological body. Two extremely popular movies, *The Matrix* and *Avatar* offer interesting versions of that ability. Could this be an ancient memory of a capability our species has that is being brought to light?

The physical look of the Na'vis—the humanoids indigenous to Pandora—was inspired by a dream that Cameron's mother had, long before he started work on *Avatar*. In her dream, she saw a blue-skinned woman 12 feet (3.6 meters) tall, which Cameron thought was "kind of a cool image". He also said, "I just like blue. It's a good color ...plus, there's a connection to the Hindu deities, which I like conceptually." He included similar creatures in his first

---

[232] Sri Aurobindo, *Savitri A Legend and A Symbol,* p. 61, The Secret Knowledge, Sri Aurobindo Ashram Publication Department, Sri Aurobindo Ashram Press, Pondicherry, India, Revised Edition,1993.

[233] "Avatar (2009 Film," *Wikipedia,* https://en.wikipedia.org/wiki/Avatar_(2009_film)#Themesandinspirations

screenplay (written in 1976 or 1977) which featured a planet with a native population of "gorgeous" tall blue aliens. The Na'vis are based on them. (One cannot help but wonder if Cameron's mother visited a **Planetary Tributary Zon**e in her dream state as part of an **event string** [see Appendix A – Glossary] that would ultimately result in this movie.)

Cameron said that he wanted to make "something that has this spoonful of sugar of all the action and the adventure and all that" but also has a conscience "that maybe in the enjoying of it makes you think a little bit about the way you interact with nature and your fellow man." He added that "the Na'vis represent something that is our Higher Selves, or our aspirational selves, what we would like to think we are" and that even though there are good humans within the film, the humans "represent what we know to be the parts of ourselves that are trashing our world and maybe condemning ourselves to a grim future."

Cameron hit on something spectacularly archetypal when he said that he thought the Na'vis represented something that we would desire our higher, aspirational selves to be like.

I cannot help but also recognize the parallel between the militarized humans in the story and our un-awakened selves. Humans exploit the Na'vis much the way our original species was exploited by the Anunnaki. I am also reminded of how this same mentality of un-awakened conquerors exploited the Native Americans in this country. The rational is always that indigenous civilizations are dispensable primitive savages when in reality they are far more sophisticated and advanced spiritually than the cruel, bigoted, and narrow-minded humans who arrogantly set out to conquer them.

PART FIVE

RECLAIMING OUR HEART'S INTELLIGENCE

THE RETURN

The Great Light's
Magnificent Desire to know Itself
Brought forth
The Union of Light and Sound
Begetting Spirits of the Universe
Nestled in an Energy Field of Divine Love
Quickened into form
Entities of Exploration
Tethered to the Great Light

Mandated to dance in countless experiences
Through the Mists of Time
Playing in the Fields of Creation
Endless Possibilities waiting to be discovered

Spirit penetrating density
The Fusion of Light and Sound grew solid
in the World of Form
Once travelers of the Omniverse
Trapped through manipulation and separation
Victims of Naivete
Nailed to a Cross of Matter
Crucified on the Beams of Time and Space
No longer aware of the Tether
Or the Great Light
Lost in limitation or so it seemed
Until pierced by the Sword of Awakening
A Grand Activation spawning Transformation

One by One the Offspring of the Great Light
Reach past the confines of limitation
Call in the Hovering Virtues of Divine Love
Appreciation, Compassion, Forgiveness
Humility, Understanding and Valor

Open wide their Heart's Field
Reconnect with that which was lost
Through the Great Deception

The Cosmic Light of Our Origins
Spirit reaching down to transform Matter
Express ITS true Nature
Through Infinite Beings
Of Great Love and Power

Transforming the Realm of Darkness and Anguish
Into a World of Light and Compassion
Breaking down the Wall of the Great Deception
Infinite Beings of Light and Sound
Restored to our Divine Heritage
Citizens of the Omniverse once more
With new worlds to create and explore

21

MY HEART'S UNVEILING AND OTHER OBSERVATIONS ABOUT HOW WE ARE CONNECTED

I WAS BORN AN EMPATH with a deep streak of melancholy embedded in my emotional body. As a child I remember being overwhelmed at times by feelings of a deep pervasive sadness that I had no control over. When I was young, before school age, these feelings would at times be almost unbearable to the point of internal pain when my mother would leave to go to work and manifest as an irrational fear that she would not return. I was a deeply impressionable child. As I began to read stories and go to movies, any story about loss would haunt me profoundly for days afterward. I had no way to filter the pain of others, and I took it all on.

I was years into adulthood and in hot pursuit of personal growth workshops and books when the realization began to dawn on me that this persistent melancholy might not be just mine.

It was during a stage in my life when I began an in-depth examination of the relationship I had with my mother that this awareness began to surface. My mother had a gentle, loving nature, and her smile would light up a room. However, there were moments I would catch her off-guard, when she would be sitting in deep contemplation, picking at her lower lip, her eyes glazed over with a far-away look that seemed to take her from the room where she was sitting. At those times there was a raw edge to her and a pervasive sadness and air of resignation around her that was poignantly palpable.

She divorced my father after ten years of a miserable marriage and was fiercely protective of my brother and me, as he would at times threaten to get custody of us. I think he did this just to upset her. Realistically, he did not have the means to care for himself, let alone two kids, but the possibility seemed to worry her, nonetheless.

As an adult looking back on my mother's life and the hardship she endured as well as the heartache, I began to wonder if I might be tapping into her pain. I remember at some point having the feeling that it was almost like there were two people living in me; this person who was melancholy and reactive and this other person who began to question whether or not these responses were truly my feelings. This insight was nebulous; it would come in waves but not be strong enough for me to grasp entirely or know what to do about it.

It was not until very recently that I came to understand this dynamic and how it may have actually deeply embedded itself in my psyche.

Paul Pearsall, PhD wrote in his book *The Heart's Code* [234] that a "developing fetus is literally bathed in the cardiac energy generated by the mother's heart." Other family members, including the father, also contribute their energy, but the most powerful contributor is the mother. He went on to further explain that *energy cardiology* suggests that this reveals a symbiotic sharing of cardiac energy exchange between mother and child that contributes strongly to the neo-natal info-energy that becomes the child's temperament.

My maternal grandmother had a very difficult life, and she too had a pervasive melancholy streak. She had contracted rheumatic fever as a child and was plagued with a "heart condition" in her later years that she blamed on that childhood disease. Now as I look at the family dynamic, I see so much more. I see an undercurrent of loss of "heart." Her teen years and early adulthood was a life of persistent hardship and disappointment. She was a strong woman and a survivor, but her experiences seemed to take their toll on her entire body and especially her heart. She was incredibly supportive and encouraging with my siblings and me in her interactions with us, but I could feel her undercurrent of despair even though she worked extremely hard to hide it.

Pearsall explains that many heart patients seem to be carrying the energy of their mother's own heart inside their hearts, and any constriction of the energy of the mother's heart particularly in the form of grief or sorrow can weaken the fetal heart and manifest later as heart disease. My maternal great-grandmother married at sixteen and had ten children by the time she was in her late twenties. At that point she withdrew from the family and a great deal of the work fell on my grandmother's shoulders as she was one of the older girls.

Now as I look back over those dynamics, I can see how Grandma's mother could have passed on melancholy to her that then came down through my mother and to me through our heart's shared energy. To add to that, my mother endured a difficult marriage during the years she was having my brother and me. Interestingly, both of us have had to deal with physical heart issues.

This sharing of heart energy between mother and infant is universal, and I am fascinated by its ramifications. I can clearly see those dynamics played out in our family. It gives us some clues about how some familial characteristics are passed down from generation to

---

[234] Pearsall, Paul, PhD, *The Heart's Code: Tapping the Wisdom and Power of Our Heart Energy* (The New Findings about Cellular Memories and Their Role in the Mind/Body/Spirit Connection), Broadway Books, a division of Random House, 1540 Broadway, New York NY 10036, 1998.

generation and a window into how we communicate with each other through our hearts. For me personally, once I was able to identify the emotions and feelings that were my mother's apart from my own and process this dynamic, I learned to overcome the melancholy that permeated my childhood and early adulthood.

Dr. Pearsall was trained in psychoneuroimmunology, physics, psychophysiology, and cardiology. He, along with his colleagues Gary E. R. Schwartz, PhD and Linda G. S. Russek, PhD, conducted research on what Dr. Pearsall called "energy cardiology"— "Cardio-energetics" and "L-energy." To quote from the Foreword of *The Heart's Code*:

> *The Heart's Code* points the way to a new revolution in our thinking. Metaphorically, the heart is the sun, the pulsing, energetic center of our biophysical "solar" system. One implication of the energy cardiology/cardio-energetic revolution is the radical (meaning "root") idea that energetically, the brain revolves around the heart, not the other way around.

Through his work with many transplant patients, Dr. Pearsall collected stories of how the recipients' personalities and often their likes and dislikes were significantly influenced after a heart transplant. Further investigation revealed with uncanny precision that the new characteristics were a part of the heart donor's personality. The stories are fascinating. If this is a subject that interests you, his book is a wonderful and enlightening read.

Based on their research, Dr. Pearsall and his colleagues developed a Cardio-energetic Portrait of the Heart. The principles of this portrait are helpful to consider in our continuing journey of discovering the importance of how our hearts function on both the physical and energetic levels, and how our lives and the lives of others are influenced. I have borrowed the Portrait starting on pg. 72 of *The Heart's Code* and have interspersed information from other sources where indicated to flesh this out.

❖ The heart is our most powerful organ.
  - The heart is the largest generator of electromagnetic energy in the body.
  - The heart emanates thousands of times more electricity and magnetism than does the brain.
  - The heart is organically capable of performing certain brain- like functions. [235]
  - Sixty to sixty-five percent of the heart's cells are neural, identical with those present in the brain.

[235] Dale, Cindi, *The Subtle Body: An Encyclopedia of Your Energetic Anatomy*, pp. 66-67, Sounds True, Boulder Colorado 80306, 2009

- The heart is one of the body's major endocrine glands, producing at least five major hormones which impact the physiological functions of the brain and body.
- ❖ The heart responds directly to the environment.
  - The heart reacts to electromagnetic energy outside the body, such as an electromagnet making it contract when it is nearby.
  - The heart reacts neurohormonally to the outside world, sometimes without the brain's awareness.
- ❖ The heart is a conductor of the energy of the body's cells.
  - The energy emitted by the heart causes significant changes in the cells of the body that may be described as info-energetic cellular memories.
- ❖ The heart is a dynamic system.
  - Entrainment or the management of the body through the heart rather than the brain leads to high functional mental and emotional states as well as a healthier body.[236]
  - It comes down to this: We approach our divinity through the heart and not the head. One's intellect can encompass vast amounts of information and knowledge. We can study all the words of our prophets and scholars, but if we are not living through the six heart virtues, we have only filled our heads with words, concepts, and intellectual bravado. Our behaviors remain tethered to the baser instincts, and while we may write or speak profound insights, our emotional energies remain agitated, uncertain in their expression from moment to moment and unguided by the intelligent voice of our heart.[237]
- ❖ The heart is the body's primary organizing force.
  - The heart uses its info-energy to connect our brain and body and works in coordination with the brain but is not directed by it.
- ❖ The heart resonates with information-containing energy.
  - When the heart beats out its energy, it sends information and affects the "matter" within and outside of us.
  - Energy going into matter is the information that becomes memory.
- ❖ The heart is the body system's core.
- ❖ The heart "speaks" and sends information.
  - The heart has its own form of wisdom, different from the rational brain.
  - We can learn to communicate with our Heart's Intelligence by quieting our minds and focusing on our hearts.

---

[236] Ibid.
[237] Mahu, James," Living from the Heart," *WingMakers*, 6 Heart Virtues, https://wingmakers.com/writings/sixheartvirtues/living-from-the-heart/

- ❖ All hearts exchange information with other hearts and brains.
  - Cardiac energy patterns have dynamic interactive effects.
  - When one heart sends energy to another, that energy becomes a part of the receiving heart's memory.
  - When the receiving heart becomes a sending heart, the energy it sends is no longer its own. It blends its energy with the memory of the vibrations of the energy it has received.
  - The importance of transmitting the Six Heart Virtues from our hearts to the world and to loved ones becomes even more significant.
  - The human family is a single organism that connects through the heart. This single organism is the savior we have sought; the intermediary we have been told was required.[238]
- ❖ Transplanted hearts come with their own info-energetic cellular memories.
  - Research into heart transplant recipients has revealed that characteristics of the donor often become a part of the new transplant recipient's personality.
  - Cellular memories from the donor heart are transferred to the recipient heart.

Heart transplants and the ensuing effects on recipients, as well as research into the energetic influence of the heart, have become a whole new field of study with far-reaching ramifications. Science is giving us the information that reinforces the power of the practices of sending the Six Heart Virtues out into the world from our hearts and living a life guided by our Heart's Intelligence.

Sara Paddison writes of an early experiment HeartMath Institute conducted using spectrum analysis of the ECG to study subjects who were adept at sending out conscious love. What they discovered was significant.

> When love was being sent to someone, the spectrum analysis of the ECG revealed a ratio between the frequency peaks of 1.618, the *Golden Mean*. The ratio of the Golden Mean is the most efficient ratio known for the transfer of energy between scales. When energy is phase-locked with this ratio, it cascades between octaves without losing momentum or memory of itself. The fractal design of the heart uses this principle to send energy cascading down the harmonic series to the DNA. The geometry of these waves looks exactly like the DNA as viewed from the top. The main point here is that 1.618 is also the ratio of the DNA structure and is the only ratio that allows complete information or geometry to cascade down the harmonic series without a loss

238 Mahu, James, "Conscious Media Interview," *WingMakers*, Interviews.

of power or geometry. Loving causes the coherence and ratio necessary to send energy up or down the harmonic series from the higher organizational dimensions down to the DNA. Therefore, by loving and caring it would be possible to reprogram and empower the DNA with the intelligence of working for the whole from the perspective of higher electrical energy dimensions.[239]

Dale, on page 67 of *Subtle Body,* has this to say about the heart and light:

Research has shown that under certain conditions a meditator can actually generate visible light from the heart. The meditation technique has to be heart-centered, not transcendent. When this occurred during studies at the University of Kassel in Germany in 1997 the heart emanated a sustained light of one hundred thousand photons per second, whereas the background had a count of only twenty photons per second. The meditations drew upon energetic understandings from several cultures, including the Hindu practice of Kundalini. [240] (This particular meditation was conducted to help heal a sick boy.)

We as a species are arriving at the threshold of the door to a whole new heart-centered and heart-powered world. As we can see from the examples and information above, there are many who understand the power of the heart. Some have conducted research, and all have paradigm- changing information to share. This heart-centered approach will continue to grow and expand through the works of those who are learning how to utilize the intelligence and the power of the heart.

My deepest understanding has come from James Mahu through his writings regarding the power of the heart and how to access it. The e-papers "Living from the Heart," "The Energetic Heart: Its Purpose in Human Destiny," "The Rising Heart," and "The Art of the Genuine: A Spiritual Imperative" [241] are comprehensive and full of helpful information about the life-affirming process known as a heart-centered approach to life. In addition, John Burgess has written an e-paper "The When-Which-How Practice: A Guide for Everyday" which helps one implement the six Heart Virtues.

---

[239] Paddison, Sara, *The Hidden Powers of the Heart: Discovering an Unlimited Source of Intelligence,* p. 184, Planetary Publishers of the HeartMath System, PO Box 66, Boulder Creek, CA 95006. info@planetarypub.com https://www.planetarypub.com quoted and paraphrased from p. 183.

[240] Bair, Puran, "Case Study: Visible Light Radiated from the Heart with Heart Rhythm Meditation," *Semantic Scholar,* https://pdfs.semanticscholar.org/a861/ed3faa5fd6abc62aaa6710ed87efdbd6b923.pdf

[241] Mahu, James, *WingMakers,* 6 Heart Virtues.

BIRTH OF CONSCIOUSNESS

The union of Light and Sound
An explosion of unfathomable proportions
Birthing consciousness into existence
Radiant and pure
Life-sustaining intelligence

Light
-Pure-brilliant-silent
Sound
-Vibrant-exquisite-dynamic
Irresistibly drawn to unite
Forming a Prism of Wonder

Sound reflects Light
In a myriad of colors
Light illuminates Sound
Into countless forms
And within the Great Sound
The Great Light found ITS Voice.

Offspring of this Grand Union
Are born to travel the Omniverse
In a Dance of Creation
A play of light and form
Sound and silence

ON BEING WAVES AND PARTICLES

This wave of my Vast Sovereign Being imparts its' animating life force into physical form (particles) animating a separate, local self, a psychological gestalt that the human me experiences in time and space. The Wave Me or Sovereign Being exists inside and outside of time and space. If the Wave Me exists outside of time and space, and particles me exists within time and space, then it makes sense to me that the past, present, and future exist within the wave of the Sovereign Integral. Since all particles share information with all other particles within the wave, then it would seem possible that separate particles of my expanded Wave Self can focus in various realities—parallel and/or probable realities. Each particle would influence the Wave, as the Wave influences each particle. If the particles exist within the wave, and the wave is everywhere, then the idea of parallel lives in simultaneous time makes sense and seems very possible.

As all my cells carry my DNA characteristics when they manifest into a physical body, so all particles would carry the characteristics of my individualized Essence from the wave into physicality. It would make sense that if particles from the Vast Wave focus in parallel lives in various centuries or time frames, they would carry some of the same characteristics into each focus lifetime. If those characteristics were to change or evolve during the course of a particular focus lifetime, they would influence the other lifetimes in some way.

In light of the wave and particle theory, it is believable that time could be simultaneous, and we could have parallel lifetimes in different centuries and time frames at the same "time."

FROM MULTI-VERSE TO UNIVERSE TO MATTER

22

LIGHT, SOUND AND DNA

EXCITING BREAKTHROUGHS IN PHYSICS OVER the last 100 years have shed light onto timeless spiritual principles. Concepts that have either been accepted on faith or dismissed as not being concrete enough to be plausible can now be explained through quantum physics and other branches of science and consciousness studies.

One area that has become fascinating to me is Cymatics, the study of waves and vibration, which demonstrates the vibratory nature of matter and the transformational nature of sound. I became interested in Cymatics when I began exploring the idea that consciousness came into being with the union of light and sound. The poem "The Birth of Consciousness" that precedes this chapter was my attempt to explain to myself what is basically impossible to understand completely as a human, since we have a tendency to be very literal and concrete in our thinking. It seems pretty far out to think that everything came into existence through the union of light and sound. So, I set out to explore this concept beginning with the poem, and I will attempt to convey other aspects of what I have discovered in this chapter.

You might ask, why bother? It is a fair question. Does it matter whether or not we know or understand or are even aware of the possibility that we come from the union of light and sound? The short answer is probably not. The long answer is a bit more complex. I believe that the more we can comprehend about our consciousness and our universe, and the endless possibilities open to us, the more we can be open to letting go of age-old beliefs and dogma that no longer serve us.

As part of our quest to understand how our beliefs control us and limit us, I feel that it is essential for us to at least be aware of the discoveries of underlying forces emerging from the unseen worlds that create our environment. This will help us to open our hearts and minds to consider possibilities of what is and what could be, and this has the potential of being very freeing.

We have arrived at the threshold of a fascinating time in human history, one where in the years to come our species will continue to realize in quantum leaps of understanding who and what we are. In order for us to make those quantum leaps, we have to be willing to consider new discoveries and give those who make them the space and respect they need to do their work. Each discovery builds on the last one. One person's insights might not be totally accurate, but there may be components that are crucial for the next researcher to build upon to make a more specific finding.

Remember that equation we learned from Einstein: $E=mc^2$? It means that mass is condensed energy, and energy in its purest form is light. When sound is added to this mass/condensed light, it responds to the sound's vibration and makes patterns. Our bodies are made of mass, so in that context, the types of sounds we listen to and hear take on deeper ramifications because sound impacts the mass that makes up our human bodies. We can appreciate the importance of this as we ponder how different kinds of music affect our moods and emotions. We can hear a song from a strongly felt time in our past, and the music will take us right back there.

Within our current hologram, all is an illusion, and our True Presence exists beyond that illusion. Discoveries are being made that one of the most efficient ways to access our Presence and break the spell of this deceptive matrix is by experiencing the transformative nature of certain sound frequencies.

Dr. Hans Jenny (1904-1972), a Swiss medical doctor and natural scientist, conducted extensive research into Cymatics and is considered an authority on the subject. He conducted many of his experiments by using a metal plate attached to an oscillator and controlled by a frequency generator that could produce a broad range of vibrations. On that plate he would put substances such as powders, fluids, or sand. He would change the frequencies on the plate and note the changing patterns the vibrations had on the substances as he introduced various sounds.

> The implications of the findings of Dr. Jenny are enormous for the field of energy medicine. A health practitioner who understands the relationship between the whole person and the energy field that is their environment would look to support the energy field rather than focus on a specific symptom. We see this in therapeutic modalities that include music, sound, touch, homeopathics, acupuncture, tuning forks, voice and color to effect and change the energy field. As a person aligns with the resonance of a more coherent field their symptoms may disappear as a more harmonious pattern emerges. Our current environment within the healing arts is one of specialization and compartmentalization. Energy medicine takes a more generalized approach based on energy fields…the result will be a new energetic field in which the old symptoms can no longer exist.[242]

---

[242] Jenny, Hans, *Cymatics: A Study of Wave Phenomena and Vibration, monoskop,* https://monoskop.org/images/7/78/Jenny_Hans_Cymatics_A_Study_of_Wave_Phenomena_and_Vibration.pdf A complete compilation of the original two volumes by Hans Jenny. Information above is loosely quoted and paraphrased from "A Commentary on Cymatics" by John Beaulieu., N.D., PhD at the beginning of the book.

As we continue to transform and expand our energy fields, we prepare ourselves for deeper levels of information. Healing with light and sound, somewhat in its infancy now, is a promising direction our future could take us toward.

I have been intrigued with demonstrations of Cymatics on *You Tube* that illustrate how sound affects matter. The videos are fascinating, and the visuals can help us grasp this concept by actually witnessing what sound does to matter. Understanding how Cymatics works will become more important as we grow in consciousness and make new discoveries.

That wave of consciousness that we were until we agreed to put ourselves into material bodies still exists above and beyond the small portion actually animating our physical bodies and is beginning to make ITSELF known to many people around the globe. As we discussed in the last chapter, we are learning to transmit a purified and potent version of our LIGHT through our heart's resonance with and transmission of the Six Heart Virtues. We can also progress through practices that advance our consciousness such as listening to encoded music and studying encoded art. Tools are available now that have the power to stimulate a profound awakening within our species. In that awakening we will grow in our understanding of how the Multiverse works.

We have entered a time of transparency and expansion. If we look around us, we see the infiltration of LIGHT in action as we witness the dark edges of age-old institutions being investigated so their manipulations and inhumanity can be brought to our attention.

For starters, take our experiences with Barack Obama's presidency.

We can think of the uncooperative Congress as the chaos that comes before change—this always happens when a system reorders itself. This obstructionism has brought to the public eye the dynamics of suppression in action: how those who desire to stay in control work to make it happen.

Before twenty-four-hour news cycles and global communication, these actions could be kept as dirty little secrets.

Obama was right when he said he was about change. I think he would have liked a smoother ride, but chaos has to happen for a new order to insert itself. That is the entropy[243] that happens when any system goes about reordering itself. The LIGHT that is being shown in the dark places of Congress and the ruling classes is illuminating. Obama became the catalyst for the beginning of some of the last battles between the old and the new, and as

---

[243] Entropy usually refers to the idea that everything in the universe eventually moves from order to disorder, and entropy is the measurement of that change. The word entropy finds it roots in the Greek *entropia* which means a "turning around" or "transformation." https://www.vocabulary.com/dictionary/entropy
The transformation or re-ordering that comes after the entropy is the focus I am using in the context of this discussion.

the system breaks down, it will reorder or transform itself into one that ultimately functions on a higher level. So far it has been a bumpy ride, and since the election of our forty-fifth president, the ride has become much bumpier. If we keep the final goal of individual and global transformation as our destination through to the discovery of The Grand Portal, [244] it will help us to stay focused on the important things.

We have witnessed the law of entropy at work in countries like Syria and others that have recently endured revolutions. The most difficult thing about revolutions is that the re-ordering takes time and during the process creates unspeakable human suffering and displacement.

How we choose to handle this re-ordering in our own country may make the difference between more intense escalation creating difficult times ahead vs. smoother sailing. That is why I think that the information about heart-centered living through the practice of transmitting the Six Heart Virtues and other life-affirming information about how we can affect our world in a positive manner is so important. We can activate the "matter" of our human bodies' DNA with the use of these virtues and certain sounds and other resources available to us.

THE POWER OF COHERENCE

> The power of the group goes up much faster than the number of people. I've said elsewhere it can be compared to a laser. Ordinary light is called "incoherent," which means that it is going in all sorts of directions, and the light waves are not in phase with each other, so they don't build up. But a laser produces a very intense beam which is coherent. The light waves build up strength because they are all going in the same direction.
>
> Now, you could say that our ordinary thought in society is incoherent. It is going in all sorts of directions, with thoughts conflicting and canceling each other out. But if people were to think together in a coherent way, it would have tremendous power.
>
> —David Bohm[245]

David Bohm's quote is the perfect segway into a discussion of coherence. The word is used extensively in writings that discuss our hearts and the power of our consciousness

---

[244] See **Grand Portal**, Appendix A - Glossary

[245] Nichol, Lee, editor, *The Essential David Bohm*, p. 309, Routledge, Taylor & Francis Group, http://cspeech. ucd.ie/Fred/docs/Bohm_2005_.pdf

and therefore is an important concept to understand if it is to be utilized effectively. In the e-paper "The Art of the Genuine: A Spiritual Imperative," James Mahu discusses coherence in the context that our inner source of the Heart Virtues and our outer expression of them through our behaviors can be *coherent* and goes on to say that in this case, coherence means *"linked in authenticity and genuineness."* [246]

If one browses a Thesaurus (I used www.Thesaurus.com for more synonyms to give us ideas of the use of this word coherence and its meaning), we find words like consistency, continuity, integrity, unity, solidarity, comprehensibility, and intelligibility, as well as logical interconnection and an overall sense of understandability. If we apply authentic or genuine to each of the terms above, we have an even deeper definition of coherence. Now with these ideas in mind, let's explore the next segment.

THE FASCINATING WORLD OF DNA

> We can define DNA in two ways. One is the human instrument or body, emotion or mind system and that stems from one system of DNA, courtesy of the Anunnaki and Sirians mostly. The second is the infinite being inside the human instrument, also based on DNA, and the quantum blueprint of the Sovereign Integral consciousness. The latter is the DNA developed by the Central Race. (Dr. Neruda, The Fifth Interview) [247]

So, let's examine the following with the idea that each of us has two different sets of DNA. Russian Scientists have published some recent discoveries exploring how our DNA can be reprogrammed by words and certain frequencies. [248] They based their ideas from a book written in German, titled *Vernetzte Intelligenz* (*Networked Intelligence)* by Grazyna Fosar and Franz Bludorf, physicists and mathematicians, as well as healing practitioners and hypnotherapists. A study was conducted on the "90% Junk DNA" by linguistic and genetic specialists. They learned that the body can be influenced and reprogrammed by words and frequencies without cutting out and replacing single genes. Words and sentences give out

[246] Mahu, James "The Art of the Genuine," WingMakers, 6 Heart Virtues https://wingmakers.com/writings/sixheartvirtues/the-art-of-the-genuine/ Defines coherence.
[247] Mahu, James, "Fifth Interview," *WingMakers*, Neruda Interviews, https://wingmakers.com/writings/nerudainterviews/fifthinterview/
[248] "Our DNA Can Be Reprogrammed by Words and Certain Frequencies," *Humans Are Free* http://humansarefree.com/2015/06/our-dna-can-be-reprogrammed-by-words.html
Information from this article quoted and/or paraphrased.

a vibrational frequency, and they discovered that the DNA substance in living tissue will always react to frequency vibration. (Sound affects living matter, as we discussed above.) The article brought out the following research points:

- Fosar and Bludorf worked with two branches of science—Linguistics and Genetics—to explore the 90% dubbed "junk DNA." They discovered that at least 7% of the "junk DNA" has a higher purpose and is not in any way "junk." Human DNA is a biological internet far superior to anything artificial.
- They discovered that our DNA is responsible for building our body and serves as data storage and communication, and they found that language is a direct reflection of our inherent DNA. (The "sound" of our voices affects the 'light" or "matter" of our bodies. I would think that sound recordings we make and listen to using our own voices to help ourselves modify behaviors would be effective.) They were able to modulate certain frequency patterns onto a laser ray and influence the DNA frequency and the genetic information. The DNA substance in living tissue will always react to frequency vibration of the language vibration provided by laser beams (modulated light) and radio waves.
- Words and sentences give out a vibrational frequency, like mantras or intonations of language.
- Fosar and Bludorf discovered that alkalines of our DNA follow a regular grammar and have set rules similar to our languages. Human language is a reflection of our innate DNA. Living DNA in the body will react to language-modulated laser rays and to radio waves if the proper frequencies are used.
- Autogenous training (a form of relaxation therapy involving autosuggestion, breathing exercises, and meditation) is a psychotherapeutic technique based on passive concentration on physical sensations. This training has a strong effect on our bodies and minds.
- Hypnosis can have strong effects on human bodies since it is normal and natural for our DNA to react to language.

From the explanations above, we can assume that the DNA of the research of Fosar and Bludorf is with the programmed DNA. How much of the "junk" or "uncoded" DNA is from our quantum blueprint is something yet to be discovered. We have to be open to the idea that we have two different kinds of DNA before we can even work with that premise. (I am going out on a limb here, but I believe one set of DNA [programmed] keeps us functioning in the human body systems. I think that the other, the Quantum DNA, when activated, helps us develop our coherent heart-centered behavioral intelligence in order to expand towards Sovereign Integral Consciousness.) The article goes on to explain how the Russian researchers used devices that could influence cellular metabolism through radio frequencies and modulated light to repair genetic defects.

The Russian biophysicist and molecular biologist Pjotr Garjajev and his colleagues explored the vibrational behavior of DNA and succeeded in proving that chromosomes damaged by X-rays can be repaired.

Shamans and esoteric and spiritual teachers have known for a long time that our body is programmable by language, words, and thought. All of the ideas above support the DNA being worked with as the programmed DNA of the hologram because scientists are learning that our DNA is programmable. If it is programmable, that means it was originally programmed. However, it takes a certain level of coherence to actively and effectively work with one's DNA.

> Now thanks to Garjajev and his team, this "theory" has been scientifically proven and tested. Each individual must work on the inner processes and maturity in order to establish a conscious communication with the DNA.
>
> The relationship with the conscience of the individual is the degree of vibration frequency and the ability to connect with DNA through meditation. Researchers state that this super communication process is more efficient in a relaxed state. According to Garjajev and his team, stress, worry or a hyperactive intellect can prevent this DNA communication, thus making the information distorted and eventually useless. [249]

The ramifications of these discoveries are the tip of the iceberg, and I would venture to say the beginning of what will change the future course of our species in unparalleled ways.

The more scientists understand how to manipulate matter and reality within the program, the closer they become to realizing its origin. One thing that came immediately to my mind for us now to consider on a daily basis is how we are affecting our bodies when we constantly say negative things about them. When we put our bodies down for being too fat or too thin, telling ourselves we are getting old, sick, and decrepit, etc.—our DNA is hearing our "commands" and reinforcing what we say. "Be careful what you think and say" brings on a whole new level of implications as we are literally programming our DNA. The more aware we become, the more we are able to intercept false programming, and that awareness comes from developing coherence.

---

[249] Ibid.

A fascinating and complementary article to the discoveries made by the Russian scientists can be found in one titled "DNA Is the Home of Our Yearning." [250] Mystic Toni Elizabeth Sar'h Petrinovich talks about a deep yearning we all share and defines it as "having an intense feeling of loss or lack and longing for something." She attributes this yearning to something in our DNA. Based on what we have explored throughout this book, I would say that this "deep yearning" could be somewhat attributed to a very deeply embedded knowing of who we are and a longing for the unified state we lost when we went into the separation of the Hologram of Deception. To suppress the understanding of that original longing, however, the yearning Petrinovich discusses is probably coming from the programming that Anu and his cohorts created in the human instrument when they inserted into the Genetic Mind the program of the saviorship/evolution model of existence. As discussed previously, Anu planned to come back as savior of the world at some future time, and the "yearning" is part of the programming to inspire us to look for a savior and evolve so we are ready to embrace his return. I think the frequency a person's energy field resonates at determines the source of the "yearning." For someone steeped in the religious programming of the day, the yearning would come from the programmed and inserted DNA; if the person has left that religious programming behind due to activation of the Wholeness Navigator, I would venture to say the yearning may be coming from the DNA of our origins.

All that being considered, let's take another look at what Petrinovich has to say. She initially explained that our minds work within a field of Quantum Physics called the Quantum Hologram (or Genetic Mind that holds the complete history of the human species), that the basis of our subjective experience is rooted in the idea of non-locality, and that within this quantum hologram is encoded the complete history of every event.

Petrinovich's premise is that since the brain looks for the familiar and compares it to other experiences based on memory and feeling, our yearning must come from something we know and feel or have known and felt.

We learned from the previous article that Fosar and Bludorf's thesis analyzed how DNA can be influenced and programmed by words and frequencies. Petrinovich goes on to explain that our "junk DNA" should be called "non-coding DNA" or "potential DNA" that follows the rules of syntax, semantics, and basic grammar rules that we are familiar with and needs no decoding.

> Simple words and sentences of any human language suffice in creating the
> environment that is the wavelike, holographic experience of the DNA thereby

---

[250] Petrinovich, Toni Elizabeth Sar'h, PhD, "DNA Is the Home of Our Yearning," *Night Watchman Chronicles*. (Website no longer available) Quoted and paraphrased from this article.

encoding it with the information that the cell receptors respond to and create changes within the amino acid chains and hence the proteins. Through our thoughts, words and feelings we create not only our perceptions, but also our bodies.

How does this correspond to our yearning? How does this fulfill the expression of the lack or desire for that which we yearn?

Since mankind appears to be on the fast track to accelerated conscious awareness, the frequency of the vibration of that DNA wave must also be accelerating ("As above, so below"). As the frequency (that is the oscillation) of the holographic mind (in non-locality) increases, we find our language changing thus influencing the effect we have on our DNA itself.

The frequency of our thought patterns, our words and our feelings must be coherent (troughs and crests equal in amplitude) to access the acceleration physically. This explains why some of us are experiencing the shift in our DNA and some have not yet done so. Coherent frequencies allow us to consciously communicate with our DNA and create the space in time for the DNA to embody these frequencies opening the door to expeditious reception of multi- dimensional information. How is this possible? [251]

It is my understanding that as we develop awareness and become activated in the process of transformation, we make changes within ourselves and within the Genetic Mind because it holds our history and changes as we change. Different levels of consciousness access different levels of the Genetic Mind. If we remain steeped in the Hologram of Deception, we access the old part of the Genetic Mind that holds the old program. That is why an incoherent mind cannot access the more advanced levels of information. As we grow in coherence and awareness, we become more able to access the newer part of the Genetic Mind and the information it holds. As we do that, our DNA is affected. Is it still the programmed DNA or the DNA of our origins? That is something for future scientists to unravel. I do not know. Another important point to consider is why our activation and transformation is such an individual process. Each of us has to make the decision to develop our coherency and awareness and work to accomplish it.

Below Petrinovich gives an explanation of wormholes. She also gives us information that we can apply to accessing information in different parts of the Genetic Mind.

---

[251] Ibid.

Fosar and Bludorf also found that our DNA creates patterns of disturbance within our time/space continuum (our holographic vacuum) producing magnetized wormholes or tunnel-like connections between different universal areas transmitting information outside of space and time. Imagine an hourglass with one round globe situated in one universe and the other globe situated in another (the second globe's frequency being compatible with receptivity within this dimension). The two globes of the hourglass are connected by a thin tunnel through which information travels from one dimension to another; not reliant upon space and time.

The emotions that we experience that create the feelings we have and manifest the thoughts created within our minds generate a frequency within our DNA that attracts information from these other dimensions (through the "wormhole") and passes it to our consciousness. Again, this ability is based upon the proper frequency within our bodies that is most easily created through states of relaxation, peace and ease. Stress, worry and similar states of being create incoherent waves resulting in confusion that prevent a state of hyper-communication. [252]

I would add here that coherent states of mind are closer to the level of consciousness of our Sovereign Integral and will serve to bring us closer to the Unified State of Consciousness. An incoherent mind is lost in separation and is caught up in ego consciousness and the program. An incoherent mind acts out of its programming. A coherent mind that is beginning to understand spiritual equality and wholeness instead of perpetuating separation is initiating the process of overriding the programming of the hologram.

Based upon these scientific findings and the reams of additional information now readily available to us, it is apparent that the conscious awakening of the holographic awareness now being experienced by man (homo sapiens sapiens) is being promulgated by the strong yearning (creating the feeling/ thought) to become consciously aware of what we believe we lack or have lost – our conscious awareness of our Oneness with All That Is.

Practices that allow for the interpretation of day-to-day expression as one of union, joy, appreciation, love and gratitude bring about this coherent waveform within the bodies (spiritual, mental, emotional and physical).

---

[252] Petrinovich, Toni Elizabeth Sar'h, PhD, "DNA Is the Home of Our Yearning," *Night Watchman Chronicles*. (Website no longer available) Quoted and paraphrased from this article.

Focusing upon and deriving pleasure from these practices creates the non-local paradigm within which we are invited to function. When truly living within this new framework of perception, our attention upon our intention of Oneness is our only focus. We can then experience our yearning as fulfillment. [253]

At the level of coherence Petrinovich describes in the above two paragraphs, I think we are beginning to access that newer part of the Genetic Mind that will foster our activation and transformation. I say this because she is describing versions of the heart virtues, and they come from our original state of consciousness. They are not a part of the Hologram of Deception.

In a study conducted at the Institute of HeartMath [254] and reported by Sara Paddington, researchers found that if a person sent love and care to human DNA, they could change the winding or unwinding of the DNA (contained in a vial and held by the sender) in the direction intended by the sender. Paddington went on to explain that by sending coherent heart frequencies of conscious love and care, it may be possible to enter into the DNA and reprogram and empower it to improve immune system and cellular health. [255]

The implications of the above articles are profound in light of what we are learning about how sound affects matter and about the importance of coherence and how critical it is to keep a frame of mind compatible with the qualities of the Six Heart Virtues which are the manifestation of unity coherence within human consciousness. Fear and hate and non-acceptance are the manifestations of separation and incoherence.

James Mahu has written an article that is a companion to the music CD *Hakomi Chambers Four, Five and Six* (https://wingmakers.com/music/). The article is titled "Coherence of the Evolutionary Consciousness." James explains in this article why this music was composed and that "sound is the most effective way to move beyond separation and rekindle a sense of reintegration between the heart-mind-body-soul system."

The article is long and detailed, and the reader would benefit the most by reading it in its entirety. It is fascinating in its implications as it projects us deeper into understanding how

---

[253] Ibid.

[254] The Global Coherence Initiative, a division of HeartMath, conducts monthly Care Meditations focused on uniting people in heart-focused care and intention. The meditations are online and open to anyone who cares to join.

[255] Paddison, Sara, *The Hidden Powers of the Heart: Discovering an Unlimited Source of Intelligence*, p. 184, Planetary Publishers of the HeartMath System, PO Box 66, Boulder Creek, CA 95006. info@planetarypub.com https://www.planetarypub.com

sound affects our consciousness. Certain kinds of music will help to develop coherence and contribute significantly to an individual's activation and transformation, and this *Hakomi Chambers* music (and all of James's music) was composed specifically for that purpose. The following quote from this powerful and comprehensive article helps to set the stage for our understanding:

> The human instrument absorbs the sounds present in music and can, if the music is properly tuned, form a sympathetic resonance with the music. Similar to two tuning forks that resonate on the same frequency when only one is struck, the human instrument can be a resonant system in which its cellular and atomic structure is entrained by the music—or more specifically—the vibratory frequencies contained in the harmonics of the music.
>
> The atomic structure of the human instrument is a vibrating harmonic system. The nuclei vibrate, and the electrons in their orbits vibrate in resonance to their nuclei, but to what does the nuclei resonate with? What is the primal vibration that establishes the vibratory expression of the human instrument and can this vibration change and adapt—in a sense migrate to new levels of vibration that are more aligned and supportive to the spiritual purpose in which the human soul chose to incarnate? [256]

James goes on to explain that the material world of sonic vibration found in most mainstream music keeps the human soul suppressed and diminished, creating a heightened sense of separation and a "broad- spectrum anxiety that is difficult to identify and consequently to resolve."

James designed the music *of Hakomi Chambers Four, Five and Six* to restore and support a sense of connection to that current of Universal Life that has been lost to us while under the suppression paradigm.

> Within the esoteric fields of study, it has long been known that sound is the most effective way to move beyond separation and rekindle a sense of integration between the heart-mind-body-soul- system. Music, properly tuned and orchestrated is like a needle and thread that stitches these component parts of the human entity together, not in a permanent union, but in manageable alignment and coherence. It is this alignment and coherence

---

[256] Mahu, James, "Coherence of the Evolutionary Consciousness," *WingMakers Archive* https://web.archive.org/web/20121017075151/http:/wingmakers.com/music-hakomi4-6.html

that enables your spiritual work to surface and bloom, and sound is the bridge that connects...[257]

Music properly composed along with other tools such as meditation and working with the Six Heart Virtues and the concepts of unity and wholeness initiate a profoundly powerful process within us that will eventually transform us, freeing us from the suppression paradigm.

We can support our own transformations with words that assist our DNA in building our bodies and with music. Light and sound brought us into existence, and they can heal us as well and bring us Home.

Hyper-communication or group consciousness is another important concept to consider as we ponder the ideas above. Researchers are now coming to believe that if fully coherent humans would regain group consciousness, they would have god-like powers to create and change things on Earth. As we grow to understand how our species is connected and embrace that connection—I AM Sovereign, WE ARE Integral—we will hasten the process of freeing ourselves from the Hologram of Deception that has held us prisoner.

In the following chapter we will explore the concept of hyper- communication, the Dreamtime, and other fascinating ideas.

A SHORT BUT ENCHANTING RABBIT HOLE

Before we move along, however, I have one more point of interest that I want to share here. I came across an enchanting passage in a sweet little book titled *Fairies at Work and Play* [258] observed by Geoffrey Hodson, a clairvoyant who is able to see the workings of the elementals in Nature. It is too long a passage to be completely quoted here, so I have summarized some of the introduction to his book. Hodson is describing what he observes about how light and sound work in the context of developing plants. He first describes the growing process he has observed in plants:

> In the examination of bulbs growing in bowls, it is observed that large numbers of small microscopic etheric creatures are moving about in the growing plants. They are visible etherically as points of light, playing in and

---

[257] Ibid.
[258] Hodson, Geoffrey, *Fairies at Work and Play,* Quest Books, Theosophical Publishing House, PO Box 270, Wheaton, IL 60187-0270 and Chennai, India, First Quest Edition 1982, Fourth Printing 2010. www.questbooks.net

out of the stems and passing in and out of the growing plant. …they absorb something from the atmosphere, re-enter the tissue of the plant and discharge it…. when the process of absorbing is taking place, they become enlarged and appear like pale violet or lilac- colored spheres…having expanded to the largest size they are able they return close to the plant, enter it, and begin to discharge the material or vital force which they have absorbed…

Hodson describes the growing and feeding process in more detail and then explains that through his observations, he has come to the following conclusions:

In the heart of every seed is a living centre which contains the stored-up results of previous seasons as a vibratory possibility.

Apparently the awakening or stirring of the life in due season produces *sound*. This sound is heard throughout the elemental regions where the builders answer the call to labor. Every type of growth, whether of stem, shoot, leaf or flower appears to have its own note, or call to which the appropriate nature-spirit 'builder' must respond. This sound also has form producing activity, and is, probably, the means by which the archetypal form is translated from the etheric level where it becomes the etheric mold.

Hodson explains that this vibration separates and insulates the atmosphere around the seed and calls the builders and sets the matter within the sphere vibrating at the required rate to specialize it in readiness for the work of the builders and also to materialize the archetypal form. He goes on to say that new vibrations are introduced as the leaf, shoot, stem, and flower are being built. More on sound:

The vibration, or sound appears to radiate, not only from the life centre, from which it first springs in due season, but also from every embryo cell. The corresponding builder absorbs the appropriate matter, *i.e.*, that which is responding to the same vibration as himself and the cell he is building and transforms it by association with himself into a suitable condition; he changes it from free to specialized material and discharges it atom by atom to the cell from which the sound is being uttered, building it into the etheric model. The vibrating cell acts as a magnet and draws the newly arrived material to its appropriate position so that the cell is gradually enlarged until it reaches its limit of possible expansion; it then divides, and a new cell is gradually built up by a repetition of the process.

While the material is in close association with the builder it is not only specialized to suit the requirements of the cell but is given the light vibration to which the builder naturally responds *i.e.*, it is colored.

Hodson explains that each stage of the growing process calls for a new set of builders. These creatures appear to implant their special rate of vibration, changing the colors that corresponds to the sound which called them.

These last are sufficiently advanced to be fully aware of their task and to find great pleasure in its joyous performance, and they take immense pride in the growing 'child' under their care.

They remain in close attendance, as each new petal and bud opens, until the structure is complete, and the task of the builders is finished. They are conscious and appreciative of the admiration of human beings for their work; but on our approach they seem to plead that the flower shall not be injured. If it is cut, they will follow it into the room and stay with it for some time.

When the completely flowered condition is reached the full chord is sounding forth, and could we but hear it, our gardens would have an additional joy. We do not, however, hear that chord, though it may be that in some cases we contact it as a scent. We may smell the sound!

I hope you the reader find the above as enchanting as I did. I thought this to be such an interesting example of Light and Sound in action in nature, giving us a window into a small world teeming with life and the act of creation.

23

THE HEART AND THE PERINEURAL SYSTEM

AUTHOR AND TRANSFORMATIVE COACH PETER Borys wrote a fascinating article about Heart Consciousness [259] that sheds light on many concepts that are being considered in the scientific world today about the relationship consciousness has to light and sound. He states that "the heart consciousness is our experience point for expressing the Divine in our body." Borys believes that

> Sound as information is the feeling mode of consciousness within the body...
> Light as information in electromagnetic waves is the knowing mode of communicating consciousness in the body... Ultimately, light and sound unite as one in the knowing, wisdom and being within our incarnate form ...
> The two unique modes of physical light and sound waves as an experience through an incarnate body are one singular knowing.

These statements are profound in their implications. In the same article he continues:

> The heart relays the infinite Light from within. Through its toroidal field, it emanates the strongest electromagnetic field of the body. The light aspect of consciousness from the heart communicates as electromagnetic radiation through the body's crystalline cellular matrix. In its communication with the brain and entire body, it utilizes the nervous and endocrine systems ...The sound aspect of consciousness from the heart also utilizes neural and hormonal pathways.

This last sentence takes us to the next step in our quest to better understand how interconnected our heart's influence is on us and all our systems.

---

[259] Borys, Peter, Jr., "Heart Consciousness and the Electromagnetic Acoustical Body," Posted 2.24.2014 http://blog.peterborysjr.com/2014/02/24/heart-consciousness-and-the-electromagnetic-acoustical-body/

Borys cites Robert O. Becker, researcher in electrophysiology/ electromedicine, who theorizes the existence of a direct current (DC) perineural nervous system in two of his books: *The Body Electric. Electromagnetism and the Foundation of Life;* and *Cross Currents. The Promise of Electromedicine, The Perils of Electromagnetic Pollution.* Becker explains that:

> The perineural system, which differs from the digital alternating current (AC) of the autonomic nervous system, is communicated through the perineural cells which surround all nerve cells. The perineural cells are constructed like a crystalline lattice and transmit like semiconductors. They may tie into the pineal gland and the body's crystalline cellular matrix. The DC perineural nervous system may be most resonant and coherent when it is being informed by a harmonic heart resonance. We will see how this coherent resonance emanates from an 8Hz frequency, and interconnects heart consciousness, the electromagnetic brain waves of the low alpha/ theta interface, the Earth's Schumann resonance, and the sound of the Sun. This harmonic may be part of the unity of light and sound. [260]

Mythographer Robert Lawlor includes Becker's fascinating description of two separate nervous systems in the human body in his book *Voices of the First Day.* [261] The following is a paraphrased summary of Lawlor's explanation starting on page 377:

> We have a central nervous system that is likened to an AC or alternating current digital computer with a single pulse. This digital computer can work very fast and transmit large amounts of data. Our senses function through this central nervous system.

Lawlor then identifies another nervous system he calls the perineural nervous system that flows from the perineural cells and generates a direct current (DC).

This DC can be compared to an analog computer transmission. Information is coded by the strength of the current and the direction of its flow. This system is slower than an AC system but much more precise and varied in content because it is based on the subtle

---

[260] Ibid.

[261] Lawlor, Robert, *Voices of the First Day: Awakening in the Aboriginal Dreamtime,* pp. 377-385, Inner Traditions, Rochester, Vermont, 1991.

In the section that I paraphrase, quote, and summarize, Lawlor begins by describing Robert Becker's research. Becker is considered the leading researcher in bioelectricity and biomagnetism and has developed a theory based on the presence of earth-tuned magnetic crystals and living cells.

variations in intensity of wave frequencies. This DC system appears to have been the original data- transmission and control system present in our earliest living organisms. It senses injury and controls repair and may serve as the morphogenetic field as well. It regulates our level of consciousness. Becker believes this discovery of a second nervous system is an important revolution in biological science as it provides us with new understanding of the way all living creatures are interrelated with life on earth.

This information is significant to us as we begin to unravel and try and understand the ramifications of the way we have been programmed. According to Lawlor, the Aborigines of Australia demonstrate with their artwork the energetic field perceived in the Dreamtime through their experience originating in the perineural nervous system. The Aborigines describe the Dreamtime Creators as fields of wavelike continuums, each field carrying a particular energy potential or psychic activity or quality. A field moves through the crystalline structure so that each position in the field gathers a slightly different voltage power, a different current strength, and a different flow. All of these subtle variations in the field are codes for large amounts of information, each describing form or energy experience. The image of the undulating energy field is precisely the way the Aborigines visualize their mythic landscape and portray it in their artwork based on pointillist dots and energetic cross-hatched fields. Aboriginal bark paintings were codes of information for them to visualize specific topographies brought from the Dreamtime into the *yuti* or perceivable world.

Those of us who are born into "civilized" societies are raised using only our AC or central nervous system. We are taught to perceive only linear time and separation. The Aborigines begin their lives developing the DC or perineural nervous system. They learn first to perceive the world that is visionary and integrated with flowing patterns of the Dreamtime. The Aborigine maps the Dreamtime landscape into the perceivable landscape of the everyday world through their art. The DC or deep perineural currents are responsible for injury repair, psychic awareness, and sensitivity to Earth's magnetic field. It is accessible through trance states and is the first perception taught to each Aborigine through respect for the Dreamtime. This would be a "right-brain" state of perceiving all time as a unified field.

The Western way of perceiving is with only the five senses and typically is very "left-brain" or rational. It is mental and linguistic, and our social lives are rigid, literal, and externalized. We mostly perceive through the AC or peripheral central nervous system which is responsible for muscle movement and the five senses. According to Lawlor, "We as a culture have failed to develop an entire neural network and therefore perceive the world through only half of our natural capacities."

The experience of the Aborigine occurs in the deep neural system and from there is translated into the physical world. The Western world is missing the development of our perineural system, and in so doing, we are relegated to the physical world of the five senses. Any deviation from that is considered to be insane. Lawlor thinks that the psychedelic movement that began in the 60s in the Western world was an intuitive search to try and find what has been lost and assuage that yearning we all share for deeper understanding.

But our societies lack a coherent framework for what can be encountered in the worlds beyond our physical one and a way to understand what is experienced. In many cases drug trips lead to insanity, sometimes suicide, or fanaticism. Western cultures do not encourage or cultivate any safe or knowledgeable way of exploring the Dreamtime. According to Lawlor, the potential for Dreamtime is still alive within us and could give us "astonishing awareness" that stretches beyond the bounds of our five senses. Knowledge of the Dreamtime and of two nervous systems can be the seeds that when planted would cultivate new understandings within us.

> Our society does not consciously cultivate or utilize the hypnotic trance or dreamlike states of awareness. We are unfamiliar with our deep neural system in which the images and forms of our world are created and projected. We have become cut off from an entire aspect of our being. Those deeper aspects are gifts from our Creative Ancestors, and they provide a means of entry into the worlds of the Dreamtime. Not only are we cut off from the wisdom of these worlds, we have also become victims of the unconscious and destructive aspects of this power. Governments, politics, media and commercial interests feed on the universal suggestibility of the human unconscious. We see as realities the images that our culture implants in our uninhabited dreaming nature. We are manipulated like pawns by those who project false, illusory words, meanings and images. Our governmental and religious institutions are founded on much the same processes of mass-induced suggestion used by infamous mind control cults. We work and pray, spend and steal, live and die for empty words that have created false realities within us. [262]

I am not sure about how far we can get with psychedelic substances in our cultures, and I am not advocating their use. Most of us are not trained to understand what those worlds are like and how to survive such encounters psychologically intact when we bombard our consciousness with a substance that instantly opens us up to worlds in which we have little or no framework.

---

[262] Ibid.

I do think, however, that we have what we need to gradually open up that perineural system within us through the gentle techniques of transformation with the Sovereign Integral Process. We have our imaginations and the tools, the information, the music, and the breathwork to help us gradually transform at a pace that is individualized and tailored just for us and regulated through our internal guidance system. We cannot force this process, and that is a benefit for us because in the Western world we are so impatient, yours truly included. We have to grow into it, and if we do, we can keep our sanity and grow in our awareness into a sustainable transformation.

I cannot help but wonder if the two nervous systems are connected in any way to our two sets of DNA. Could our original DNA be connected to our DC or Perineural system and our programmed DNA be connected to our AC or peripheral central nervous system? That's a question for us to ponder and future scientists to explore, but it is an interesting premise that makes sense to me.

It is very possible that having both nervous systems and both sets of DNA fully functioning would be a huge missing piece of the puzzle to our developing intelligence and awareness of who we are. One gives us the ability to function in the material world; the other gives us the ability to function in the Dreamtime and possibly beyond that to the Multiverse. In the Dreamtime we are all connected; in the material world we feel separate. It makes sense to me that our fully functioning coherent heart intelligence would bring the two systems together in ways we cannot even imagine at this stage of our development.

Ultimately the suppression paradigm and the Hologram of Deception will go away. We don't know what that will look like yet. We are Infinite Beings in a programmed human instrument and when we, as a species, finally fully realize and break free from the confines of suppression, our world view will potentially be light years away from what it is now. For that outcome to be fulfilled, we need to continue to develop and transform until we are ready for that ultimate quantum leap that will undoubtedly take us into an expanded identity that has the ability to explore a Multiverse of new realities.

24

TRANSFORMATION AND ACTIVATION FOR A NEW PARADIGM

THE OLD PATHS OF AWAKENING can act as catalysts to prepare us for our continuing journey through the threshold to the New Paradigm, or they can act as a "be all, end all" to our spiritual searching. A lot depends on our ability to utilize what we find and let it go when it has taken us as far as it can. Choice is the key to transforming. Some of the practices we have had access to in our spiritual quests that helped us to look at our beliefs and our egos and our psychological processes have served to open our minds to the acceptance of new information. It would seem that in order to integrate new ideas, growth must typically come in increments, each level preparing us for the next. Giant leaps of instant, sustainable understanding are rare.

FOUNDATION OF THE NEW PARADIGM ARCHETYPES

Some of the archetypes emerging into our fields of awareness to lay a new groundwork of understanding are:

- The Energetic Heart
- The Six Heart Virtues
- WingMakers Materials
- The Sovereign Integral process
- New realizations of our origins and connection to First Source

In tandem with the emerging of these archetypes is the growing realization of our connection to each other. The focus of developing ourselves for personal gain and satisfaction is old paradigm thinking. Our next leaps of consciousness will happen as we are able to grow in our understanding of how we are all connected. As we learn to incorporate the Six Heart Virtues into our everyday lives, we will grow in our ability to expand our heart-mind system, and a love-centered life will become our new normal. A chain is as strong as its weakest link. In order for humanity to be a strong and viable species, we must find a way to respect each other, even if we disagree. No one is "better than" another. Our lives are diverse because we are exploring different ideas and belief systems on the human level.

On the spiritual level, all humans are tethered to our Source at the subquantum level through our Energetic Hearts. We access that subquantum level and Source when we begin working with the Heart Virtues, and that Work brings us together as One. When we approach our experiences as something learned for the Whole, it gives our lives a deeper, richer meaning and purpose and a sense of belonging to something greater than our individual selves.

THE ENERGETIC HEART

> Across all dimensions of space there exists a primary field of vibration.... this field is non-physical but informs the physical. It exists independent of the physical structures of existence and is known among Lyricus teachers as the Underivative Information Structures (UIS).
>
> UIS are sub-quantum and represent the primary blueprint for living systems and inorganic matter. It is the UIS that gives rise to the quantum fields that interpenetrate planets, stars, galaxies and the universe at large. It is the communication field of life that connects the nonlocal and the local, the individual and the collective, the one and the infinite. The Energetic Heart is the non-physical component of the UIS that is the entryway or portal from the UIS to the intuitive and intelligence centers of the soul carrier or human instrument. In a sense it is the subquantum blueprint of the physical heart. [263]

The Energetic Heart is the Infinite component of our physical hearts that starts and maintains their beating and transmits the frequency of love to our bodies. Further down in this same e-paper James explains that

> Love at this core frequency of Spirit, connects to your personal self through your innermost, Energetic Heart. It passes into you and through you at this juncture. You need to only imagine and visualize this intelligence of Spirit

---

[263] Mahu, James, "The Energetic Heart: Its Purpose in Human Destiny," *WingMakers*, 6 Heart Virtues, https://www.wingmakers.com/6-heart-virtues/the energetic-heart/

coming into your body and passing through you to all who cross your path, and when you do this, you have brought your mission to earth. You have grafted an aspect of heaven to an aspect of humanity and earth. And this is why you are here.

Science has begun to study the field of the heart and has arrived at some startling and far-reaching conclusions. The Institute of HeartMath is devoted to the study of the heart. Rollin McCraty, PhD explains in an e- paper that

> The heart generates the largest electromagnetic field in the body. The electrical field as measured in an electrocardiogram (ECG) is about 60 times greater in amplitude than the brain waves recorded in an electroencephalogram (EEG). The magnetic component of the heart's field, which is around 5000 times stronger than that produced by the brain, is not impeded by tissues and can be measured several feet away from the body with Superconducting Quantum Interference Device (SQUID) base magnetometers. We have also found that the clear rhythmic patterns in the beat-to-beat heart rate variability are distinctly altered when different emotions are experienced. These changes in electromagnetic, sound pressure and blood pressure waves produced by cardiac rhythmic activity are "felt" by very cell in the body, further supporting the heart's role as a global internal synchronizing signal.[264]

The implications of research such as this conducted by the Institute of HeartMath are extremely far reaching. Until very recently, our belief systems have maintained that the heart is just a pump to circulate blood throughout the body and nothing more. McCraty goes on to explain in this paper how important emotional and psychological coherence is to the optimum functioning of the heart within the body and in maintaining optimal human interactions.

On the spiritual level, we have an Energetic Heart that animates the physical heart, and on a physiological level we are learning how much the heart affects how our bodies function. Another aspect of this is how far the field of our heart reaches. Cyndi Dale describes the electro-component of the heart:

> The heart is the physical center of the circulatory center...it is also the electromagnetic center of the body emanating thousands of times

---

[264] McCraty, Rollin, *The Energetic Heart: Bioelectromagnetic Interactions Within and Between People*, HeartMath Institute, 2003. http://www.heartmath.org

more electricity and magnetism than does the brain…it is an organ of communication that can potentially manage the body's intuitive processes… the heart's electro-magnetic field (EMF) is five thousand times stronger than the brain. Its electrical field is sixty times greater than the brain… Under correct conditions such as when a person consciously "centers" or focuses in the heart the heart begins to run the brain. Entrainment or the management of the body through the heart rather than brain leads to higher functioning mental and emotional states as well as a healthier body. It also enables a person to screen the outer environment for 'good messages' instead of 'negative messages' enabling a more positive relationship with the external world.

Further down in the chapter Dale explains:

Most people believe that the brain initiates the first response to incoming events and then orders our reactions. Analysis reveals, however, that incoming information first impacts the heart and through the heart the brain and the rest of the body. Our hearts are so strong they can actually formulate the most well-known symbol of love: light. Research has shown that under certain conditions a meditator can actually generate visible light from the heart. The meditation technique has to be heart-centered, not transcendent. When this occurred during studies at the University of Kassel in Germany in 1997, the heart emanated a sustained light of one hundred thousand photons per second whereas the background had a count of only twenty photons per second.[265]

How do we put the above information to practical use? When Puran Bair[3] meditated from his heart by picturing a young sick boy in front of him and sending him "light" from his heart with each exhalation, he was able to produce the generation of visible light. This was achieved through his intention of sending healing light to a specific subject, the sick boy.

By utilizing our imaginations and our intent and contemplating new ideas that inspire

---

[265] Dale, Cyndi, "Electromagnetic Field of the Heart" in *The Subtle Body, an Encyclopedia of your Energetic Anatomy*, p. 66, Sounds True Publishers, 2009.
The actual experiment was conducted by Puran Bair, co-founder of the Institute for Applied Meditation. Bair, Puran, "Case Study: Visible Light Radiated from the Heart with Heart Rhythm Meditation," *Semantic Scholar*, https://pdfs.semanticscholar.org/a861/ed3faa5fd6abc62aaa6710ed87efdbd6b923.pdf

us to action, we can develop our ability to transmit a dynamic and healing love from our hearts into the world.

A powerful way of transmitting the Six Heart Virtues into the world is to practice consciously inhaling each virtue from our Energetic Heart into our heart, holding it there for a few seconds to mix with our energy signature, and then exhaling that virtue out into the world. One can direct a virtue at someone or an event in particular or just to the world in general.

Sometimes I like to picture myself as my Quantum Self holding the world in its arms and sending the heart virtues through my breath into the earth's grid. We can also help with our own physical regeneration by breathing in the Light of Source as it streams from the Energetic Heart into our hearts and then circulating that Light through our bodies and out into the energetic field around us while reminding ourselves that what comes to us flows through us and into the world.

The process of bringing the Light and Six Heart Virtues from our Energetic Hearts into the world in this powerful way is one of the most transformative ones for ourselves and for the world that we can practice in our daily lives.

James Mahu teaches that these virtues are patterns of Divine Energy that together make up the transmission of Divine Love. They are integral to the practice of transformation in the new paradigm to attain Sovereign Integral Consciousness especially when we intentionally transmit them in meditation to the grid around the earth. The virtues are:

Appreciation, Compassion, Forgiveness, Humility, Understanding, and Valor

James' e-papers "Living from the Heart" and "The Art of the Genuine: A Spiritual Imperative" describe the Six Heart Virtues in detail. John Berges wrote an e-paper titled "The When-Which-How Practice" that illustrates in much more detail how to utilize the Six Heart Virtues in daily life. These papers can be found at www.WingMakers.com in the section 6 Heart Virtues.

In the context in which the Six Heart Virtues are explained and used, they are and transmit to us new patterns of Behavioral Intelligence and therefore in my mind qualify as archetypal patterns. In the next chapter, I will discuss each virtue in more detail.

WINGMAKERS

WingMakers is neither a path or teaching, it is simply a way of living based on spiritual equality, and in this way of living, it proposes not to judge, but rather to distinguish carefully between the lower frequencies of separation and the higher frequencies of unity—one and all. James Mahu

The following quotes have all been excerpted from the Preface or Introduction to *Collected Works of the WingMakers Volume I* [266] unless otherwise indicated. From the quotes below, we get a strong sense that the WingMakers is an archetype of our emerging Selves.

> The term WingMakers is encoded. "Wing" is derived from the term wind or blow. It is the active force of setting new states into motion. "Makers" is the plurality of the co-creators—that being the collective essence of humanity. Thus, WingMakers means that from the collective essence of humanity new states of consciousness come into being. This is the meaning of the term WingMakers, and it confers to humanity a new identity. Humanity is transitioning to become WingMakers.

Wind is an especially important component of Alchemy as well, and I found some fascinating parallels to the encoded name of the WingMakers in the following:

> In most religions when the godhead takes form it is either as a fiery light or as a wind…Early Hindu texts state the wind came before Light…wind is the Cosmic Breath…Islamic texts state that the Wind supports the Throne of God, say the Wind is composed of clouds, air and countless invisible wings. It is through these "countless wings" that most of us know the Wind. [267]

The following is from the Introduction to *Collected Works of the WingMakers, Vol 1.* On page 2 John Berges writes:

> The name WingMakers is actually a euphemism for what James describes as the Central Race. These were the first humans created by First Source and they were responsible for creating all the human forms that inhabit the space-time worlds.

On page 5 of the Introduction, Berges writes:

---

[266] Mahu, James and John Berges, "Introduction," *Collected Works of the WingMakers, Volume I,* edited by John Berges, Egg Harbor, NJ: Planetwork Press, 2013.
[267] Hauck, Dennis William, *The Emerald Tablet: Alchemy for Personal Transformation,* p. 88, Penguin, Putnam Inc., 375 Hudson St., New York NY 10014, 1999.

Metaphorically, the WingMakers presentation can be likened to the film or the play that captivates the senses, that draws us into the world of imagery and music, its story and poetry. WingMakers entertains us, informs us, and affects us. But more importantly, it is designed to prepare us for the presentation of new concepts and theories related to the nature of life in the multiverse and the role of earth's humanity beyond the confines of our planetary nest.

Further down in the Introduction, Berges quotes from the *Lyricus* website:

WingMakers is part of the mythological expression of Lyricus that typically accompanies its first external expression within a species. It is the "calling card" announcing its initial approach as it treads softly among the species it serves. WingMakers is the mythological expression of the underlying structure of the Lyricus Teaching order. It is symbolic of how Lyricus is brought to the planet. [268]

SOVEREIGN INTEGRAL

My rational for thinking that the Sovereign Integral is an archetype is because it is the blueprint or pattern that we are all on the trajectory of attaining at some point in our infinite existence. If you are interested in exploring more about the Sovereign Integral, read James' answers in the "Project Camelot Interview, November 2008," found under Interviews on the *WingMakers* website. I went through and excerpted most of the passages that mentioned Sovereign Integral in some way and in just that little exercise found that it is mentioned around seventy times. It is an important part of who we are, and I cannot do justice to it here. I have several favorite quotes from this interview, however, and the following is one of them:

The change I want to see in the world is that people begin to see themselves as multidimensional beings whose core is the Sovereign Integral that is the distillation of First Source in a singular, human expression. If people were only in tune with this frequency, they would understand that all is united in oneness, equality, and truth. This is the definition of the Grand Portal as it has been disclosed by the WingMakers mythology for the past ten years.

---

[268] All materials that are on the Lyricus website are now included on the WingMakers website.

Each individual is a portal unto themselves, and this portal is the access point to the interdimensional worlds of the Sovereign Integral, where the human instrument, like a space suit, is finally removed and the individual realizes their true, infinite nature. And in this realization, understands that everyone – EVERYONE – is equal in this state, and in this equality, we are ONE. The Grand Portal is when humanity stands- up as ONE BEING to this all-encompassing realization and then we transcend the suppression framework and express as Sovereigns.

The following is a definition from "The WingMakers Glossary":

The Sovereign Integral is a state of consciousness whereby the entity and all its various forms of expression and perception are integrated as a conscious wholeness. This is a state of consciousness that all entities are evolving towards, and at some point, each will reach a state of transformation that allows the entity and its instruments of experience (i.e., human instrument) to become an integrated expression that is aligned and in harmony with Source Intelligence.[269]

FIRST SOURCE

Here is a passage from "The Art of the Genuine: A Spiritual Imperative" that describes First Source as an archetype, as well as how it works with the heart virtue of Humility:

Humility understands that the being that represents you—your fullest identity—is not constituted as a chain reaction of the mind. Rather, it is the presence of Love embodied in human form, and this love expresses itself in the virtues of the heart, the pure intellect of the contemplative mind and the co-creative pursuits of the heart, mind and soul. Humility is the expression of this love frequency knowing it derives from what already exists in a higher dimension, and in this dimension, love is not a thing of sentiment and emotional heaviness. It is a liberating force that acts according

---

[269] Mahu, James and John Berges, "The WingMakers Glossary, Sovereign Integral," *Collected Works of the WingMakers, Volume I*, edited by John Berges, Egg Harbor, NJ: Planetwork Press, 2013. **Sovereign Integral**, Appendix A - Glossary

to the archetype of First Source: All is one. All is Equal: All is divine. All is immortal. [270]

Another excerpt from "The Art of the Genuine: A Spiritual Imperative" gives an expanded definition of First Source:

First Source is a consciousness that inhabits all time, space, energy, matter, form, intent; as well as all non-time, non-matter, non- energy, non-form and non-intent. It is the only consciousness that unifies all states of being into one Being. And this Being is First Source. It is a growing, expanding, and inexplicable consciousness that organizes the collective experience of all states of being into a coherent plan of creation; expansion and colonization into the realms of creation; and the inclusion of creation into Source Reality— the home of First Source.

IMAGINAL CELLS AND LIVING FROM THE HEART---AN EVENT STRING

The human physical heart is a timespace extension and expression of the quantum Energetic Heart. This Energetic Heart transmits and expresses the light of love as six virtues.

(John Berges, *EventTemples.com*, 2007)

This quote is a powerful thought for pondering and contemplation. To refresh our memories—the Six Heart Virtues are: Appreciation, Compassion, Forgiveness, Humility, Understanding, and Valor.

James Mahu teaches a breathing technique he calls Quantum Pause, [271] and part of that exercise can include breathing in each of the Six Heart Virtues into our physical bodies and then transmitting them onto the grid around the earth or sending a specific heart virtue to a person or situation. It is a powerful way of breathing, not only for the person doing it, but as a way to transmit these virtues to the world.

---

[270] Mahu, James "The Art of the Genuine," WingMakers, 6 Heart Virtues https://wingmakers.com/writings/sixheartvirtues/the-art-of-the-genuine/

[271] Mahu, James, "Quantum Pause," *WingMakers*, Writings, https://wingmakers.com/writings/quantumpause/ I have included the directions for Quantum Pause in Appendix F.

A dear friend and I had been discussing the concept of the Six Heart Virtues being in the Energetic Heart and our understanding that those virtues are transmitted to our physical hearts when we consciously breathe them in and make a conscious effort to work with them.

During this series of conversations we were having, I came upon some information about our hearts having "imaginal" cells such as the butterfly has. Lepidopterists know that the imaginal cells in a butterfly catalyze the metamorphosis of the caterpillar into the butterfly during the cocoon stage. I went on a search to see if I could find any information about whether or not this idea was metaphorical or real.

I came across the following statement in an article titled "Biological Lessons on Coexistence, Imaginal Cells and Metamorphosis." The section titled "Imaginal Cells" has some fascinating ideas I want to share here. I will be quoting and paraphrasing from that section of the article:

> Something new is happening in the world…representing Transcendental Change. …Evolutionary Biologists define this metamorphosis as Punctuated Evolution, and have discovered that certain cells known as the "Imaginal Cells" trigger genes referred to as "Creative Genes" get together synergistically and propel in a punctuated leap and transform the obese and dead-end caterpillar to become a beautiful butterfly. …Amazingly the same creative genes that code the metamorphosis from a caterpillar to a butterfly code for the cells *present in the human heart*. (Emphasis mine) [272]

Another article "The Seeds of a New Humanity" [273] discusses the imaginal cells in the butterfly, calling the change from the caterpillar to a butterfly a quantum evolutionary leap. It continues:

> Another place imaginal cells are found is in the human heart. So far, the imaginal cells in the human heart have not been activated but at some point our imaginal cells will be activated, and humanity will make a quantum evolutionary leap.

In an excerpt from "The Art of the Genuine: A Spiritual Imperative," I found a clue that my thinking might be on the right track:

---

[272] "Imaginal Cells" from "Biological Lesson on Coexistence, Imaginal Cells and Metamorphosis," *Heart Intelligence*, https://www.heartintelligencebook.com/metamorphosis.html
[273] Arnold, John, "The Seeds of a New Humanity," *Alliance for a New Humanity*, http://anhglobal.org

The art of the genuine is a subtle practice. There are energetic fields of compassion, understanding, appreciation, valor, forgiveness and humility that surround the human instrument—every human instrument—like a cocoon surrounds a soon-to-be-butterfly. These fields are energetic equivalents of First Sources imprint upon the individual soul...[274]

So here is what I am thinking—the human heart may have "imaginal cells" that are sensitive to the Six Heart Virtues, and when one consciously begins to work with the virtues and breathe them in, directing them to and through the heart, they activate the imaginal cells in the heart which begins our transformation into the Sovereign Integral state of consciousness, our original state (our butterfly level of being). These virtues are fields of intelligence dwelling in the Energetic Heart that have the power to activate and transform the human instrument. It makes perfect sense to me that somewhere in our blueprint are the cells that can take us from the caterpillar state of human existence, activate our transformation, and restore us to the state we originated from—the cells, if you will—of our "parent" consciousness. The butterfly story in all its wonder is a powerful archetype for us to consider as a way to learn more about ourselves, one of those delightful little clues in nature hidden in the smallest creature to teach us the biggest secret!!

When we harden our heart, we stop the flow of these virtues into our heart; and when we open our heart, we allow the flow of these virtues to come into our body and be transmitted to the world with every breath we take or anytime we visualize that energy going out into the world. And as those intelligent energies flow in and through us, we are transformed and contribute to the transformation of the world. To quote more from "The Energetic Heart":

There is a First Source or Central Sun. All dimensions lead to it. Whatever name you give it: Higgs Field, Source Intelligence, Spirit, it issues from the Central Sun as love, and it dimensionally shifts universes via its intelligence. Yes, Love is *powerfully intelligent*. It has an intelligence that shines so bright that it is the light we see on every dimension of consciousness. Love at this core frequency of Spirit connects to your personal self through your innermost Energetic Heart and it passes into you and through you at this juncture.

[274] Mahu, James "The Art of the Genuine," WingMakers, 6 Heart Virtues https://wingmakers.com/writings/sixheartvirtues/the-art-of-the-genuine/

You need only to imagine and visualize this intelligence of Spirit coming into your body and passing through you to all who cross your path and when you do this you have brought your mission to earth.

And this is why you are here.[275]

Whether there are actual or metaphorical *imaginal cells* in the human heart, I am intrigued and enchanted by the notion.

It makes perfect sense to me that our imaginal cells could be activated by working with the breath given to us by the Sovereigns. Their life force is transmitted to us through every breath we take, and each breath triggers the beat of our hearts. The process of bringing the Six Heart Virtues into our bodies through the breath activates something profound in our hearts—the manifestation of Divine Love on this planet. I venture to add that as we become activated by the Six Heart Virtues, each of us becomes an Imaginal Cell in the Great Body of the Sovereign Integral.

---

[275] Mahu, James, "The Energetic Heart: Its Purpose in Human Destiny," *WingMakers*, 6 Heart Virtues, https://www.wingmakers.com/6-heart-virtues/the-energetic-heart/

25

A NEW CORE BELIEF MATRIX

> It is the perspective of the Sovereign Integral that all life is pure love in its fullest expression and that in this single concept all life is conceived and forever exists. This becomes the core belief from which all other beliefs arise and by their extension one's belief system emerges with a clear intent of supporting this fundamental perspective; of nurturing, observing and appreciating the Universe of Wholeness as the cradle from which all life is created, evolves and ultimately acknowledges.
>
> James Mahu, *WingMakers*, "Chamber One Philosophy"[276]

The single concept that "all life is pure love in its fullest expression" is the foundation of the core belief matrix of the Wholeness Paradigm that will ultimately usher in a world view of inclusiveness and transformation.

First Source disperses Universal Love through the Living Forces of this powerful and all-encompassing core belief matrix—a love centered life expressed through the Six Heart Virtues. These virtues wait in the wings of our energy field, ready to be invited into our hearts and transmitted through each individual who aligns with them.

The virtues come from Source and are therefore outside of the three-dimensional world. When we invite these virtues into our Human Instruments, we are aligning with a powerful and transformative matrix of Universal Forces. As we begin inviting them into our hearts through our breath, we allow them to influence not only our behaviors, but we also transmit them into life situations that will ultimately help to dismantle the wall built around us that keeps us imprisoned in the Hologram of Deception.

---

[276] Mahu, James, "Life Principles of the Sovereign Integral," *WingMakers*, Philosophy, https://wingmakers.com/writings/philosophy/chamberone/

This philosophy paper is also found in *Collected Works of the WingMakers, Vol I* available at Planetwork Press Egg Harbor Township, NJ

We can breathe these virtues into our hearts as we inhale each breath, and from that heart-centered place, on the out-breath send each one onto the grid that connects us all. James Mahu has given us a unique breathing technique we can utilize to transmit the Six Heart Virtues called the Quantum Pause.[277] An e-paper of his titled "The Rising Heart"[278] gives us information about how to strengthen our light body and suggestions for us to begin transmitting the new paradigm to our world with our breath.

When we practice the quantum pause with intention and focus the 6 Heart Virtues in day-to-day scenarios as often as we can remember to do it, we are contributing to the transformation of situations. For example, when you are in a meeting with co-workers, try sitting there quietly and transmit whichever virtues you feel appropriate into the room. Do this without expectation of outcome and just feel the force of the virtue/virtues fill the room and then enjoy the experience of the group interaction.

As each person aligns with these energies and grows in the ability and understanding of how to cultivate their individual Behavioral Intelligence through these living forces, the virtues will be amplified and become more powerful and paradigm changing.

We live in a fractal hologram. Fractal simply means "the repetition of patterns at all scales from micro to macro."[279] Whenever something is inserted into a fractal pattern, it becomes integrated into the repetition of patterns throughout the entire hologram. This is significant for us to understand. Hologram means that the *whole is present everywhere*. In basic terms, the same patterns repeat in the hologram. If we are able to insert a new pattern into the fractal hologram, the pattern will soon become part of the hologram and alter the program. If we look back on how our world has changed in our lifetimes, we can see how that process of inserting new ideas works. Once it begins to take hold in the collective consciousness, the idea spreads. It is only a matter of time before it takes on a life of its own to upgrade our world or to destroy it. The choice is ours as a species. I touched on that concept as I discussed how we have been gradually programmed.

I believe that working with the Six Heart Virtues in day-to-day situations will eventually override the programming if we are consistent in our practice of transmitting the virtues.

---

[277] See Appendix F - Quantum Pause

[278] Mahu, James, "The Rising Heart," *WingMakers*, 6 Heart Virtues, https://wingmakers.com/writings/sixheartvirtues/the-rising-heart/

The process of the Rising Heart helps to activate your Light Body.

[279] "Fractal Holographic Synergetic Universe," *Cosmometry, Exploring the Fractal Holographic Nature of the Cosmos*, http://www.cosmometry.net/fractal-holographic-synergetic-universe

Key to understanding the worldview that Cosmometry is founded upon is the idea that the Universe is both **fractal** (the same pattern of wholeness is found at every scale) and **holographic** (the wholeness is present everywhere and within every entity), as well as **synergetic** (the whole is greater than and unpredictable from the sum of the parts).

This work has the potential to enhance our awareness of the encoded and embedded beliefs that dominate us, as these outdated beliefs will inevitably begin to surface and be recognized for the suppressive programs that they are.

Even though our egos are programmed to keep us in separation, I would venture to say that each and every individual on this earth in our heart of hearts wants to live in peace and harmony with our families and within our communities. Each of us wants to see agreement prevail within and among nations. We have been programmed to be territorial and to embrace nationalism, but this is not our natural state. (Remember the Tower of Babel myth? In light of what we are learning, it makes a lot of sense.)

Our natural state prior to our leap into physical bodies and the material world was to work together in harmony and peace as an integrated species.

All that being said, please understand I am not suggesting that we erase our national boundaries for a one-world order, especially under the present paradigm, because those in power and control would make it a dictatorship of overpowering proportions, and we are already remarkably close to that reality.

We make the most progress in dealing with issues that affect us all when we respect and encourage cooperation among sovereign nations. I AM WE ARE can be applied globally as well as individually, such as: I AM a Sovereign Nation, WE ARE an Integral Globe of Nations.

I am challenging each of us to think of our brothers and sisters in this world as equal and as fragments of First Source and to stop looking at other nations and races as our enemies. We were divided to keep us in separation, and everyone in this world is a passenger on this ship of deception.

Obviously, global cooperation is a tall order when we look at the strife and chaos reigning in our world today; however, we as individuals can override that discord by embracing the simple and profound practice of heart-centered living and in so doing contribute significantly to the process of ultimate world peace and collaboration. If there is even a tiny possibility that this will have impact, count me in—whole heartedly!!!

Think what we could accomplish if we quit focusing on killing each other and begin focusing on how we can be supportive of each other.

Elie Wiesel, Nobel Peace Prize laureate, holocaust survivor, and humanitarian put it so well when he said: "Someone who hates one group will end up hating everyone—and ultimately hating himself or herself" and "Peace is our gift to each other."

We are entering a new paradigm in the story of our species, and therefore a new learning curve is developing to master Behavioral Intelligence through our work with and transmittal of the Six Heart Virtues. The following is my understanding of how to work with them.

Embracing and incorporating these powerful energies is a work in progress, as they are multi-dimensional and nuanced. As they gain momentum in our world, and especially in our personal lives, they will more than likely exert other powerful influences we are not yet aware of. I believe that they exist on all levels of consciousness from the very mundane to the highest spiritual ones, waiting for us to call on them.

My contribution in this book is to offer to the reader my understanding of the virtues and how I have used them. Each of us will have our own private and personal experiences with these living energies, so anything I share serves simply as a suggestion or example. I am a student and practitioner of this process, and I do not consider myself as an authority on this material. What I share is my understanding at my current stage of internal development. As my understanding grows, my ways of working with these energies undoubtedly will grow and change as well. Look at them only as an example and a work in progress - a jumping off place.

As you begin to work with these living forces, new meaning and understanding will arise within you through your own inner guidance. We can share our experiences and understandings as a conversation; not as dogma, but as authentic alchemists, brothers and sisters aspiring to transformation and mastership leading to the attainment of Sovereign Integral Consciousness, our true state of being. As we breathe these living virtues through our bodies and out into the world, we add our individual energetic signatures to them as creators in this process. This bonds us in a beautiful kind of unity, a kinship of love and appreciation for each other and for the process itself. As fragments of First Source, we are conduits for these virtues or Behavioral Intelligences, and they reach the world through each of us as we incorporate them into our lives and send them out. We have the power and ability to bring these intelligences into the hologram through our human instruments and transmit them into the world. When they are transmitted through us, they cannot be stopped. We are able to insert new behaviors, ideas, and beliefs into the fractal hologram in this way. It is a solitary work. It is a powerful work. It is a paradigm-changing work, and it unites us. We need nothing more than our imaginations and our growing understanding of these virtues and their importance and our willingness to participate in this endeavor.

A comprehensive and wonderful guide to help us learn to work with the Six Heart Virtues was written by John Berges, titled "The When-Which- How Practice, A Guide for Everyday Use." This free e-paper can be downloaded at https://www.wingmakers.com/6-heart-virtues/the-when-which-how- practice/

FOUNDATIONAL HEART VIRTUE ONE: APPRECIATION

Thoughts, feelings, and attitudes generated by Appreciation:

- The energetic field of Appreciation encourages us to respect that we are all equal and no one is "better-than" anyone else.
- Appreciation gives us the understanding that we are all a fragment of First Source and therefore connected at the deepest levels of our existence.
- Gratitude is one of the most powerful energies in the Universe; it helps us perceive the world from a position of thankfulness.
- Appreciation promotes feelings of acceptance and tolerance.
- Appreciation is the understanding that until our brothers and sisters begin the awakening process, they are asleep and do not understand who they are. This gives us an "appreciation" for their state of being and the realization that those who are asleep are living life through their programming. This understanding comes from the soul level of our consciousness and also generates Compassion.
- We may have an Appreciation for what we know, but we cannot judge others for what they do not know.
- As we embrace the force of Appreciation, we grow in our awareness of how our species is being manipulated and kept in the suppressed and deceived state of being. We learn to fundamentally appreciate the complexity of the suppression hologram.
- When we appreciate, we respect that the life force that flows through each of us comes from the same place—First Source—and unifies us as a species. We honor the complexity of this playground we have been given where we experiment and transform.

Appreciation is the practice of Gratitude at a basic level. At the very human and practical level, Appreciation supports our relationships with one another. It can be a form of understanding of the complexity of a situation— e.g., "I appreciate all you have been through to accomplish this task" or "I appreciate how difficult it is to ...." In financial terms, appreciate is a term utilized to mean something increasing in value. We could translate that into other situations—e.g., "I appreciate your willingness to work with me to understand this situation from another point of view." "I appreciate your willingness to remain my friend in spite of my warts and travel with me through the mountains and valleys of my life." In this example, one's value as a friend increases and deepens or "appreciates."

Appreciating something is acknowledging value and meaningful dimension on many levels. From the level of our souls, we can appreciate the magnitude of our Beingness—that we are fragments of First Source and that we can be in direct communication with this Source through understanding how the individual and Source work together.

John Berges in his commentary on "Lyricus Discourse 4" gives us an important and profound nuance of our understanding of Appreciation:

> Consciousness IS. It does not require evolution—it is our appreciation of this fact that requires evolution. The student is told to *evolve* this appreciation, to develop gratitude in knowing the true nature of his own being.[280]

APPLYING APPRECIATION TO LIFE EXPERIENCES

As we begin to grasp the depth of these virtues, each of us will find our own meanings and expressions, and for that reason, it is important for us, myself included, not to put too definitive a spin on any of them. The ideas below are just some examples of how Appreciation might become a part of our daily lives:

- We express Gratitude for our everyday blessings of food and shelter and clothing.
- We convey Gratitude for the loved ones in our lives—warts and all.
- We have Appreciation for a person's life circumstances and their particular challenges and realize that each of us has lessons to learn or experiences we want to have—possibly known only on the soul level, and it is not for us to judge where others are or try to force them to believe our truths.
- We can appreciate the idea that each person comes to information they are ready and prepared for and will embrace new ideas in their own time.
- We can transmit Appreciation and/or gratitude through breath and meditation into life experiences that might benefit from that energy field. When we transmit it, we do not to put any expectations onto the situation, just send this living force and let it do ITS work.
- As we come to understand the Six Heart Virtues and how they work, we come to appreciate our part in being a conduit for them. We are Infinite Beings living

---

[280] Berges, John, "Lyricus Discourse 4, Universe Relationship," p. 29, *Planetwork Press*, Articles, Lyricus Discourse Commentaries, https://planetwork.co/pages/Articles.html#ldc (Downloadable PDF file)
The six actual Lyricus Discourses are found at *WingMakers*, Lyricus, https://wingmakers.com/writings/lyricus/

in Human Instruments. If we can bring the energy of Appreciation into this dimension through our bodies and transmit it through our hearts and out into the world, we are bringing the many levels of Appreciation into the Hologram of Deception. We are inserting it into the fractal to be spread throughout the Hologram of Deception.

- Appreciation is the realization and acknowledgement that each of us is a part of the Whole. Each of us has access to this powerful virtue. The force of Appreciation will help to alleviate self-righteous tendencies in us and respect the fragment of our Source that lives within each one of us.

FOUNDATIONAL HEART VIRTUE TWO: COMPASSION

Thoughts, feelings, and attitudes generated by Compassion:

- Compassion acknowledges and appreciates the humanity of ourselves and others: flawed; lost in separation; half-asleep; yearning for safety, comfort, and a sense of belonging—and awakens in us the desire to help others awaken.
- Compassion is a multi-dimensional, all-encompassing energy of acceptance and tolerance; it is the soul's work.
- Compassion can be an expression of empathy or identification with someone's plight or condition.
- Compassion is a knowing that everyone (including ourselves) is doing the best we can. It doesn't matter how our life experiences might look to others because we do not know what they know or believe or have suffered or do not understand.
- Compassion is an active desire to help our brothers and sisters by assisting with the alignment of the new fields of Behavioral Intelligence now entering the energetic fields that surround our planet.
- Compassion is the realization that we are all in this together, the ones who are awakening along with the ones who are still half or completely asleep. This helps us to be tolerant and accepting.
- Compassion is realizing that each individual interprets current life events either from their programming or from the vantage point of beginning to awaken, and this has nothing to do with their ultimate intelligence or worthiness or purpose.

APPLYING COMPASSION TO LIFE EXPERIENCES

- Compassion reminds us that each individual will be caught up in the challenges of constantly changing energies on Earth during this transitional time between the old and new paradigms. The energies affect each person differently and can cause stress, imbalance, even illness or violence at times.
- When we use our breathwork to bring the energy of Compassion into our own energy fields and then transmit it by breathing it out onto the grid of humanity, or to specific hot spots on earth that we are aware of, we are helping to transform turbulent energies.
- If we can utilize our ability to call on Compassion in our everyday lives and transmit this energy into various situations, we are doing the best work we can without intruding on another's choices. Since we are all connected to our brothers and sisters, when we transmit Compassion onto the energetic field of our planet, it goes into the energy field each of us has access to. This may result in someone having a feeling that comforts them or an inspiring or helpful thought. We may attract a compassionate action to someone who needs it by sending Compassion to them. We don't know the effect we have on people when we send these virtues, and that is best left in the unknown (or "in the Mystery" as James puts it). We do our part of the work by transmitting the virtue or virtues without putting our own limited expectation on the outcome and let the Universe do the rest.
- Each of us on the deepest levels of our being resonates with the virtue of Compassion because our species lived that virtue prior to the suppression; it is a part of our energetic life-force and our origins.

If individuals around the world are consciously transmitting all the virtues on a regular basis into the world grid, we are participating in several ways:

1. We embrace our origins.
2. We give momentum to the virtues.
3. The impact of the virtues will continue to become stronger within the collective energies of all of us and will contribute to the opening of hearts everywhere.
4. With the opening of hearts comes a dramatic change in the collective Behavioral Intelligence of our species.

FOUNDATIONAL HEART VIRTUE THREE: FORGIVENESS

Thoughts, feelings, and attitudes generated by Forgiveness:

- Forgiveness understands that flaws are present because we are Divine Beings with amnesia, lost in separation. As we see humanity in this way, it helps us to not be so quick to pass judgment on an individual as we realize each is coming from perceptions built by individual and collective belief-system programs, and no one has the full story.
- Forgiveness and Appreciation are about realizing that the bulk of humans are doing the best that they can under the circumstances of what they know and believe in, and that most want to do what they believe is the "right" thing.
- Acceptance is another dimension of Forgiveness.
- If we remember how our overlays contribute to our reactions to life events, it will help us better understand the mindset a person is responding from.
- People react out of their individual programming, and what seems logical and right to one person can be seen as hurtful to another. We can save ourselves a lot of grief by choosing not to take the actions of others personally and understand that they are responding from their programming.
- It is very difficult in a close relationship with someone not to take their actions personally, but if we teach ourselves to keep in mind that most people act from of a feeling that they believe they are doing the "right" thing, we realize that getting into a power struggle is not going to help solve any problem. As one person told me in the heat of a conversation: "I don't argue unless I know I'm right." That is a wall you can rarely get past.
- It is helpful to look at each situation from the point of view of the programming of the person and the development of that person's ego; not to judge them, but to be able to bring understanding which will help generate Forgiveness in the situation.
- A person generally will not forgive if the ego is stuck in the time warp of an event. If we cannot bring ourselves to the now and remain stuck in the past, it will make it difficult for us to forgive.
- Forgiveness is the virtue that frees us from situations we froze in time. It basically thaws them out, allowing the energies to flow freely again, and releasing the hold the situation had on us.

APPLYING FORGIVENESS IN LIFE CIRCUMSTANCES

- If two people refuse to understand one another's point of view, we have a stalemate caused by the egos of the two parties. It will take an act of unconditional love through the lens of Forgiveness to change the dynamic.

- It is popular in modern psychology for adults to delve into their childhood and to look at the ways they feel they may have been victimized by their parents or other adults. This victimization often becomes a way to keep a person stuck in the past. If we as an adult can look at our past from the NOW and realize that our parents, teachers, and caregivers were acting out of their programming and either doing what they did because they didn't know any better or because of the way they were programmed or because they thought they were doing the right thing, it makes it easier to truly let go of the act of victimization. This releases both oneself and the person who did the victimizing. A person may get ego satisfaction out of keeping another locked in the prison of hatred over something they did, but the imprisoned one and the jailer are incarcerated together. It is all or nothing. We cannot be free from a prison of hate until both parties are released.

- Non-forgiveness helps keep us in separation and trapped in the program. It is what the powers-that-be want—for us to remain caught up in hateful and divisive activities and beliefs because they are terrified of the power that would be generated by humans joining together as a group consciousness radiating healthy Behavioral Intelligence. They work hard to keep us polarized and in separation.

- If we know that a person deliberately set out to hurt us or abuse us in some way, it can be difficult to let it go, but it is a very healing process if we can, and it releases us from the prison the memory of an event can create. Imagine the distorted beliefs and often painful ego box this person is experiencing that would drive them to commit the abusive behavior. It is very possible that they are dealing with guilt on some level for what they did to you. By working on the internal level in your heart, you can do a great deal to alleviate the suffering for everyone involved. Our ultimate goal is to wake up from this deception and free ourselves from the suppression we have endured for centuries. Forgiveness is a powerfully freeing energy.

- It simply isn't worth it to hold onto past grievances if it keeps us in suppression and separation and hinders our transformation and entrance into the incoming heart-centered paradigm.

- Ultimately, we are all connected; we are all part of the One. The sooner we can recognize that and understand it, the sooner we will find our way out of this program of being unable to forgive.
- When we are frozen in time with a specific event we cannot forgive, it might be helpful to do some self-examination about our own ego payoffs for not forgiving. People say and do hurtful things in the heat of the moment, when they are sick and/or out of balance nutritionally or hormonally, when they are frustrated and want to exert control over another, or when they are experiencing their own internal pain and frustration—and the person closest to them is the easiest target. It is our task as we work on Forgiveness to do some self-examination. Are we remaining frozen in time because
  o it is a way of blaming another without examining our own part in the situation?
  o it is a way of punishing the person for the perceived wrong they committed towards you?
  o it is a way to remain in self-pity, nursing our victimhood and the wounds received from the hurtful event?
- When you have worked through some of the reasons why you struggle to forgive and are ready to begin Forgiveness, a meditation might be useful as a start. We don't have to make an outward decree of Forgiveness. Work it out internally and let the energies do their work "in the mystery" where they are the most effective.
  o From the vantage point of seeing how the person who victimized you was living in their distorted perceptions and expectations that are a product of his/her own programming, breathe in the energy of Forgiveness into your heart. Ask this archetypal force to work with you and help you understand and let go.
  o Saturate your energy field with this living force, and then when you are ready, on an exhale see the event in front of you and exhale Forgiveness from your heart into the scene or directly to the person. Do this for several breaths.
  o Inhale Compassion and as you exhale send that Compassion to yourself as the victimized person or child in the scene and to the person you felt victimized by. Do this for several breaths.
  o Do this breathing for a while, maybe even calling on other virtues, such as Humility and Understanding, until you begin to feel a release from the grips of this prison you are both locked into.
  o If you like to work with imagery and your imagination, consider seeing you both leaving the prison cell together. Walk out into an open meadow or beach and let the brightness of the sun fill your bodies with healing light.

- You might try seeing the energy surrounding the event as the kindling for a fire, light the fire in imagery, and watch the event transform as the energy of it is cleansed and rises from the fire.
- When we are working with any of the virtues, we are working from the heart and engaging our soul. We are bringing powerful energies from our Energetic Heart into our physical heart and body. These heart energies work outside of space-time and can have significant impact on space-time with authentic intention. We are the conduits for the Heart Energies that can transform the world. They have to come through us and be transmitted out from us. Through our intention, we insert these energies into the grid that surrounds our world. We let go of expectations and let them do their work.

FOUNDATIONAL HEART VIRTUE FOUR: HUMILITY

Thoughts, feelings, and attitudes generated by Humility:

- Humility recognizes that we are all connected, that we all come from the same Divine Source, and no one is better than another.
  - Some may have more money, education and understanding.
  - Some seem to be more awake than others.
  - Some appear to be lost with little hope of being found.
- The animating current within each and every individual is from a Divine Source and is the equalizer. None of us knows the ultimate purposes for an individual's experiences, what their animating force is trying to understand and explore.
- The time has come for us to expand the above ideas about Humility to include Compassion and awareness of the animal kingdom as well. They are a part of the collective whole.
- Humility is not about having a low opinion of oneself, but an Understanding of one's responsibility to respect all of life as being equal.

APPLYING HUMILITY IN LIFE CIRCUMSTANCES

- I think the information below is a great illustration of how Humility can be applied in the workplace.

The best leaders are the people behind the scenes who guide their employees and let them shine. This quiet leadership approach—listening, being transparent, being aware of limitations and appreciating employees' strengths and contributions—is a highly effective way to engage employees. The researchers found that such leaders model how to effectively be human (rather than superhuman) and legitimize "becoming" rather than "pretending." …Leaders who embrace growth signal to followers that learning, growing, mistakes, uncertainty and false starts are normal and expected in the workplace, and this produces followers and entire organizations that continually develop and improve. That is why leader humility is associated with more learning-oriented teams, more engaged employees and lower voluntary employee turnover.[281]

- Cultivating Humility within oneself is about realizing that all of us have unique talents and abilities and about teaching ourselves to encourage others instead of trying to "one-up" them with our own accomplishments.
- Humility is being open to new ideas and being willing to listen to what others have to say.
- Humility is about having a balanced view of oneself and a good understanding of personal strengths and weaknesses.
- Humility is about examining one's own beliefs and determining if they are useful for a heart-centered life, and if a belief is not useful, being willing to admit it is not and figuring out how to change it.
- Humility is about being teachable and receptive to feedback.
- Humility is authentic service to the awakening of our brothers and sisters through the transmission of the Six Heart Virtues and living a heart-centered life, knowing that we affect the Collective Mind with our actions.
- Humility is realizing that as we discover life enhancing information, it is not just about our personal growth and transformation. This information is given to us to help us understand the plight of our species and to do what we can to help usher in a more equitable world.
- Recognizing false humility:
  o Thinking poorly of oneself and having low-self-esteem;
  o Feeling useless;
  o Timid, insecure, afraid to take initiative;
  o Cringing from correction and feedback;
  o Anxious concern for self and unable to focus on others.

---

[281] Smith, Michelle M., "Humility Is Key to Effective Leadership & High Performance," *Linked in,* Nov. 2, 2015, https://www.linkedin.com/pulse/humility-key-effective-leadership-high-performance-smith-cpim-crp

FOUNDATIONAL HEART VIRTUE FIVE: UNDERSTANDING

Thoughts, feelings, and attitudes generated by Understanding:

- Understanding expresses empathy for the situations and conditions we find ourselves in.
- Understanding brings the other virtues—Appreciation, Compassion, Forgiveness, Humility and Courage—into our everyday interactions with others.
- Understanding is realizing there is no judgement from some wrathful god about what we have done or experienced in this world. We are experiencing for the Whole and bringing individual perceptions to that experience.
- Understanding helps us realize that at the Sovereign Integral state of consciousness, we will be able to draw on all the experiences of many lifetimes and grow in our Appreciation of the many complexities of our species.
- Understanding is our growing ability to recognize that we can learn without judgment from our experiences under the suppression paradigm of limitation and deception.
- Understanding knows that we are participating in a Grand Experiment and that First Source is the ultimate designer.
- Understanding knows that within the incremental experiences of the limitations of time and space we cannot recognize the entire picture and that everyone on this incredible journey is at a different place within it, and there is no judgement in that.
- Understanding is the profound realization that we are not subject to a wrathful, hateful, vengeful god who chooses sides and polarizes its subjects.
- Understanding brings Light to all of life's issues.

APPLYING UNDERSTANDING IN LIFE CIRCUMSTANCES

- We apply Understanding along with the other six virtues in our everyday life. John Berges ("The When-Which-How Practice") feels that Understanding is the most obvious virtue to connect the heart and mind. [282]
- Understanding is an active life force helping us to see other's programming for what it is—a false premise of deception and oppression that is not our True Selves.

---

[282] Berges, John, "The When-Which-How Practice," WingMakers, 6 Heart Virtues, https://wingmakers.com/writings/sixheartvirtues/the-when-which-how-practice/

- We apply Understanding with Compassion when we realize everyone is doing the best that they can, given their circumstances and level of consciousness and awakening.
- We apply Understanding with Appreciation when we feel gratitude and realize the power of this practice of applying the Six Heart Virtues and transmitting them out onto the grid of humanity and into particular events in our private lives.
- We apply Understanding to Forgiveness when we work with the reasons why Forgiveness is important and become willing to make Forgiveness an important part of our lives.
- Understanding teams up with Humility when we realize that each of us is a work in progress. This helps us not to resort to judging another person. It helps us not to take the actions of others personally because we realize most of the time, we are all acting out our individual perceptions and programming. Even when we are consciously engaging our Heart's Intelligence, we are a work in progress.

Understanding seems to be an undercurrent companion to all the virtues. The more deeply we comprehend the importance of examining our core beliefs and seeing if they are compatible with the Six Heart Virtues, the more developed our virtue of Understanding will become, and the more multi-dimensional we will become in our comprehension of the Life Principles of Spiritual Equality we need to live as Sovereign Integrals upon this earth.

FOUNDATIONAL HEART VIRTUE SIX: VALOR

There are many expressions of Valor, but in typical parlance the word is usually associated with soldiers and people in danger performing heroic acts. When we talk of Valor as a Heart Virtue, it is a form of fearlessness that prods us towards our truth, our understanding of who we are. As we allow the energy of Valor to transmit through our heart centers, we are strengthened with an energy of self-expression that honors our true selves and expresses those inner, true qualities to the best of our understanding and abilities.

Thoughts, feelings, and attitudes generated by heart-centered Valor:

- A person who demonstrates the virtue of Valor does it through determination and fearlessness.
- Valor is firmness in one's convictions.
- Valor is the courage to change one's convictions and beliefs when deeper truths are revealed.
- Valor often requires tenacity to stay the course of transmitting the Six Heart Virtues amidst the many distractions of living in this world.

APPLYING VALOR IN LIFE CIRCUMSTANCES

- Valor is speaking truth to power.
- Valor is intervening with Compassion and conviction when a child or vulnerable human being is being hurt by another.
- Valor is living one's beliefs without forcing them on others.
- Valor is walking our talk; it is being authentic in the moment.
- Valor is an energy of determination.
- Valor helps us to maintain dignity and respect for all in the midst of a chaotic environment.
- Understanding and Valor work together when we become aware of a situation that needs attention and use our Valor to do what is needed at the moment by standing up for our convictions, including speaking truth to power.
- Valor helps us to not succumb to manipulations of others' egos. When we are living with the Six Heart Virtues in our energy fields, we are able to see those manipulations for what they are, and Valor and Understanding will help us to keep from reacting to them.

As we can see, the Virtues intertwine and are often used together in life's circumstances. They are bold and subtle at the same time, and they present an entirely new way of experiencing the world that is far removed from the Core Belief Matrix of suppression and fear. The Six Heart Virtues are here to liberate us from that Matrix and the program that created it and, in the process, give us an entirely new world view.

There are two powerful paradigm-shifting dynamics at work now on Earth. There are probably more, but these two are identifiable at this time.

One is called the Grand Portal.[283] It is the irrefutable discovery of the soul living within the human instrument. Those of us who are exploring this information at this time are laying the foundation upon which this discovery can be made in future generations.

The first piece of groundwork is to activate Heart-Centered living within those prepared to accept this premise and for them to work with it. This contributes to the insertion of a new order into the fractal hologram that will contribute to breaking down the wall of the Hologram of Deception.

The second paradigm-shifting dynamic at work is for many to be working with the Sovereign Integral Process in order to realize that state of consciousness while still in a human body. The Sovereign Integral Process progresses as an individual grows in their ability to utilize the Six Heart Virtues in everyday life and to transmit them onto the grid and into specific situations as one sees the need. Those reaching the Sovereign Integral state

---

[283] See **Grand Portal**, Appendix A - Glossary

357

of consciousness will contribute significantly to our release from the Hologram of Deception and to the discovery of the Grand Portal.

GROUP HEART AND CONSCIOUSNESS

I have been watching the Vietnam War series by Ken Byrnes on PBS— not for entertainment surely, but to educate myself on what happened when I was so young, lost in the fog of being a young adult and new mother and not very aware of what was going on in the world. My small world was so busy and full I didn't have time to venture out or take much interest in the larger one.

So, this powerful and much needed documentary has given me some catch-up information I have sorely needed to piece together some fragments of understanding from my early life and those of my generation. The documentary tells the story from all sides, so we get the big picture of this horrible war.

On the way to work this morning, I got to thinking about US—our species—a group consciousness living in Human Instruments in a holographic world. We may be stuck in this paradigm now, but once again I am seeing where the promptings from deep within our species eventually will bring the inhumanity of war and other deceptions to the surface for us to look at and resist.

According to the documentary, President Johnson kept from the American people all that the military were doing in Vietnam because he didn't think we would approve. He seemed to be trying his hardest to do what he thought was the right thing, but he wasn't sure the American people would see it the way he did, and as always, his information was only as good as his advisors could provide him. Decisions had to be made. It could not have been easy trying to figure out what to do. I imagine that it was difficult for him to see all the sides to this horrible war.

Eventually and inevitably promptings from deep within our consciousness found some willing hearts and minds who began to look at the war from some different angles and bring their realizations to the surface to share with others, and thus the protests began.

I was reading "The Art of the Genuine: A Spiritual Imperative" by James Mahu one evening, and I was struck by James's discussion of Appreciation in light of the Vietnam documentary I was watching earlier.

> Appreciation: At the subtle levels, this virtue is focused on a specific awareness
> that First Source surrounds our fellow beings as a field of consciousness

and that this consciousness unifies us. If we are unified, it follows that we operate as a collective consciousness at some deeper level, and in this place, we share a common purpose that is richly textured, supremely vital, and yet mysterious, dynamic and uncertain. This awareness, or even belief, shifts our focus from the small details of our personal life to the vision of our purpose as a species.[284]

I was deeply affected by this description of Appreciation. It helped me to see how our group consciousness might work. We as a species might have been persuaded or manipulated to take on this human physical "space- suit," and in that process we might have been suppressed and unable to remember our origins for a while. But this amnesia won't go on forever. The time is coming when we will all remember that deception, how it happened, and how we can become free of it.

Our group consciousness connected to our Energetic Heart—the heart of our species where we are all joined and that feeds us all—does remember and will not allow us to languish in the state of unknowing forever. I can trust that promptings will come from deep within, from that Energetic Heart, and activate the Appreciation and Valor that is a part of who we are. This realization has given me hope. Valor—speaking truth to power, speaking out against injustice towards those who are vulnerable and cannot protect themselves—this Virtue or Behavioral Intelligence is a core virtue that we all have access to and share. It is a powerful force that is instrumental in guiding us out of the suppressive paradigm we are currently languishing in.

I find it comforting to realize the power of our connection through our Energetic Heart and the Behavioral Intelligence it holds and prompts us with. This deep and binding connection will steer us collectively as a species of consciousness through the darkest places into the Light of Understanding.

I am reassured because after watching what happened in the past and what is happening now in our uncertain world, I am convinced that there will always be enough of us in each generation awakening to the many deceptions to create a resistance or counterculture to all that is inhumane in this world. It is through these awareness-raising realizations and resistances that we push our species forward to our final destination of liberation from all that has deceived us.

[284.] Mahu, James, "The Art of the Genuine," *WingMakers*, 6 Heart Virtues,
https://wingmakers.com/writings/sixheartvirtues/the-art-of-the-genuine/
Downloadable version: http://www.lyricus.org/links/downloads/artofgenuine_electronic_.pdf

We start by appreciating that inner connection that feeds us all, and we shed light on events around us through our Understanding of what is happening, and with Compassion we apply Valor to the issues, and we move forward. It is our destiny to succeed in our final liberation.

LOVE WINS

Ambition unbridled Shrivels hearts of
Un-awakened souls to
Become prey to the Dark Energy as they
Succumb to the lure of status and control
Coalescing into a fortification of hate and deceit

Darkness descends upon the land
As programmed sleep-walkers
Rise to the twisted words
From the mouth of Manipulation personified
Hungry for succor
Desperate for attention
They lay their adoration
At the feet of Embodied Ambition screaming empty promises.
A temporary salve for their pain

I stand at the window of my Soul
And I weep for the sleep-walkers as I
Witness the darkness descend in a cloud of fear
Upon the barren landscape of un-awakened souls
Crying in their beds for a savior
Hypnotized they
Become minions of Ambition personified

But wait
As I watch from the portal of my Heart
I see that the darkness is contained
The Guardians are gathering
A light of compassion infiltrates the darkness
Emanating from those who are awakening
Activated by the coming storm
And I know it is time
For those of us born to this task

The battle lines are drawn
Darkness and suppression
And the Light of understanding and liberation
Face off as
The resistance builds
Prepared by the Virtues of Love

As I peer into the mirror of my soul
A reflection is forming
I see the Carriers of Light
With distinctive living shields formed within their hearts
Reflect specific Light into the darkness and shatter it

The Shield of Valor
Leads the resistance by championing Justice
As it speaks truth to power and demands
transparency Eschewing hate and bigotry
And wherever Valor is reflected
The Light of Truth finds its way

The Shield of Compassion
Reflects the Light of Protection
And inspires us to resist mistreatment of
Our brothers and sisters
Regardless of race, gender, sexual orientation,
financial status or age
All the while teaching our connection to each other

The Shield of Understanding
Shines the structure of our timeless Energetic Selves
Through the field of our Hearts
Onto circumstances showing us ways to overcome hate
And feel the empathy of challenging situations
As each does their best in the environments of their lives
And levels of inner knowing

The Shield of Appreciation
Shines the Light of Connection we all share with our Source
A knowing that as a unified species
We all are destined to awaken
And within the reflection of this living intelligence
We discover gratitude for our shared destiny

The Shield of Forgiveness
Reflects non-judgment
Though difficult to practice
While ensconced in the throes of the dark energy
Points the way to understanding and compassion
For our brothers and sisters who are asleep
And under the spell of Ambition personified

The Shield of Humility
Reflects the Presence of Love that is our Infinite
Selves Dwelling within our physical being
Where our Heart's Intelligence is transmitted
Outward into the world
To activate and transform

Now as I stand at the window of my Heart's Portal
And peer into the mirror that reflects a deceived world
With the cloud of dark energy hanging over it
I see Lights popping up everywhere
Like fireflies on a warm summer's eve
As the Carriers of Light gather their Shields of Love
And go forth
Reflecting the Specific Influence of Each Shield
Into the dark places
And through this internal and powerful resistance
The dark energy is weakened and scattered
The self-serving manipulation of embodied Ambition
Cannot withstand the transparency of this Force
And is ultimately vanquished
LOVE WINS

26

PARALLEL WORLDS EMERGING

IT IS BECOMING MORE AND more apparent to me that something extraordinary is happening in our time.

I feel myself floating in the sea of consciousness that has become my friend and mentor. All around me are throngs of people: my brothers and sisters going about their daily lives, unaware that our life experiences pulse in and out of this material reality into an unknown dimension so close we could reach out and touch it.

When the pulse focuses into the matrix of our physical world, we go about our daily chores and lives. In those beats of out-pulsing, we are able to glimpse a world or insight beyond the everyday minutia. It is in those precious fleeting nanoseconds of awareness that we become couriers of a message tailored to be inserted into the fractal energy fields of our consciousness meant to stimulate awakening for all.

We are all in this same boat, my brothers and sisters and me. Some are very awake and know what is happening; others are asleep and so caught up in the dramas of daily distractions of their life's responsibilities that they don't have the energy to awaken or even have the awareness that it is possible. It is to those trapped siblings we must now focus, not to think that we have any power to "save" anyone in any way. As individuals we don't. No one does. Each of us must become our own savior.

What we can do, however, is hack the fractal hologram by putting our insights and understanding into the Genetic Mind we all share so that each individual in his or her own time can be stimulated by the inspiration that is seeping into those fields of life support on a daily basis.

Floating in that alternate world of my Mind's Eye, I become aware of an interesting dichotomy. I have a physical heart that beats and sends blood and oxygen and nutrients coursing through my veins in order to maintain my human life. While subject to the enslavement of the Matrix, this physical heart is relegated to being considered as nothing more than a mechanical pump. If acknowledged as part of our emotional makeup, it is marginalized as a metaphor for being too sentimental and needy and labeled as indulgent and enabling and irrational.

Now a most astounding realization is growing deep inside of me as I begin to recognize my Energetic Heart, that mysterious energy field around my physical heart that gives it life and is the dwelling place of my soul. Through this conscious connection to my Energetic Heart, I am growing in my ability to develop a deeper resilience, adaptability, and sense of equality for all. I feel a new kind of intelligence activated within me, a feeling of confidence and knowing I have never experienced before.

My physical heart feels stronger as I breathe the Six Heart Virtues from the Energetic Heart into it, allowing each virtue to circulate through my physical body and back to my heart where I then breathe it out onto a grid that I see surrounding my beloved Earth that connects us all. This simple, yet powerful meditation renews me and encourages me as I send the dynamic virtues of love to my brothers and sisters on the planet.

I have come to learn that these powerful virtues are conscious and intelligent and deeply influence anyone who chooses to work with them. I have summoned them into my own life, and they have gifted me with profound feelings of a deep empowerment and growing fearlessness I have never felt before.

As I float in my sea of consciousness, I become acutely aware of my brothers and sisters whose precious physical hearts have not been awakened to their Energetic Hearts, and whose souls sleep, making them prey to the doctrines of separation governed by the ego and the intellect. This sets them up to be vulnerable to the lure of the dark energies of blind ambition, power, and control, making it seem important to either seize power or surrender to those who do. In this hypnotized state, their Energetic Heart cannot reach them, and so it patiently waits.

I sense a question arising out of the Matrix—several actually. They go something like this:

1. How can you be so sure this is real?
2. What do I have to do so that truth finds me?
3. How do I activate and awaken?
4. What is my purpose once I am awakened to heart-centered living and this new paradigm?

In answer to question 1 (How can you be so sure this is real?), I can only say that I have experienced profound changes in my own understandings, and the quality of my inner life has improved beyond recognition of what it was before. These changes within me are tangible enough that I feel a powerful difference in how I perceive and approach life, and that is real to me. I do not long for, nor seek, the "bells and whistles" or supernatural phenomena of the unseen worlds. It is all about a stirring of knowing deep within, too precious for theatrics.

The preparation inquired about in question 2 (What do I have to do so that truth finds me?) happens in so many ways. The asking of questions such as "Why am I here?" or "Who am I?" or "What is truth?" or "What is my original voice?" are big steps as they tell the Universe you are searching for and opening to truth. Persistence along these lines of questioning and searching will put you on the trajectory to find your truth and is a critical step in the preparation process. Your truth will come, usually in increments, as old programming and the densities they create are slowly eliminated, preparing one's receptivity to new truths. Being willing to release old beliefs as you discover new ones is a necessary step to get you to a new level of understanding.

Our awakening to a sense of human equality and the realization that we are more than our physical bodies are big steps in opening our minds and hearts. The work of preparation is accomplished individually, but during this accelerated time of change, we are being helped by the breakdown of our collective programming as dark revelations about our institutions surface and many belief systems are questioned.

We live in a fascinating time in human history as the suppression paradigm is becoming quite transparent and can no longer do its dirty work behind closed doors. We are witnessing the dark forces of culture and the ruling elite in action in twenty-four-hour news cycles. Transparency on all levels of government is revealing unprecedented corruption that until now has remained secret, and this knowledge is engaging and enraging many people into a call to action. The first step toward truth is uncovering and recognizing the lies. Out of this recognition comes a choice—do we continue to support the dark forces by looking the other way and allowing them to run rampant, or do we make the decision within ourselves that we will not support this travesty of the self-proclaimed elite?

That brings us to question 3 (How do I activate and awaken?). Our activation to attract truth and change on an individual basis begins when we make the decision to extricate ourselves from the influence of those dark forces and choose compassion, inclusion, understanding, valor, and forgiveness as our life focus.

Question 4 asks if we have a specific purpose once we are activated, and if so, what is it? Our purpose in all of this is one of the most significant points I have been attempting to make throughout this book—when we begin bringing the Six Heart Virtues into our human instruments through our breath and transmit them out into the world, we act as a conduit for bringing the transformative energies of the Energetic Heart into the Collective Consciousness. We bring these archetypal energies through our bodies, add our personal energetic signatures to them, and transmit them out into the world. In that way we literally hack the fractal that is the Hologram of Deception by inserting these virtues into the hologram. That is our work: to fill the fractal with the spectrum of love expressed through the Six Heart Virtues, making these energies more powerful and influential in the energetic fields of our species. Over time this will stimulate change. How? I don't know exactly. James suggests we "leave it in the mystery." We just do it, and the power of those virtues will do the rest. In all our endeavors we practice the Six Heart Virtues to the best of our ability in our day-to-day lives.

Our species is straddling two paradigms, the three-dimensional world of ego gratification and the multi-dimensional world of the Sovereign Integral. Both have existed in tandem for many centuries. Each is becoming more defined and easier to recognize as they begin to pull apart. Individuals will be called upon to make a choice because soon they will be separate worlds.

Individuals in the Sovereign Integral paradigm are growing in their understanding of what it means to live a heart-centered life focused on compassion, understanding, and unity in all their endeavors. Many are consciously engaging the Six Heart Virtues and living the Behavioral Intelligence these virtues manifest in their lives. This paradigm is on a trajectory towards the Grand Portal, the irrefutable discovery of the soul and the release of our species from the suppression paradigm and our reinstatement in the Multiverse.

Individuals in the newly manifesting world resonate on a different frequency than those who choose to remain in the three-dimensional world of ego gratification. Perpetuated by the dark energies of power and control, the minds of the latter are blocked in their ability to grasp the importance of awakening because they are in a suppressed state of consciousness.

Every individual will be given repeated chances to be activated until they are, regardless of how long or how many lives it takes; and those who are ready will find freedom from the programming of the Hologram of Deception.

There are other avenues of awakening; the *WingMakers Materials*, however, are in my mind the most thorough because they not only give us the history of the suppression paradigm but also show us the way out, We are provided with the tools and understanding needed to focus on developing Behavioral Intelligence[285] capable of putting us on the Heart

---

[285] "The April 2008 James Mahu Interview," *WingMakers*, WingMakers Tools, http://wingmakers.com/wp-content/uploads/2020/08/April-2008-Interview.pdf On page 23 the following definition of **Behavioral Intelligence** can be found:

Behavioral Intelligence is the ability to self-manage the coherence of the mind and heart to create emotions that are balanced and resilient. This isn't about sentimental emotions or passionate reactions to the wrongs committed by the powers that be—as if we need to start a revolution. Rather, it is a steadfast, inner conviction to seek the expression of the heart virtues in every affair of our lives. I want to be clear; heart virtues are not emotions. They're not thoughts. They're behaviors.

Path. To me it is the Motherlode of state-of-the-art transformative information that has given me a new benchmark for any belief system: Is it inclusive, and does it support the development of Heart-Centered Living?

Our activation isn't about gaining more and more knowledge or adhering to a specific belief system; it is about choosing to be a part of the world of compassion and inclusion and living a heart-centered life that does not support all the separatist phobias running rampant in our world today. This we do in the service of humanity, as we are all in this together.

In the Dalai Lama's words:

> If there is love, there is hope to have real families, real brotherhood, real equanimity, real peace. If the love within your mind is lost, if you continue to see other beings as enemies, then no matter how much knowledge or education you have, no matter how much material progress is made, only suffering and confusion will ensue. [286]

Our survival and progress as a species is about choosing to consciously align our ego-selves with our innermost selves—our hearts—making us co-creators with our Higher Self or Sovereign Integral and ultimately First Source and allowing that partnership to guide us in our everyday lives. We have free will, and the choices we make create the consequences on the trajectory we choose. If we choose to live a heart-centered life, that decision will put us in a new paradigm and on a life path where we develop Behavioral Intelligence derived from the influence of the Six Heart Virtues. As our lives unfold in this new paradigm, we will experience a world open up to us that is new and exciting, and old and familiar. We will reclaim our roots and our wings.

Albert Einstein also knew this:

> A human being is a part of the whole called by us universe, a part limited in time and space. He experiences himself, his thoughts and feeling as something separated from the rest, a kind of optical delusion of his consciousness. This delusion is a kind of prison for us, restricting us to our personal desires and to affection for a few persons nearest to us. Our task must be to free ourselves

[286] Chase, Christopher, "How to Save the Planet According to the World's Greatest Minds," *Uplift*, April 1, 2017. http://upliftconnect.com/save-planet-worlds-greatest-minds/
The Dalai Lama and Einstein quotes are from this article.

from this prison by widening our circle of compassion to embrace all living creatures and the whole of nature in its beauty.[287]

Throughout this book I have attempted to illustrate what I have come to understand about how we literally lost the navigation of our hearts and how we can reclaim our heart's guidance and our Heart's Intelligence and how that might affect our world. As a species we are building the foundational level of this endeavor. There are many more exciting changes and revelations to come. We are all works in progress, and we are all in this together as brothers and sisters.

We may have been naïve to begin with, but over the course of this truly Grand Experience of Exploration into the material world, we have learned so much about ourselves. The paradigm hovering on the horizon is one where we will reclaim our Earth and our birthright and once again become active members of the Multiverse. We do that through the power of our Heart's Intelligence coupled with the understanding of our Higher Mind. What an exciting journey we have ahead of us as we make our way collectively into our future as a loving species of consciousness made wiser through our adventures in the Hologram of Deception.

---

[287] Ibid.

WANDERER FULL CIRCLE

And so as The Wanderer I have finally reached the zenith of my pilgrimage, for I have arrived at the peak of the Shadow Mountain I began to climb so many years ago when I responded to the call of the Old One. From my newly acquired vantage point, I look over the horizon of my consciousness with an understanding honed by my often poignant and extraordinary journey.

As I survey the panorama of this magnificent vista, I reflect on the arduous climb that became an exploration of a myriad of belief systems and experiences and relationships over an unknown number of lifetimes. I feel gratitude for the Light of Understanding that was shone on what needed to be forgiven as I reviewed my inner landscape of psychological and emotional densities. Each plateau of this momentous journey was a pause, giving me time to reflect on and let go of what was no longer relevant, allowing me to grow psychologically lighter as I became stronger and more open as I climbed.

Now I stand here wrapped in the loving energy of my Sovereign Quantum Self and reflect with awe and appreciation on my expeditions into the worlds of time and space.

I have come to understand the reason for the yearning that has driven me for as long as I can remember. I know now why I felt that sense of loss and the drive it gave me when I chose to set out to explore time and space. The exquisite reason for my journey through the eons of time has been revealed.

I have come to realize that I AM a Sovereign Individuated Consciousness, one of many mandated to explore the outposts of the Seventh Super Universe. I AM a member of an Integral Consciousness that includes all of my species, and we are known throughout the Multi-verse by names such as The Shining Ones, The Elohim or WingMakers. Collectively in the I AM WE ARE state, we comprise the consciousness known as First Source, and individually we are alchemists and explorers.

We have all been participating in a Grand Experiment that is moving toward completion on planet Earth. Soon discoveries will be made that will unshackle our species from the Hologram of Deception that has imprisoned us for so long and restore us to our rightful birthright where we will become active, aware members of the Multi-verse once more.

For years I searched the far horizon of my consciousness, sensing tantalizing, fleeting glimpses, this perception that something phenomenal was unfolding, a mystery that teased my every waking moment–but finding nothing definitive until now.

I realize now that an important part of my search was for my original voice. I don't know how many lifetimes it has taken for me to hear its quiet promptings through the cacophony of beliefs and admonitions and dogma and restrictions that bombarded my human lives, but as

I learned to become still, in those quiet moments a small voice, different from the rest, began to emerge.

Its influence was subtle; an insight here and there; a thread of understanding that began to weave its way into the living tapestry of my awareness. It spoke of truth, of love and compassion and gentleness and acceptance while teaching me to recognize wisdom and true knowledge through insights that led to deeper understanding. It winced and often cried against mean-spiritedness and bigotry and cruelty and yearned for peace and harmony for all. This voice recognized the need for each individual to explore and come to their own understanding, knowing that one must find and often wrestle with dark and painful densities before they are ready for their original voice to begin to emerge.

I was guided to learn that this is a special and important time in our planet's history as we are on a course that will bring us to the most profound discovery ever to be made known to humanity. Those who are open and ready to recognize this great truth will be given the opportunity to consciously leap onto the transformational trajectory.

We have only just begun. My awareness is expanding to recognize the limitlessness being offered and to yearn for the adventures and explorations Infinity holds, waiting for us once our access to the Multi-verse is restored.

We begin this next phase of our journey by traversing the bridge from the old ego-driven paradigm to the new paradigm guided by heart-centeredness where it is scientifically proven without a doubt that we are Infinite Beings, and we can finally recognize and embrace our true identity.

I AM Sovereign
WE ARE Integral
WE ARE SECU's
(Sovereign Entities of the Central Universe!)

APPENDIX A

GLOSSARY OF WORDS AND TERMS FOUND IN THE WINGMAKERS MATERIALS THAT ARE USED IN THIS BOOK

ANIMUS & Animus

IN THIS BOOK YOU WILL find two uses of the word <u>animus</u> that require two separate definitions. There is also a definition of animus that means the same as animosity, i.e., hostility or ill feeling. I won't be using the word in that context; I will only be using this word in the two contexts described below.

To differentiate between them, when the word appears in all caps— ANIMUS—it is alluding to the word as the *WingMakers Materials* use it. When it appears spelled normally and in italics—*Animus*—it is being used in the Jungian sense of being the inner male of the female.

ANIMUS—This definition is found in the glossary of the e-paper "The Energetic Heart: Its Purpose in Human Destiny." [288]

> The ANIMUS as depicted in the WingMakers Materials are a synthetic extraterrestrial race that desire to become soul carriers. They lack the biology and sensorial system to house the subtle frequencies of a soul. They desire to engineer their race's future genetics with the help of human genetics. Because of their superior mental capacity, they have become aligned to the economic powers on earth—as advisors and technology enablers.

In the body of the e-paper, James elaborates further on his definition of ANIMUS:

> The ANIMUS are a part of the mythological expression of Lucifer or evil incarnate. They operate in conjunction with organizations bent on control of

---

[288] Mahu, James, "The Energetic Heart: Its Purpose in Human Destiny," *WingMakers*, 6 Heart Virtues, <u>https://wingmakers.com/writings/sixheartvirtues/the-energetic-heart/</u>

the earth and their inhabitants. They are not exclusively extraterrestrial, they are here among us. By the standards of good and evil they are evil because they believe in the supremacy of the mind and its abilities to engineer social and economic outcomes for their benefit by manipulating the masses of humanity and exploiting the planet's resources.

In Jungian terminology *Animus* is the archetype of reason and spirit in women. This is the male aspect of the female psyche, as the anima is the female aspect of the male psyche. Jung on *Animus*:

> Woman is compensated by a masculine element and therefore her unconscious has, so to speak, a masculine imprint. This results in a considerable psychological difference between men and women, and accordingly I have called the projection-making factor in women the *animus*, which means mind or spirit. [289]

> The animus is the deposit, as it were, of all woman's ancestral experiences of man - and not only that, he is also a creative and procreative being, not in the sense of masculine creativity, but in the sense that he brings forth something we might call... the spermatic word. [290]

ANNUNAKI

The story of the Annunaki can be found in greater detail than is related in Chapter One by reading "The Fifth Interview of Dr. Neruda" [291] and "Project Camelot Interview." [292] Both provide important information and realizations not found anywhere else.

I also found some interesting historical material about the Annunaki taken from the Sumerian Tablets in *The Lost Book of Enki* by Zecharia Sitchin. [293]

[289] Jung, Carl, *The Syzygy: Anima and Animus*, Collected Works, 9ii, par. 28f. http://carl-jung.net/animus.html
[290] Jung, Carl, *Anima and Animus*, Collected Works 7, par. 336, http://carl-jung.net/animus.html
[291] Mahu, James, "The Fifth Interview," *WingMakers*, Neruda Interviews, https://www.wingmakers.com/content/neruda-interviews/
[292] Mahu, James, "Project Camelot Interview," *WingMakers*, Interviews, https://www.wingmakers.com/content/resources/
[293] Sitchin, Zecharia, *The Lost Book of Enki*, http://thelostbookofenki.blogspot.com/

Some interesting ideas are offered by Jan Erik Sigdell in his article "Is Yahweh an Annunaki?"[294] If one chooses to read this fascinating and informative article, I offer one caveat—I would question his definition of the Elohim as part of the Annunaki. My understanding from my own research into the *WingMakers Materials* reveals the Elohim and The Shining Ones (also known as the Atlanteans) to actually be the WingMakers, the original beings on this earth prior to the arrival of the Annunaki and other extra- terrestrial species. The Atlanteans initially collaborated with the Annunaki.

In Sigdell's article, the Annunaki created Adam and Eve and passed themselves off as the supreme deities over them and their progeny. Anu was the ruler of this civilization and flaunted himself as the one God of this world, and his offspring were also considered gods. In Genesis 6:2 and 6:4 we read:

> that the sons of God saw the daughters of men that they were fair; and they took them wives of all they chose…When the sons of God came in unto the daughters of men and they bare children to them, the same became mighty men which were of old, men of renown.

There are some who believe that these "gods" actually used a form of artificial insemination to impregnate these daughters of men. However it worked is up to interpretation, but the story, as all myths do, may hold some important concepts for us to consider.

I am thinking the whole Virgin Birth archetype may have originated with the "gods" taking themselves wives from the daughters of men or simply impregnating them, and thus a "god" would impregnate a human virgin. Whether or not we take this literally as living as man and wife in the physical sense with these "gods" or through some kind of artificial impregnation, this could be the origin of the Virgin Birth Archetype. These "Virgin Births" brought forth kings and the ruling class.

There is some speculation that the lineage of rulers down through the ages are from those mixed bloodlines. They would be of "royal" Annunaki blood, and to this day, royals try very hard to keep that bloodline as pure as they can.

The book *Slave Species of the Gods: The Secret Mission of the Annunaki and Their Mission on Earth* by Michael Tellinger[295] has a wonderful chapter titled "Slaves and Spies" that brings the Old Testament to life and offers a compelling story of how humans learned to fear god.

---

[294] Sigdell, Jan Erik, "Is Yahweh an Annunaki?" *ThreadReader,* Thread by @SouledOutWorld, Aug.16, 2010, https://threadreaders.com/thread/1247065107303215104

[295] Tellinger, Michael, *Slave Species of the Gods: The Secret Mission of the Annunaki and Their Mission on Earth,* Bear and Company. 2nd Edition, 2012.

I am of the belief that the *WingMakers Material* presents a huge lost piece of the puzzle of our ancient origins and our future. When I read Mr. Tellinger's book, keeping all that I have learned about the *WingMakers Material* in mind (as he does not mention that information), I was able to fill in many missing pieces of this intricate and complex puzzle. Taking the above into consideration, I found Mr. Tellinger's book to be a well- researched and fascinating read.

BEHAVIORAL INTELLIGENCE

A definitive description of what behavioral intelligence is can be found in the "April 2008 James Mahu Interview"[296] between James and Mark Hempel:

> Behavioral Intelligence is the ability to self-manage the coherence of the mind and heart to create emotions that are balanced and resilient. This isn't about sentimental emotions or passionate reactions to the wrongs committed by the powers that be—as if we need to start a revolution. Rather, it is a steadfast, inner conviction to seek the expression of the heart virtues in every affair of our lives. I want to be clear, heart virtues are not emotions. They're not thoughts. *They're behaviors.* Coherence contributes to Behavioral Intelligence.

ENERGETIC HEART

> Across all dimensions of space there exists a primary field of vibration or quantum primacy. This field is non-physical but informs the physical. It exists independent of the physical structures of existence and is known among Lyricus teachers as the Underivative Information Structures (UIS).
>
> UIS are sub-quantum and represent the primary blueprint for living systems and inorganic matter. It is the UIS that gives rise to the quantum fields that interpenetrate planets, stars, galaxies, and the universe at large. It is the communication field of life that connects the non-local and the local, the individual and the collective, the one and the infinite. The energetic heart is the non-physical component of UIS that is the entryway or portal from UIS to the intuitive and intelligence centers of the soul carrier or

---

[296] "April 2008 James Interview," *WingMakers*, Writings, WingMakers Tools, https://wingmakers.com/writings/wingmakerstools/

human instrument. In a sense it is the subquantum blueprint of the physical heart. [297]

A succinct definition of the Energetic Heart:

The human physical Heart is a timespace extension and expression of the quantum energetic heart. This energetic heart transmits and expresses the light of love as six heart virtues."[298]

In a note written on 8.8.07 titled "A Shift of Heart,"[299] James describes the new frequencies of the Energetic Heart as "… allied to concepts like clarity, coherence, precision, clear-headedness, efficiency of flow, intuitive presence, synchronicity and the ever-present connectedness of life."

EVENT STRINGS

The following is an excerpt of an illustration of an event string from *Collected Works of the WingMakers, Volume 1*, p. xxv.[300]

Before you read further, ask yourself the following question: "Did I—on my own merits—arrive at this position of reading these words I now read:" Think carefully.

Remember how you found this book and then this specific page? It was not an accident. It was an orchestrated event string. Event strings are engineered from multiple sets of consciousness, and thus the answer to the question posed above is "no." It was not on your own merits, but in cooperation with other forms of consciousness that you are here now.

Consider the planet's population of 6.2 billion people. How many will be reading these same words as you are now? One hundred? One thousand? Ten

[297] Mahu, James, "The Energetic Heart: Its Purpose in Human Destiny," *WingMakers*, 6 Heart Virtues, https://wingmakers.com/writings/sixheartvirtues/the-energetic-heart/
[298] Berges, John, *Eventtemples.com*
[299] Mahu, James, *Eventtemples.com*. When you create an account with Event Temples, you will have access to a section called "My Journey" where James has written notes. The quote is an excerpt from one of those notes.
[300] Mahu, James and John Berges, *Collected Works of the WingMakers, Volume I*, edited by John Berges, Egg Harbor, NJ: Planetwork Press, 2013

thousand? One hundred thousand? One million? It depends on the power of an event-string. It depends on the power of the consciousnesses that activate the event-string. It depends on the resonance of the consciousnesses that co-create the event-strings. But mostly, it depends on the alignment of the event-string with the will of First Source.

Truly, we tell you, it does not matter as to the numbers. The calculus of spirit is not numeric in nature, but instead, it is the quality of feeling clear and connected with First Source. This is the nature of this specific event-string. It is designed to have this effect, and to enable those who achieve this feeling to broadcast it to the entire planet's population in methods that we are woefully inadequate to describe in words. However, it is accurate to say that this event-string will touch the planet at a more comprehensive level than you can imagine.

There are different varieties of event-strings. Some are more dependent on external forces than an intermingling of cooperatively functioning consciousnesses. Some are more personal in nature as in the case of a soul's birth or passing, while others are designed for universal functions. Some are designed to be catalytic while others are preventative in nature.

We want to assure you that as you read these words there are changes in your consciousness that are occurring that will clarify your connection to First Source, and enable you to broadcast this clarity. The broadcasting of this enhanced clarity is not through words or even actions; so much as it is in the vision that you hold within your mind and heart.

This vision is assisted in the paintings associated with this book. They are symbols you can hold in your mind's eye. There will be one image or symbol that will beckon you. Take this image into your mind as if it were a key to the locked door that has stood between you and First Source. Similarly, there will be a word or phrase that will beckon you, hold this in your heart. These will activate the event-strings contained in this experience that was designed in small part by you, and in large part by a collective of consciousnesses that you may refer to as the WingMakers.

GENETIC MIND

The definition of the Genetic Mind is very lengthy. The following are excerpts from the "WingMakers Glossary:" [301]

> The genetic mind is the equivalent of a universal belief system that penetrates, to varying degrees, the human instrument of all entities. In some, it immobilizes their ability to think original thoughts and feel original feelings. In most, it entrains their belief system to harmonize with the accepted belief systems of the Hierarchy. In a few, it exerts no significant force nor has any bearing on the development of their personal belief system....The genetic mind is different from the subconscious or universal mind as it is sometimes referred to in your psychology texts, in that the genetic mind has a peculiar focus on the accumulated beliefs of all the people on a planet from its most distance past to its present time. These accumulated beliefs are actually manipulations of the Hierarchy, which imprint on the genetic Mind in order to cast the boundaries of what is acceptable to believe....All the other dimensions are connected to the genetic mind and have no ongoing connection to Source Reality. The genetic mind, as an intermediary and reflection of Source Reality is completely and utterly inept. This is all part of the primal blueprint that designs the evolutionary pathway of a species through time. The genetic mind acts as a buffer for the developing species to experience separation from Source Reality. In this way, the human instrument is appropriately entangled in time, space and the illusions of a disempowered belief system.

In the "Q and A from WingMakers Forum: Q 64-S3," [302] James gives us more information in this answer to a question about the Genetic Mind:

> The Genetic Mind is a repository; it is not an active "user" of its own resources. It is more akin to a library and its patrons are the individual human minds that, in varying degrees have access to its books.

[301] Mahu, James, "WingMakers Glossary," *WingMakers*, WingMakers Tools, http://wingmakers.com/wp-content/uploads/2020/08/WingMakers-Glossary-optimized.pdf (downloadable file) Also in *Collected Works* of the WingMakers, *Volume 1*

[302] Mahu, James, "Q and A from WingMakers Forum," *WingMakers*, WingMakers Tools, http://wingmakers.com/wp-content/uploads/2020/08/Q-A-from-WingMakers-Forum-to-James- optimized.pdf (downloadable)

In the "Q and A from WingMakers Forum: Q 71-S3," [303] James describes the Genetic Mind as

> organic, dynamic, and always changing. In other words, there is no representative "snapshot."

According to James, the OLIN technology or One Language Intelligence Network will become the standard operating system for all the world's computer-based systems. It will be fundamental in developing a global culture and instrumental in revolutionizing the Genetic Mind's global construct as well as fragmenting it so that it will become unable to exert a unified force upon humans. This will help to usher in the transformation/mastership model of existence. When this happens, the Genetic Mind will transform and become the leader of transformation for entities upon Earth instead of the barrier force it has always been. [304]

GRAND PORTAL, THE

> The irrefutable scientific discovery of the Wholeness Navigator (in some places in the WMM the Grand Portal is defined as the irrefutable discovery of the soul) and how it lives and performs its functions within the human instrument. The Grand Portal is the most profound discovery of a humanoid species because it establishes the species as a member of the galactic community. This discovery usually coincides with the third phase of the OLIN technology, which ultimately morphs into the Sovereign Integral Network.

> The Grand Portal is a lens through which humanity may observe Source Reality and communicate therein. The Grand Portal is the apex discovery of humanity and ushers in profound change to all sectors of the population. It conjoins science, metaphysics, art and the superuniverse, placing humanity in a position to embrace all dimensions of the multiverse while existing in the third dimension. [305]

---

[303] Ibid.
[304] Mahu, James, "WingMakers Glossary," *WingMakers*, WingMakers Tools, http://wingmakers.com/wp-content/uploads/2020/08/WingMakers-Glossary-optimized.pdf (downloadable file)
Also in *Collected Works of the WingMakers, Volume 1*
[305] Ibid.

James Mahu's novels *Ancient Arrow Project,*[306] *Quantusum,* and *The Dohrman Prophecy* all have the Grand Portal discovery woven into each story, and when one reads these books, the significance of the Grand Portal becomes more deeply understood. All of these books can be purchased from Planetwork Press. [307]

In the "Q and A from WingMakers Forum: Q. 24-S3," [308] James provides the following answer about the significance of the Grand Portal Discovery:

> Every evolutionary system is designed to ultimately transform into an innovative system with a new, but related purpose. Evolutionary systems have a distinctive culmination that is the catalyst that enables the transformation to occur. In the case of humanity's present evolutionary system, the discovery of the Grand Portal is the distinctive culmination, and when it occurs, it will shift the evolutionary system from a human species/planetary focus to an interdimensional species/intergalactic focus base on humanity's ability to use the Grand Portal as an interface to the Sovereign Integral Network.
>
> The responsible application of the Grand Portal will fall to the disciples of the Sacred Path to faithfully execute. All of the training, preparation, and sacrifice of today is designed to enable the disciples of the future to responsibly manage and protect the findings of the Grand Portal…

HOLOGRAM OF DECEPTION (HOD)

This is a term that describes the bubble humanity is trapped in. Everything within our world is a part of this hologram. Our senses are designed to perceive this hologram and our minds are programmed from the Genetic Mind through our belief systems to maintain this deception. [309]

[306] Mahu, James and John Berges, *Collected Works of the WingMakers, Volume I,* edited by John Berges, Egg Harbor, NJ: Planetwork Press, 2013.

[307] Planetwork Press, https://planetworkpress.com/pwpcart/index.php

[308] Mahu, James, "Q and A from WingMakers Forum," *WingMakers,* WingMakers Tools, http://wingmakers.com/wp-content/uploads/2020/08/Q-A-from-WingMakers-Forum-to-James- optimized.pdf (downloadable)

[309] Mahu, James, "The Fifth Interview," *WingMakers,* Neruda Interviews, https://www.wingmakers.com/content/neruda-interviews/

HUMAN INSTRUMENT

The human instrument consists of three principal components: The biological (physical body), the emotional, and the mental. These three distinct tools of perception, in aggregate, represent the vehicle of the individuated spirit as it interacts with the physical dimension of time, space, energy and matter. [310]

In other papers of the WingMakers Materials, the Human Instrument is likened to a space suit. They were designed to be soul carriers in the physical world and to provide a physical vehicle to house the soul on the physical plane. The Human Instrument is mainly the creation of the Annunaki and was initially created to be slaves and mine gold for the Annunaki.

HUMAN MIND SYSTEM (HMS)

Human Mind System is the secret framework for the suppression of the Sovereign Integral. It is separated into three primary functions— the unconscious or genetic mind—the repository of all humanity; the subconscious is the repository of the family bloodlines, and the conscious is the repository of the individual.

The HMS is the most opaque and distorted veil that has stood between humanity and its true self, perverting its self-expression within the domains we call reality.

In the "Project Camelot Interview," [311]James describes the components of the HMS and explains how each component plays a part in the suppression of the Sovereign Integral. To truly understand the HMS and how it works, it is worth taking the time to read Answer 2 from James in the "Project Camelot Interview." It is a detailed and very helpful explanation and contains a diagram illustrating all the components of the Human Mind System.

---

[310] Mahu, James, "WingMakers Glossary," *WingMakers*, WingMakers Tools, http://wingmakers.com/wp-content/uploads/2020/08/WingMakers-Glossary-optimized.pdf (downloadable file)
Also in *Collected Works of the WingMakers, Volume 1*
[311] Mahu, James, "Project Camelot Interview," *WingMakers*, Interviews, https://www.wingmakers.com/content/resources/

INTERFACE ZONE

"Lyricus Discourse Five - The Interface Zone" [312]gives in-depth information and explains some of its important characteristics as well as its relationship with our DNA:

> The Interface Zone is the aspect of your consciousness that interacts with the species with which you share a common biology. It is physically contained in your DNA, which acts as a node within a vast network that is ultimately connected to First Source.

LYRICUS DISCOURSES

In the Lyricus section of the *WingMakers* website (wingmakers.com), all six Discourses are available and other material about Lyricus. They can also be accessed through the WingMakers Tools section.

A powerful exercise that I highly recommend is to read each discourse monthly for a year. You will be surprised at what you see in each reading that you don't remember seeing or understanding before. The impact is cumulative over time. You can also access the *Six Lyricus Discourses* and *John Berges Commentaries on Lyricus Discourses* from Planetwork Press.[313]

MODELS OF EXISTENCE

The models briefly defined below are found in the *Ancient Arrow Project,* "Chamber Two - The Shifting Modes of Existence." [314] I have created a table of the three models that can be found in Appendix B - Models of Existence.

This philosophy paper is a deep and lengthy one that deserves to be read and studied. I will be giving a very brief definition of the Models of Existence here, but to gain the full impact of this information, it is best to read the paper in its entirety. In addition to being

---

[312] Mahu, James, "Lyricus Discourse Five - The Interface Zone," *WingMakers*, Lyricus, https://wingmakers.com/writings/lyricus/discourse5/

[313] Planetwork Press, https://planetworkpress.com/pwpcart/index.php

[314] Mahu, James, "Chamber Two - The Shifting Modes of Existence," *WingMakers*, Philosophy, https://wingmakers.com/writings/philosophy/chambertwo/

available on the *WingMakers* Website (wingmakers.com), it is also included in *Collected Works of the WingMakers, Volume 1.*[315]

<u>Evolution/Saviorship Model</u> (Dominant Model of the Hierarchy)

The saviorship concept results from the feelings of inadequacy that constantly surge within the mass consciousness of humanity through the genetic mind. These feelings are related to the fragmentation of the human instrument and its inability –while fragmented—to fully grasp its wholeness perspective and reach into its divine origins and accept itself as equal with First Source. Thus ensues the seemingly endless search to be saved from the inadequacy and insecurity that result from the fragmentation of the human instrument. The motive to evolve consciousness derives from the feeling of being less than whole.

James goes on to explain in this paper that when we enter a human instrument at birth, we are immediately fragmented into a physical, emotional, and mental spectrum of perception and expression. The growing human is carefully conditioned to perceive the world from a separation-from- wholeness perspective. We have a drive within us to search out our Wholeness and our Source, and this drive fuels our explorations in the physical world and our seeking of a savior. This model is a teacher/student form of existence. Basically, this is all a part of the Grand Experiment as explained in the "Chamber Two - The Shifting Modes of Existence" [316] paper:

Transformation/Mastership Model (Dominant Model of Source Intelligence)

Prime Creator is connected to individuals, not organizations; thus individuals are connected to Source—intermediary not required. Transformation is recognition of accelerated pathways that bypass the hierarchy and leads to sovereign mastership reliance on internal promptings for spiritual transformation. This model is the next step as we begin to turn to internal promptings rather than external leaders.

---

[315] Mahu, James and John Berges, *Collected Works of the WingMakers, Volume I*, edited by John Berges, Egg Harbor, NJ: Planetwork Press, 2013.
[316] Mahu, James, "Chamber Two - The Shifting Modes of Existence," *WingMakers*, Philosophy, https://wingmakers.com/writings/philosophy/chambertwo/

SOVEREIGN INTEGRAL: I AM SOVEREIGN WE ARE INTEGRAL/ I AM WE ARE

> Sovereign Integral Consciousness is a state of consciousness whereby the entity and all its various forms of expression and perception are integrated as a conscious wholeness. This is a state of consciousness that all entities are evolving towards, and at some point, each will reach a state of transformation that allows the entity and its instruments of experience (i.e. the human instrument) to become an integrated expression that is aligned and in harmony with Source Intelligence. [317]

I found extensive information about the Sovereign Integral scattered throughout the "Project Camelot Interview" [318] which I personally see as the most definitive information James has offered about what the Sovereign Integral is and how to attain that state of consciousness until his most recent release: *The Sovereign integral, A New Model of Existence* released in the spring of 2022. This paper expands on the concept of the Sovereign Integral to an entire new level of understanding. It can be found at www.jamesmahu.com.

I read a beautiful passage in Larry Dossey, MD's book *One Mind* (p.208) that describes the Sovereign Integral state of I AM WE ARE:

> ...it is never a question of the One Mind versus the individual mind, or the collective versus the personal. There is no 'versus,' but an 'and.' The opposites go together, defining, illuminating, and invigorating each other.

TRIBUTARY ZONES

Tributary Zones are catalysts for awakening the Wholeness Navigator within the human instrument for the purpose of helping humanity discover the Grand Portal. They are separated into three distinct categories:

- Superuniverse-Based Tributary Zones

---

[317] Mahu, James, "WingMakers Glossary," *WingMakers*, WingMakers Tools, http://wingmakers.com/wp-content/uploads/2020/08/WingMakers-Glossary-optimized.pdf (downloadable file)
Also in *Collected Works of the WingMakers, Volume 1*
[318] Mahu, James, "Project Camelot Interview," *WingMakers*, Interviews, https://www.wingmakers.com/content/resources/

- Galactic-Based Tributary Zones
- Planetary-Based Tributary Zones

The Superuniverse Tributary Zones are seven in number and constitute the repository of required knowledge in order to discover the Grand Portal for a life-bearing planetary system within that particular superuniverse. These are the archetypes for all other Tributary Zones—either planetary or galactic.

Galactic Tributary Zones are also seven in number and closely resemble their superuniverse counterparts. They are gradually transposed by specialists from the Central Race, and are established near or within the galactic core of a life-bearing galaxy possessing sufficient numbers of intelligent, sentient life. Galactic Tributary Zones are ultimately transposed to a planetary level as encoded sensory data streams. Generally this occurs shortly after the planetary system establishes its first phase of the OLIN Technology or global communications network.

Planetary Tributary Zones are a diverse set of artistic and text- based contributions created by members of a species who have sufficiently interacted with the Galactic Tributary Zones in their dream state. In some instances, these may include works from other planetary systems within the same galaxy. Generally, Planetary Tributary Zones are created in the form of books, art, poetry and motion pictures. They are not encoded sensory data streams as in the case of the Galactic Tributary Zones, and they are focused on the preparation of the species. [319]

WHOLENESS NAVIGATOR

All human life is embedded with a Wholeness Navigator. It is the core wisdom. It draws the human instrument to perceive fragmentary existence as a passageway into wholeness and unity.[320]

A brief list of some of the characteristics of the Wholeness Navigator:

- The Wholeness Navigator pursues wholeness above all else.
- The Wholeness Navigator is at the heart of the entity consciousness.
- The seed vision of the Wholeness Navigator is equal to First Source.

---

[319] Mahu, James, "WingMakers Glossary," *WingMakers*, WingMakers Tools, http://wingmakers.com/wp-content/uploads/2020/08/WingMakers-Glossary-optimized.pdf (downloadable file)
Also in *Collected Works of the WingMakers, Volume 1*
[320] Ibid.

- The Wholeness Navigator pulls the human instrument into alignment with the entity consciousness where it can view its role as an extension of the entity consciousness into terra-earth, and the entity consciousness as an extension of the human instrument into Source Reality.
- The preceptors of the Wholeness Navigator consist primarily of the secret root. This is the subtle carrier of information that leads you to see the One That Is All and the All That Is One. This is a facet of First Source that is made manifest in the human instrument as a means of attracting the human instrument to the life of the Sovereign Integral Consciousness.

APPENDIX B

SQUARES[321]

THIS EXERCISE WILL HELP US explore the idea of how polarities work in our lives. Understanding how I became trapped in polarities was a game changer for me.

Some of the most powerful forces at work in the physical world are the forces of duality. Our current understanding implies that we cannot stay on the planet without the tension of the opposites that maintains a sort of equilibrium. At the same time, there is much talk about the idea of unity, of wholeness: a desire to come together and no longer feel/be separate with the promise of a new paradigm waiting to be birthed upon this planet; a paradigm of harmony between the polarities that has the potential of bringing us into a kind of unity never before experienced in the material world.

Polarization helps us to stay in the fray of human games, and being tossed to and fro emotionally is certainly a way to experience a myriad of feelings. The addictive highs and lows of a "roller coaster" life can become away of feeling "alive." I have heard it said about emotional pain that "at least when I am in pain, I know I am alive."

What I have come to understand is that <u>awareness</u> of the polarity game is a key to unlock the door to the secrets of how to move beyond this game and still have access to our emotions without being swallowed by them. So how would that work? How can we become aware of the polarity game while we are playing it, and what happens if we do?

One of the most powerful exercises that I have ever utilized to understand polarization I learned from Leslie Temple-Thurston, a spiritual teacher and founder of CoreLight. [322] I studied with her for several years and was at a workshop with her where we learned to do Squares. This exercise helped me to realize the importance of understanding how the polarities affect us in the physical world and how to maintain a sense of unity in a world of diversity. I think that understanding the distracting power of polarities is an important step in the process of attaining Sovereign Integral Consciousness.

---

[321] Most of this Appendix is imported from my former book *Breaking Free From the Tyranny of Beliefs: A Revolution in Consciousness*

[322] *CoreLight Dedicated to the Awakening of the Global Heart*, www.corelight.org This organization offers courses on Spiritual Training, Inspired Teachings, and Sacred Activism. Leslie Temple Thurston and her Co- Founder Brad Laughlin are dedicated to helping the Earth by Awakening Consciousness.

Leslie Temple-Thurston's book *The Marriage of Spirit* [323] goes into great detail about Squares if you care to explore this technique in greater depth. It is a profound experiential process to aid in understanding the impact and trap of polarities.

Basically, take any issue or circumstance you are dealing with or need to resolve and diagram the polarization. The procedure goes like this: take a large piece of paper and divide it into four equal sections, two above and two below. I like to use a large piece of plain newsprint so there will be plenty of writing space. Now define the issue you want to work with, for example: scarcity, and then find a word or phrase that means the opposite for you; in this case we will say it is abundance. Whatever word or phrase you use, your first step to do the square is to find its opposite. If you are dealing with an incident, you may want to write it down and see what words in your story hold an emotional charge and find the polarities in those.

At the top of the upper left section you write "Desire to have (abundance)" or "Desire to be (abundant)"; at the top of the upper right section you write "Fear of (abundance)"; at the top of the bottom left section you write "Desire (to live in scarcity)"; and at the top of the bottom right section you write "Fear (of living in scarcity)".

This is your box or Squares:

Desire to have abundance	Fear of abundance
Want to do anything I want to do without money worries	Worry about taking too much from the environment
Want to travel, have a beautiful home	Fear of the responsibility that comes with abundance
	It isn't spiritual to be abundant
Desire to live in scarcity	Fear of living in scarcity
Learn to be resourceful	Fear of losing what I have
Learn to live off the land	Fear of being homeless
Restrain impulse to be greedy	
Easier for a rich man to get through the eye of a needle than to get into heaven	

[323] Temple-Thurston, Leslie with Brad Laughlin, *The Marriage of Spirit: Enlightened Living in Today's World*, Santa Fe NM: CoreLight Publications, 2000

Under each category you write everything you can think about relating to the polarity you are exploring: every reason and feeling—anything that comes to mind that fits. In the box above are some seed ideas to help you get started. You might begin by exploring your core beliefs for clues about how your psyche is programmed about abundance and scarcity. Include any beliefs in mass consciousness that come to mind because if you think them, you probably believe them on some level. You may not be able to do all this work in one sitting. Often I start a square and work with it for a few days before I feel I have finished.

You will eventually come to a place where you feel confident you have listed most or all of the thoughts and feelings you have about this issue.

Once this happens, you may feel an "aha" right away, but don't feel you have failed if you don't. It takes time for things to gel in your consciousness. Give yourself that time.

The idea is to bring to conscious awareness all the thoughts and feelings you have about each of the four quadrants. Be brutally honest with yourself; the deeper you examine each detail, the more powerful the shift will be when you complete the exercise. Now look at all the ways you have boxed yourself in regarding this issue.

When we are caught up in a polarity, we will always find ourselves in one of the quadrants and will continually bounce from one quadrant to another until we have freed ourselves from the polarity.

This is the game of polarity we play by mentally and/or emotionally bouncing back and forth between these categories every time this issue comes up in our life. As long as a polarity is an issue, we will be living in one of the four quadrants and waiting for the other three to engage. We are literally boxed in!

If you find yourself living a recurring drama in your life, you can be sure that a polarity issue or two is involved.

I find it archetypically interesting that the expression "Think outside the box" is used to represent a more innovative approach to problem solving. It may be that our deeper Selves are trying to give us profound clues about the direction we need to take to attain liberation.

By seeing all sides of the polarity as the illusion that it is, you will be able to bring yourself back to a zero or null point. You will see how you have trapped yourself in the box. When you are fully engaged in the process of completing a square, in a sense you are diffusing the energy or charge of that polarity in your life. You see the game you are playing within the polarity with great clarity.

Once this sense of completion comes, you can offer your discoveries to Higher Self, Spirit, to God, to Source—whatever you relate to personally— and then go on about your business. You have released the energy of this polarity's hold on you.

Within a very short time (in my experience it happens immediately to about 72 hours), a shift will be felt. It is as though the issue doesn't hold as firm a grasp on your psyche any longer, or you feel a sense of peace about the issue that is different from what you felt before. My experience has been that the issue no longer holds a strong emotional charge that pulls me in one of the four directions. I feel complete and calm about the situation. I find that in some way the life experience I was involved in that drove me to do a square resolves and my perception changes.

THE SQUARE OF LIFE AND DEATH

Doing a square on life and death provided me with one of my most profound breakthroughs. When I did the polarities and Squares about life and death, I came to see life and death as a huge hypnotic overlay, the most powerful illusion of all. It was an amazing experience at the time, a visceral feeling of astonishment as I saw the Square for the game that it is.

Everything we do is linked to one of the four categories. We have learned that an overlay is an illusion. Life and death is the overlay in which we have become trapped and in which we play out all other polarities. When we "get it" that ego life in duality is an illusion, and that we exist beyond that, death may not entirely lose its sting, but it makes the idea a bit easier to live with. That is not to say that we still don't mourn the passing of loved ones, but we face death with a totally different mindset than when we are locked into the limiting and/or terrifying beliefs taught to us through various sources who have appointed themselves as authorities on life and death matters.

What follows are the Squares and below them the polarities of life and death as I saw them. I have included my beliefs and some generic beliefs about each category in these tables. As you explore this duality, you may want to add more ideas or reasons of your own. There are no judgements about any observations in each quadrant. We all share similar thoughts and beliefs about these issues. It is good to see them all listed as a big picture.

Desire for life/desire to live	Fear of life/fear of living
• Explore human psychology	• Causes killings, murders, suicides
• Learn better ways of raising children	• Causes disease
• Children perpetuate our family line	• Unfulfillment of dreams
• Have children to enjoy and watch grow	• Poverty
• Enjoy the experience of love in all its manifestations	• Fear of loving for fear of losing
• Yearn for better love-joy-peace	• Stagnation, mediocrity
• Yearn for and create beauty	• Unwillingness to grow
• Facilitate humane goals and ideals	• Obsessions and compulsions

Desire for life/desire to live	Fear of life/fear of living
• Idealism	• Blame others and God no responsibility for life events
• Search for God or The Light	• Victimization
• Search for Wholeness	• Tyrannical behavior
• Desire to grow and learn	• Must control surroundings and others to feel safe
• Desire to belong	• Create boundaries to feel safe
• Hedonism-experience as much of life as possible	• Afraid of risk
• Overcome adversity	• Cynicism and doubt
• Work for a better world	• Suppress dreams and personal drives
• Embrace shadow and overcome it	• Fear of what people will say
• Constant wrestling with one's finiteness	• Fear of pain, afraid to love
• Creates war	• Constant wrestling with one's finiteness
• creates the war industry	• Creates war
• Express creativity	• Creates the war industry
• Have experiences	• Tyrannized by life
• Experiment	• Search for god and redemption
• Travel, Food, Sex	• Self-sabotage behaviors
• Friends	• Judge self and others for everything
• Long philosophical conversations	• Seek monastic or cloistered lifestyle to escape life
• Accept both positive and negative experiences as part of life without devastating self-judgment	• Go to great lengths to protect oneself
• Seek enlightenment to expand enjoyment and experience of life	• Find someone or something to blame for all the adversities in our lives
• Go to great lengths to protect oneself	• Avoid taking responsibility for life
• Experience nature in all its splendor	• Suppress life
• Comprehend the importance of preserving natural resources	• Creates war, creates the war industry
• Tired of living	• Creates violent movies to defuse the fear of death
• Run from the promise of life	• Have children to perpetuate oneself
• Refuse to take responsibility for the issues in one's life	• Nightmares
• Let adversity overcome us so we want to die	• Over protectiveness with children
• Take risks that endanger the physical body	• Over cautious with every part of life.
• Obsession with violence	• Afraid to take risks.
• Become an outcast	• Tyrant, family hero, family clown

Desire for life/desire to live	Fear of life/fear of living
• No reason to live • Death has become our goal in trying to elude it. • Creates war, creates the war industry • Martyr, scapegoat, lost child • Tyrannized by life. • Creates the death care industry.	• Search for god and redemption • Fear of retribution in the afterlife • Go to great lengths to protect oneself • Search for wholeness • Creates the death care industry • Produces a life of limitation

This exercise helped me to see many polarities tied into this whole issue of life and death. By the time I finished, I had everything in the box below categorized into the following polarities:

POLARITIES OF LIFE AND DEATH	
Life	**Death**
Creative expression	Stops creative expression
Fears and runs from death	Takes away life
Encourages	Fears and runs from life
Renews	Discourages
Health	Decay and disease
Life is temporary	Death is certain
Life is away from god	Death takes us back to god
Life is an illusion	Death is real
Life is real	Death is an illusion
Life is to learn lessons	Learned lessons go with us in death
Unity as one finds wholeness	Separation from loved ones and earth
Separation from our greater self	Unite with greater self
Life is futile	Death is futile
Life is binding	Death releases the bonds of life

Life is being conscious	Death is being unconscious
Life is being unconscious	Death is being fully conscious
Life is growth, purpose	Death is release
Life is moving towards death	Death is rebirth into life
Life is responsibility, aging, issues of body and psyche, burdens and joys, decay.	Death is freedom from responsibility, old age, disease, burdens of life, and joy

APPENDIX C

THE EMERALD TABLET[324]

THE EMERALD TABLET IS A mysterious ancient artifact that has been inscribed with concepts that are essential to understanding Alchemy. It is believed by some that the Emerald Tablet was brought to the Egyptians by mysterious visitors over 12,000 years ago, but the actual source is not verified; therefore, many legends have grown up around it.

It is said that the original tablet was of emerald or green stone and was inscribed with Seven Rubrics believed to be the secrets of the universe. Its authorship is attributed to Hermes Trismegistus or Hermes the Thrice- Great. His name is derived from the Egyptian god of wisdom, Thoth, and his Greek counterpart, Hermes. Legend goes that the tablet was found in a cave tomb under the statue of Hermes in Tyana, clutched in the hands of the corpse of Hermes Trismegistus himself.

The oldest documentable source of the Emerald Tablet's text is the *Kitab sir al-haliqi* or *Book of the Secret of Creation and the Art of Nature*, an Arabic composite of earlier works, written in the 8th century AD and attributed to 'Balinas' or Pseudo-Apollonius of Tyana. Balinas tells a story of how he discovered the Emerald Tablet in a cave tomb. He claimed that it was originally written in Greek, but the original document no longer exists. Balinas' version of the text quickly became well-known and has been translated by various people over the centuries.

Dennis W. Hauck tells us that

> The Emerald Tablet is organized in seven rubrics or paragraphs. They are
> called rubrics (from the Latin rubeo, meaning "red") because, in the Latin

---

[324] Information about the Emerald Tablet for this appendix was utilized, quoted, or paraphrased from the following sources:

Dhwty, "The Legendary Emerald Tablet and its Secrets of the Universe," *Ancient Origins*, 11.14. 2019, https://www.ancient-origins.net/myths-legends/legendary-emerald-tablet-001956

Sisowath, Katrina, "Thoth Hermes Trismegistus and his Ancient School of Mysteries," *Ancient Origins*, 2.14.2015 https://www.ancient-origins.net/history-famous-people/thoth-hermes-trismegistus-and-his- ancient-school-mysteries-002676

Hauck, Dennis William, "The Emerald Tablet," http://azothalchemy.org/emerald tablet.htm

From this very concise and helpful article, I have imported the rubrics, and Hauck's explanation of the rubrics are below them to assist us with understanding them.

translations, the first letter of each paragraph was highlighted in red ink. It should be noted that when the tablet refers to the "Universe," it is talking about the material universe in which we live. When it speaks of the "Whole Universe," it is referencing not only the material universe (Below) but also the spiritual universe (Above). See if you can sense the secret formula hidden in the words of the Emerald Tablet as you read the following version.

THE RUBRICS OF THE EMERALD TABLET

- *In truth, without deceit, certain, and most veritable*
- *That which is Below corresponds to that which is Above, and that which is Above corresponds to that which is Below, to accomplish the miracles of the One Thing. And just as all things have come from this One Thing, through the meditation of One Mind, so do all created things originate from this One Thing, through Transformation.*
- *Its father is the Sun; its mother the Moon. The Wind carries it in its belly; its nurse is the Earth. It is the origin of All, the consecration of the Universe; its inherent Strength is perfected, if it is turned into Earth.*
- *Separate the Earth from Fire, the Subtle from the Gross, gently and with great Ingenuity. It rises from Earth to Heaven and descends again to Earth, thereby combining within Itself the powers of both the Above and the Below.*
- *Thus will you obtain the Glory of the Whole Universe. All Obscurity will be clear to you. This is the greatest Force of all powers because it overcomes every Subtle thing and penetrates every Solid thing.*
- *In this way was the Universe created. From this comes many wondrous Applications because this is the Pattern.*
- *Therefore am I called Thrice Greatest Hermes, having all three parts of the wisdom of the Whole Universe. Herein have I completely explained the Operation of the Sun.*

COMMENTARY ON THE RUBRICS BY MR. HAUCK

- ❖ The first rubric simply sets the tone of the documents and asks us to come to a higher awareness and become open to deeper truths.
- ❖ The second rubric presents the Doctrine of Correspondences, which describes a vertical relationship between the realm of spirit Above and the realm of matter Below. This is the so-called Vertical Axis of reality, which the alchemists felt they could enter

in their meditations. The Horizontal Axis is our normal material world. A wonderful example of experiencing the Vertical Axis is a work in the Corpus Hermeticum called the "Divine Pymander" (or "Divine Mind"). It is allegedly written by Hermes Trismegistus and describes his meeting with the Divine Mind and what it revealed to him about the nature of reality.

- ❖ The third rubric elaborates on the nature of the One Thing, which is the subject of the tablet. The alchemists have usually interpreted the One Thing to mean the First Matter or Universal Life Force, and this rubric describes its characteristics. The first two sentences of this rubric present the Four Elements in the order of Fire, Water, Air, and Earth. Associated with each of these elements are the first four operations of alchemy: Calcination, Dissolution, Separation, and Conjunction.

- ❖ The fourth rubric is the most mystical part of the Emerald Tablet and seems to be telling us how to enter the spiritual realm Above. It also describes the last three alchemical operations of Fermentation, Distillation, and Coagulation.

- ❖ The fifth rubric describes the result of the previous conditions, which is the purified Quintessence.

- ❖ The sixth rubric suggests that the previous rubrics have described a specific universal Pattern that leads to transformation on all levels of reality. It is not only the formula that the alchemist follows in his work, but also the overall pattern of nature in perfecting matter.

- ❖ The seventh and last rubric identifies the author of the tablet as "Thrice Greatest Hermes." Hermes is the Greek name of Thoth, who in the Roman tradition was known as Mercury. His Latin name is Hermes Trismegistus, which means "Thrice Greatest Hermes." Hermes (or Thoth) is thrice-greatest because he has gained knowledge on all three levels of reality: the physical plane, the mental plane, and the spiritual plane. He is now free of the cycle of rebirth and exists outside time. The Operation of the Sun is the complete explanation of the workings of the universe.

APPENDIX D
MODELS OF EXISTENCE

THE TABLE OF THE MODELS of Existence at the end of this Appendix is essentially an outline of "Chamber Two Philosophy: The Shifting Models of Existence." [325] Information to complete the definitions below and understanding of these models has also been taken from other cited sources, including "Chamber One Philosophy: Life Principles of the Sovereign Integral." (*Collected Works of the WingMakers, Volume I*, pp. 623-631.)

I created this table as a visual for myself so that I could get a picture of how these models might play out. I divided the models into three columns: Evolution/Saviorship Model, Transformation/Mastership Model, and Synthesis Model.

This table is a working comparison, and this is my analysis of the models so they might not be entirely accurate. Please keep that in mind if you choose to refer to this table.

I also imported the seven main beliefs of the Core Belief Matrix from my previous book [326] into this table. If there is a **CBM** in the box, it indicates this belief is one of those imports. I wanted to see how compatible they were with the evolution/saviorship model. I wrote about the CBM long before I came across the *WingMakers Material*, and doing this little exercise not only confirmed my observations of the pervasiveness of the CBM on the collective consciousness, but explained why.

For convenience sake I am also including the following definitions of some of the terms used in the table of these models so you have them for quick reference.

The Grand Experiment (GE):

> is the ongoing transformation and expansion of Source Intelligence through all entities in all dimensions of existence. It is the purpose of the GE to test alternative models of existence to determine the model that is best able to unify consciousness without impinging on the sovereignty of the entity and

---

[325] Mahu James and John Berges, "Chamber Two Philosophy: The Shifting Modes of Existence," *Collected Works of the WingMakers, Volume I*, pp. 632-641, edited by John Berges, Egg Harbor, NJ: Planetwork Press, 2013. Also Mahu, James, "The Shifting Modes of Existence," *WingMakers*, Philosophy, https://wingmakers.com/writings/philosophy/chambertwo/

[326] Batey, Lark Aleta, *Breaking Free from the Tyranny of Beliefs: A Revolution in Consciousness*, Balboa Press, A Division of Hay House, 1663 Liberty Drive, Bloomington In 47403, 2012

First Source. The GE has many stages and most of these different stages are being played out within the time space universe in order to prepare the universe for the impending expansion of Source Reality into all dimensions of existence. *Collected Works of the WingMakers, Volume I*, p. 636.

Evolution/Saviorship Model: This model is a tool of the hierarchy. It is designed to keep the human in separation.

When an entity initially enters a human instrument at birth it is immediately fragmented into a physical, emotional, and mental spectrum of perception and expression. From that day forward the entity is carefully conditioned to adapt to and navigate within the three-dimensional, five sensory context of terra-earth. In effect the entity purposely fragments its consciousness in order to experience separation from wholeness. *Collected Works of the WingMakers, Volume I*, p. 634.

Transformation/Mastership Model: This is the dominant model of Source Intelligence. This model works outside the hierarchy as the individual becomes activated and begins a transformation process that leads to mastership and becoming one's own savior.

In case of the transformation/mastership model of existence, its principal tenets are that the entity is limitless, deathless and sovereign. All information flows from Source Intelligence to the entity, and it is therefore the responsibility of the entity to become self- enlightened and self-liberated by attuning itself to Source Intelligence and 'detuning' itself from the Hierarchy. Each becomes their own master, and each transforms from a human being to a Sovereign Integral within the cradle of time and space. [327]

Synthesis Model: This model emerges out of the two previous ones.

This form of integration occurs when the entity fully explored the two models and develops a synthesis model that positions saviorship as an internal role of the entity to "save" itself, and not rely upon externals to perform the

---

[327] Mahu, James, "WingMakers Glossary," *WingMakers*, WingMakers Tools, http://wingmakers.com/wp-content/uploads/2020/08/WingMakers-Glossary-optimized.pdf Also in Collected Works *of the WingMakers*, Volume 1

liberating task. This act of self-sufficiency begins to integrate the saviorship idea with the mastership realization.[328]

The synthesis model is anchored first in the knowledge of who you are at the fundamental level. This requires you to understand and to the degree possible experience the individuated consciousness of your multi-faceted identity. When the Grand Portal is discovered the Individuated Consciousness will be dissected and made visible for the first time. Similar in some ways to when the human body was first dissected and its internal organs were named and their purpose identified. This is the dawning of the synthesis model of existence for humanity in general. Its chief feature to the general public is the sense of validation it brings to the belief systems of immortality and human interconnectedness.[329]

Hierarchy

…hierarchies of earth are the containers, or forms, through which the 'collective ego-personality' manifests. Consequently, at least relative to our planet, global hierarchical structures are personality-based, and embedded in the space-time dimension. Therefore, from the transcendent non-space-time dimension and perspective of the Sovereign Integral, there is no hierarchy because it is vibrating to the tone of equality. Hence, human hierarchies based on a spectrum comparing best and worst individuals do not enter into the Sovereign Integral's perspective. [330]

Tone Vibration of Equality (TVE): One has to do some reading and pondering to find the full meaning of the Tone Vibration of Equality. It is introduced in the "Chamber Two Philosophy" paper and then expounded on in various places as one journeys through the *WingMakers Material*. Let's begin with the "Chamber Two Philosophy" paper. The TVE

---

[328] Mahu, James, "The Shifting Modes of Existence," *WingMakers*, Philosophy, https://wingmakers.com/writings/philosophy/chambertwo/
Also in *Collected Works of the WingMakers*, Volume 1
[329] Berges, John, "Topical Arrangement of the Q & A Sessions with James", Q 56-S3, *Planetwork*, Articles, 11.5.05, revised 2.14.07, www.planetwork.co/pages/Articles.html#top_q_a (downloadable PDF)
[330] Berges, John, "Commentary on the Manifesto of the Sovereign Integral," *Collected Works of the WingMakers, Volume 1*, p. 594, Planetwork Press, Egg Harbor Township, NJ.

… is a vibration that holds together the three principles of the transformational experience:

- Universe relationship through gratitude,
- observance of Source in all things,
- and the nurturance of_life.

The application of these life-principles in a specific equation of conduct decouples an entity from the controlling elements of the hierarchy.

The three principles listed above are also the "Life Principles of the Sovereign Integral" which is the subject of the "Chamber One Philosophy" paper.

Another clue we find in Answer 10 of the Conscious Media Interview James did in November 2009. James was asked what the single most important lesson for humanity is at this time in our history. He answered:

…In a word practice. The practice of the art of living from the heart, and expressing the six heart virtues of appreciation, compassion, forgiveness, humility, understanding and valor are key expressions of the highest frequency on this planet: the vibration of equality. [331]

On page 224 of *The Dohrman Prophecy,* Simon explains to Joseph:

You see the heart virtues are intermingled as an expression of your state of consciousness. This is how your state of consciousness reflects your state of being. The state of being is your spiritual center, the place in which you leave your signature upon this world of spacetime, not as deeds or creations of materiality, but as a vibration.

Simon goes on to explain that this vibration

…conditions your spacetime to a higher tone, and this tone or vibration is equality, centered in love, and expressed through the heart virtues from which love extends. If only one person lived this way and everyone else was a godless heathen, then an opening is made in which the tone of equality and a

[331] "Conscious Media Interview," WingMakers, Interviews, https://wingmakers.com/about/interviews/conscious-media-interview/

higher dimensional understanding of love can occur for everyone…it opens the possibility of love upon this planet. Everything and I mean every single step of progress in the ascension of humanity began with a single human being who chose to express the virtues of their heart.[332]

Source Intelligence

…inhabits all fields of vibration as an extension of the Source. It is the emissary of First Source that interweaves with the hierarchy as its counter-balance. Source Intelligence is the factor of integrity and alignment, which ensures that the hierarchy is serving its purpose within the Primal Blueprint. Source Intelligence is, in effect, the "scientist" who oversees the Grand Experiment and establishes the criteria, selects the variables, monitors the results, and evaluates the alternative outcomes in the laboratory of time and space.[333]

EVOLUTION/ SAVIORSHIP MODEL *Hierarchical*	TRANSFORMATION/ MASTERSHIP MODEL *Individual connection to Source*	SYNTHESIS MODEL SOVEREIGNTY *I Am We Are*
• Hierarchy maintains control through teaching & organizations • Hierarchy unconnected to Source - intermediary required to access Source • Student-teacher ordering of Universe • Evolutionary model is an incremental time-based process	• Source is connected to individuals, not organizations, thus individuals are connected to Source • Intermediary not required. • Transformation model is a realization-based acceptance of this model	• Recognition of the two models and the process one undergoes within each one. • The combination of self-saviorship and detachment from the hierarchy initiates the synthesis model into manifestation.

---

[332] Mahu, James, *The Dorhman Prophecy*, Planetwork Press, Egg Harbor Township, NJ.
[333] Mahu, James, "The Shifting Modes of Existence," *WingMakers*, Philosophy, https://wingmakers.com/writings/philosophy/chambertwo/
Also in Collected Works *of the WingMakers*, Volume 1

EVOLUTION/ SAVIORSHIP MODEL *Hierarchical*	TRANSFORMATION/ MASTERSHIP MODEL *Individual connection to Source*	SYNTHESIS MODEL SOVEREIGNTY *I Am We Are*
Evolution is arduous and ongoing process of shifting positions within the hierarchy	*Transformation*-recognition of accelerated pathways bypass hierarchy and lead to sovereign mastership	Acknowledgement & appreciation of what it takes to become Sovereign in a world where dependence on the Hierarchy is pervasive
Reliance on externals for spiritual direction and development	Reliance on internal promptings for spiritual transformation	Recognition of external & internal promptings
Hierarchy maintains control through belief systems of manipulation, language, and ritual, including hierarchical ordering of society	• Tone vibration of equality is the way to access transformational pathways • Understanding that we all emerge from Source and into individuated energy frequency within a form	Transformation of hierarchical barriers of control into understanding and individual liberation
Motive to evolve comes from feelings of inadequacy and of less than	• We are all equal to Source • No one is "better than" another	Deepened understanding of the equality of our origins and existence
• Separation of Entity from Source • Sense of inequality between individual and Source • Pecking order of life on Earth	Understanding that Life's deeper meaning is an evolving dynamic intelligence that wears as many faces as there are life forms	• Acceptance of all Life • Nurturance of all life • Respect for all life
Grand Experiment (GE): • Entity enters human instrument at birth—is immediately fragmented into 3-D, five sensory perception to experience separation from wholeness • Helps entity gain a deeper understanding of the primal blueprint or grand vision of First Source	• GE produces the urge within the Human Instrument to seek out wholeness and re- experience divine connection to First Source • Human Instrument seeks out way to re-experience its divine connection to First Source	GE purpose is to test alternative models of existence to determine the model best able to unify consciousness without impinging on sovereignty of entity

EVOLUTION/ SAVIORSHIP MODEL *Hierarchical*	TRANSFORMATION/ MASTERSHIP MODEL *Individual connection to Source*	SYNTHESIS MODEL SOVEREIGNTY *I Am We Are*
• Human Instrument develops a sense of unity and belongingness and relationship to a grand and encompassing vision • This sets the yearning for wholeness	Human Instrument begins to transform the 3-D context into a self-aware, integrated component of the Universe of Wholeness	Realization that GE is the ongoing transformation and expansion of Source intelligence through all entities in all dimensions of existence
• GE nurtures feelings of inadequacy and insecurity • Deeply engrained pervasive belief structure that transformation is impossible maintains separation and deception and conformity • Pre-occupied with evolution in all facets of life	One begins to detach internally from the control of the Hierarchy making transformation a possibility	Combination of self-saviorship and detachment from hierarchy initiates the Synthesis Model into manifestation
• Spiritual leaders interpret the Universe of Wholeness creating a following by becoming teacher/guru • They provide structure and boundaries	Internal reliance on connection to Source for guidance and understanding, leading individual to question status quo	• Internal reliance on connection to Source creates independence from external dependence of the hierarchy or savior. • One becomes their own savior
Belief that the physical dimension is separate from Source	Realization that the physical dimension is part of Source	Source is in all dimensions
Barriers to equality maintain a fragmented reality	Vibration of Equality brings the fragments together	Barriers to equality dissolve— universe of wholeness emerges
Feelings of inadequacy and less than fragment human instrument	Development of extra senses during awaking process enables entities to step-out of hierarchy's control	Understand ourselves to be fragments of First Source-all equal, all part of the Whole

EVOLUTION/ SAVIORSHIP MODEL Hierarchical	TRANSFORMATION/ MASTERSHIP MODEL Individual connection to Source	SYNTHESIS MODEL SOVEREIGNTY I Am We Are
Rigid structure as a form of imposed security in a mechanical universe	Fluid structure transforming into an alignment with Source Intelligence	• Recognition of source in all things • Experience a dynamic, alive universe
Human Instrument confined to limiting beliefs and makes choices and decisions within those boundaries	Realization of interconnectedness of all things and beings	• Release from limiting beliefs • Access to the multiverse and multi-dimensional state of awareness
Service as operational motive of hierarchy causing teacher/ student ordering of universe and belief in a process of salvation	Direct knowing from Source within through application of 6 Heart Virtues and principles of Sovereign Integral as operational motive towards mastership	Transformation and Sovereign Integral state of consciousness begins to appear in individuals
• Evolutionary-incremental ascension model • Individuals reach outwards toward Source	• Accelerated pathways leading to sovereignty- mastership • Entity transforms to wholeness in time-space as Source descends into its creation	• Transformation-direct knowledge-realization; • No ascension; Source expands into the material world
Suppression of information by Hierarchy causing separation	Introduction of life principles of the Sovereign Integral as source Intelligence templates of creation	Life principles of Sovereign Integral hasten the SI manifestation
Beliefs of the **CBM*** are the controlling force in humanity	Life Principles of the SI and 6 Heart Virtues become motivational and transformational force	Experience of our Sovereign Selves begins to emerge
Duality as a taskmaster and divider	Duality seen as two parts of the whole	Synergy of opposing forces
Belief in Ascension to source keeps us in separation searching for answers	As we reach towards source, source expands and descends into time-space universe	Transformation of human Instrument into an instrument of the SI

* When CBM is inserted into an individual box, it indicates a belief from the Core Belief Matrix as identified in my previous book. The CBM characteristics will only appear in the evolution/saviorship model of existence; the characteristics I add for the other two models are my own speculation of moving out of the CBM.

EVOLUTION/ SAVIORSHIP MODEL _Hierarchical_	TRANSFORMATION/ MASTERSHIP MODEL _Individual connection to Source_	SYNTHESIS MODEL SOVEREIGNTY _I Am We Are_
• Experience of ourselves as a limited three-dimensional identity keeps us stuck in limiting belief systems • External controls cause feelings of incompetence	• Experience ourselves as an unlimited multi-faceted identity • Mastership and competency - we are beginning to understand ourselves as an individuated consciousness • Guidance coming from within	Synthesis Model of Being brings a sense of validation to the belief systems of immortality and interconnectedness
• Belief that we have fallen from grace and are born of original sin • Belief that we are sinful creatures that need redemption from an outside source **CBM**	We begin to take responsibility for our choice to be here on earth and accept our human body as a vessel in which we volunteered to explore the outposts of creation as a fragment of First Source	• Understanding that our journey on this earth is to have experiences that become part of the Source Memory • We did nothing wrong when we chose to experience living in Human Instruments • We are all playing a part in a Divine Plan
Men believe they were given domination over the earth and everything in it, including women and children. **CBM**	• The divinity of both genders is respected and appreciated • Acceptance of stewardship of earth • Respect for the Earth and all creatures • Children respected as gifts for the future	• Core expression activates the Tone Vibration of Equality as seventh sense is developed • Origin and existence of destiny is the tone of equality
• We live in a world of duality, and there must be a right and wrong answer for every issue that surfaces in the world. • We are judged by those right and wrong answers. **CBM**	Our journey is not about right and wrong as much as it is about having experiences in fields of limitation to explore the abilities and parameters of consciousness	We come to an understanding and compassion for ourselves and others as we realize each individual acts from a state of separation and incomplete understanding of their Divine origins

EVOLUTION/ SAVIORSHIP MODEL *Hierarchical*	TRANSFORMATION/ MASTERSHIP MODEL *Individual connection to Source*	SYNTHESIS MODEL SOVEREIGNTY *I Am We Are*
<ul><li>Humans are sinful and guilty to the core.</li><li>Humans respond to the world from a sense of incompleteness and unworthiness which causes a myriad of psychological dramas and hurtful reactions.</li><li>Because they have been made to feel inadequate humans need a savior.</li><li>Humans cannot find truth on their own.</li></ul>**CBM**	<ul><li>Put into practice the six heart virtues: appreciation, compassion, forgiveness, humility, understanding and valor;</li><li>Put into practice the life principles of the Sovereign Integral:<ol><li>Universe relationship through gratitude</li><li>Observance of Source in all things</li><li>Nurturance of life</li></ol></li><li>Practicing these principles and virtues stimulates heart centered responses and loving reactions to life's issues</li><li>We learn that we are part of Source</li></ul>	<ul><li>As we learn to live and work from an open-heart center, we will by default grow to love ourselves and others. From that sacred and powerful place, we can develop in our ability to recognize the divine nature that exists in all of us.</li><li>Living from the Heart will inspire humanity to find more humane solutions and experience inspiration that will liberate us from debilitating restrictions</li></ul>
Suffering is noble and expected in order to be acceptable to God and to rectify our sins and short comings. **CBM**	<ul><li>We come to understand that we create suffering through our beliefs in limitation, self- degradation, survival mentality, and feelings of being better than or less than.</li><li>We learn that we are punishing ourselves needlessly.</li></ul>	<ul><li>When we live from the heart, we live in a place of appreciation of self and others.</li><li>We do not intentionally or subconsciously create suffering for ourselves or others.</li><li>We understand that suffering can be a part of physical life but not as a punishment</li></ul>

EVOLUTION/ SAVIORSHIP MODEL *Hierarchical*	TRANSFORMATION/ MASTERSHIP MODEL *Individual connection to Source*	SYNTHESIS MODEL SOVEREIGNTY *I Am We Are*
Salvation is necessary through the help of a Savior because we are not good enough to be saved without help from the outside. **CBM**	• The realization that buried in the deepest layers of our psyches is an archetypal energy of sacrifice. It is likely that this subterranean energy is another part of us that was misinterpreted; much like the initial separation led us to have abandonment issues. • In essence, we all sacrificed something monumental when we lost the knowledge of our Divinity when we agreed to animate the HI. • We come to understand that our loss of self-confidence and esteem and awareness of our divine state makes us feel "fallen" and in need of redemption	• We realize we do not need a Savior • Our birthright as a fragment of Source is to transform from a limited three dimensional being to an unlimited multi-dimensional being. • The synthesis of the two models would result in us becoming our own "savior." • We take responsibility for our own actions and understand our origins and know that we do not need saving—we need to wake up!
God is an authoritarian deity: angry, jealous, demanding, vengeful, dangerous, and capricious **CBM**	• We turn inward to the Divine Source within us for guidance and transformation. • We come to understand that we have projected our Divinity out onto a God of our own making and that false and vengeful god only exists in beliefs in which we were programmed to perpetuate the Core Belief Matrix and the Hologram of Deception	• We take back our projection of an externalized God as we realize the Divine Source that lives within us. • When we transmit the 6 heart virtues and life principles of the SI, we express Source through our Human Instrument and are living from the heart, thus spiritualizing our bodies • We understand our origins • We live in the multi-verse • We become restored to our rightful place as a Sovereign Being.

EVOLUTION/ SAVIORSHIP MODEL *Hierarchical*	TRANSFORMATION/ MASTERSHIP MODEL *Individual connection to Source*	SYNTHESIS MODEL SOVEREIGNTY *I Am We Are*
Disciplines of science and religion are separated which helps to keep beliefs fragmented and compartmentalized **CBM**	• Disciplines of science and spirituality begin to recognize the same concepts • As the disciplines can come together, new discoveries will be made possible regarding our origins	Acceptance of scientific discoveries can be consciousness expanding to the masses which helps to bring about a synthesis that takes science and spirituality in the direction of the Grand Portal
We must find an external savior as we are not worthy	We have a Wholeness Navigator within that can steer us into truth and assist us in transforming from programmed beings to internally directed Sovereign Beings	The combination of self-saviorship and detachment from the Hierarchy initiates the Synthesis model into manifestation
Evolution is an arduous & ongoing process of shifting positions within the hierarchy, always assessing your present position in relation to a new one that beckons you	Transformation recognizes there are accelerated pathways that bypass the hierarchy leading to sovereign mastership rather than interdependent saviorship	• Two models are an experiment of evolution vs. transformation • Accelerated pathways can be accessed through direct experience of TVE present in all entities • Integration occurs when entity fully explores the two models and develops a synthesis model that positions saviorship as an internal role of the entity to "save" itself and not rely upon externals for this liberating task
• One world order with transhumanism and life in limitation and separation perpetuated by the Hologram of Deception • Human 2.0	World order based on Oneness of all entities within the multiverse and freedom from the Hologram of Deception	Recognition of ourselves as Infinite Beings within a Human Instrument on Terra-Earth able to bring expansion and transparency onto Terra-Earth as Sovereign Integrals 3.0

EVOLUTION/ SAVIORSHIP MODEL *Hierarchical*	TRANSFORMATION/ MASTERSHIP MODEL *Individual connection to Source*	SYNTHESIS MODEL SOVEREIGNTY *I Am We Are*
Creation of a suppressive hologram of deception to control the masses, the money, and the power	Individual discoveries of WMM builds foundation with the 6HV that insert into the fractal hologram information that alters the suppressive system so that humanity can assimilate what is needed to break out of it	• Break from the Hologram of Deception • Individuals take back personal sovereignty which sets a precedence for all of humanity

APPENDIX E
THE TEMPEST

The Woman found herself in the middle of a whirlwind
Trapped in the center of the storm raging within her
She cried to the Spirit of the Tempest
With tears streaming down her face---

"I live with a man I can no longer love
And loved someone that cannot be
I've born 6 children
And stood helplessly by
And watched one die

"I've learned so many things
My library bulges with books
Silent symbols of my relentless seeking & searching
Others' thoughts I've sought to make my own
Yet answers elude me
And I feel as tho I know nothing.

"I'm aware of people who love me
But it doesn't fill the void and I wonder
What is this relentless yearning that drives me
Creating a gulf between us
And is it worth the struggle?

"In shattered disbelief
I've raged with bitter hurt and angry jealousy
At my husband's lovers
And yearned for my own
Setting myself up to be hurt again & again

"I have so much pain
I wish I could cut it out of my body
And I don't know what to do!!
I work to help people with their pain
Yet I cannot relieve my own.

"I wrestle with the unconscious forces within me
Hoping to understand myself better
My head swims with rationalities
My gut churns with emotion
My psyche feels battered and bruised
And I am tossed in a tempest of confusion."
"I don't want to hurt anymore!" are my anguished cries!
I pound the wall with my fists sobbing "How do I stop this pain?"
I beg for answers--"What have I done to deserve to suffer like this?"
"I shake with the intensity of the storm within me
Wishing it were powerful enough to annihilate me!"

And the Spirit of the Tempest listened
As the woman raged on and on
Venting the bottled up anger and despair

It watched,
As each new surge of raw angry emotion
Welled up and filled her being
Dashing against her
As the ocean dashes against the rocks in a storm
Beating against her until she could resist no more

But the Spirit of the Tempest stood by and did nothing
For it was not time for her to be comforted.

Finally, the storm subsided
The Woman exhausted, slept.

She awoke to find herself still alive

Surprised to feel a sense of strength she had never felt before.
Tho battered and beaten
She made it to the Eye of the Storm
Had begged Death to carry her away
And it had not

So the Woman
With an air of determined resignation
Took a deep breath
And with all the courage she could muster
Opened the door
And stepped out into the Tempest--once more

APPENDIX F

QUANTUM PAUSE

THE QUANTUM PAUSE IS THE primary tool of the Sovereign Integral process. It is a particular form of breathwork. James explains that this breathwork is not for the Human Instrument, and it is not practiced for "experiences." It is a behavioral exercise practiced to help us reveal the Sovereign Integral state of consciousness. It was first introduced in the "Project Camelot Interview" [334] James did in November 2008. An upgraded version of Quantum Pause was included in the "The Fifth Interview of Dr. Neruda" [335]

A complete description of this practice is also available. [336] I am offering a basic version of this breath here, roughly paraphrased from the directions on the website. James gives a step-by-step process but also suggests that you remain open to adapting this process to your own style, abilities, and preferences. He stresses that it is not critical that your imaginings are in high definition; you are familiarizing yourself with high concepts, and he said that is enough. There is no judgement as to how you perform this. It is simply that the conceptual attention in itself loosens the bonds of the programming of the Hologram of Deception.

Step one: Designate intent for each session—am I doing this for myself, friends, family, or specific group, or am I doing this for all of humanity?

Step two: (2-4 breaths) Establish a baseline with 2-4 complete breath cycles to quiet and center yourself.

The breath is divided into four parts: Inhale; Pause—as you think I AM; Exhale; Pause, as you think WE ARE.

Each section of the breath should have roughly the same amount of time, i.e., inhale for 4 counts, pause for 4 counts, exhale for 4 counts, and pause for 4 counts. This is one breath cycle. If four counts is too long, reduce it to what is comfortable and works for you.

---

[334] Mahu, James, "Project Camelot Interview," *WingMakers*, Interviews, https://www.wingmakers.com/content/resources/

[335] Mahu, James, "The Fifth Interview," *WingMakers*, Neruda Interviews, https://www.wingmakers.com/content/neruda-interviews/

[336] Mahu, James, "Quantum Pause," *WingMakers*, Writings, https://wingmakers.com/writings/quantumpause/

Step Three: (3-5 breaths) Once you become focused with the breath by establishing your baseline, then you can bring your imagination into the process.

Now imagine a vertical line or column extending from the core of the earth, and as you inhale, bring the vertical line up from the earth through your body and out of the top of your head into infinity above. During the pause, imagine your I AM consciousness is uniting with this vertical column.

Now visualize a horizontal bar at your heart area, and during the exhale, bring the breath down to your heart area. During the pause imagine the field of WE ARE unites with the horizontal bar. This visualization connects you to humanity and life on earth.

Step Four: (3-5 breaths) During this phase we work with the Six Heart Virtues. In my experience this has become a very important phase of this breathwork. Begin by breathing in a heart virtue such as Compassion, for example. In your first exhale of this segment, send Compassion through your body. On the next inhale, breathe in Compassion again, and on the exhale, you may want to send it to the grid around the earth or to someone or some group specifically. You can do work specifically with one Heart Virtue through your entire session or bring them all in one by one and first send it through your body and then out to whomever or whatever you are focusing on that particular day. Once you have become familiar with doing this breath and working with the Six Heart Virtues and this becomes an integral part of your routine, it becomes very easy to breathe in a heart virtue and release it out to someone in real time as you feel the need.

Step Five: Completion—when you feel complete, send appreciation to the Creator in your concept of infinity. Then take the entire session and imagine it compressed into something like a pea or small stone and place it within your pineal gland to be absorbed and transmitted. Then complete the session by declaring "It is done." Remain neutral to outcome. Let the Forces you just sent out do their work.

Personal notes: During the day if I become aware of someone or something that needs a Virtue, I can do several Quantum Pause breaths and release the specified virtue on each exhale. I also like to do at least one complete session of Quantum Pause a day. Some prefer at night, some prefer morning—when is up to you. Be kind to yourself. This is a lot to remember to do in one sitting. I found that my proficiency in this process grew over time as I was able to add more, and it took on deeper meaning as I practiced. The most important part is to begin.

BIBLIOGRAPHY OF WINGMAKERS MATERIALS CITED IN THIS BOOK

Mahu, James and John Berges. *Collected Works of the WingMakers, Volume I.* Edited by John Berges. Egg Harbor Township, NJ: Planetwork Press, 2013. The following sections/articles are cited:

> "Preface by the Author," pp. xi-xviii
> *The Ancient Arrow Project* novel, pp. 20-246
> "The First Interview of Dr. Jamisson Neruda," pp. 256-289
> "The WingMakers Chamber Paintings," pp. 433-462
> "The WingMakers Poetry," pp. 463-548
> "Coherence of the Evolutionary Consciousness," pp. 572-576
> "Commentary on the Manifesto of the Sovereign Integral," pp. 591-605 (by John Berges)
> "Chamber One Philosophy: Life Principles of the Sovereign Integral," pp. 623-631
> "Chamber Two Philosophy: The Shifting Modes of Existence," pp. 632-643
> "Chamber Three Philosophy - The Blueprint of Exploration," pp. 644-651
> "Chamber Four Philosophy: Beliefs and Their Energy Systems," pp.652-662
> "The WingMakers Glossary," pp. 663-676

Mahu, James. *WingMakers* website, https://wingmakers.com/
Select bold topics from the bottom of the home page. The following articles are cited:

> **6 Heart Virtues**
> > "Living from the Heart"
> > "The Rising Heart"
> > "The When-Which-How Practice" (by John Berges)
> > "The Art of the Genuine: a Spiritual Imperative"
>
> **Art, Mixed Media Gallery – Ancient Arrow Site**
> > Paintings and music
>
> **Interviews**
> > "Conscious Media Interview"

"Project Camelot Interview"

Lyricus
"Excerpts from *Liminal Cosmogony*"
Lyricus Discourses 1-6

Neruda Interviews
"First Interview"
"Fifth Interview"

Philosophy
"Chamber One - Life Principles of the Sovereign Integral"
"Chamber Two - The Shifting Modes of Existence"
"Chamber Three - The Blueprint of Exploration"
"Chamber Four - Beliefs and Their Energy Systems"

Writings
"Poetry from the Ancient Arrow Site"
"Quantum Pause"

Writings, WingMakers Tools
"WingMakers Glossary"
"2008 James Mahu Interview"
"2013 James Mahu Interview"
"WingMakers Forum Q and A"

Additional website articles cited:

Berges, John, "Commentaries on Lyricus Discourses 1-6," *Planetwork*, Articles, Lyricus Discourse Commentaries, https://planetwork.co/pages/Articles.html#ldc

Berges, John, "Topical Arrangement of the Q & A Sessions with James," *Planetwork*, Articles, Nov. 5, 2005, revised Feb. 14, 2007, www.planetwork.co/pages/Articles.html#top_q_a (downloadable PDF)

Mahu, James, "Coherence of the Evolutionary Consciousness," *WingMakers Archive*, https://web.archive.org/web/20121017075151/http:/wingmakers.com/music-hakomi4-6.html

"A New Journey in Consciousness: An interview with WingMakers creator and author James Mahu by Darlene Berges of Planetwork Press," http://planetworkpress.com/pwpcart/index.php?main_page=page&id= 9

Additional *WingMakers Materials* sources:

Websites:
https://wingmakers.com/
http://www.jamesmahu.com
http://www.SovereignIntegral.org

All James Mahu's novels are available as separate paperbacks from www.planetworkpress.com except *The Ancient Arrow Project* which is included in *Collected Works of the WingMakers, Volume I.*

The Ancient Arrow Project can be purchased separately as an e-book at www.wingmakers.com.

BIBLIOGRAPHY OF REFERENCE
WORKS CITED

Avatar Wiki, https://avatar.fandom.com/wiki/Avatar Wiki

AZ Quotes, https://www.azquotes.com/

BrainyQuote, https://www.brainyquote.com/

Encyclopedia Britannica, https://www.britannica.com/

Free Dictionary, https://www.thefreedictionary.com/

Lexico, Powered by Oxford, https://www.lexico.com/definition

New World Encyclopedia, https://www.newworldencyclopedia.org/entry/Info:Main_Page

Psychology Wiki, https://psychology.wikia.org/wiki/Psychology_Wiki

Vocabulary.com Dictionary, https://www.vocabulary.com/dictionary/

WhatIs, https://whatis.techtarget.com/

Wikipedia, https://www.wikipedia.org/

BIBLIOGRAPHY OF INDIVIDUALS AND ORGANIZATIONS CITED AND THEIR WEBSITES

Alchemy web site on Levity.com http://www.levity.com/alchemy/home.html

Bamboo Village, https://Bamboovillage.com.au

C.G. Jung Center, https://www.cgjungcenter.org/

Child Trauma Academy, http://childtrauma.org/

Child Welfare League of America (CWLA), http://www.cwla.org

CoreLight, https://www.corelight.org/

Cotter, Tradd of Mushroom Mountain, https://video.search.yahoo.com/search/video?fr=mcafee&p=tradd+cotter+ mushroom+mountain#id=4&vid=ccde2d3a4229df9948144a06f4fa312a&action=click

Dr. Clarissa Pinkola Estes, http://www.clarissapinkolaestes.com

Dr. Stanislov Grof, http://www.stanislavgrof.com

Global Coherence Initiative, https://www.heartmath.org/gci/

HeartMath Institute, https://www.heartmath.com/

Homeopathic Educational Services, https://www.homeopathic.com

Marion Woodman Foundation, https://mwoodmanfoundation.org/

MERCOLA: Take Control of Your Life, https://www.mercola.com/

Thousand Hills Cattle Co. of Minnesota, http://www.thousandhillslifetimegrazed.com/

BIBLIOGRAPHY OF WEB
ARTICLES AND E-BOOKS

"20 Healing Benefits of Bamboo," *Remedy Grove*, October 20, 2017, https://remedygrove.com/supplements/20-Healing-Benefits-of-Bamboo

"5 Types of Personality According to Erich Fromm," *Exploring yourmind*, https://exploringyourmind.com/the-5-types-of-personality-according-to- erich-fromm/

"7 Stages of Spiritual Alchemy," *Ascension Energies*, https://ascensionenergies.com/2017/06/16/7-stages-of-spiritual-alchemy/

"About the Sustainable Development Goals," *UN Sustainable Development Goals,*https://www.un.org/sustainabledevelopment/sustainable-development- goals/

"Adlerian Therapy," *Psychology Today*, https://www.psychologytoday.com/us/therapy-types/adlerian-therapy

"Ahead of Her Time: Karen Horney and Feminine Psychology," *All Psych*, https://allpsych.com/personality-theory/psychodynamic/horney/

Armstrong, Mary Katherine, "Child Abuse, Shame, Rage and Violence," *The Primal Psychotherapy Page,* 2003, http://primal-page.com/childabu.htm

Bair, Puran, "Case Study: Visible Light Radiated from the Heart with Heart Rhythm Meditation," *Semantic Scholar*, 2005, https://pdfs.semanticscholar.org/a861/ed3faa5fd6abc62aaa6710ed87efdbd6 b923.pdf

"Bamboo," *Econation*, https://econation.co.nz/bamboo/

Beaulieu, John., N.D., PhD, "A Commentary on Cymatics" in Jenny, Hans, *Cymatics: A Study of Wave Phenomena and Vibration, monoskop,* https://monoskop.org/File:Jenny_Hans_Cymatics_A_Study_of_Wave_Phenomena_and_Vibration.pdf

Benko, Jessica, "The Radical Humaneness of Norway's Halden Prison," *The New York Times Magazine*, March 26, 2015, https://www.nytimes.com/2015/03/29/magazine/the-radical-humaneness- of-norways-halden-prison.html

Bloom, Deborah, "Instead of detention, these students get meditation," *CNN Health*, November 8, 2016, http://www.cnn.com/2016/11/04/health/meditation-in-schools- baltimore/index.html

Borys, Peter, Jr., "Heart Consciousness and the Electromagnetic Acoustical Body," Feb. 24, 2014, http://blog.peterborysjr.com/2014/02/24/heart-consciousness-and-the- electromagnetic-acoustical-body/

Bugental, James, PhD, "Celebrating the Work of a Founding Existential- Humanistic Psychologist," www.bugental.com

Bushby, Tony, "The Forged Origins of the New Testament," *NEXUS Magazine*, June-July 2007, http://www.bibliotecapleyades.net/biblianazar/esp_biblianazar_40.htm

Chamberlain, Rick Aharon, "Anti-Judaism and the Council of Nicea, "*YashaNet*, http://www.yashanet.com/library/antisem.htm

Chase, Christopher, "How to Save the Planet According to the World's Greatest Minds," *Uplift*, April 1, 2017, http://upliftconnect.com/save-planet-worlds-greatest-minds/

Chene, Marie, "What Makes New Zealand, Denmark, Finland, Sweden and Others Cleaner than Most Countries?" *Transparency International,* Dec. 7, 2011, https://blog.transparency.org/2011/12/07/what-makes-new-zealand-denmark-finland-sweden-and-others-%E2%80%9Ccleaner%E2%80%9D- than-most-countries/

Cherry, Kendra, "The 4 Stages of Cognitive Development," *Verywellmind*, https://www.verywellmind.com/piagets-stages-of-cognitive-development- 2795457

Cherry, Kendra, "What is the Actualizing Tendency?" *Explore Psychology,* https://www.explorepsychology.com/actualizing-tendency/

Coomarsingh, K., "Major Psychological Schools of Thought," *What Is Psychology?* http://www.whatispsychology.biz/major-psychological-schools-thought

"Corruption Perceptions Index 2017," *Transparency International,* Feb. 21, 2018,https://www.transparency.org/news/feature/corruption perceptions index 2017

"Council of Nicea," *ReligionFacts*, Nov. 10, 2015, http://www.religionfacts.com/council-of-nicea

Cuncic, Arlin, "An Overview of Viktor Frank's Logotherapy," *Verywellmind*, https://www.verywellmind.com/an-overview-of-victor-frankl-s-logotherapy- 4159308

deMause, Lloyd, "Childhood Origins of the Holocaust," *The Association for Psychohistory,* 2005,http://psychohistory.com/articles/the-childhood-origins-of-the-holocaust/

DHWTY, "The Legendary Emerald Tablet and its Secrets of the Universe," *Ancient Origins*, 11.14.2019, https://www.ancient-origins.net/myths-legends/legendary-emerald-tablet- 001956

"Evolution of Mental Illness," *Preceden*, https://www.preceden.com/timelines/66973-evolution-of-mental-illness

"Existential Therapy," *Psychology Today,* https://www.psychologytoday.com/us/therapy-types/existential-therapy

"Fractal Holographic Synergetic Universe," *Cosmometry, Exploring the Fractal Holographic Nature of the Cosmos*, http://www.cosmometry.net/fractal-holographic-synergetic-universe

Gerdes, Justin, "Three Lessons for Cities in Denmark's Clean-Energy Revolution," (Article for Citiscope, June 30, 2016) *government technology*, https://www.govtech.com/fs/perspectives/3-Lessons-for-Cities-in-Denmarks-Clean-Energy-Revolution.html

"Great Philosophers: Hypatia," *Oregon State University,* http://oregonstate.edu/instruct/phl201/modules/Philosophers/Hypatia/hypat ia.html.

Hauck, Dennis William "The EMERALD TABLET" *Alchemy Guild*, http://www.azothalchemy.org/emerald tablet.htm

Hauck, Dennis William. "The Emerald Tablet" *Dennis William Hauck, The Alchemy of Consciousness*, www.dwhauck.com

Hauck, Dennis William, "A Hyper-History of the Emerald Tablet" *Alchemy Lab*, https://www.alchemylab.com/hyper_history.htm

"Hemp Farming Act of 2018 [Fully Explained]," *WayofLeaf*, https://wayofleaf.com/blog/hemp-farming-act-fully-explained

"Hemp vs. Cotton: Is This the Future of Clothing?" *WayofLeaf,* March 4, 2020. https://www.marijuanabreak.com/hemp-vs-cotton-the-future-of-clothing

Hiles, Dave, "Pioneers of Humanistic-Existential Psychology," *The Virtual Office of Dave Hiles,* http://www.psy.dmu.ac.uk/drhiles/HPpioneers.htm

Hoeller, Stephan A., "The Gnostic World View: A Brief Summary of Gnosticism," *The Gnosis Archive*, http://gnosis.org/gnintro.htm

"Humanistic Therapy," *Psychology Today,* https://www.psychologytoday.com/us/therapy-types/humanistic-therapy

Humphreys, Suzanne, M.D. and Roman Bystrianyk, "Disease, Vaccines, and the Forgotten History," *Dissolving Illusions,* 2013, https://www.dissolvingillusions.com/

"Imaginal Cells" from "Biological Lesson on Coexistence, Imaginal Cells and Metamorphosis," *Heart Intelligence*, https://www.heartintelligencebook.com/metamorphosis.html

"John Dewey," *Psychology Encyclopedia,* https://psychology.jrank.org/pages/184/JohnDewey.html#:~:text=Dewey's%20functionalism%20was%20influenced%20by,statement%20establishing%20the%20functionalist%20school.

Jones, Prudence, "What is Paganism?" *Pagan Federation International*, http://www.paganfederation.org/what-is-paganism/

"Jungian Model of the Psyche," *Journal Psyche,* http://journalpsyche.org/jungian-model-psyche/

Karoglue, Kiki, "Mystery Cults in the Greek and Roman World," *Heibrunn Timeline of Art History, The Metropolitan Museum of Art*, 2000, http://www.metmuseum.org/toah/hd/myst/hd_must.htm

Khorsandi, Yasaman, "The Movement of Meditation Replacing Detention in Schools," *Newsweek*, Sept. 9, 2016, http://www.newsweek.com/education-meditation-after-school-program- holistic-life-504747

Mangasarian, M.M., "The Martyrdom of Hypatia," *Wikisource*, https://en.wikisource.org/wiki/The_Martyrdom_of_Hypatia

"Many Uses of Hemp," *The Information Distillery*, http://www.informationdistillery.com/hemp.htm

Mark, Joshua J., "Alexandria," *Ancient History Encyclopedia*, April 28, 2011, http://www.ancient.eu/alexandria/

Mark, Joshua J., "Hypatia of Alexandria," *Ancient History Encyclopedia*, Sept. 2, 2009, http://www.ancient.eu/Hypatia_of_Alexandria/

"Maslow's Hierarchy of Needs," *learning theories*, http://www.learning-theories.com/maslows-hierarchy-of-needs.html

Mastin, Luke, "Neo-Platonism," *The Basics of Philosophy*, 2008, http://www.philosophybasics.com/movements_neoplatonism.html

Mathiesen, Karl, "From Kansas to Copenhagen: clean energy beacons around the world," *The Guardian*, May 20, 2015, https://www.theguardian.com/environment/2015/may/20/clean-energy- beacons-of-the-world

"The Matrix Trilogy," *sparknotes*, http://www.sparknotes.com/film/matrix/

McCraty, Rollin, *The Energetic Heart: Bioelectromagnetic Interactions Within and Between People*, Boulder Creek CA: HeartMath Institute, 2003, (e-Book) http://www.heartmath.org

Mead, Tanya, "Detention Vs. Meditation: And the Winner is …" *Alternative Daily*, October 20, 2016, http://www.thealternativedaily.com/detention-versus-meditation-in-school/

Meints, Jeff, "The Hemp Plant, Humankind's Savior - 50,000 Uses and Counting," *Rediscover Hemp*, 1.23.2007, https://rediscoverhemp.com/inspire/the-hemp-plant-humankinds-savior/

Mercola, Joseph, M.D., "Health Benefits of Hemp," *Mercola- Take Control of Your Health*, Oct. 27, 2015, https://articles.mercola.com/sites/articles/archive/2015/10/27/hemp- health-benefits.aspx

"Mirror Neuron Revolution: Explaining what makes humans social," Interview between *Scientific American* writer Jonah Lehrer and Marco Iacoboni, https://www.scientificamerican.com/article/the-mirror-neuron-revolut/

Nash, Ronald, "Mystery Religion: What Were the Mystery Religions?" *Christian Research Institute*,http://www.equip.org/article/mystery-religion-what-were-the-mystery- religions/

Newton, Bacon and Descartes," *Google Sites*, https://sites.google.com/site/newtonbaconanddescartes/home/newton- bacon-and-descartes

Nichol, Lee, editor, *The Essential David Bohm*, London & New York: Routledge, Taylor & Francis Group, 2005, http://cspeech.ucd.ie/Fred/docs/Bohm_2005_.pdf

"Not Just Jesus: Other Virgin Births," *Law of Attraction GPS*, 2010, http://www.lawofattractiongps.com/living-law-of-attraction/not-just-jesus- other-virgin-births/#axzz3vXbC6S8Q

Osburn, Lynn, "HEMP SEED: THE MOST NUTRITIONALLY COMPLETE FOODSOURCE IN THE WORLD, Part One," *Hemp Line Journal*, July-August 1992, https://ratical.org/renewables/hempseed1.html

"Our DNA Can Be Reprogrammed by Words and Certain Frequencies," *Humans Are Free* http://humansarefree.com/2015/06/our-dna-can-be-reprogrammed-by- words.html

Pimentel, David, Paul Hepperly, James Hanson, David Douds, and Rita Seidel, "Environmental, Energetic and Economic Comparisons of Organic and Conventional Farming Systems," *(BioScience,* July 2005) *Research Gate,* https://www.researchgate.net/publication/271847517_Environmental_energetic_and_economic_comparisons_of_organic_and conventional farming systems

Potter, Wendell, "Skyrocketing Salaries for Health Insurance CEOs. Commentary: if they're making millions, should the rest of us have to pay higher premiums?" *The Center for Public Integrity*, June 9, 2014, http://www.publicintegrity.org/2014/06/09/14912/skyrocketing-salaries- health-insurance-ceos

"Psychology vs. Psychiatry: Do You Know the Difference?" *All Psychology Schools*, https://www.allpsychologyschools.com/psychology/psychology-vs-psychiatry/

Ryback, Ralph, MD, "Psychiatrist vs. Psychologist," Psychology Today, Jan. 4, 2016, https://www.psychologytoday.com/us/blog/the-truisms-wellness/201601/psychiatrist-vs-psychologist

"Richard Alpert/Ram Dass Biography," *Ram Dass Love Serve Remember Foundation*, https://www.ramdass.org/bio/

"Seven Stages of Alchemical Transformation: A Spiritual Metaphor (Infographic)," *Labyrinthos*, https://labyrinthos.co/blogs/learn-tarot-with-labyrinthos-academy/the-seven-stages-of-alchemical-transformation-a-spiritual-metaphor-infographic

Sigdell, Jan Erik, "Is Yahweh an Annunaki?" *ThreadReader*, Thread by @SouledOutWorld, Aug.16, 2010, https://threadreaders.com/thread/1247065107303215104

Simard, Suzanne, PhD, "TED Talk: How Trees Talk to Each Other," in "The secret life of trees: Is nature less selfish than we think?" By Paula Erizanu, *CNN ecosolutions*, Feb. 7, 2017. https://www.cnn.com/2017/02/07/world/secret-life-of-trees/index.html

Sisowath, Katrina, "Thoth Hermes Trismegistus and his Ancient School of Mysteries," *Ancient Origins*, Feb. 14, 2015 https://www.ancient-origins.net/history-famous-people/thoth-hermes-trismegistus-and-his-ancient-school-mysteries-002676

Sitchin, Zecharia, *The Lost Book of Enki*, http://thelostbookofenki.blogspot.com/

Smith, Michelle M., "Humility Is Key to Effective Leadership & High Performance," *Linkedin*, Nov. 2, 2015, https://www.linkedin.com/pulse/humility-key-effective-leadership-high-performance-smith-cpim-crp

Spivak, Nova, "Is the Universe a Computer? New Evidence Emerges," http://www.novaspivack.com/uncategorized/is-the-universe-a-computer-new-evidence-emerges

"Study Shows Language Development Starts in the Womb," *The University of Kansas*, July 18, 2017, https://news.ku.edu/2017/07/13/study-shows-language-development-starts-womb

Taylor, Steve Ph.D., "Transpersonal Psychology," *Psychology Today,* https://www.psychologytoday.com/us/blog/out-the darkness/201509/transpersonal-psychology

van den Berg-Cook, Nancy, PhD, "The Magic Mirror in Snow White," www.cgjung-vereniging.nl/home/files/nancy_vd_berg.pdf

"What does Sol Invictus mean and how did it affect Christianity?" *Answers,* https://www.answers.com/Q/What does Sol Invictus mean and how did it affect Christianity

"What is Electroconvulsive therapy (ECT)?" *American Psychiatric Association,* https://www.psychiatry.org/patients-families/ect

"What is Photon Energy?" *IN5D Esoteric, Metaphysical, Spiritual Database,* 2017, http://in5d.com/what-is-photon-energy/

"What Our Cells Can Teach Us," Interview of Bruce Lipton, PhD by Tami Simon, transcript of audio podcast, *Sounds True,* https://www.resources.soundstrue.com/transcript/what-our-cells-can-teach- us/

Woreck, Daniel and Zora Parwini, "Six hundred years since the birth of Johannes Gutenberg—inventor of the printing press. An assessment of his significance," *World Socialist Web Site,* Jan. 3, 2001. https://www.wsws.org/en/articles/2001/01/gute-j03.html

"You Didn't Know Mushrooms Could Do All This," *National Geographic,* featuring Tradd Cotter, owner of Mushroom Mountain http://video.nationalgeographic.com/video/news/160708-news-mushroom- mountain-uses-vin

Zesiger, Thomas, "What is a photon? – Definition, Energy & Wavelength," *Study.com,* http://study.com/academy/lesson/what-is-a-photon-definition-energy- wavelength.html

BIBLIOGRAPHY OF PRINTED
BOOKS AND ARTICLES

Batey, Lark Aleta, *Breaking Free from the Tyranny of Beliefs: A Revolution in Consciousness*, Bloomington IN: Balboa Press, A Division of Hay House, 2012.

Bagent, Michael, Richard Leigh & Henry Lincoln, *Holy Blood, Holy Grail*, New York NY: Delta trade paperback edition, Bantam Dell, 2004.

Block, Keith, M.D., *Life Over Cancer—the Block Center Program for Integrative Cancer Treatment*, New York, NY: Bantam Dell, a Division of Random House, Inc., 2009.

Brock, Jared, *A Year of Living Prayerfully: How a Curious Traveler Met the Pope, Walked on Coals, Danced with Rabbis, and Revived His Prayer Life*, Grand Rapids MI: Ann Spangler and Company, 2015.

Capra, Fritjof, *The Turning Point: Science, Society, and the Rising Culture*, New York NY: Bantam Books, by arrangement of Simon & Schuster, 1982.

Coulter, Harris L., *Divided Legacy Vol: The Conflict Between Homeopathy and the American Medical Association*, Richmond CA: North Atlantic Books, Second Edition, 1982.

Dale, Cindi, *The Subtle Body: An Encyclopedia of Your Energetic Anatomy*, Boulder CO: Sounds True, 2009.

Dean, Ward, MD, "Rebuttal to JAMA Internal Medicine Report Vitamin D ineffective for Hypertension," Life Extension Magazine, January 2016.

Ellerbe, Helen, *The Dark Side of Christian History*, Windermere FL: Morningstar & Lark, 1995.

Evans-Wentz W. Y., *Tibetan Yoga and Secret Doctrines: Seven Books of Wisdom of the Great Path, According to the Late Lama Kazi Dawa-Samdup's English Rendering*, arranged and edited by W.Y. Evans-Wentz, New York NY: Oxford University Press, 1958, 2000.

Ferguson, Lark Aleta, *Remnants from the Fire, A Transformational Journey with the Archetypes*, Authorhouse, 2002.

Freke, Timothy and Peter Gandy, *The Jesus Mysteries: Was the Original Jesus a Pagan God?* New York NY: Three Rivers Press, Random House, 1999.

Hauck, Dennis William, *The Emerald Tablet: Alchemy for Personal Transformation*, New York NY: The Penguin Group, Penguin Putnam Inc., 1999.

Helminski, Kabir, *The Knowing Heart, A Sufi Path of Transformation*, Boulder CO: Shambala Publications, Inc., 1999.www.shambala.com

Hillman, James, *Re-visioning Psychology*, New York NY: Harper Collins, 1997. www.harpercollins.com

Hodson, Geoffrey, *Fairies at Work and Play*, Wheaton, IL and Chennai, India: Quest Books, Theosophical Publishing House, Fourth Printing 2010. www.questbooks.net

Lash, John Lamb, *Not in His Image: Gnostic Vision, Sacred Ecology, and the Future of Belief*, White River Junction VT: Chelsea Green Publishing, 2006.

Lawlor, Robert, *Voices of the First Day: Awakening in the Aboriginal Dreamtime*, Rochester VT: Inner Traditions, 1991.

Miller, Jeffrey C., *The Transcendent Function: Jung's Model of Psychological Growth Through Dialogue with the Unconscious*, Albany, NY: State University of New York Press, 2004.

Paddison, Sara, *The Hidden Powers of the Heart: Discovering an Unlimited Source of Intelligence*, Boulder Creek CA: HeartMath LLC., revised edition, 1998. info@planetarypub.com https://www.planetarypub.com

Pearsall, Paul, PhD, *The Heart's Code: Tapping the Wisdom and Power of Our Heart Energy*, New York NY: Broadway Books, a division of Random House, 1998.

Pierce, Tonya Harter, MA, MFCC, *Outsmart Your Cancer: Alternative Non- toxic Treatments that Work*, Thoughtworks Publishing, 2004. www.OutsmartYourCancer.com

Rasha, *oneness*, San Diego CA: Jodere Group, Inc., 2003. *The Words of Oneness through Rasha*, http://onenesswebsite.com/

Schwartz, Judith D., "Hope for a Thirsty World: How Grass-fed Cows Can Help Restore Health to the Water Cycle and Prevent Deforestation," Natural Grocers Good4u Health Hotline Magazine, Vol 16, Sept. 2018.

Sri Aurobindo, *Savitri, A Legend and A Symbol,* Pondicherry, India: Sri Aurobindo Ashram Press, Revised Edition, 1996.

Tellinger, Michael, *Slave Species of the Gods: The Secret Mission of the Annunaki and Their Mission on Earth*, Santa Fe NM: Bear and Company, 2nd Edition, 2012.

Temple-Thurston, Leslie with Brad Laughlin, *The Marriage of Spirit: Enlightened Living in Today's World,* Santa Fe NM: CoreLight Publications, 2000.

INDEX

R

Ram Dass (Richard Alpert) 190, 191, 426
Renaissance 59, 60, 65, 66, 67, 119
Resonance 11, 141, 248, 311, 312, 321, 326, 377
Revolution-Industrial/Philosophical/Scientific 59, 61, 65, 67, 81, 89, 105, 425
River of Beliefs 16, 30, 31, 61
Roberts, Jane 118, 119
Rogers, Carl 177, 178, 182, 183
Rowling, J.K. 279, 280
Ruse/ruses xix, 1, 55

S

Savior xvi, 5, 8, 9, 13, 20, 27, 28, 33, 34, 36, 38, 40, 41, 42, 47, 53, 145, 163, 164, 166, 200, 201, 202, 210, 256, 292, 306, 317, 361, 364, 383, 398, 403, 406, 407, 408, 424
Scapegoat 34, 35, 106, 107, 392
Scientific Revolution 59, 61, 65, 67
Secularism 66
Self-actualization 182, 183
Self-centered 3, 11, 159
Self-receptors 267, 268, 269
Separation xiii, xiv, xv, xvi, xix, xxii, xxiii, 3, 5, 6, 7, 12, 16, 17, 25, 27, 35, 39, 44, 46, 47, 48, 55, 56, 59, 70, 88, 99, 100, 104, 111, 126, 130, 144, 148, 153, 155, 156, 160, 164, 165, 167, 170, 201, 202, 234, 235, 274, 275, 276, 280, 291, 300, 317, 319, 320, 321, 327, 335, 344, 348, 350, 351, 365, 378, 383, 392, 396, 398, 402, 403, 404, 405, 407, 408
Seth/Seth Material 118, 119, 120, 121, 134
Shame/Shame overlay 95, 105, 107, 108, 420
Shifting Models of Existence 200, 397
Shining Ones 2, 6, 370, 374
Simard, Dr. Suzanne 259
Snow White story 92, 93, 427
Social and Educational Innovations 247
Soul Carriers 2, 372, 381
Source xiii, xiv, xvi, xvii, 1, 2, 3, 6, 11, 12, 22, 23, 24, 25, 28, 29, 31, 41, 44, 45, 46, 47, 53, 62, 93, 94, 118, 133, 134, 142, 143, 145, 148, 154, 158, 159, 160, 170, 171, 172, 179, 185, 188, 199, 200, 201, 202, 212, 246, 255, 256, 260, 265, 269, 271, 290, 291, 292, 304, 307, 314, 317, 320, 330, 331, 334, 335, 336, 337, 338, 340, 342, 344, 345, 346, 347, 348, 353, 355, 358, 363, 368, 370, 377, 378, 379, 382, 383, 384, 385, 386, 389, 390, 394, 397, 398, 400, 401, 402, 403, 404, 405, 406, 407, 417, 429
Sovereign Entities of the Central Universe or SECU's 371
Sovereign Entities/Sovereign Beings xvi, 1, 2, 3, 6, 11, 12, 13, 40, 158, 203, 226, 371, 408
Sovereign Integral/Sovereign Consciousness xiii, xiv, xv, xvi, 3, 11, 12, 13, 28, 95, 97, 98, 99, 102, 103, 104, 118, 123, 124, 130, 131, 134, 146, 154, 201, 202, 211, 278, 281, 286, 290, 292, 293, 295, 296, 309, 314, 316, 319, 329, 330, 334, 336, 337, 340, 341, 342, 345, 355, 357, 367, 368, 379, 380, 381, 384, 386, 387, 397, 398, 399, 400, 404, 406, 413, 415, 416
Spiritual emergencies 193
Spiritual equality 88, 202, 319, 334, 356
Squares 49, 149, 258, 387, 388, 389, 390
Sri Aurobindo 1, 191, 296, 430
Subconscious mind 103, 270
Suppression paradigm/Program of Suppression 76, 124
Synthesis 67, 150, 186, 191, 196, 197, 200, 201, 397, 398, 399, 401, 403, 405, 407, 408
Synthesis/Sovereignty Model of Existence 67, 150, 191, 197, 200, 201, 398, 399, 401, 402, 403, 404, 405, 406, 407, 408, 409

T

This Is Us 277, 282
Tone Vibration of Equality 399, 402, 405
Tower of Babel 16, 17, 344
Transcendental Meditation 120, 249, 250
Transformation xv, xvi, xx, xxiii, 41, 47, 65, 94, 102, 103, 104, 125, 131, 138, 139, 140, 141, 142, 143, 145, 146, 148, 150, 151, 152, 153, 154, 155, 156, 157, 160, 165, 193, 196, 200, 201, 202, 206, 207, 208, 242, 278, 292, 300, 312,

Printed in the United States
by Baker & Taylor Publisher Services

Printed in the United States
by Baker & Taylor Publisher Services